Practice Theory and Education

Practice Theory and Education challenges how we think about 'practice', examining what it means across different fields and sites. It is organised into four themes: discursive practices; practice, change and organisations; practising subjectivity; and professional practice, public policy and education.

Contributors to the collection engage and extend practice theory by drawing on the legacies of diverse social and cultural theorists, including Bourdieu, de Certeau, Deleuze and Guattari, Dewey, Latour, Marx and Vygotsky, and by building on the theoretical trajectories of contemporary authors such as Karen Barad, Yrjo Engestrom, Andreas Reckwitz, Theodore Schatzki, Dorothy Smith and Charles Taylor. The proximity of ideas from different fields and theoretical traditions in the book highlight key matters of concern in contemporary practice thinking, including the historicity of practice; the nature of change in professional practices; the place of discursive material in practice; the efficacy of refiguring conventional understandings of subjectivity and agency; and the capacity for theories of practice to disrupt conventional understandings of asymmetries of power and resources. Their juxtaposition also points to areas of contestation and raises important questions for future research.

Practice Theory and Education will appeal to postgraduate students, academics and researchers in professional practice and education, and scholars working with social theory. It will be of particular interest to those who wish to move beyond the limiting configurations of practice found in contemporary neoliberal, new managerialist and narrow representationalist discourses.

Julianne Lynch is Senior Lecturer in Curriculum and Pedagogy at Deakin University, Australia. Her research focuses on curriculum innovation and the everyday practices of teaching and learning, particularly in relation to new media and new communication technologies.

Julie Rowlands is Senior Lecturer in Education Leadership at Deakin University, Australia. Her research takes a critical sociology of education approach, drawing particularly on the theories of Pierre Bourdieu, to examine higher education systems, governance, leadership, academic work and organisational change.

Trevor Gale is Professor of Education Policy and Social Justice at The University of Glasgow, where he heads the School of Education. He is a critical policy sociologist researching social justice in contexts of influence and of practice in education.

Andrew Skourdoumbis is Senior Lecturer in Education (Pedagogy and Curriculum) at Deakin University, Australia. His research engages with matters of curriculum theory encompassing policy analysis, teacher practice and educational performance. Andrew is interested in global reform efforts in education that impact teacher practice and the way that exacting methods of research govern school education policy and teacher performance.

Practice Theory and Education

Diffractive readings in professional practice

Edited by Julianne Lynch,
Julie Rowlands, Trevor Gale and
Andrew Skourdoumbis

Routledge
Taylor & Francis Group

LONDON AND NEW YORK

First published 2017
by Routledge

2 Park Square, Milton Park, Abingdon, Oxfordshire OX14 4RN
711 Third Avenue, New York, NY 10017

Routledge is an imprint of the Taylor & Francis Group, an informa business

First issued in paperback 2018

British Library Cataloguing in Publication Data
A catalogue record for this book is available from the British Library

Library of Congress Cataloging-in-Publication Data
A catalog record has been requested for this book

ISBN: 978-1-138-19139-6 (hbk)
ISBN: 978-1-138-61027-9 (pbk)

Typeset in Bembo
by Apex CoVantage, LLC

MIX
Paper from responsible sources
FSC   FSC™ C013985
www.fsc.org

Printed in the United Kingdom by Henry Ling Limited

'*Practice Theory and Education* explores and maps relatively uncharted territory, to problematise and theorise practice. An impressive range of theoretical resources (including Bourdieu, Vygotsky, Deleuze) are mobilised to bring *practice* into question. This is a creative, adventurous and significant collection of papers, written by outstanding scholars, which marks a step-change in how we understand and research practices in education. Really exciting stuff!'

Stephen J. Ball, Professor, University College London, UK

'Insightful, wide-ranging, scholarly, and innovative, this book is a welcome addition to the growing body of work on practice theory and professional education. An important contribution, breaking new theoretical ground, it rewards careful and attentive, *diffractive* reading!'

Bill Green, Emeritus Professor, Charles Sturt University, Australia

'This stunning collection troubles all the clichés about practice that structure and weigh down an applied field like education, especially the theory/practice and research/practice binaries. Authors convince us that theory, practice, and research function in an onto-epistemological arrangement in which they are not distinct but completely imbricated. They encourage us to experiment in this arrangement to produce difference, the exceptional, rather than to repeat the same, the pedestrian, the normal they refuse.'

Elizabeth Adams St. Pierre, Professor and Graduate Coordinator, University of Georgia, USA

'The need to theorise practice in education has never been greater than it is today. It is through theoretical analysis leading to the development of cogent critique that we should be able to resist the vagaries and short-termism of so many recent interventions into education policy. This volume brings together contributions from leading scholars around the world who draw on a wonderful array of theories to demonstrate the power of such research.'

Ian Menter, Emeritus Professor, University of Oxford, UK

'In an age when education practice has become routinized and confined to "best practices," the contributors to this volume challenge how we connect theory and practice. The authors build on a diverse range of theorists to suggest numerous paths to reconceptualizing the theory-practice connection. The ideas are invigorating and, therefore, the book warrants a close reading and rereading.'

David Hursh, Professor, University of Rochester, USA

'This is an important and timely book. I especially welcome its emphasis on drawing from many traditional sources, yet at the same time problematising their established canons and taken for granted assumptions. In the spirit of disruption, this overall approach creates a sense of resonance and dissonance while celebrating alterity and renegotiating what practice theory is all about. A much needed perspective at this time of turmoil and crisis in education and beyond.'

Anna Stetsenko, Professor, The Graduate Center of The City University of New York, USA

Contents

Figures and tables

Figures

Tables

Preface and acknowledgements

The seeds of this volume were sown during a series of symposia presented by members of The Warrnambool Collective – a group of education, arts, humanities and social sciences researchers, first established under the mentorship of Trevor Gale, that meets regularly in the regional Australian city of Warrnambool to write and engage in research endeavours away from the everyday demands of university life. These meetings are generously funded by the Deakin University Faculty of Arts and Education and play a special part in the research lives of all who participate.

Across 2013 and 2014 numerous symposia were held where members of The Warrnambool Collective presented work drawing on different practice theories and theorists. These presentations challenged The Warrnambool Collective to think more critically about practice, about the past and potential contributions of practice theories, and about possible resonances and dissonances between and amongst them. This edited collection grew from that series of presentations and many of the presenters therefore appear as authors within this volume, together with other scholars from outside of the group who were invited to contribute based on their particular areas of expertise. We wish to thank each of the authors for their contributions, all of which challenged us to think about the distinctive contribution of practice theory within their particular areas of interest. We also thank the thirty-three 'blind' reviewers whose work enhanced the quality of the volume through their astute engagement with early drafts and who so generously contributed much time and expertise.

A special thank you to Kristoffer Greaves who worked diligently with the management and formatting of files, and whose flair for all things technical helped us to work through numerous challenges. We also thank the Deakin University Faculty of Arts and Education for funding that supported the preparation of the final manuscript.

Contributors

Michael W. Apple is John Bascom Professor of Curriculum and Instruction and Educational Policy Studies at the University of Wisconsin-Madison, Madison, WI, USA.

Julia Coffey is a lecturer in sociology at the University of Newcastle. Her research is focuses on gender, youth, health and the body. Julia has published on young people's body work practices and identity, health and the body, and pedagogy. She is the author of two books, *Body Work: Youth, Gender and Health* (2016, Routledge) and *Learning Bodies: The Body in Youth and Childhood Studies* (Springer, 2016, edited with Shelley Budgeon and Helen Cahill).

Russell Cross is senior lecturer in language and literacy education at the Melbourne Graduate School of Education. His research focuses on the social, cultural, historical and political nature of teachers' work from a Vygotskian perspective.

Anne Edwards is professor emerita at the University of Oxford, where she co-founded the Oxford Centre for Socio-cultural and Activity Theory Research (OSAT). She has examined professional practices through a cultural-historical analytic lens for the last twenty years.

Joseph J. Ferrare is assistant professor of education policy and sociology at the University of Kentucky, Lexington, KY, USA.

Trevor Gale is professor of education policy and social justice at The University of Glasgow, where he heads the School of Education. He is a critical policy sociologist researching social justice in contexts of influence and of practice in education.

Kristoffer Greaves PhD is a research fellow with the Faculty of Arts and Education at Deakin University. As a lawyer interested in legal education, he draws on sociological and cultural theories of practice to study research- and practice-based approaches to education for the professions.

David Harris is a doctoral student at Deakin University, Australia. His research explores the engagement of Australian literature with ecological crises and how fiction might enable resistance to and renewal amidst these devastations.

Ailsa Haxell is head of school of Interprofessional Health Studies at the Auckland University of Technology, New Zealand. She has an educational focus on practice development within the broader health context.

Steven Hodge is a lecturer in the School of Education and Professional Studies at Griffith University, Brisbane, Australia. He has broad research interests, including philosophy of education, curriculum theory and practice theory.

Michelle Ludecke is a lecturer in the Faculty of Education at Monash University, working in the areas of professional studies and practice, and performing arts education. She was awarded her PhD from Deakin University, and her thesis is titled 'Firsts: Performing ways first year teachers experience identity transformation'. Michelle's work in teacher education centres on identity, pedagogy and the transition to teaching.

Julianne Lynch is senior lecturer in curriculum and pedagogy at Deakin University, Australia. Her research focuses on curriculum innovation and everyday teaching and learning practices, particularly in relation to new media and new communication technologies.

Tebeje Molla is a postdoctoral researcher in the School of Education at Deakin University. His areas of research include education policy analysis, transnational policy processes and social justice in and through education.

Stephen Parker is a research fellow in the School of Education at the University of Glasgow, UK. His research interests include higher education policy, social justice in education, and social theory.

Michael A. Peters is professor in the Wilf Malcolm Institute for Educational Research at Waikato University, Emeritus Professor at the University of Illinois at Urbana-Champaign and Professorial Fellow at James Cook University. He is the executive editor of *Educational Philosophy and Theory* and founding editor of several other journals, including the *Open Review of Educational Research* and *The Video Journal of Education and Pedagogy*.

Jessica Ringrose is professor of sociology of gender and education, at the Institute of Education, University of London. Recent research includes projects on feminism in school and youth digital sexual cultures and activism. She is the author of over fifty journal articles and book chapters, and four books including *Post-Feminist Education? Girls and the sexual politics of schooling* (2013, Routledge) and *Deleuze and Research Methodologies* (EUP, 2013, edited with Rebecca Coleman).

Julie Rowlands is a senior lecturer in education leadership at Deakin University in Australia. Her research takes a critical sociology of education approach, drawing particularly on the theories of Pierre Bourdieu to examine higher education systems, governance, leadership, academic work and organisational change.

Peter H. Sawchuk is a professor of adult education and industrial relations at the Ontario Institute for Studies in Education (University of Toronto, Canada). Recent publications include *Contested Learning in Welfare Work: A Study of Mind* and *Political Economy and the Labour Process* (Cambridge University Press).

Andrew Skourdoumbis PhD is a senior lecturer in education (pedagogy and curriculum) at Deakin University, Australia. His recent research engages with matters of curriculum theory encompassing policy analysis, teacher practice and educational performance. Andrew is interested in global reform efforts in education that impact teacher practice and the way that exacting methods of research govern school education policy and teacher performance.

Catherine Smith is a PhD student at Deakin University. Her research focuses on care in education policy and teaching practice from a critical philosophical perspective.

Dorothy E. Smith PhD is an adjunct professor of the Department of Sociology of the University of Victoria, British Columbia, Canada and Professor Emeritus of the Ontario Institute for Studies in Education of the University of Toronto, Canada. Working with students and colleagues, she has made and works with a sociology known as Institutional Ethnography.

Marek Tesar is a senior lecturer at the University of Auckland, specialising in philosophy of education, childhood studies and early childhood education. He is Editor-in-Chief of the journal, *Policy Futures in Education*.

Chapter 1

Introduction

Diffractive readings in practice theory

Julianne Lynch, Julie Rowlands, Trevor Gale and Andrew Skourdoumbis

Introduction

In recent years many works have been published with the term 'practice' in the title. Some focus on notions of 'best practice' and 'evidence-based practice', or 'how to' practise within specific professional fields. Others draw on limiting distinctions between theory and practice, or practice and policy, or they do not explicitly engage with the notion of 'practice' but instead take it to be an already understood and unproblematic concept/object. However, practice theories proceed from the premise – emphasised by Green (2009a) – that 'practice' should not be taken for granted, elevating it for explicit consideration. *Practice Theory and Education* contributes to this growing interest in practice theories by focusing on how they might be deployed in different contexts and to what end.

Reference to the word 'education' within the title of this volume points to the close but sometimes fraught relationship between practice theory and education research. In part this is because of persistent questions, from those within the field and those without, about the potential for and the significance of gaps between theory and educational practice. However, it is precisely because practice theory is integral to much education research that the field of education research has contributed significantly to the development and evolution of practice theory. Indeed much contemporary practice theory used within research more broadly arises from or has its origins at least in part within the field of education research. This is evident when, for example, authors writing on diverse topics well beyond education nonetheless draw on the theories of Bourdieu (1977), Reckwitz (2002), Schatzki (1996) and Kemmis (Kemmis et al. 2013) among others, all of whom developed theories of practice but also wrote about education directly (although not always exclusively). Indeed, Schatzki argues that Pierre Bourdieu was one of the founding practice theorists and that he and Anthony Giddens (1979) are 'leading exponents of practice theory' (2012, p. 13), together with philosophers such as Charles Taylor and Jean-Francois Lyotard, who also wrote about education directly (see Lyotard 1984). Bourdieu's work is particularly influential in this regard because he wrote extensively about education and researched school education, universities and education fields more broadly (see for example, Bourdieu 1988, 1977). His work also serves to remind the reader that education practice does not only take place in classrooms, or indeed, within education institutions (Bourdieu & Passeron 1977).

The contributors to *Practice Theory and Education* – drawn from the fields of governance and leadership, literary theory, school education and teaching, higher education, counselling, social theory and research methodology – explicitly engage with the notion of 'practice' in order to push theoretical boundaries, to challenge and rethink how we understand practice as an object of inquiry, and to examine and illustrate what this means for researching professional practice in a variety of contexts. *Practice Theory and Education* moves beyond the most commonly cited professional fields to include chapters on literary practices, policy as practice, gender as practice, words as practice and research practices. The collection also includes chapters working outside of particular practice fields, focusing on practice philosophy and extending particular manifestations of practice theory and practice-focused research methodology. Within these works, practice theories are engaged and developed as a possible means of seeking to understand social and professional practice, and as a way of speaking back to the limiting configurations of practice found in, for example, structuralist, liberal-humanist, neoliberal capitalist or narrowly representationalist research traditions.

Most publications focused on practice theory dedicate some discussion to terminology and the different referents of the word *practice*. This work is similarly taken up by each of the chapters in this collection as they engage with particular theoretical traditions. This is important because *practice* is a word in common use and used in diverse ways even within a single context. The principal distinction often made within practice theory publications is between *practice* as an uncountable noun (this is the object of *practice theorists* who ask 'what is practice?' and then find themselves engaged in onto-epistemological considerations) and *practices* as a countable noun (the/a practice) that points to particular configurations of bodies acting with and on other bodies in particular settings. However, further distinctions are usually required and made, particularly in relation to the countable *practice/s*. For example, Reckwitz (2002, p. 250) distinguishes between a routinised practice or *way of doing*, and the unique actions of an individual who effectively 'carries' that practice; that is, the practices through which ways-of-doing manifest. Schatzki (2001, p. 56) makes similar distinctions between what he refers to as 'organized nexuses of activity' (e.g., farming practices), 'actions' (e.g., building fences) and 'doings', 'sayings' and 'relatings' (e.g., hammering), which manifest in the unique performances that are usually the object of empirical studies. Within particular practice theories, frameworks for theorising particular *practice/s* are usually underpinned by explicit ontological considerations, and diverse practice theories share characteristics that contribute to the ontological sense of practice theory. For example, Feldman and Orlikowski (2011, p. 1240) explain that central to practice theory is an understanding of social life as an 'ongoing production' that emerges through people's recurrent actions. Thus a tension with which practice theories engage is between the productive and repro- ductive flows of the social, and this tension serves as a key ontological engine for provoking new understandings: the social is constituted via manifestations that are both singular in their materiality yet recognisable in a formal sense *as practices*.

So the terminology of practice theory is slippery, and precision of terminol- ogy within particular theories and deployments of theories is important, but this is not the only source of slipperiness when working with practice theory. The object of inquiry itself is theorised as one that is difficult to nail down. Green (2009b, pp. 39–40) usefully characterises *practice theory* as 'a distinctive post-Cartesian strand of thinking about practice, one that is sceptical about and seeks to problematise modernist views of both representation and subjectivity, linked in turn to received notions of knowledge and identity', thus pointing to the epistemological problematics engaged by practice theory. Scholars working with practice theory often postulate alternative, non-representational configu- rations of practice that focus on, for example, materiality, embodiment, situated- ness and relationality, with some theoretical trajectories challenging the notion of individual human subjects and the distinction between subject and object in social research. In this book, such challenges are performed with reference to theorists such as Barad, Bourdieu, de Certeau, Deleuze, Latour, Charles Taylor and Vygotsky. These theorists problematise the methodological presumptions of modern sociology by identifying risks associated with reflective research logics and tools that seek to represent practices, and by raising questions about what and how we might know. Here the risk is that research methods and representations merely reproduce established conceptual frameworks and fail to capture aspects of practice that escape the net of such frameworks. Thus practice is theorised as an object of study that calls for new methods of inquiry and presentation.

Some scholars working with practice theory have noted methodological trends within practice approaches, through which empirical researchers seek to capture the temporal-spatial enactments and transformations of practices without losing a sense of the complexity and dynamism of practice. For exam- ple, Miettinen et al. (2009, p. 1314) write of a 'methods agenda' within practice theory, noting the examples of ethnography, ethnomethodology and Cultural Historical Activity Theory (CHAT) as approaches for studying 'a living practice "here and now"'. Others have developed particular methodological approaches that they believe respond to practice ontologies – for example, *practice-focused ethnography* as described by Trowler (2014). These methodological approaches have been developed in response to a desire to move away from the reductivism of realist, idealist and relativist approaches to researching practice.[1] Others have expressed concerns about taking established methodologies as a starting point. For example, St Pierre (2014), in her work on post-qualitative inquiry, has argued that considerations of ontology are more fruitful than engagements with particular methodologies. In this vein, Green and Hopwood (2015, pp. 5–6, citing Kemmis) describe a trend in practice research towards what they call 'philosophical-empirical inquiry', where researchers 'bring together conceptual sophistication with empirical rigour'. Many of the chapters in this collection engage with these methodological challenges, and some deploy or advocate for particular 'philosophical-empirical' strategies that attempt to respond to these challenges.

Challenges relating to how we might *know* practice are taken up in the chapters in this collection, with some employing noted practice theories and methodologies in relation to particular empirical contexts and others providing close, critical engagements with the onto-epistemological writings of eminent practice theorists and philosophers. In this chapter, we draw on the concept and practice of *diffraction* to introduce and provide a productive reading of the fifteen contributions that constitute *Practice Theory and Education*.

Diffraction: Reading *through* the chapters

In her much cited 1992 essay *The Promise of Monsters*, Haraway described the interference patterns produced by diffracting rays of light. She employed this concept to write against the reproductive logics of science – the logics of reflection – and to invoke an ontology of emergence and contingency, where 'very rarely does anything really get reproduced' (Haraway 1992, p. 299). Diffraction is a physical phenomenon that can be observed when light, water or particles encounter some sort of interference or move from one medium into another, generating new forms and movements. The term diffraction is also used to describe the process that occurs when waveforms encounter other forces (an object or another wave), or move from one medium to another, resulting in a transfer and transformation of forces and the production of new waveforms. Referring to waveforms in water, Huygen's Principle states that every point on any wave can be regarded as a new source of secondary waves. These productions only occur through encounters, and encounters necessarily produce new forms. Within the humanities and social sciences, diffraction provides a disruptive metaphor and has been taken up by many who seek to pursue non-representational research agendas and non-representational (affirmative, productive, advocative) research ethics. In relation to practice, an ontological grounding that assumes an immanent logic of interference and the production of difference is particularly attractive because of the promises it holds for social change and emancipation from relations of domination. If practices are not simply reproduced, then they can be done differently. In fact, they are always done differently.

The diffraction metaphor has been taken up by diverse cultural and literary theorists as an attempt to move away from representational logics of analysis where texts are scrutinised for their referents or meanings, or where texts are compared with other texts to determine which is the 'truer' representation of the object of concern. Instead, diffraction suggests approaches that attend to what is produced when two or more entities encounter each other – for example, the bodies of readers with texts, texts with other texts. Feminist theorists have argued that diffraction is not only a useful metaphor but is also an ontological precondition of all *material-discursive becomings* (e.g., Barad 2007). They point to both the methodological and ethical implications of an onto-epistemology of immanence constituted via diffractive encounters, in which presumptions to represent are not only feeble and ill-informed, but can also be damaging, and where attempts to overcome the shortcomings of representationalist intentions via, for example, self-reflection or reflexivity are naive (Haraway 1992).

In this chapter, we take up diffraction as a material strategy for presenting the contents of the book. This approach was employed by Barad when she proposed to read Foucault and Butler *through* Bohr in the service of new productions. We do not, therefore, look at these texts to work out what they mean or what they show us or in what ways they are *true*. Instead, we ask, *What 'patterns of resonance and dissonance'* (Barad 2007, p. 195) *are produced as we encounter and assemble these texts, and where does this take our understandings of practice?* Thus our engagements with these chapters do not aim to be 'transcendent and clean' (Haraway 1996, p. 439) as though we have taken the role of honest and balanced commentators, but – more honestly than that – we *work* the chapters to see what is produced through and for us. In what follows, we offer four diffractive readings produced by the proximity of chapters within each of the four sections of the book: (1) discursive practices; (2) practice, change and organisations; (3) practising subjectivity; and (4) professional practice, public policy and education. These themes provide the structure for the remainder of this introductory chapter, and allow us to read across chapters drawing on diverse theories, empirical settings and methodological approaches to see what are produced as the key matters of concern in contemporary practice thinking in relation to professional practice, education and change. This grouping risks overplaying the commonality between chapters, as well as failing to leverage potentially generative connections between grouped chapters and those in other sections. Thus are the constraints of a linear text! We start each section below by offering a sense of the chapters – possibly contrived as a representational move, but heartened by Barad's (2014, p. 185) note that 'reflection and diffraction are not opposites, not mutually exclusive, but rather different optical intra-actions highlighting different patterns, optics, geometries that often overlap in practice'.

Section 1. Discursive practices: Practising words, writing and theory

Dorothy Smith opens Section 1 with an experimental chapter, where she identifies different practices of words and how 'word-referent relations are implicated in organising what people do' (Smith 2017, p. 25). Moving us through a tour of five 'specimens', Smith illustrates some of the different ways in which *words as practices* – while accommodating divergent pathways – also organise complexes of possible, intelligible responses. This tour is intended to open the way for ethnographers to treat words in new ways: as concrete presences that enter into material relations. In the second chapter, Steven Hodge and Stephen Parker examine the works of philosopher Charles Taylor to discuss how theories and practices interact and how these interactions can effect changes in the *social imaginary*. Hodge and Parker (2017) argue that Taylor – like other practice theorists – sought anti-idealist explanations of the social, but that – unlike other practice theorists – he sought to provide a systematic account of the efficacy of theory. This account distinguishes a meaning-giving *background* of practices which Taylor goes on to describe in terms of *social imaginaries*. Taylor's analysis suggests that it is the infiltration of theories into the social imaginary that accounts for the apparent efficacy of theory in the realm of practice. The chapter by Julianne Lynch and Kristoffer Greaves focuses on research-writing practices, drawing on Michel de Certeau's conceptualisation of *everyday practice* to characterise these discursive practices as a dialogue between reproductive and productive operations. Employing de Certeau's conceptualisation of *reuse*, they write of the interplay between the normative meta-narrative structures and conventions of research-writing products and the spaces for play produced by the emergent nature of practice. In the final chapter in this first section, David Harris draws on Deleuzian and new materialist thought to provide a critique of representationalist ambitions in and analyses of literary practices with respect to ecological crises. Harris moves forward from this critique to theorise other *intensive* functions of literature, providing examples from contemporary Australian fiction.

In reframing the deployment of discursive materials (words, theories, research writing, literature) as implicated in and imbricated with practices – bound together with the movements of other materials in dynamic and mutually constitutive ways that are both singular and recognisable – each of these chapters attribute work to discursive materials that move beyond representations of referents. In Smith's chapter we see a move away from the temptation to treat words as mimetic within ethnographic research towards words as practices that assemble and organise bodies (human and non-human, child and table). Hodge and Parker examine the different ways theories manifest in the realm of practice, the effects they might have within specific historical contexts, and how this might interact with the social imaginary. Lynch and Greaves (2017) write of the reproductive tendencies served by the conventional forms and logics of research-writing practices, where the meta-narrative structures of research writing reproduce representationalist epistemologies. And, Harris points to these reproductive tendencies of writing in relation to representational literature when 'representations blind us to the world's complexity and to its unrepresentability' (Harris 2017, p. 72). Thus, each chapter offers a critique of representationalist assumptions in discursive practices and points to how such assumptions can serve claims to power and powerful bodies (the American military, governing elites, the author-researcher, capitalism). Just as a word like 'body count' can be deployed in materially co-constitutive ways, particular theories can be perpetuated in the service of particular material configurations (and the interests of particular groups); the meta-narrative structures of research writing can reproduce representationalist epistemologies; and representationalist literary practices can perpetuate the very assumptions and relations they seek to challenge and change.

Consistent with the sensibilities of practice theory, each chapter also allows for the more-than-representational (Lorimer 2005) work of discursive practices to support new productions and a reconfiguring of relations. Smith sees the assembling and organising effected by words as practices as constraining, but not determining. The precondition of Smith's (2017, p. 23) discussion is an ontology where 'nothing is ever quite the same as it was before or will be', yet forms of co-ordination persist. Co-ordination persists because it is actively practised and produced through practices. This contingent view of relations brings with it the possibility that things might be different because they might be practised differently. Similarly, for Hodge and Parker, theories do not have a determining relation to practices: their penetration of the social imaginary depends on how they are appropriated and practiced within historically specific situations through, for example, the work of elite groups, and some theories prove to be more efficacious than others. Thus, both of these chapters posit a dynamism that provides for the possibility of resistance and change. Within this section, the chapters by Lynch and Greaves and by Harris proceed explicitly from an ontology where singularities proliferate, and the authors of both speculate about possible ways to escape the reproductive logics of representation. Lynch and Greaves embrace de Certeau's celebration of alterity as they move from a critique of representationalist research-writing logics towards suggesting possible strategies for research writing to produce discomforting affects in readers. And Harris elaborates an ontology of immanence and material-discursive entanglement from which to theorise literary practices that might enable us to 'renew our capacities to imagine worlds beyond the current state of affairs' (Harris 2017, p. 78).

The attribution of more-than-representational force to discursive material leads us to refigure how we understand agency, positing agency in an inter-individual space – as movements and matterings that unfold via relations between bodies. This move away from agency as an attribute of individual human bodies is shared across diverse practice theories, though the extent to which individual agency – and indeed human agency – is given up as a foundational concept varies between theories (and chapters). Within the four chapters that comprise this section, agency is written as an outflow of encounters between discursive and material things (words, narrative structures, theories, human bodies, objects, hyperobjects[2]). This resonance between chapters strikes us even when individual chapters might be seen as very divergent in their philosophical foundations, subjects and purposes: discursive material, in relation with other bodies (human or nonhuman; alive, dead or ostensibly inanimate within human scales of time) contribute to the way things are done and known, and indeed to the *what* of doing and knowing. This relational view of agency leads us to consider models of transformation, where change does not proceed as an orchestrated human endeavour, or as developments located in or undertaken by individual bodies, but instead emerges through complex, mutually constitutive relations as they are practiced, including relations between discursive materials and other bodies/materials.

Section 2. Practice, change and organisations

Although we have chosen to name this section in relation to 'organisations', the four chapters within it do not share a common definition or understanding of what an organisation is or even agreement that such a definition can or should exist. Despite this, all four chapters in this section speak to practice within the context of organisations and organisational change, in whatever forms these are understood or characterised. Thus, Rowlands and Gale's chapter draws on Bourdieu to consider the practices required of academics to comply with research output calculation models within universities. Although it is generally understood that the habitus is reflected in practice, Rowlands and Gale (2017) seek to extend this by highlighting that the habitus is also shaped by one's own past practices. That is, research output calculation models have the potential not only to have a direct impact on academics' own research practices but also to potentially play a role in reshaping the academic habitus within the higher education field.

In the following chapter, Ferrare and Apple draw on theorisations of policy networks to analyse the role of venture philanthropism in education policy. They argue that a significant effect of venture philanthropism is the tendency towards isomorphism or convergence within education policy, centred on market-based reform. However, Ferrare and Apple also conceptualise the ways in which power relations within an organisational field, such as education, can lead to instability and transformation. They show how the process of building and mobilising a policy network as employed by philanthropic organisations constitutes an organisational practice that can influence education in ways that reflect a philanthropic organisation's policy objectives.

Edwards explicates a cultural historical account of practice drawing on the legacies of Vygotsky and Leont'ev. Within this theoretical context the chapter demonstrates the usefulness of the dialectic between personal agency and societal conditions in overcoming three specific problems of practice: transition across practice boundaries; changing or creating practices; and collaborating across boundaries. The chapter also highlights the practical challenges associated with the transformation of institutional practices and the importance of motivated actor agency. In contrast, Haxell draws on the explicitly non-dialectical theoretical resources of actor-network theory (ANT) and the example of the development of text counselling practices through a youth helpline to highlight the co-evolution of human and non-human actors as practices are reconfigured. The chapter theorises practice not as being generated within a particular reality but as generating multiple situated realities within which there are divisions that are arbitrary and therefore 'can be renegotiated' (Haxell 2017, p. 153).

In all four chapters, practice is not additional – it is central to understanding and being in the world. Indeed, in different ways, each chapter portrays practice as something that makes or *is* the world, however differently that world may be comprised or understood. Moreover, practice is complex and multifaceted. Thus, within both the Ferrare and Apple and Haxell chapters, practice is not linear or the consequence of conscious decision-making by agents or actors. This is consistent with the account given by Rowlands and Gale, who state that for Bourdieu, practice is 'the outcome of internalised knowledge . . . which manifests as an agent's skills, proficiencies and competencies' (2017, p. 93). At the same time, practice is not a mechanical reaction (Rowlands & Gale 2017) or 'a set of actions that one carries out' (Edwards 2017, p. 128). That is, practice is more than a set of actions and not all actions are practice. Within these four chapters there is also a relationship between people and practice in that '[p]eople are therefore shaped by practices, but may also shape them' (Edwards 2017, p. 127) even though not all chapters describe this relationship explicitly and for Haxell, drawing on ANT, the relationship involves not only people but also things.

Experiencing the world through the lens of various practice theories opens up possibilities for change or transformation within practices, although none of the authors naively assume that such change would necessarily be positive or 'good'. Moreover, Haxell (2017, p. 152) usefully points out that there is as much work in 'keeping things the same' as there is in changing them. Nonetheless, change is complex. This is at least partly because practices arise out of history, of what has come before, as well as what is happening now and what may or may not happen in the future or futures. Thus, Edwards describes practices as 'historically constructed' and therefore not subject to change 'simply through shifts in what people do in activities' (2017, p. 133). Similarly, for Rowlands and Gale, practices are 'borne from history' (2017, p. 93), although Haxell asserts that this is a history that is not always visible to us. This necessarily raises questions about how change might take place.

The Ferrare and Apple, and Rowlands and Gale chapters each draw on aspects of Bourdieu's theory of practice as a lens through which to consider two new forms of governance, namely policy networks and academic workload models. In different ways, these two chapters seek to challenge or extend understandings of Bourdieu's theory of practice by highlighting that such governance regimes are not neutral and can play a key role in shaping and reshaping aspects of education practice in ways that align more closely with the market-based philosophies of education from which they are derived. Ferrare and Apple use the notion of isomorphism arising from institutional theory to explain homogeneity within policy network funding strategies among philanthropists. Rowlands and Gale also hint at isomorphism within the higher education field that they depict, relating to the rapid spread of academic workload models and their effects on research practices. That is, one way that practices can change is to create a closer alignment with the surrounding organisation or organisations.

However, in reading the chapters across or against each other, what is also evident is the potential for practices of disruption or reform. Thus, organisations and interactions between organisations are 'sites of intersecting practices' (Edwards 2017, p. 135) separated by divisions that are arbitrary, held together by ongoing negotiations and therefore open to renegotiation (Haxell 2017). Such intersections have the potential to create spaces for challenge and reform in the 'cracks and contradictions' that naturally arise (Ferrare & Apple 2017, p. 123). They open the way for what Rowlands and Gale describe as 'reflexive and disruptive' practices; that is, practices that disrupt by responding to opportunities that arise *in the moment*. Returning to our earlier observation that practice is something that makes the world, the notion of deliberately and reflexively disruptive practice is therefore suggestive of possibilities that if the world as we know and understand it is made, it can also be remade.

Section 3. Practising subjectivity

Section 3 brings together four chapters that raise questions about how we might understand *subjectivity* as a central concern in research into practice. Not all of these chapters explicitly take up subjectivity as a central focus, but they each imply configurations of subjectivity as they engage with notions about matters such as human consciousness, tacit knowledge, mediated agency and the agency of the more-than-human. The first chapter, by Peter Sawchuk, is a theoretical exposition of the warrant for what he describes as an *expansive material dialectical* approach to the study of human practices. This is followed by three differently theorised site studies: Julie Coffey and Jessica Ringrose draw on posthuman concepts from Deleuze and Guattari and from Barad (2007) to analyse 'gendered becomings' in two different research settings: one focused on cosmetic surgery and the other on a school-based feminist club. Michelle Ludecke draws on the theoretical work of Reckwitz (2002), Schatzki (2001) and Kemmis (2010) to characterise what she has named the *practice of survival* among beginning school teachers employed on short-term contracts. Catherine Smith and Russell Cross employ concepts from CHAT to conceptualise the practice of care in a disadvantaged secondary school setting.

There are resonances between these chapters: their conceptualisation of practice, how human subjectivity features within that conceptualisation, and what approaches to theorising and empirical inquiry are found to be efficacious. Across all four chapters we see a critique of conventional conceptions of the discrete, rational human subject and of intentionality as a key driving force behind practice and human agency. While Sawchuk (2017, p. 159) explicitly refuses to give up the existence of 'the thinking, feeling, knowing, choice-making and acting subject', he uses the CHAT concepts of *activity*, *operation* and *mediation* to provide a critique of modernistic views of human practice as goal-oriented actions. He notes, 'people always act on (and are acted upon), think about, feel, perceive and know the world *as mediated by artefacts or tools of some kind*' (p. 8, emphasis added). In his chapter, 'artefacts' such as cognitive or affective schema – commonly associated with human subjectivity – appear among a list that includes extra-individual artefacts such as physical objects and divisions of labour. While Sawchuk uses the concept of *activity* to critique individualist views of human practice, Coffey and Ringrose (2017) use the Deleuzo-Guattarian notion of *assemblage* together with Barad's concept of *intra-action* to deploy a post-human view of practice. Through their research accounts of body practices, the authors trace complex, relational assemblages that involve dynamic, constitutive connections between 'more than human, trans-human and posthuman' entities that are constantly in flux (Coffey & Ringrose 2017, p. 176, citing Currier). Their chapter provides accounts of subjectivity that invoke relations between human bodies (their corporeality, their affects, their cognition), other physical bodies (breast implants, dolls), particular spatio-temporal settings (the beach, the shower) and contested societal norms about what gendered bodies should be and do. Ludecke's (2017) account illustrates how beginning teachers' *practice of survival* is produced through interconnections between material-economic agents (the contract), discourses (ways of talking about beginning teachers), mental activities (expectations, perceptions, misconceptions) and bodily activities (taking on extra-curricular duties, applying for other jobs). In Smith and Cross (2017) – which is theoretically aligned with Sawchuk in its engagement with activity theory – we see an application of Engström's (1999) formulation of an activity system, in which the subject or *human do-er* (Hasan & Kazlauskas 2014) (in their case, the teacher) is understood as emerging in relation to that subject's object (students). Within the activity system, this relation between subject and object can only be understood in relation to all aspects of the activity system (artefacts, rules, divisions of labour) and contradictions between these.

The roles of both conscious mind and unconscious mental activity have been central to philosophical debates about human subjectivity and practice, and are particularly significant for projects that seek to inquire of or promote social change or changes to professional practice. Although the chapters vary in the degree to which they countenance or reject the notion of discrete human agency, each speaks to notions of intentionality, tacit knowledge and the habituality of practices, as well as implications of these for changing practices. Sawchuk (2017, p. 170) refers to 'un-self-conscious responses to immediate symbolic and material conditions of activities'. Similarly, Ludecke takes up the concept of unconscious or tacit knowledge and its role in professional practice. She argues that change agendas focused on beginning teachers' practices need to involve strategies enabling them to develop more explicit understandings of their tacit knowledge of survival practices. Indeed, we can speculate that the teachers involved in Ludecke's study will have developed more explicit understandings of their previously tacit knowledge through their participation in the research project. This type of change is referred to in Coffey and Ringrose's (2017, p. 190) chapter as 'the re-assembling of subjectivity', observed in girls involved in the feminist group on which they report. The group provided spaces for new types of relations between bodies and objects, where the plasticity of bodies and objects allowed possibilities for doing gender differently. Similarly, Smith and Cross (2017) evidence explicit attempts to interrupt the habituality of practice by employing a data collection approach that purposefully sought to intervene by engaging teachers in different ways with their own professional practice and that of others.[3]

In reading these chapters together, it becomes clear that there are benefits of understanding human subjectivity as produced *within or via complexes* that exceed human bodies and include extra-individual agents and materials (physical and discursive). This complexity brings challenge in terms of inquiries into practice or agendas to change practice, but it also brings opportunities for transformation. As well as the resonances produced by the proximity of these four chapters, significant onto-epistemological dissonances are also evident. Sawchuk (2017, p. 159, citing Ollmann) writes of a philosophy of internal relations that is explicitly dialectical, with reality depending on 'the inter-penetrating connections of parts and whole'. This ontology is evident in the chapter by Smith and Cross, who apply concepts discussed by Sawchuk. In contrast, the theoretical resources used by Coffey and Ringrose contribute to a refusal to countenance a material 'whole', except as a concept that may be deployed in practices. New materialist thought sees distinctions between and boundaries around entities as constitutional 'cuts' made by analysts and their apparatuses (Barad 2007), a conceptualisation that problematises the prefiguring in research accounts of a whole or a background, or distinctions between, for example, the micro and macro. The degree to which a context, background or whole brings affordances or constraints to inquiries into practice is a contested space among practice theorists.

Section 4. Professional practice, public policy and education

The final section of *Practice Theory and Education* brings together three chapters focused on formal education and educational research. Each chapter engages critically with neoliberal understandings of educational practice that are premised on maximising the freedoms and skills of individual human agents as a sufficient prerequisite for institutional change by way of market- and competition-based reforms (Harvey 2005). These understandings are intertwined with the development of new managerialist approaches to governing professional practice, where the formal locus of power within institutions is effectively relocated from practising professionals to policy makers via systems of audit and surveillance (Davies 2003). As well as providing a critique of such framings, each chapter also proposes generative means for moving beyond them. This is important work in times when practices of new managerialism threaten to push into, and to define, all aspects of social and professional life, while simultaneously being understood as inadequate to the challenges of current times.

Michael Peters and Marek Tesar start this section by offering a genealogical account of how practice has emerged as a central concern within educational research and policy. They describe the relative influence of historical figures like Thorndike and Dewey, and how tensions between educational paradigms have played out across the twentieth century and can be seen to continue to influence current educational landscapes. The chapter by Trevor Gale and Tebeje Molla then engages with the notion of the *deliberate* professional as it appears in the conventional literature on professional practice, critiquing the focus on intentionality in thinking and action and arguing for a reformulation of *deliberativeness* in professional practice as a capacity that is both intentional *and thoughtful*. Gale and Molla conceptualise *deliberative* professionals as taking time to make considered decisions and judgments, avoiding acting on impressionistic or intuitive knowledge, and instead acting on their convictions in a purposeful way. Finally, Andrew Skourdoumbis and Julianne Lynch examine teacher effectiveness research (TER) by drawing on a 'practice perspective' – citing Reckwitz (2002), Thrift (1996, 2007) and Schatzki (2012) – to provide a critique of TER's scientometric configurations of teaching that isolate teacher behaviours as major contributors to enhancing the learning outcomes of students. They argue that TER promotes reductive views of teaching and subjectivising views of teachers; that the sensibilities of contemporary practice theory support more productive engagements with the complexities of teaching; and, through this, that practice theory is more likely to support professional transformation than understandings offered by TER.

Each chapter contributes to an understanding of how, in current times, political motivations demand *practical* solutions to educational problems. Each also provides a critique of this emphasis on the practical and of the technicist approaches it often supports, where the behaviours of teachers and students become codified in simplistic and normative ways. Peters and Tesar (2017) highlight the historicity of educational research, describing the 'birth' of educational research as interconnected with the development of techniques of statistical analysis found in behavioural psychology. They argue that these origins contributed to the development and influence of current mechanistic views of teaching and learning and related statistical techniques which emphasise *evidence* in public education and what they term *State-istics*. Peters and Tesar warn (citing William James and John Dewey) against 'scientistic' approaches to developing generalizable solutions to educational problems. In relation to professional practice, Gale and Molla (2017) argue that, while the capacity for deliberation is critical for developing responses to perennial educational challenges (e.g., educational inequity), it is unlikely to be achieved via the codification and teaching of the pre-deliberated functions associated with deliberation. This is because 'the deliberative nature of action is called into question when professional actions are always the same'. Similarly, Skourdoumbis and Lynch (2017, p. 273) argue that, through its focus on the codification of *effective* classroom-based pedagogic actions, the processes and products of TER enact 'reductions and elisions', where teachers are the easy targets of educational policy reform, and where underlying systemic factors contributing to inequality (e.g., socio-economic status) are 'accounted for' but not positioned as open to policy influence. Taken together, these chapters suggest that the ways of knowing and representing teaching and learning that currently dominate school education policy reflect particular politico-historical positionings that must be addressed before adequate responses to educational challenges can be developed. This point is taken up elsewhere by Gale and Parker (forthcoming) in relation to teacher education policy, where they argue policy pressure in countries like Australia, England and Scotland promotes a foregrounding of the practical that serves political purposes, but which also undermines much needed theoretical work.

As well as providing accounts and critiques of influential ways of understanding educational professional practice, each chapter in this section also constitutes a call to reconfigure and to intervene in the knowledge cultures that are currently influential within public education policy and teacher education. Peters and Tesar raise questions about how researchers and practitioners might be supported to better interrogate, discuss and reflect on their own practice with a view to increased professional independence. Gale and Molla describe particular methods for stimulating greater critical consciousness among teachers and school leaders, arguing that this is 'slow' work (citing Kahneman), involving pedagogies of discomfort (citing Boler and Zembylas). Similarly, Skourdoumbis and Lynch argue that, while 'quick fixes' are attractive to policy makers, there are no quick fixes to educational problems. They speculate that the products and processes of TER would better support teacher professionalism and educational transformation if, instead of serving as normative frameworks to which teachers are subject, they were positioned as generative materials with which teachers actively engaged and experimented.

Compared with chapters in other sections, there are fewer dissonant tones produced by the proximity of these three chapters. This is not surprising given the persistent (though marginalised within public policy) chorus of critique found within education scholarship that decries the de-professionalising influence of current approaches to the management and governance of schools found in many Anglophone countries. However, a point of difference (also found among other chapter groupings in this collection) is the degree to which possible solutions are seen to depend on conscious thought and reflection.

Conclusion

The arrangement of the chapters in this book produces groupings that are an artefact of the genre with which we work. Each of the fifteen chapters speaks to or has implications for the themes we have used to structure the text as a whole and, as noted earlier, almost any arrangement would have offered both coherence and disconnects. Reading across theories, settings and accounts has also produced what we might claim as key matters of concern in contemporary practice thinking in relation to professional practice, education and change. Thus, a process of crystallisation has occurred and certain shared foci have solidified. Points of resonance include a focus on:

- The nature of change and how change in practices occurs or might be supported, together with the flipside of this: how things persist or remain the same;
- The historicity of practices and their entanglement with what has come before, what is happening now and what may or may not happen in the future;
- The place of discursive material in practice, where materials like words, theories and research accounts have material effects beyond supposed representation;
- The efficacy of refiguring conventional understandings of subjectivity and agency to account for their production via complexes of entities that include the discursive, and that exceed individual human bodies; and,
- The capacity for theories of practice to disrupt conventional understandings of asymmetries of power and resources.

Our process of reading diffractively across the chapters within each section also highlights points of onto-epistemological contestation because proximate chapters have drawn on diverse theoretical resources to communicate understandings of what constitutes reality(ies), what we might know about this, and how the concept of *practice* articulates with such understandings. Noted areas of contestation included:

- The degree of influence ascribed to human intentionality, deliberative action and reflexivity in professional practice and in the disruption of institutionalised practices. While some perspectives caution against the risk of privileging individual agency and human rationality, others see human practices such as reflexivity as keys to transformation, and still others posit that these positions are not mutually exclusive;

- The efficacy of conceptualising the social as unfolding in relation to a broader context, background or whole, and associated sociological distinctions between, for example, the micro and the macro. Some perspectives see such concepts as critical for supporting understandings of practice, while others see them as artefacts of specific practices that need to be explained; and,
- The efficacy (or otherwise) of dialectical understandings of the relationship between personal agency and broader societal conditions should they be countenanced.

Important questions have been raised for future work, which deal with the challenges associated with changing practices and the creation or emergence of new practices. This is particularly pertinent to the transformation of institutionalised practices (for example, within formal education settings), where practice theory might be unattractive to policy makers who seek short-term or programmable solutions. While political interests are easily criticised, they nevertheless are a powerful part of the practice assemblage with material implications for change agendas. The challenges of changing practices or the emergence of new practices are also relevant to projects of social change (for example, in relation to gender equality or recovery from environmental degradation). In these instances the task ahead might seem insurmountable, but practice theory can offer ways of thinking and being that might invoke and embolden new solutions and indeed new practices.

We commenced this chapter by focusing on the work that practice theory does, how it might be deployed and to what end. Practice theories support critique, but critical scholarship will not in and of itself remake the world in the ways imagined by these chapters. More powerfully, practice theories unsettle and make it difficult for us to think, read and write in habitual ways. There is hope that these difficulties might also provoke struggle and through this disrupt the repetition of inequity and injustice. We invite you to consider the readings we have offered as stimulus for your own productive engagements with the chapters in this collection, and hope that in reading our account (and possibly revisiting it after you have read the chapters), you are primed to engage critically with the notion of practice and with approaches to apprehending and presenting practice in your research.

Acknowledgements

Thank you to David Harris, Steven Hodge and Stephen Parker for providing feedback on sections of this chapter.

Notes

1 See discussion in Trowler (2014) in relation to ethnography.
2 Harris (2017) draws upon this concept from Morton.
3 These strategies are also discussed by Gale and Molla (2017).

References

Barad, K 2007, *Meeting the universe halfway: Quantum physics and the entanglement of matter and meaning*, Duke University Press, Durham, NC & London.

Barad, K 2014, 'Diffracting diffraction: Cutting together-apart', *Parallax*, vol. 20, no. 3, pp. 168–187.

Bourdieu, P 1977, *Outline of a theory of practice*, R Nice (trans), Cambridge University Press, Cambridge.

Bourdieu, P 1988, *Homo Academicus*, P Collier (trans), Polity, Cambridge.

Bourdieu, P & Passeron, J-C 1977, *Reproduction: In education, society and culture*, Sage, London.

Coffey, J & Ringrose, J 2017, 'Boobs and Barbie: Feminist post human perspectives on gender, bodies and practice', in J Lynch, J Rowlands, T Gale & A Skourdoumbis (eds), *Practice theory and education: Diffractive readings in professional practice*, Routledge, London, pp. 175–192.

Davies, B 2003, 'Death to critique and dissent? The policies and practices of new managerialism and of "evidence-based practice"', *Gender and Education*, vol. 5, no. 1, pp. 9–103.

Edwards, A 2017, 'A cultural-historical approach to practice: Working Within and Across Practices', in J Lynch, J Rowlands, T Gale & A Skourdoumbis (eds), *Practice theory and education: Diffractive readings in professional practice*, Routledge, London, pp. 127–140.

Engström, Y 1999, 'Activity theory and individual and social transformation', in Y Engeström, R Miettinen & RL Punamaki (eds), *Perspectives on activity theory*, Cambridge University Press, Cambridge, pp. 19–38.

Feldman, MS & Orlikowski, WJ 2011, 'Theorizing practice and practicing theory', *Organization Science*, vol. 22, no. 5, pp. 1240–1253.

Ferrare, J & Apple, M 2017, 'Practicing policy networks: Using organisational field theory to examine philanthropic involvement in education policy', in J Lynch, J Rowlands, T Gale & A Skourdoumbis (eds), *Practice theory and education: Diffractive readings in professional practice*, Routledge, London, pp. 108–126.

Gale, T & Molla, T 2017, 'Deliberations on the deliberative professional: Thought-action provocations', in J Lynch, J Rowlands, T Gale & A Skourdoumbis (eds), *Practice theory and education: Diffractive readings in professional practice*, Routledge, London, pp. 247–262.

Gale, T & Parker, S (forthcoming), 'The prevailing logic of teacher education: privileging the practical in Australia, England and Scotland', in M Peters, B Cowie & I Menter (eds), *A companion to research in teacher education*, Springer, Dordrecht.

Giddens, A 1979, *Central problems in social theory: Action, structure and contradiction in social analysis*, University of California Press, Berkeley.

Green, B 2009a, 'Introduction: Understanding and researching professional practice', in B Green (ed.), *Understanding and researching professional practice*, Sense Publishers, Rotterdam, pp. 1–18.

Green, B 2009b, 'The primacy of practice and the problem of representation', in B Green (ed.), *Understanding and researching professional practice*, Sense Publishers, Rotterdam, pp. 39–54.

Green, B & Hopwood, N 2015, 'Introduction: Body/practice', in B Green & N Hopwood (eds), *The body in professional practice, learning and education*, Springer, Dordrecht, pp. 3–14.

Haraway, D 1992, 'The promises of monsters: A regenerative politics for inappropriate/d others', in L Grossberg, C Nelson & PA Treichler (eds), *Cultural studies*, Routledge, New York, pp. 295–337.

Haraway, D 1996, 'Modest witness: Feminist diffractions in science studies', in P Galison & DJ Stump (eds), *The disunity of science*, Stanford University Press, Stanford, CA, pp. 428–441.

Harris, D 2017, '"Gestures towards": Conceptualising a literary practice for crises of ecologies', in J Lynch, J Rowlands, T Gale & A Skourdoumbis (eds), *Practice theory and education: Diffractive readings in professional practice*, Routledge, London, pp. 71–88.

Harvey, D 2005, *A brief history of neoliberalism*, Oxford University Press, Oxford.

Hasan, H & Kazlauskas, A 2014, 'Activity theory: Who is doing what, why and how' in H Hasan (ed.), *Being practical with theory: A window into business research*, THEORI, Wollongong, AUS, pp. 9–14.

Haxell, A 2017, 'The development of a text counselling practice: An actor-network theory account', in J Lynch, J Rowlands, T Gale & A Skourdoumbis (eds), *Practice theory and education: Diffractive readings in professional practice*, Routledge, London, pp. 141–155.

Hodge, S & Parker, S 2017, 'Accounting for practice in an age of theory: Charles Taylor's theory of social imaginaries', in J Lynch, J Rowlands, T Gale & A Skourdoumbis (eds), *Practice theory and Education: Diffractive Readings in Professional Practice*, Routledge, London, pp. 39–54.

Kemmis, S 2010, 'What is professional practice? Recognising and respecting diversity in understandings of practice', in C Kanes (ed.), *Elaborating professionalism: Studies in practice and theory*, Springer, London, pp. 139–165.

Kemmis, S, Wilkinson, J, Edwards-Groves, C, Hardy, I, Grootenboer, P & Bristol, L 2013, *Changing practices, changing education*, Springer, Singapore.

Lorimer, H 2005, 'Cultural geography: The busyness of being "more-than-representational"', *Cultural Geography*, vol. 29, no. 1, pp. 83–94.

Ludecke, M 2017, 'The practice of survival: Reflexivity and transformation of contract-employed beginning teachers' professional practice', in J Lynch, J Rowlands, T Gale & A Skourdoumbis (eds), *Practice theory and education: Diffractive readings in professional practice*, Routledge, London, pp. 193–210.

Lynch, J & Greaves, K 2017, 'Michel de Certeau: Research writing as an everyday practice', in J Lynch, J Rowlands, T Gale & A Skourdoumbis (eds), *Practice theory and education: Diffractive readings in professional practice*, Routledge, London, pp. 55–70.

Lyotard, J-F 1984, *The postmodern condition: A report on knowledge*, University of Minnesota Press, Minneapolis, MN.

Miettinen, R, Samra-Fredericks, D & Yanow, D 2009, 'Re-turn to practice: An introductory essay', *Organization Studies*, vol. 30, no. 12, pp. 1309–1327.

Peters, M & Tesar, M 2017, 'Bad research, bad education: The contested evidence for evidence-based research, policy and practice in education', in J Lynch, J Rowlands, T Gale & A Skourdoumbis (eds), *Practice theory and education: Diffractive readings in professional practice*, Routledge, London, pp. 231–246.

Reckwitz, A 2002, 'Toward a theory of social practices: A development in culturalist theorizing', *European Journal of Social Theory*, vol. 5, no. 2, pp. 243–263.

Rowlands, J & Gale, T 2017, 'Shaping and being shaped: Extending the relationship between habitus and practice', in J Lynch, J Rowlands, T Gale & A Skourdoumbis (eds), *Practice theory and education: Diffractive readings in professional practice*, Routledge, London, pp. 91–107.

Sawchuck, P 2017, 'Parsing and re-constituting human practice as mind-in-activity', in J Lynch, J Rowlands, T Gale & A Skourdoumbis (eds), *Practice theory and education: Diffractive readings in professional practice*, Routledge, London, pp. 159–174.

Schatzki, TR 1996, *Social practices: A Wittgensteinian approach to human activity and the social*, Cambridge University Press, Cambridge.

Schatzki, TR 2001, 'Introduction: Practice theory', in TR Schatzki, K Knorr Cetina & E von Savigny (eds), *The practice turn in contemporary theory*, Routledge, London pp. 1–14.

Schatzki, TR 2012, 'A primer on practices: Theory and research' in J Higgs, R Barnett, S Billett, M Hutchings & F Trede (eds), *Practice based education: Perspectives and strategies*, Sense, Rotterdam, pp. 12–26.

Skourdoumbis, A & Lynch, J 2017, 'The temptations and failings of teacher effectiveness research: Provocations of a "practice perspective"', in J Lynch, J Rowlands, T Gale & A Skourdoumbis (eds), *Practice theory and education: Diffractive readings in professional practice*, Routledge, London, pp. 263–279.

Smith, C & Cross, R 2017, 'Classroom activity systems and practices of care', in J Lynch, J Rowlands, T Gale & A Skourdoumbis (eds), *Practice theory and education: Diffractive readings in professional practice*, Routledge, London, pp. 211–228.

Smith, DS 2017, 'Exploring words as people's practices', in J Lynch, J Rowlands, T Gale & A Skourdoumbis (eds), *Practice theory and education: Diffractive readings in professional practice*, Routledge, London, pp. 23–38.

St Pierre, EA 2014, 'Post qualitative inquiry', keynote lecture presented to the Joint Conference between Australian Association for Research in Education and New Zealand Association for Research in Education, Queensland University of Technology, Brisbane, 2 December 2014.

Thrift, N 1996, '"Strange country": Meaning, use and style in non-representational theories', in *Theory, culture & society: Spatial formations*, Sage Publications Ltd, London, pp. 1–51.

Thrift, N 2007, *Non-representational theory: Space, politics, affect*, Routledge, London.

Trowler, PR 2014, 'Practice-focused ethnographies of higher education: Method/ological corollaries of a social practice perspective', *European Journal of Higher Education*, vol. 4, no. 1, pp. 18–29.

Discursive practices

Practising words, writing and theory

Chapter 2

Exploring words as people's practices

Dorothy E. Smith

This exploration originated in an obscure contradiction arising in institutional ethnography. Institutional ethnography is a sociology that begins and works from people's actual doings viewed as they are coordinated. Starting with the ongoing of people's actualities means that nothing is ever quite the same as it was before or will be, though many if not most changes may be imperceptible. Hence institutional ethnographers are always investigating a historical process shaped by what has been going on before and projected into what's coming next. There is no place for a concept such as *social organisation* that rides outside the particularities of people's actual lives and doings. At the same time institutional ethnographers do use it. It allows a movement of representation in the ethnographic text that goes beyond the detail of raw observation to recognising forms of co-ordinated activities as recurring or being 'the same' as what is done at other times and by other people. And those, indeed, are what the ethnographer is going after.

This chapter does not encounter this difficulty directly. Nor does it propose a general solution. In a sense, it sidesteps the contradiction. In exploring words as people's actual practices, it is discovering something that people do in particular local settings and at particular times which generalises beyond the local particularities of the time and place in which they are uttered. In what people say or write, hear or read, we can find at least one important dimension of social organisation as a local accomplishment; words as uttered (in Bakhtin's sense which includes both speech and writing (Bakhtin 1981)) transgress everyday particularities.

The dialogue I'm proposing here takes up institutional ethnography's commitment to learning from and about actual people's actual doings (including in language) as they co-ordinate with one another. Conceptualising words as people's actual doings or practices proposes a direction of study into how words engage us, as practices, in ways that are quite ordinarily available to observation and description. I am interested in opening up a region for discovery that will be useful in learning how people are putting our worlds in common together in the ongoing of our everyday lives. In what follows, five specimens of words seen as people's actual practices are explored empirically.

There is, of course, a monstrous literature on language in anthropology, linguistics, literary theory, semiotics, philosophy of various kinds including ordinary language philosophy, discourse studies, ethnomethodology, and so on. But here, though I draw from time to time on thinkers or researchers in one or other of these regions, I want to move away from more technically developed modes of investigating and theorising language, to what allows us to see what we ourselves do and to be able to attend to words as we practice them. It's a move rather like that made by J. L. Austin (1962), the ordinary language philosopher who decided to step outside the constraints of philosophical discourse and look at how people use words. But it goes further because it adopts institutional ethnography's move to return to our own bodily being just where we are, recognising, of course, that what we're doing is practising the words of our discourse. But we can look around and we can learn from the ordinary just as Austin did.

In moving towards an ethnography of words as uttered (spoken, written, read), we encounter the problem of our implicit dialogue with the discourses in which what people are doing in words gets expressed as nominals that dispense with the presence and doings of actual individuals. We want to be able to make observations of words as people practise them; we want to be able to see how they are working; we want observations both of what people say, write or read, but also of words as they go on inaudibly and invisibly inside the bony walls of the skull. What we have somehow to do is to avoid displacing the presence of people by replacing them with nouns such as 'meaning', 'sense', 'thought', 'mind', and so on (including Mead's term 'response' [Mead 1962]). They are odd terms because although they can be assigned grammatically to work as the subjects or objects of sentences, they have no referents beyond the text in which they are uttered.

The distinctively social character of words has perhaps been most boldly established by George Herbert Mead (1962), whose account of language conceives it as essentially social. In his critique of Darwin's account of how animals respond to gestures, he developed a distinction between gestures as direct responses to the moves initiated by another animal and significant symbols – or words – that evoke the same response in speaker and hearer. Thus, significant symbols are essentially social practices. Building on Mead's thinking is a radical alternative to models of communication that picture meaning translated into sound (or presumably written words) that travels between individuals to be translated from sound to meaning when it gets to the other side. Mead's conception of word as a conventionalised sound (or written form) that evokes the same response in speaker and hearer enables us to see how words bring into being among people what V. N. Volosinov has called 'interindividual territory' (1973).

The inter-individual territory that will be examined using the small collection of specimens that follows focuses on words practiced as referring to something or some event. To frame the topic, I start with A. R. Luria's (1961, 1976;

Luria & Yudovich 1971) observations of how, when they come into play, words for objects standardise perception of how a named object is perceived. Here is an account in which Luria and his associate, Yudovich, describe how children learn to focus on the generalised features of named objects[1].

> The mother's very first words when she shows her child different objects and names them with a certain word, have an indiscernible but decisively important influence on the formation of his mental processes. The word, connected with direct perception of the object, isolates its essential features; to name the perceived object "a glass", adding its functional role "for drinking", isolates the essential and inhibits the less essential properties of the object (such as its weight or external shape); to indicate with the word "glass" any glass, regardless of its shape, makes the perception of this object permanent and generalized.
>
> (Luria & Yudovich 1971, p. 23)

Luria calls this the phenomenon of *verbal generalisation systems*. He is emphasising how words relating us to referents organise a standardisation of responses across the particularities of time, settings and people. These are the practices in words that are taken up in what follows. We work through five very different specimens of people's practices of relating words to referents. We begin with two specimens that refer to actual objects (*table* and *bus*) – Luria's focus – but then move to others (*chemistry lecture, indecent exposure* and *body count*) in which the generalising function of naming has a more complex relation to what is referred to. Each is small ethnography describing how the words organise our doings – including, of course, doings in words. No claim is being made that this is comprehensive or a systematic collection. I have learnt as I examined each of them that learning has been incorporated into the accounts. The specimens' viewing words as practices are intended simply to break open a region that furthers ethnographic exploration. I've drawn on various sources as specimens, some of my own experience of word practices, others based on ethnographic and/or historical studies done by others.

The specimens also began to make observable how word-referent relations are implicated in organising what people do. The first of the specimens is the word *table* observed not as practised on a particular occasion, but following a procedure rather like that described by Mead in his 'dog' story, to bring out what 'came to mind' as I took up the word. In writing this specimen, I was producing in practice the very phenomena on which it focuses and, as readers read, they may notice instances of their own experience of practising this word coming to mind.

In the first and second specimens, the referent is a definite material object with a generalisable appearance. The first, the word *table*, brought into view more than an organisation of perception. The material object referred to conforms in very various styles to the part tables play in Western culture. The standardised material object provides for distinctive ways in which people co-ordinate. The second specimen, *bus*, draws attention to how the standardised appearance of an object evokes the word. In both these specimens of word-referent relations, there's a definite material object with a generalisable appearance; just the actual physical presence of such an object can evoke its name and how it might be taken up into what we are doing and how implicitly we may be participating in organisation beyond what's perceived. But specimen three, *the chemistry lecture*, is a shift. First, of course, the referent as an actual event is to be found in people's collectively coordinated activities. Yes, there are events or occasions involving people in collectively co-ordinated actions that are directly observable; yes, they do take some standardised generalised form. However, with *the chemistry lecture* there's another dimension present in any such occasion and that is how it is articulated, as what is in the institutional organisation of the university or college, as well as in the complex relations of chemistry discourse which is tied into the actual delivery of the lecture – what in a sense makes it a *chemistry* lecture. In this context, then, the word-referent relation has to be examined as it is grounded in the institutional categories defining the operations of university or college and in the everyday work organisation of the people involved in administration, teaching, research, studying and so on. Implicit in the phrase *chemistry lecture* are sequences of institutionally co-ordinated actions hooking up many others in institutionally authorised positions – students, faculty, administrative staff, electronic technicians and so on.

The chemistry lecture, however, is only a first step into the deep complexities of textual realities, those forms of word-referent relations that are organised textually. The categories of law, policy, management and other modes of governing discourse do refer, but do not directly identify, an actual object, person, event and so on that will fit. Institutionally authorised categories, such as *acts of indecency* in Ontario's 'bawdy' house law or the *body count* as a US military managerial category, discover referents only as appropriately authorised agents go to work to produce some kind of account drawn selectively from actualities that will fit them. The word-referent relation becomes a relation between the authorised category as frame and a textual representation drawn from but displacing actualities as experienced. The logic of Luria's observation of how words naming objects govern how the latter are perceived is at work here: 'The term that is successfully imposed will occupy the field of meaning' (Warner 2015, p. 10).

Specimens

I Table[2]

In taking up the word *table* as our first specimen of a practising word referring to an object, I'm following a practice described by George Herbert Mead

(1962) when he's making visible the fundamentally social character of language. Here's a passage in which he uses as an example the word *dog*.

> If one asked what the idea of a dog is and tried to find that idea in the central nervous system, one would find a whole group of responses which are more or less connected together by definite paths so that when one uses the term 'dog,' he does tend to call out this group of responses. A dog is a possible playmate, a possible enemy, one's own property or somebody else's. There is a whole series of possible responses. There are certain types of these responses that are in all of us, and there are others that vary with the individuals, but there is always an organisation of the responses that can be called out by the term 'dog.' So if one is speaking of a dog to another person he is arousing in himself this set of responses that he is arousing in the other individual.
>
> (Mead 1962, p. 71)

In how I've taken up this exploratory practice, hunting down the various 'responses' and the paths that connect them, I've done it in the process of writing, or in that obscure interplay between what's getting done 'in skull' and what emerges on the screen or page. Of course I'm dumping the notion of 'idea' but otherwise my writing practice of the word *table* follows Mead's 'in skull' account of how the word *dog* organises a complex of possible responses and connecting pathways.

'Responses' and connections are in this context framed and hence organised by the focus on word-referent practices, on *tables* as organising what the term refers to, its objects. Luria has the child learning to focus on named objects selectively so that s/he attends to generalised aspects. But taking off with the word *table* directs attention also to how objects may be created in generalised formats. A table separates floor at foot level from actions on a surface within reach of the upper part of the body. Built into the word as we practice it is a social organisation. We can imagine a table merely as a physical object, stripped of its social organisation, if we think of a child crawling on a wooden surface raised above the floor and of how the legs and surface of a table might appear to children playing underneath (my five-year-old granddaughter likes to hide there). But, as children learn to treat and recognise tables, they are learning social organisation not just of perception but also of coordinated doings among people. When my older granddaughter, Calla, was little she would sometimes climb on a chair and crawl across the dining room table, and her father would call out, 'Calla, get off the table!' Over time she's learning that whole bodies aren't welcome on the surface of the table used for eating. She's learning, as her father speaks, a practice of the word *table* that designs how she uses the object it locates. She learns also that mealtimes at the table are practices just for the upper part of the body.

So the word *table* can do more than organise how an object is perceived; it organises people's practices. When people come together and sit at a table their legs and genitals are discreetly suppressed though things, such as sexual touching, may go on, unobserved but not unfelt, under the table. In public settings – in a restaurant, for example – separate tables group people eating together, establishing a temporary appropriation of discrete territories. And imagine someone moving into a new living space who has a friend coming to dinner; her furniture delivery got delayed and she hasn't a table. 'What could I use as a table?' she says to herself; she finds a sturdy packing box, spreads a cloth on it, and, as a final touch, puts a water glass with a flower in the centre, arranging pillows around it to sit on.

Attend in your reading to how you activate the word 'table'; instances from your own experience may come to mind. Reading a text is a silent conversation (Smith 2005). What you've been reading will have engaged your own practices of the word *table*, organised by the same verbal generalisation and making other connections following different paths.

II The bus

This is an experiential account. Like all accounts of experience, it becomes what is told in dialogue with a particular verbal context – an ordinary conversation, an academic discourse or speech genre. Here, of course, the discourse is that of institutional ethnography. It is an account drawn from observation, from a conscious looking at something or someone's doings that is then told in terms referring the reader to the original actuality.

I was out walking my dog in Vancouver when I met my grandson near the sports field. He'd been coaching a junior rugby team. We stopped to talk at the corner of 12th Avenue and Vine Street. While he was telling me about what he'd been doing, I happened to glance east on 12th and saw a bus passing across a street two blocks away. The 'in-skull' dialogue went on as shown below. The words in bold are those that I can remember actually practising. In brackets are those aspects of the 'in-skull' dialogue that were not explicitly verbal.

> [a bus crosses 12th Avenue] **bus** [unuttered question: what street?] **Arbutus** [unuttered question: what bus?] **number 16** [unuttered question: where does it go after 12th?]

It was as if the word *bus* that kicked in when I was actually seeing its referent generated further words that had at that moment no visible referents. It went into practice as organiser of a sequence of connections related to transit buses – they travel definite routes along nameable streets. All this was fast, a momentary distraction from my conversation with my grandson.

This account was introduced to take up the connection Luria observed between a word and the standardisation of perception of an object because it raises further questions of how this connection is organised as actual practices. Luria's verbal standardisation goes from word to an organisation of how a thing is perceived as its object. In this story, we find a reverse sequence. The first moment is my perception of an object that is standardised in how it appears. I see a recognisable transit bus crossing an intersection. A transit bus is recognisable by its standardised shape and coloring; it's not a Greyhound or a truck or van.

Thus, in this story we can begin to get a take on the word-referent organisation that works both ways when objects are standardised in some way to evoke the word. Once the word *bus* is in play, it organises a dialogue that builds on my *under*-standing of the transit system in Vancouver – buses have numbers that identify routes. Seeing a bus travelling at a particular place can suggest a number and that then orients to a question of where it goes next. I emphasise the 'under' in 'under-standing' because it is presupposed but never explicit as I go from *bus* to street name to bus number to a question about where it's going. My mini 'in-skull' dialogue as it maps the street and the number 16 bus route southward co-ordinates with the institutional organisation of the local public transit system.

III The chemistry lecture

I chose the term *chemistry lecture* in part because I'd been re-reading Harold Garfinkel's (2002) chapter recounting his and his associates' (David Sudnow and Melinda Baccus) ethnographies of chemistry lectures in the 1970s. Their observational focus was on lecture occasions as a sequence of action among participants that, governed by an underlying and implicit social order analogous to that discovered in Conversational Analysis, 'produces' the lecture as an event. The several observations of particular chemistry lecture events at different universities are assembled into an account of the practices of what Garfinkel calls the 'local order-production cohort'. It becomes '*the* chemistry lecture'. He takes for granted that occasions or events produced in people's practices are unproblematic as 'phenomena'.

> These are recurrencies in productions of immortal, ordinary things – traffic jams, service lines, summoning phones, blackboard notes, jazz piano in a cocktail lounge, talking chemistry in lecture format, police protection of an ambulance run, good work in Tibetan Buddhist debates – phenomena that *exhibit* along with their other endogenously accountable details, endogenously accountable populations that staff their production.
>
> (Garfinkel 2002, p. 124)

As stated in introducing the topic of this chapter, what is done is always historical in the sense that it's happening in an ongoing everyday, always in change however minutely. Yet ethnographies rely on how people are acting and coordinating what they are doing in ways that fit the generalising word or words that name an event, occasion and so on. Ethnomethodology's explications of the local production of events shows how people do bring into being what can be named using the same standardising categories. Here, however, the issue is how a term like *the chemistry lecture* can be used to refer to some kind of occasion when people come together in a co-ordinated sequence of action that they – or others – can name as such. We're opening up here the problem of how word (or phrase) is practiced in institutional settings. The references of institutional terms are not as directly identifiable as words for materially given objects such as a table or a passing bus. Janet Giltrow (1998) became interested in the prevalence of nominalisations in managerial discourse. Nominalisations are nouns constructed out of active verbs. When she set about 'unpacking' them to discover the active agents implicit in them, she found a fundamental ambiguity: once unpacked, the agents could not be identified as a particular person or as the same person. Take a statement such as 'the creation and implementation of institutional arrangements' (Giltrow 1998, p. 341) and unpack it into its implicit active statements.

> Now agency is visible. Some actual individual, w, creates, and another, x, implements; or, w creates and yet another, y, implements. But a fundamental ambiguity remains: we can't be sure if it's a single actor or set of actors linked in a chain of action: are w, x and y the same entities or different ones?
> (Giltrow 1998, pp. 341–342)

What Giltrow uncovers is a case of a more general problem in institutional discourses. In making the transition from word/term to referent, we have to travel through the textual mediations of institutional organisation. Take the term 'undergraduate' which appears in the title to Garfinkel's (2002) chapter on the chemistry lecture. 'Undergraduate' locates a complex of textual specifications of a category of persons. How are students differentiated from people who are not students? They are registered in the university or college registration system; they have probably paid or provided for the payment of their fees; they are signed up for a program; and so on and so on. And for the students who come to the chemistry lecture, it is only one piece in the sequence of the course they're taking and in which their performance as evaluated will result in a grade registered in the university records.

Then there's the problem of what is 'chemistry' and here we're launched into the complex of text-mediated discourses located in actual people's work in multiple sites in universities and colleges; in various corporations relying on chemical research; at conferences and conventions; and so on and so on. Ethnomethodological interest in explicating local productions of social order makes sense of reducing multiple observations of chemistry lectures to 'the chemistry lecture'. However our turn towards taking up the word-referent organisation as actually practised has to recognise that the term carries implicit connections extending beyond any particular occasion so named. And we recognise also that the term *chemistry lecture* may be used to refer to an actual event, taking place at a scheduled time and period in a room with a definite and probably numbered identity; it is what it is – each time – for those who participate – the lecturer who's working to get whatever step in teaching undergraduate chemistry his or her lecture carries to the students; and the students are using the lecture, with varying attention, as work for a course for which they've registered. Not so different, after all, from the number 16 bus I saw crossing Arbutus and travelling south.

Garfinkel's (2002) version of the referent for the words 'chemistry lecture' is analogous to the bus that passes the intersection of 12th and Arbutus in our second specimen. It attempts to ground the term in something that can actually be observed and studied. But somehow what the term refers to slips away. A chemistry lecture is one in a sequence of collective events that contribute to an undergraduate course. Nothing is actually what it is, no one is actually who they are, without reference to the scientific discourse that is being locally practiced as the lecturer and undergraduate students come together in a class built into a course that has been authorised in the university's regulatory process. In any occurrence of a chemistry lecture – an actual event – these relations were also present in the 'work organisation' of the chemistry lecture as an actual happening. Once we attend to how the word (term)-referent organisation enters into co-ordinating people's actions institutionally, we can recognise that any actual occasion identified as a *chemistry lecture* implicates a nexus of relations co-ordinating students' and instructors' work in the chemistry course with other work in which students or faculty or administrative staff are active, in and beyond the particular university or college site, with the complex relations of the scientific and technical discourses of chemistry.

IV Acts of indecency

George Smith (1988) wrote an ethnography describing how when gay men were found enjoying sex in a steambath in Toronto, the manager in charge and the owner of the steambath were charged with 'acts of indecency' under Ontario's 'bawdy house' law.[3] But what is being referred to by the term 'acts of indecency'? The referent has no concrete features that can be identified in definite times and places or as performed by specific individuals. Nothing like the *table* or the *bus* here; nothing like a *chemistry lecture* when it's actually happening. So now we have to go deeper into the textually mediated worlds of institutional and large-scale organisation; we have to look for word-referent practices in which a 'governing' word or term establishes a frame that textual representations of what actually is or has been happening have to fit. The referent of the word/term has to be actively produced as a textual reality that, as referent, the word/term of a governing or, as I sometimes call it, boss text.

By boss or governing text I'm referring (and notice my word practices here) to texts that are established as authoritative independently of the authority of local practices – the 'bawdy house' law is an instance as is also the fifth specimen – the managerial 'body count' evaluation established for the US military during the Vietnam War. They establish textual frames that the representations of actualities have to be fitted to enable or be relevant to mandated courses of action. There are definite procedures for generating texts, such as legislation, policy-making committees and so on that produce authoritative texts without identifying them with particular individuals. They are then legitimated as having been approved by a governing body to stand independently of those involved in their production, set up to be enforced by procedures, and agents are designated to take on that job. The wording of the governing text may implicate varied interests and have to be carefully negotiated.[4]

However the term 'acts of indecency' was established, there it is in Ontario's 'bawdy house' law. If someone can be shown in an appropriate textual representation as having been engaged in an act of indecency, he or she can be charged under the law. Hence when two officers visited the steambath undercover to observe and report the sexual activities of the gay men present with a view to bringing charges, their report had to characterise what they saw as fitting the shell of *acts of indecency*. Here's a passage from the police report:

> When the officers first entered the premises they walked around and noted the lay-out of the premises as well as any indecent activity that was taking place at that time. It was at this time that both officers saw a number of men laying (sic) nude in the private booths with the door wide open. Some of these men were masturbating themselves while others just lay on the mattress watching as other men walked about the hallways. The officers took periodic walks about the premises and they saw that the same type of indecent activity was taking place each and every time.
>
> (Quoted in Smith 1988)

'Acts of indecency' under this law are not a specific type of sexual activity; they are any overt sexual activity *performed in public*. Nothing wrong with masturbating, but notice how the officers are careful to mention the booths with doors wide open, the men watching other men masturbating and so on. In producing their account the officers picked out what could count as *acts of indecency* and hence enable charges to be brought against those involved.

Another clause of the 'bawdy house' law sets up the terms under which '[e]veryone who ... agent or otherwise having charge or control of any place or any part thereof to be let or used for the purpose of a common bawdy house, is guilty of an offence ...' (quoted in Smith 1988) and can be charged. Again the officers' account includes selective observations of the steambath's manager's actions that show him as aware of the 'public' character of the sexual activities going on.

The police report and its processing become the textual reality on the basis on which an institutional course of action – charging the owner and manager of the steambath and those found in it and then the subsequent legal moves – is enabled. Actualities as those involved were experiencing them are displaced; they are irrelevant; there's no place in the 'shells' of the bawdy house law in which their own experiences could fit.

V *The* body count

With this final specimen we are examining a word-referent relation in which the referent has in a sense no actual existence out there; it does not happen. When we looked at the legal category 'acts of indecency', the business of the police officers was to make observations (and report) what was going on among people that would fit the legal frame. Here, however, though there are people in action, the textual representation is not of what they are or were doing, but in how an outcome of their doings can be *counted* and contribute to statistical representations at a managerial level.

James William Gibson (1986) has written a historical study of the Vietnam War, *The Perfect War: Technowar in Vietnam*. His concept of 'technowar' is of war governed in its objectives, appraisal of forces and numbers, and material costs by managerial methods of statistical data collection and analysis. Robert McNamara was the major figure in introducing these technical statistical methods of managing contemporary warfare to the United States. He had been appointed to the position of US Secretary of Defense by President Kennedy. Trained and taught at the Harvard University Business School, he had during World War II 'developed statistical techniques of systems analysis for the War Department as management tools in controlling large organizations' (Gibson 1986, p. 14). Before his defense appointment, he had been the General Manager of the Ford Motor Company.

McNamara introduced new concepts of managerial rationality into the Department and into the conduct of the Vietnam War. A discourse was developed proposing a microeconomic analogy for victory in Vietnam. McNamara held that:

> 'Transforming the world into discrete quantities is . . . a necessary first step in all reasoning about warfare.' . . . It was proposed that computer simulations based on the model of profit maximization could be used to evaluate 'different combinations of ships, planes, and ground troops . . . to find the most 'cost-effective' victory.
>
> (Gibson 1986, pp. 79–80)

Ratios of numbers of US forces and the combined forces of North Vietnam (NVA) and the Vietcong (VC) were used to evaluate effectiveness. The long-term objective and the winning of the war were defined as the reduction of the NVA and VC to the point where they were no longer able to replace casualties and eventually would give up. Hence the establishment of the 'body count' as an on-the-ground objective contributing directly to the statistical data evaluating progress of the war.

This specimen of a textual reality is distinctive in that what fits has to be countable. A body count seems straightforward since each dead body can be registered simply as an individual unit to be included in the count; the numbers accumulated can then be manipulated statistically in various ways.

> Different formulas were used, but the commitment to war as a rational production process was common to all. General Ewell, for example, set up standards to determine satisfactory "kill ratios" for different units. . . . Normal production rate for Ewell's units was . . . killing ten enemy soldiers for every US soldier killed! Rewards and punishments [for the officer corps] were distributed around that norm. . . .'
>
> (Gibson 1986, p. 113)

Producing the body count was a developed organisational performance. 'Commanders set up systems of calculating ratios of body counts. Ratios were of losses, sometimes simply of US versus Vietnamese, at other times more complex' (Gibson 1986, p. 112). It was not always clear who was enemy and who just civilian Vietnamese.

> At times the US forces saw rules of engagement not as constraints upon their activities but as categories to be appropriated for deliberately killing people who they knew were noncombatants. Identifications rules became a 'cover' for perverse killing.
>
> (Schell 1968, p. 137)

In the previous specimen, we saw the use of the categories of the boss text of Ontario's 'bawdy house' law as a 'shell' that representations had to be fitted to. Here we find that actualities to be fitted to the shell of the 'body count' had to be 'performed'. For example, attacks could be launched to provoke a response from the enemy and hence enable killing. Here is a personal account of this as a 'body count' performance:

> Night movement, that was a suicidal patrol. That was one of the worst patrols you could ever go out on. The purpose of it was for you to walk up on Charlie and for him to hit you, and then for our hardware to wipe them out. We were used as scapegoats [sic] to find out where they were. That was all we were − bait. They couldn't find Charlies any other way. They knew there was a regiment out there. They weren't looking for just a handful of VC. Actually, they'd love for us to run into a regiment which would just wipe us out. Then they could plaster the regiment and they'd have a big body count. The general gets another damn medal. He gets promoted.
>
> (Stan Goff, quoted by Gibson 1986, p. 111)

This is an early development in the progressive extension of corporate management practices to the public sector (Griffith & Smith 2014). Integral to these forms of management are technologies translating the actualities of people's work into forms of textual reality in which they become 'accountable'.

Discussion

We have scanned five specimens of word-referent relations. Starting with Luria's observation of how word naming an object standardises how the object is perceived, we have extended observations to the more general frame of word-referent relations and discovered other aspects of how such relations can be organised. The specimens raise some other issues: Luria does not consider how objects may be manufactured or otherwise shaped to fit generalised forms; nor do issues arise of some of the different ways in which the referent 'appears'. The first two specimens were of words, *table* and *bus*, that referred to material objects, as does Luria's observation. The sequence of specimens went from referents that were material objects in people's presences to *the chemistry lecture*, a word-referent relation locating a collective site in a complex of institutional relations, and two others, *acts of indecency* and the *body count*, in which the referent is produced textually and becomes a textual reality displacing actualities.

Examining these specimens suggests that when we look at words as actually practised, they can be seen to organise. I'm using the word 'organise' here as bringing into view generalised forms of coordinating what people do – including, of course, what they do in language whether spoken, written or 'in-skull'. The very writing up of the *table* specimen was organised as I brought the word into practice. In examining the *bus* specimen I can see how that word-referent relation articulated my 'thinking' to the Greater Vancouver's transit system. I tracked, in-skull, from seeing/naming the bus with its regional transit markings to the street name and the bus route number. The actual passing of the bus brings the word into play but then the word as it is taken up organises the little in-skull conversation that activates my local mapping of the transit system of routes. The *chemistry lecture* locates a setting and time where people active in intersecting institutional courses of action come together – students taking a chemistry course as part of a university program, a faculty member whose course presentation participates in the discourses of chemical science whose co-ordinated work in this site is producing a particular university course in chemistry.

In the specimens of textual representations produced to fit governing categories, the bawdy house law and the body count, we can see how the categories *organise* the work of producing representations to fit them. That fit becomes the grounds on which institutionally mandated courses of action can go ahead. The gay men enjoying their sexuality in a steambath can be charged with *acts of indecency* which are then to be recognised and taken up as offences under the 'bawdy house' law. Of course, such practices are actual; during the war in

Vietnam, producing body counts was the work of people involved in a complex hierarchic organisation. Producing the textual representations rendering what becomes the working reality within the governing texts is itself an organisation of people's work; the mandated courses of action to which such textual representations articulate happen in the real world. Real people were killed and counted in Vietnam even though military practices could not clearly differentiate those who were 'enemy' from civilians.

In these modes of organising word-referent relations as actual practices, we can begin to discover ethnographically how such text-based *verbal generalising systems* (Luria 1961) are put together as people's local practices and can be entered thereby into institutional courses of action. In the managerial imposition of statistical methods of evaluating American military progress in Vietnam, a grand imaginary (Jessop 2013) had been created in which many died, on both sides.

Inconclusion

In all these specimens we are discovering how words, as people practice them, enter into social organisation. Their verbal generalising from person to person, from one situation to another, from place to place, inserts sameness, recurrence, reproduction into the immortal ongoing historicity of actualities, where we live in our bodies. I've called this an 'inconclusion' because I have opened up these five specimens only to introduce the potentialities of recognising words as people's practices, enabling them to be incorporated in very ordinary ways into institutional ethnographies, or indeed any ethnography. In their various ways, they exemplify what comes to light as we are freed up to make observations of people's practices with words in our/their everyday lives. Allowing the ethnographer simply to observe and examine how words are practiced by people in their everyday and particularly their working lives moves away from conceptual and research strategies that isolate language to enclose it in a specialised and technical discourse.

Returning, however, to the contradiction built into institutional ethnography's ontology, the specimens of word-referent organisation do have something to tell us about how what can appropriately be described as social organisation. In a sense inadvertently the word-referent exploration has brought into view the generalised object or event as organising what people do. While the word that refers to whatever it is, is integral to how the object or event becomes organised in a recognisable and standardised mode, the word doesn't have to be actually brought into practice for the generalisation it organises to operate. Think, as an example, of the *sidewalk* and of how people concert their movements on paving that is differentiated from the street. Just this morning I'm out walking my dog and I meet a bunch of maybe a dozen male teenagers coming towards me and jamming up the sidewalk. One of those in front turns sideways without stopping and, speaking to all in a commanding voice, says 'Share the sidewalk!' Clearly they get his message because the whole group closes up to my left, making room for me and my walking stick. And clearly they know right away what he's referring to as the *sidewalk*.

I don't mean to suggest that every word people practice has to be explored to discover social organisation and, of course, word-referent organisation is only one of many identifiable practices. Nonetheless observing words as practices directs ethnographic attention to what, following Luria, we might describe as the 'verbal generalising'. Our five specimens suggest one mode in which social organisation can be located in people's local historical practices and can thereby be given concrete ethnographic presence.

Notes

1 Luria originally observed this phenomenon incidentally to an experimental study with children. I was unable to locate the original observation since it was not itself the topic and Luria's experimental work has been more or less buried – perhaps because his experimental procedures don't test hypotheses but aim rather at isolating and making aspects of children's learning observable.
2 This account of the word *table* was first written as a passage in earlier work of mine (Smith 1990). I haven't reproduced it exactly though I have incorporated some of the examples I used in the original.
3 In the terms of Ontario's law, "a common bawdy house is a place . . . that is kept . . . for the practice of acts of indecency" (GW Smith 1988).
4 Lauren Eastwood (2014) describes the work of a civil society organisation behind the scenes of a meeting of the International Forestry Forum scanning the text of a proposed agreement to ensure that it preserves key terms of the 1992 Rio de Janeiro United Nations Conference on Environment and Development. If preserved in the final and official document, the relevant terms would then frame how governments involved in the agreement could represent their forest management practices and outcomes.

References

Austin, JL 1962, *How to do things with words*, Harvard University Press, Cambridge, MA.
Bakhtin, MM 1981, *The dialogic imagination: Four essays*, M Holquist (ed.), University of Texas Press, Austin.
Eastwood, L 2014, 'Negotiating UN policy: Activating texts in policy deliberations', in DE Smith & SM Turner (eds), *Incorporating texts into institutional ethnographies*, University of Toronto Press, Toronto, pp. 64–89.
Garfinkel, H 2002, *Ethnomethodology's program: Working out Durkheim's aphorism*, A Warfield Rawls (ed.), Rowman and Littlefield, Lanham, MD.
Gibson, JW 1986, *The perfect war: Techno war in Vietnam*, Grove/Alantic, New York.
Giltrow, J 1998, 'Modernizing authority, management studies, and the grammaticalization of controlling interests', *Technical Writing and Communication*, vol. 28 no. 4, pp. 337–358.
Griffith, AI & Smith, DE 2014, *Under new public management: Institutional ethnographies of changing front-line work*, University of Toronto Press, Toronto.
Jessop, B 2013, 'Recovered imaginaries, imagined recoveries: A cultural political economy of crisis construals and crisis-management in the North Atlantic financial crisis,' in M Benner (ed.), *Beyond the global economic crisis s: Economics and politics for a post-crisis settlement*, Edward Elgar, Cheltenham, UK, pp. 234–254.

Luria, AR 1961, *The role of speech in the regulation of normal and abnormal behaviour*, Pergamon, New York.

Luria, AR 1976, *Cognitive development: Its cultural and social foundations*, Harvard University Press, Cambridge, MA.

Luria, AR & Yudovich, R 1971, *Speech and the development of mental processes in the child*, Penguin, New York.

Mead, G H 1962, *Mind, self, and society from the perspective of a social behaviorist*, University of Chicago Press, Chicago.

Schell, J 1968, *The military half: An account of the destruction of Quang Ngai and Quang Tin*, Vintage, New York.

Smith, DE 1990, *The conceptual practices of power: A feminist sociology of knowledge*, Northeastern University Press, Boston.

Smith, DE 2005, *Institutional ethnography: A sociology for people*, AltaMira Press, Lanham.

Smith, GW 1988, 'Policing the gay community: An inquiry into textually mediated relations', *International Journal of Sociology and the Law*, vol. 16, pp. 163–183.

Vološinov, VI 1973, *Marxism and the philosophy of language*, IR Titunik (trans), Academic Press, New York.

Warner, M 2015, '"Learning my lesson": Marina Warner on the disfiguring of higher education', *London Review of Books*, vol. 37, no. 6. pp. 8–14.

Chapter 3

Accounting for practice in an age of theory

Charles Taylor's theory of social imaginaries

Steven Hodge and Stephen Parker

Introduction

The 'practice turn' is a label Schatzki (2001a) uses to describe a shift across several social scientific disciplines to viewing practices as 'the primary generic social thing' (2001a, p. 10). Theorists whose research can be characterised in this way include Marx, Wittgenstein, Bourdieu, Giddens, Foucault and Canadian philosopher Charles Taylor. According to Schatzki, 'practice approaches promulgate a distinct social ontology: the social is a field of embodied, materially interwoven practices centrally organised around shared practical understandings'. He adds that,

> This conception contrasts with accounts that privilege individuals, (inter) actions, language, signifying systems, the life world, institutions/roles, structures, or systems in defining the social. These phenomena, say practice theorists, can only be analyzed via the field of practices. Actions, for instance, are embedded in practices, just as individuals are constituted within them. Language, moreover, is a type of activity (discursive) and hence a practice phenomenon, whereas institutions and structures are effects of them. Needless to say, practice theorists have different understandings of these matters.
>
> (2001a, p. 12)

One of the differences is in the way practice theorists understand the role of theory in the social world. Since Marx, pure theory has been regarded with suspicion by researchers aligned with the practice approach. 'Idealism' is a common term for the view that ideas have an autonomous and constitutive role in shaping practice. From at least Plato (c. fifth century BC), theory has been considered the primary reference point for understanding human life and society. On this view, ideas are independent of practice, while the practical realm generally represents the degradation and confusion of ideas. Modern social theory, including practice theory, challenges this ontology.

As Schatzki points out, 'practices at once underlie subjects and objects, highlight non-propositional knowledge, and illuminate the conditions of intelligibility' (2001a, p. 10). In other words, practices enable theory but are not constituted by it. Practices contain their own conditions of intelligibility (they cannot be explained with reference to external ideas) and they generate ideas and are the ultimate reference point of them. An example of this anti-idealism is provided by Marx (1977), who argues that the practices of the capitalist classes produce ideas and these ideas underpin theoretical claims on behalf of *all* practices and classes. He uses the term 'ideology' to refer to theoretical productions of practice and 'idealism' to highlight the over-blown claims of theory to account for the social world. For the critical project of Marx, therefore, practice is the primary focus for understanding society and idealism is fundamentally erroneous although it serves the interests of some groups. Practice theory can be interpreted as a contemporary form of social analysis that underwrites the anti-idealist cause.

Drawing on the work of Heidegger, Wittgenstein and Merleau-Ponty, Taylor's theory of practice takes a different line on the theory-practice relationship. As a practice theorist, Taylor subscribes to the anti-idealism characteristic of the approach. That is, he rejects the notion that theory is the autonomous locus of intelligibility vis-à-vis practices in history and society. However, Taylor's research uncovers a problematic that challenges this standard form of anti-idealism. Standard anti-idealism – originating in Marx's writings and present in nuanced form in Foucault's and Bourdieu's practice theories – has it that theories make pretensions to account for practice but that such claims are always illusory at base. In this form of anti-idealism, other mechanisms account for the intelligibility of practices. For Marx the material conditions of production furnish the rationale, while for Foucault it is disciplinary or governmental techniques that articulate knowledge and power. On these explanations, ideas as such have no prior or special claim to explain the world. But for Taylor, while it is true that ideas do not possess the autonomy and priority granted by idealism, the modern world – the empirical focus of much of his research – is marked by prevalence of, and deference to theory. He declares that 'Ours is an inescapably theoretical civilization' (1985b, p. 106). Taylor describes the efficacy of theory on the social world, including the potency of flawed social theory (Taylor 1985b) and the impact of ideas on modernity itself (Taylor 2002a). For Taylor, then, a challenge for practice theory is how to account for social practices in a theory-laden age wherein the efficacy of theory can be demonstrated. How, in other words, can the anti-idealism of practice theory be maintained in the face of the prevalence and apparent power of theory in our world?

In this chapter we examine Taylor's theory of practice and his strategies for avoiding idealism in the context of a theoretical civilization. We begin with an overview of Taylor's claim that we live in a 'theoretical civilization' (1985b,

p. 106) and introduce his examples of the influence and efficacy of theory that demonstrate the pervasiveness of theory in contemporary practices. Taylor's strategies for avoiding idealism are examined next. Here, the case for the efficacy of flawed theory investigated in his 1985 work is considered as well as the large-scale phenomenon of the influence of theory analysed in his post-2000 studies. The final section returns to the concept of social practices and reviews Taylor's account of practice in the broader context of theory and the transformation of modern social imaginaries.

The pervasiveness and efficacy of theory

Charles Taylor (b. 1931) has written on a range of seemingly disparate topics including multiculturalism, human rights, modern identity and political philosophy. Throughout much of this work there is a unifying concern with philosophical anthropology – the features that he views are essential to human agency in the modern age – and the historical development of ideas and social phenomena. As such, a theory of practice is not Taylor's main focus with little of his writings directly concerned with practice per se. This would appear to make Taylor a curious choice for this topic. But there is a sense in which Taylor is clearly a practice theorist, earning him the attention of Schatzki (2001a, 2001b).

Taylor's theory of practice differs from mainstream practice theory in its insistence on the need to account for the influence of theory at an empirical level. For Taylor, the contemporary social context of practices is marked by the pervasiveness of theory. He explains that

> Ours is a very theoretical civilization. We see this both in the fact that certain understandings formulated in modern theories have become incorporated in the common understandings by which political society operates in the West, and also in that, however simplified and vulgarized these theories may become in attaining general currency, an important part of their prestige and credibility reposes on their being believed to be correct theories, truly validated as knowledge, as this is understood in a scientific age.
>
> (1985b, p. 105)

This is to say that, contrary to the standard, dismissive view of theory associated with practice theory, any analysis of social practices must acknowledge the influence of theory. Taylor asserts that theories have become 'incorporated' into the way Westerners understand their political society. He stresses that these theories must be translated – 'simplified and vulgarized' – to become effective in practice, but more importantly that they owe their effectiveness to their being accepted as valid knowledge, according to the norms of our scientific age.

Taylor (1985b) illustrates the influence of theory on practice with reference to the theory of behaviourism. Early on in his career, Taylor (1965) published a critique of behaviourism in which he exposed the fallacies upon which the behaviourist account of human action is built. This theory of behaviour is familiar to researchers in the social sciences as the now-discredited explanation of learning that methodologically avoids consideration of consciousness, intentions, meaning and purposiveness. Behaviourism arrives at its conclusions by reducing the rich phenomena of human being and society to simpler constituents from which it seeks to build up theory. Taylor's voice joined the chorus of powerful criticism of behaviourism. In his mind at least, the limitations and distortions of behaviourism were clear for all to see and its influence on theory and practice could only wane.

Two decades later, in the opening discussion of Volume 2 of his *Philosophical Papers*, Taylor (1985b) reveals his perplexity in the face of the persistence of the theory of behaviourism and related reductive theories that he loosely terms 'naturalism', and their continued influence on social theory and practices. Naturalistic theories, Taylor argues, are united by 'a certain metaphysical motivation' (1985b, p. 2) and aspire to replicate the methods and epistemologies of the natural science. In particular, this 'family' of theories is characterised by the assumption that humans 'can be seen as a part of nature . . . [which] is to be understood according to the canons which emerged in the seventeenth-century revolution in natural science' (1985b, p. 2). Subsequently, analysis of the social world 'must avoid anthropocentric properties . . . and give an account of things in absolute terms' (1985b, p. 2). For Taylor, these approaches are unsatisfactory for a number of reasons including that they are reductive in their attempt to 'know' social life in terms of a neutral, scientific language. Scientific approaches to understanding human life, Taylor insists, cannot capture the self-interpretations and background of distinctions of worth that are essential to full human agency.[1] Taylor's concept of 'background' is influenced by the work of Heidegger, Wittgenstein and Merleau-Ponty (Taylor 2006). These thinkers were critical of naturalistic accounts of human being that assume an objective standpoint can be adopted for the study of human being. We will elaborate on the significance of the 'background' later, but for the moment it is sufficient to emphasise Taylor's argument that the epistemologies of the natural sciences are not suitable for the social sciences. Further, Taylor argues that these accounts of human being have been shown to rest on implausible and inadequate epistemologies that are themselves non-scientific and are inconsistent with their own epistemological commitments (1985b). Despite this criticism (which is not unique to Taylor, but has a long history in philosophy, the sociology of knowledge and related disciplines), the natural science model remains dominant.

In later studies, Taylor (2002a, 2004, 2007) introduces another example of the pervasiveness and influence of theory that emerges in the context of his extended analyses of 'modernity'. According to Taylor (2002a, p. 91), modernity is the 'number one problem of modern social science'. By modernity, Taylor means,

> that historically unprecedented amalgam of new practices and institutional forms (science, technology, industrial production, urbanization), of new ways of living (individualism, secularization, instrumental rationality), and of new forms of malaise (alienation, meaninglessness, a sense of impending social dissolution).
>
> (2002a, p. 91)

For Taylor, the key to comprehending this 'unprecedented amalgam' is that a new conception of the 'moral order' of society is at play. He says the concept of a moral order of society first took shape in the minds of theorists such as Hugo Grotius and John Locke. In Grotius it is the idea that human beings are 'rational, sociable agents who are meant to collaborate in peace to their mutual benefit' (Taylor 2002a, p. 92). Grotius' theory was originally constructed to describe and explain the nature of political society in a time of upheaval. But as Taylor explains, theories of this kind promulgate a normative account of how we should behave toward each other. In other words, social theories such as those of Grotius and Locke have both descriptive and prescriptive dimensions. They seek to account for the social world and also convey a sense of how we ought to behave toward each other. For Taylor, theories with this dual character have the potential to expand beyond their initial setting in the thought, conversation and machinations of elite groups and permeate society more broadly. In the case of the theory of the moral order elaborated by Grotius and Locke, Taylor says it entered on a trajectory that saw it undergo a double expansion, so that more and more people lived according to it, and secondly it intensified, making more differentiated and stronger demands on society.

With this explanation of the character of modernity and its origins, Taylor (2002a) magnifies the problem of the social efficacy of theory well beyond its purview in the 1985 papers. In his earlier work, the problem was confined to the inroads of naturalistic assumptions into social theory and practice. It was a problem there because the theories in question were inherently flawed as accounts of social practices but meet with broad acceptance. In Taylor's later analysis of modernity, however, the problem of the efficacy of theory assumes larger proportions and greater moral ambiguity. The concern is that the modern moral order, which functions ontologically at level of the background of distinctions of worth and associated images posited in the 1985 papers, is itself largely determined by theory. And it is theory that can be attributed to the authorship of individual actors and enjoys pure development and internal coherence in the context of discursive practices. The problem of the efficacy of theory identified in Taylor's 1985 writings is thus transposed to a new and wider arena of application in his later work wherein 'high' theory created by famous scholars transforms the very background of society. This account of modernity leaves Taylor with a substantial challenge. The efficacy of theory implied by his account of modernity clearly smacks of idealism.

Banishing the spectre of idealism

Taylor (2004) is well aware that any attempt to explain practices in terms of the influence or efficacy of theory invites the charge of idealism. Practice theory is hostile to social theory that prioritises theory and theorists or positions practices as shaped or formed by theory. For instance, Bourdieu (1990, p. 380) criticises what he calls 'the scholastic point of view' that is adopted by intellectuals who believe they operate outside and free of the imperatives of practice and create context-free and therefore 'true' statements about the social world. Foucault's researches present another example. His *archeological* approach, for instance, rejects any attempt to position a theory or theorist as the originator of discourses that are the source of the intelligibility of practices (Gutting 1989). But Taylor's researches reveal a society that is permeated by and even celebrates theory and the theorists who create it, and he analyses cases that demonstrate the efficacy of theory on practices. Taylor therefore faces a special challenge as a practice theorist: how to maintain an anti-idealist stance while giving ideas a substantial role in shaping society. Taylor devotes considerable effort to reconciling the claims of traditional, mainstream practice theory with his observations of contemporary social practices that demonstrate the infiltration of theory. In this section of the chapter, we spell out Taylor's strategies for avoiding the charge of idealism. We begin with the strategy he offers to account for the efficacy of the flawed naturalistic social theory and then move to his strategy for dealing with the larger problem posed by his analysis of modernity.

The first of Taylor's anti-idealist strategies for accounting for the efficacy of theory is elaborated to explain the influence of flawed social theory. As described above, Taylor's (1985b) hermeneutic picture of the human rules out the application of natural scientific theory to human being. But lack of theoretical coherence does not interfere with the spread and acceptance of naturalistic theory. The question then is: How, given the withering critiques of his and others of these theories, could theory and practice continue to be so influenced? Naturalism, in Taylor's estimation, must owe its continued appeal to something other than theoretical cogency. 'If the scientific and epistemological arguments are so poor', asks Taylor (1985b, p. 6), 'what gives them their strength?' In general terms, Taylor argues that naturalism maintains its dominance due to 'very strong preconceptions' (1985b, p. 5) that result in its 'moral motivation' overriding its own epistemological basis (1995b, p. 7). Taylor's critique goes beyond acknowledging the limitations of the language of naturalistic paradigms to argue that such approaches have significant implications for how we understand human agency. He continues:

> I believe that they derive their force from the *underlying image of the self*, and that this exercises its hold on us because of the *ideal of disengagement and the images of freedom, dignity and power which attach to it*. More specifically, the claim is that the more we are led to interpret ourselves in the light of the disengaged picture, to define our identity by this, *the more the connected epistemology of naturalism will seem right and proper to us*. Or otherwise put, a commitment to this identity generates powerful resistances against any challenges to the naturalist outlook. In short, its epistemological weaknesses are more than made up for by its moral appeal.
>
> (1985b, pp. 5–6; emphasis added)

To explain these implications Taylor turns to the 'image' of human agency held by 'modern' humans that has 'great moral appeal' (1985b, p. 6), explaining that

> behind and supporting the impetus to naturalism . . . viz. the understandable prestige of the natural science model, stands an attachment to a *certain picture of the agent.* This picture is deeply attractive to moderns, both *flattering and inspiring*. It shows us as capable of achieving a kind of disengagement from our world by objectifying it.
>
> (1985b, p. 4; emphasis added)

The key to the appeal of this image is the 'ideal of disengagement' he says is definitive of modern culture. It is to the power of this image of ourselves that Taylor attributes the resilience of naturalistic theories. He explains that 'behind and supporting' naturalistic accounts of humans such as behaviourism is the picture and ideal of the disengaged human. He says 'this image of agency . . . *offers crucial support* to the naturalist world-view' (1985a, p. 5; emphasis added).

Taylor associates these images with the 'background' introduced earlier in this chapter. Naturalistic accounts of human being are appealing to the extent that they reinforce the image of ourselves as a disengaged agent. For a theory to be effective in this sense – to have a powerful influence over practice – it needs to reinforce, resonate and cohere with 'a background of distinctions of worth' (1985b, p. 4). Taylor's argument here is that as self-interpreting beings, humans draw on an underlying system of values. He explains that

> our self-understanding essentially incorporates our seeing ourselves against a background of what I have called 'strong evaluation'. I mean by that a background of distinctions between things which are recognized as of categoric or unconditioned or higher importance or worth . . .
>
> (1985a, p. 3).

These backgrounds partly constitute self-understandings – the ways in which humans interpret their social worlds and understand their place in it – that are an 'essential or primary property of [human] existence' (Abbey 2000, p. 154). But despite being so central, these self-understandings can be regarded as wrong, incoherent or misleading, and can demonstrate the influence of a flawed theory, such as the image of the disengaged agent that emanates from naturalism.

From Taylor's explanation of the efficacy of naturalistic social theory we are able to discern his anti-idealistic argument. Theories can appear to present adequate explanations of social practices, and furthermore, through this appearance of adequacy may actually shape social practices. However, the presuppositions of theories may conflict with the ontology of social practices. In the case of naturalistic social theory, humans and their practices are assumed to conform to a stable underlying structure, much like natural objects in their diversity exhibit the stable characteristics of the substances that compose them. However, ontologically humans are self-interpreting which means that there is no stable matrix of expressions of human being and social practices. Naturalistic social theory therefore makes invalid assumptions about the nature of human being. This theory is incoherent as theory. Its efficacy is not attributable to its own validity, and therefore must refer to something else: the prevailing image of the disengaged agents, which Taylor associates with another structure, the background of distinctions of worth.

Taylor's second anti-idealist strategy for explaining the efficacy of theory emerges in the context of his analyses of modernity. In these researches, Taylor (2002a, 2004, 2007) argues that modernity is decisively influenced by theory while acknowledging that his argument seems haunted by the *spectre of idealism*. His answer to this concern involves two conceptual innovations. On the one hand he reconceptualises the background of distinctions of worth (with its associated images) in terms of *social imaginaries*. The problem of the efficacy of theory in the context of Taylor's analysis of modernity becomes the problem of how theory affects the social imaginary. The second innovation is a new account of the efficacy of theory itself. In this revised account, theory is always associated or 'packaged' with practices, but theories and practices are able to separate and recombine in the context of social-historical processes.

The way Taylor uses the term 'imaginary' is influenced by debates in social theory that assume a non-individualistic reading of the concept of imagination. This approach is part of a wider move in social theory to establish a collective basis for imagination opposed to the classical, romantic and psychological notions of imagination that give it a distinctively individual basis (Bottici & Challand 2011). Writers such as Anderson (1991), Castoriadis (2010) and Appadurai (1996) have found use for the concept in their analyses of social phenomena, positing in different ways a collective interpretation of imagination. Anderson's (1991) theory of *imagined communities* is often cited as a seminal contribution, and Taylor (2004) explicitly acknowledges his debt to Anderson. Anderson uses the idea to help make sense of the problem of modern nationhood, a notion that he located in a common imaginary, thus paving the way for a social reading of the imagination concept. Taylor (2002a) appropriates this collectivist account of imagination and uses it to articulate that part of his social ontology that had previously been described and analysed in terms of the concepts of 'background' and 'images' in his 1985 works. These concepts are consistently associated, but it is not made clear in the 1985 papers whether the background is to be taken as a fundamental category with images somehow serving to articulate aspects of it, or whether the two ideas are to be taken as complementary translations of the same thing. However, with the theory of social imaginaries, Taylor (2002a) overcomes such difficulties by identifying a fundamental social-hermeneutic feature of human being that could serve as a background with both moral and imagistic dimensions.

In Taylor's revised social ontology, an 'immediate background understanding' is introduced that people draw on to make sense of 'particular practices' (2004, p. 25). Practices are thus comprised of activities in which we engage on the basis of immediate norms and understandings that give us a sense of how this practice should go and why. Beyond these immediate understandings and norms enabling practice is the social imaginary:

> What I'm calling the social imaginary extends beyond the immediate background understanding that makes sense of our particular practices. This is not an arbitrary extension of the concept, because just as practice without the understanding wouldn't make sense for us and thus wouldn't be possible, so this understanding supposes, if it is to make sense, a wider grasp of our whole predicament: how we stand to each other, how we got to where we are, how we relate to other groups, and so on.
>
> (2004, p. 25)

Taylor's social ontology thus posits a double-hermeneutic process whereby the social imaginary underwrites immediate understandings, which in turn underwrite the meaning of particular practices. Practices are enabled by two levels of background – primarily by the immediate background understanding, and secondarily by the social imaginary presupposed by the immediate understanding. The social imaginary also serves as the wider background of the norms of particular practices. In this case it is the fact that the social imaginary harbours images of moral order that supports the norms of a practice.

The social imaginary is thus a heterogeneous social formation that informs the immediate understanding and norms of particular practices. Taylor (2004, p. 23) stresses that the social imaginary is *not* a social theory. This declaration may be read as an assertion that the social imaginary is not a garbled or distorted theory, and cannot be reduced to theoretical propositions. It is this assertion that announces the anti-idealism of Taylor's post-2000s account of the efficacy of theory. What gives sense to our practices is not any kind of 'pre-theory', not a tacit theory inherently open to idealisation, but is rather evident in 'images, stories, and legends' (2004, p. 23).

At the same time as Taylor draws a sharp distinction between social theory and the social imaginary as the basis of sense-making in practice, he has to account for his own far-reaching claim that theories authored by individuals such as Grotius can affect the social imaginary. In his analysis of the trajectory of early modernist social theory into the social imaginary, Taylor explains that individuals such as Grotius who engaged in the 'discursive practice of theorists' (2004, p. 33) were reacting to social upheavals of their time. This part of Taylor's analysis is murkier than usual, for here he seems to be saying that (discursive) practice is the source of the theory that transformed the social imaginary which proves to be requisite for any practice. However, Taylor does not believe a linear account of the relationship between theory and practices is possible. He says that 'Because human practices are the kind of thing that makes sense, certain ideas are internal to them; one cannot distinguish the two in order to ask the question Which causes which?' (2004, p. 32). The relationship between theories, practices and imaginaries can be understood, rather, on the pattern of the 'hermeneutic circle'. There is no sense in which one of them causes others, but that they are always co-implicated. If anything, Taylor (2004) locates social imaginaries and practices as chronologically prior to theory, but in modernity it clearly makes no sense to relate these terms in a linear fashion.

The theories that emerge from the discursive practices of theorists appear not to have any predetermined trajectory, but it is a prerequisite that if they are to 'infiltrate' the social imaginary, theories need to have both descriptive *and* normative aspects. Presumably, any theory with this character is a candidate for penetrating the social imaginary. Taylor (2004) argues that historically these theories circulate and are on hand, particularly to elite groups and perhaps as a consequence of the latter having the leisure to study and debate ideas. In this process, first, elite groups appropriate ideas to make sense of practices of concern to themselves under new conditions such as those produced by social upheaval. There can be new practices constructed for new conditions or existing practices that need to be understood in new ways in changing social contexts. Either way, practices and ideas are 'repackaged' so that practices under new conditions bear along with them new ideas. The work of elite groups – such as scholars – to rationalise practices in times of change contributes to the social imaginary of these groups. These groups are concerned to make sense of practices and conditions and in the process transform their own imaginary. For example, the nobility at the end of the feudal era in Britain and France transformed from a class of warrior chieftains to educated and centralised courtiers engaged in advising the crown. In Britain the process was smoother, in France less so, but in each case the practices of elites are transformed and it is the theories of the moral order that are appropriated to furnish the meaning of these changes.

At least in the context of the spread of the modern ideas of the moral order, elite groups engage in constructing and reconceptualising practices that eventually become widespread. The dissemination of these ideas was facilitated by revolutions in America and France. Taylor (2004) explains that in America the spread was eased by the existence of state assemblies in which voting was used to make decisions. These practices – constituted under different conditions according to different understandings – were 'made over' to the new ideas, creating popular assemblies with mechanisms for combining individual decisions to reach a collective decision. In contrast, in France the process was fraught since no existing practices were available and had to be constructed in bloody struggle. For Taylor, it is crucial that the theories of Grotius and Locke were on hand to give sense to these existing and new practices engaged under new conditions. Members of elite classes formalise and explain the practices following the lights of their own social imaginary. By this process old practices are repackaged with new ideas and these packages are adopted more and more widely. Taylor explains that

> The modern theory of moral order gradually infiltrates and transforms our social imaginary. In this process, what is originally just an idealization grows into a complex imaginary through being taken up and associated with social practices, in part traditional ones but ones often transformed by the contact. This is crucial to . . . the extension of the understanding of the moral order. It couldn't have become the dominant view in our culture without this penetration/transformation of our imaginary.
>
> (2004, pp. 28–29)

The infiltration of the theories of moral order into the social imaginary is accompanied by the emergence of new forms of self-understanding and social practices underpinned by the sense of moral order that underwrites the assumption that it is legitimate to combine individual decisions in a certain way to arrive at a binding collective decision. The modern theory of moral order becomes packaged with democratic practices understood as mutually beneficial and an expression of collective agency.

Modern social practices

Social practices play a pivotal role in Taylor's accounts of the efficacy of theory and his anti-idealistic strategies in relation to theory. In this concluding section we review the features of practice in Taylor's social ontology and clarify their role with respect to theory and social imaginaries. Theory-led transformation of the social imaginary of the modern world can occur when practices facilitate the penetration of theory. Taylor (2004) suggests that practices promote the extension and intensification of theory, through which the social imaginary is gradually infiltrated and changed. This occurs when new and/or existing practices under new historical conditions (such as the end of the religious wars) are explained in terms of certain kinds of theory (i.e., theory with both explanatory and normative potential). Governing elites, whose own class imaginary has been infiltrated by the theory, contrive or re-conceptualise practices initially. They are groups that have a strong interest in the promotion of a particular kind of order and who happen to be close to the discursive practices of theorists. Explaining how the theory extends beyond the contrivances and imagination of elite groups and into society more broadly, Taylor says,

> For the most part, people take up, improvise, or are inducted into the new practices. These are made sense of by the new outlook, the one first articulated in the theory; this outlook is the context that gives sense to the practices. Hence the new understanding comes to be accessible to the participants in a way it wasn't before.
>
> (2004, p. 29)

The 'outlook' identified here by Taylor is something 'articulated' by the theory. It suggests a summary or digest of the theory. Presumably, the outlook is elaborated when elites advocate and debate certain explanations of conditions. From the discursive practices of theorists to the rhetorical and administrative practices of governing classes, it is understandable that considerable didactic work is done with what may be abstruse theory to make it comprehensible within and beyond the elite class. It is clear that people one way or another adjust to the new or reconceptualised practices and accept the outlook articulated by governing actors.

Taylor's articulation here of the role of intellectual elites in shaping practice is both an extension and a deviation from his 1985 works. His earlier arguments insisted that high social theory proper – such as that developed by political theorists – has the potential either to strengthen, reinforce and legitimise existing practice, or to undermine them by making explicit the incoherence of the pre-theoretical understandings implicit in them. That is, social theories 'do not just make our constitutive self-understandings explicit, but extend, or criticize or even challenge them' (1985b, p. 94). Taylor argues that, in certain circumstances, such theories can prompt changes in practice because:

> The disruptive consequences of the theory flow from the nature of the practice, in that one of its constitutive props has been knocked away. This is because the practice requires certain descriptions to make sense, and it is these that the theory undermines.
>
> (1985b, p. 98)

In these circumstances, '[t]heory in this domain transforms its own object' (1985b, p. 101). In this earlier incarnation, Taylor is less specific about how this transformation occurs and how an externally derived theory can percolate through self-understandings, background distinctions of worth, and eventually practice. Taylor's later work is more instructive about how social theory can do this with reference to the immediate background and the social imaginary.

Taylor discerns a second way social practices interact with theory. With reference to his claims about the use of theory to make sense of new practices, he says,

> this process isn't just one-sided, a theory making over a social imaginary. In coming to make sense of the action the theory is glossed, as it were, given a particular shape as the context of these practices. Rather like Kant's notion of an abstract category becoming "schematized" when it is applied to reality in time and space, the theory is schematized in the dense sphere of common practice.
>
> (2004, pp. 29–30)

Here, Taylor describes the essential process of the extension of theory and with it the penetration of theory into the social imaginary. To make sense of particular social practices, the theory/outlook has to be modified. Social practices are complex, and creative work is required to see how the generalities of an outlook connect with particular activities, practice roles and the relationships between them. The theory is 'glossed' or re-articulated to produce a closer fit to the intricacies of practices. It is 'schematised' or transformed creating unique configurations of theory dictated by the imperatives and structures of different practices. Taylor draws on the work of Kant (1929) who argued that the intellect contains pure concepts that relate to the empirical world via schemata that contain a blend of pure and sensory characteristics. Taylor explains that practices react back on infiltrating theories creating local variants the theory that can in turn affect the original theory.

A third way practices and theory relate is when established, long-standing practices give rise to theory: practice-led transformation. In Taylor's (2004) analysis of modernity he contrasts the process by which theory of the modern moral order transforms the social imaginary with the process by which the 'economy' emerges as a distinctive modern social formation. His analysis suggests that the transformation of the social imaginary in relation to the economy was practice-led. Taylor's analysis here brings to light another pervasive idea that complements that of the modern moral order in shaping the social imaginary, the idea of objectification. This concept played an important role in Taylor's (1985a) analysis of the appeal of naturalistic scientific theory such as behaviourism. He argued then that objectification is a key feature of the modern disengaged self who, through the perspective opened up by objectification, could view itself as both free of authority and free to control. The analysis of the emergence of the formation of the market economy as an element in the modern social imaginary offers an explanation of the emergence of the idea of objectification. In this case, pre-existing commercial practices contained within them understandings associated with the role of the merchant as surveyor and controller of resources.

The idealisation to emerge from these pre-existing practices was articulated by theorists such as Locke and Adam Smith. Taylor (2004) highlights that the peculiar form of self-understanding associated with the idea of economy is that of an order that goes on 'behind the back' (2004, p. 77) of agents. Smith's 'invisible hand' (Taylor 2004, p. 76) is an image of this sort of order that arises from the very nature of atomistic individuals engaged in commercial activity with regard only to their own interests. For Taylor, this is an alternative, 'objectifying' image of social life that both enters into conflict with images central to the public sphere and democratic self-rule, and facilitates the development of objective theories of society that draw on assumptions that society can be approached as a natural phenomenon amenable to scientific analysis. These two sets of images – one linked with an objective stance on society and another with collective agency – constitute what Taylor calls the 'modern bifocal' (2004, p. 77). He indicates that there is a range of intermediate positions and that tensions emerge between the objectifying and collectivist extremes. There are also attempts to merge the two ideas such as we witness in neoliberalism, where proponents endow objectifying images such as the invisible hand of the market with moral overtones. This kind of effort confuses distinct forms of modern self-understanding.

Reviewing these three, intertwined variations on the relationship between practice and theory, it becomes clear how practices impact on the social imaginary. Because the imaginary, like the immediate understandings and norms, is always carried by practices, interactions between theory and practice must have repercussions for the imaginary. According to Taylor's analysis of the infiltration of theories of the moral order, practices react in different ways to theory and these reactions are reflected in the imaginary. Practices can be made sense of in terms of a new outlook, and they schematise the theory, producing localised variants. But as we have seen, practices can transform the social imaginary in their own right as Taylor's analysis of economic objectification suggests. In this case, practices connected with commercial activity give rise to both modifications to the imaginary and new forms of theory.

Taylor's theory of the social imaginary and its modes of transformation is an important contribution to practice theory. We have argued that the theory of social imaginaries is part of Taylor's strategy for maintaining the anti-idealistic stance of practice theory. The need to buttress the anti-idealism of practice theory has not been as high a priority in work of other practice theorists. But for Taylor, the pervasiveness and efficacy of theory that characterises modernity poses a challenge to practice theory that cannot be met by the dismissive anti-idealism that has long been associated with the practice approach. Taylor's painstaking analyses of social and historical processes present accounts of the influence of theory, from flawed naturalistic social theory (e.g., behaviourism) to theories of the modern moral order of Grotius and Locke that circulated at the beginning of the modern era. The pervasiveness and influence of theory on social practices is a feature of our civilization that cannot be denied, and the standard anti-idealism of practice theory cannot account for it. Taylor's theory allows practices to remain a unit of analysis for social research yet accommodates what is surely an overarching feature of contemporary society.

Acknowledgements

We are grateful to the editors of this book for their invitation to contribute this chapter. This work would not exist without this opportunity to engage with the complex and stimulating ideas thrown up by this invitation. We also thank The Warrnambool Collective, which was the original impetus for this chapter, early versions of which were presented to the collective in 2013 and 2015. We also acknowledge the two anonymous referees who provided useful comments. We give special thanks to Rodney Fopp for his critical appraisal of the chapter.

Note

1 This has been an ongoing issue for Taylor. For his later critiques of the use of natural science models in the human sciences, see Taylor 1995 (especially Chapter 1) and 2002b. See also Chapter 9 of Fopp (2008).

References

Abbey, R 2000, *Charles Taylor*, Acumen Publishing, Teddington, UK.

Anderson, B 1991, *Imagined communities*, Verso, London.

Appadurai, A 1996, *Modernity at large: Cultural dimensions of globalization*, University of Minnesota Press, Minneapolis, MN.

Bottici, C & Challand, B 2011, 'Introduction', in C Bottici & B Challand (eds), *The politics of imagination*, Taylor & Francis, Hoboken, NJ, pp. 1–15.

Bourdieu, P 1990, 'The scholastic point of view', *Cultural Anthropology*, vol. 5, no. 4, pp. 380–391.

Castoriadis, C 2010, 'Imaginary significations', in E Escobar, M Gondicas & P Vernay (eds), *A society adrift. Interviews and debates, 1974–1997*, Fordham University Press, New York, NY, pp. 45–68.

Fopp, R 2008, *Enhancing understanding: Advancing dialogue: Approaching cross cultural understanding*, ATF Press, Adelaide.

Gutting, G 1989, *Michel Foucault's archaeology of scientific reason*, Cambridge University Press, Cambridge, UK.

Kant, I 1929, *Immanuel Kant's critique of pure reason*, N. Kemp Smith (trans), Macmillan Education Ltd, Houndsmills, UK.

Schatzki, TR 2001a, 'Introduction: Practice theory', in TR Schatzki, K Knorr-Cetina & E von Savigny (eds), *The practice turn in contemporary theory*, Routledge, London & New York, pp. 10–23.

Schatzki, TR 2001b, 'Practice minded orders', in TR Schatzki, K Knorr-Cetina & E von Savigny (eds), *The practice turn in contemporary theory*, Routledge London & New York, pp. 50–63.

Taylor, C 1965, *The explanation of behaviour*, Routledge & Kegan Paul, London.

Taylor, C 1985a, *Human agency and language: Philosophical papers I*, Cambridge University Press, Cambridge.

Taylor, C 1985b, *Philosophy and the human sciences: Philosophical papers II*, Cambridge University Press, Cambridge.

Taylor, C 1995, *Philosophical arguments*, Harvard University Press, Cambridge, MA.

Taylor, C 2002a, 'Modern social imaginaries', *Public Culture*, vol. 14, no. 1, pp. 91–124.

Taylor, C 2002b, 'Understanding the other: A Gadamerian view on conceptual schemes', in J Malpas, U Arnswald & J Kertscher (eds), *Gadamer's century: Essays in honor of Hans-Georg Gadamer*, MIT Press, Cambridge, MA, pp. 279–297.

Taylor, C 2004, *Modern social imaginaries*, Duke University Press, Durham, NC.

Taylor, C 2006, 'Engaged agency and background in Heidegger', in C Guignon (ed.), *The Cambridge companion to Heidegger* (2nd ed.), Cambridge University Press, Cambridge, UK, pp. 202–221.

Taylor, C 2007, *A secular age*, The Belknap Press of Harvard University Press, Cambridge, MA. & London.

Chapter 4

Michel de Certeau
Research writing as an everyday practice

Julianne Lynch and Kristoffer Greaves

Introduction

> . . . no text or institution could ever 'hold' to the place where the drone of machines continues to murmur, where the noise of tools, kitchens, and a thousand and one creative activities is heard. These infinite lexicons and foreign vocabularies are silenced as soon as the museum of writing seizes these fragments in order to make them speak in our interests
>
> (de Certeau 1997, p. 139).

The impact of de Certeau's writings on cultural studies and beyond is widely recognised, with his contribution to cultural studies attracting much positive attention as well as criticism[1]. In particular, concepts operationalised in his characterisation of everyday practice have been widely deployed in fields such as culture studies, policy studies and education research[2]. However, Certeau-ian scholars have at times criticised the reception of his work, arguing that certain of his ideas have often been taken up to the neglect of others, and in reductive ways (Buchanan 2000; Highmore 2007; Rothbauer 2010). Referring to the popularity of de Certeau's formulation of *strategies* and *tactics*, Highmore (2007, pp. 14–15) observed, 'the export of this figuration has been so successful that at times the name de Certeau simply seems coterminous with the idea of "strategies and tactics"' and Buchanan (2000, p. 2) refers to these terms as 'unruly orphans'. Buchanan (2000) argued that many who appropriate these terms in anti-theoretical ways overlook de Certeau's broader onto-epistemic theory and associated methodological sense as explicated and demonstrated in his writings. This might be seen as a more general neglect of the ontological engagements of the 'posts' as has been noted by St Pierre (2013, p. 653) who, drawing on the example of Deleuze and Guattari, argued that their concepts 'are so immediately useful that it is too easy to pluck one or two . . . out of a dense system of imbricated concepts and wrongly insert them into a humanist ontology'. Similar criticisms can be made of the uptake of de Certeau's most popular concepts. In this chapter, we engage with de Certeau's neglected onto–epistemology, and use his ideas to render research writing as an *everyday practice*.

The chapter is organised into three parts. First, we reference de Certeau's writings as well as secondary texts[3] to tease out three, interrelated ideas: practice as *productive*; practice as *emergent*; and the character of *the tactical practitioner*. In so doing, we make representations of some of the best-known terms that de Certeau operationalized in his work: foremost his particular usage of *place* and *space* and the related concepts of *strategies* and *tactics*. Our purpose is two-fold: first to provide an exposition of de Certeau's theory of practice that provides a basis for the remainder of the chapter; and, second, through our approach to this exposition, to emphasise the nuanced formulations that lie behind commonly used and sometimes misused terms, nuances that contribute to the distinctiveness of de Certeau's theory of practice. In the second part of the chapter, we apply this view of practice to the field of social research, discussing the strategic, place-making operations that characterise research-writing conventions as everyday practices. Finally, we look to see what de Certeau's theory of practice provides us in terms of a way forward for living with, but also moving beyond, the onto-epistemological doubt that dogs social inquiry. We do this to raise questions about how the project of social inquiry might be reconceptualised as *a mode of operating on the world*, and to suggest potential trajectories of a research-writing practice that – moving beyond representational purposes and claims – is openly an advocacy research. Although in this writing we start from a performance of explication and then proceed to employ (re-employ) de Certeau terms and ideas, our own working with de Certeau is necessarily coloured by our own practices of discursive violence, for – as we move across the words and works of de Certeau – we perform selections and exclusions, rearrangements and redeployments, amplifications and smoothings-out, that serve the production of our own 'pretty order' (de Certeau 1988, p. 4) and that perform the narrativity that we also seek to critique.

De Certeau's characterisation of everyday practice

Practice as productive

> Bubbling out of swamps and bogs, a thousand flashes at once scintillate and are extinguished all over the surface of a society. In the official imaginary, they are noted only as exceptions or marginal events. An ideology of property isolates the "author," the "creator," and the "work". In reality, creation is a disseminated proliferation. It swarms and throbs. A polymorphous carnival infiltrates everywhere, a celebration both in the streets and in the homes for those who are unbended by the aristocratic and museological model of durable production.
>
> (de Certeau 1997, pp. 139–140)

De Certeau used spatial metaphors to examine relations of power. Many theorists draw on distinctions between space and place as they theorise the social, usually making a distinction between some sort of pre-conceptual abstract space and the production of meaning through a material-semiotic inhabitation of this space. De Certeau drew on Merleau-Ponty's distinction between geometric space and anthropological space for this primary distinction, as discussed in Buchanan (2000 pp. 109–112). Buchanan (2000) argues that this (commonly made) distinction is the implicit ontological pre-condition of de Certeau's theoretical work, but that it should not be confused with the way that de Certeau ultimately went forward to operationalize the terms *space* and *place*, each as operations of power in dialogical relation with each other. For de Certeau *place* refers to the *proper place*, the place colonised by those seeking to control usage and to keep alterity out. The determination of place involves *strategic operations*, where strategies are defined by a will to power and manifest in attempts to 'tabulate', to 'manage' (de Certeau 1984, pp. 30, 36, respectively) and to extinguish uncertainties: to render the world readable. De Certeau points to the 'syntax' of economic systems, social hierarchies, language, customs and psyche as examples of this type of place-making (de Certeau 1997, p. 145). His most well-known example and analogy for strategic operations is the work of city planners who attempt to anticipate and influence the usage of urban spaces through a from-above mapping of routes and zones (see de Certeau 1984, Chapter Seven, 'Walking in the citiy'). But this is the theoretical city, the city as can only be seen once you are removed from it. The view-from-above provides only 'the fiction of knowledge' (de Certeau 1984, p. 92). The *practiced* city cannot be subject to a totalizing view because everyday practice 'patiently and tenaciously restores a space for play' (de Certeau & Giard 1998, p. 255). Through practice, places are traversed, co-opted and remade as a continually evolving surface of singularities. In this way, place and space engage in ongoing dialogical interplay, with the production of each being dependent on, and the contradiction of, the other.

The everyday practices of users are characterised by *tactical operations* that do not emanate from, or seek to establish, a *proper* place. Instead, places serve as the raw material of the everyday tactical operations that transform them. Tactical operations cut across the demarcations of place and produce effects in the established order, they: 'deform, erode, and slowly change the equilibrium of social constellations' (de Certeau 1997, pp. 145–146). Across de Certeau's writings, *tactics* and *everyday practices* are for the most part synonymous. Everyday practice is characterised by *reuse*, that is, by the appropriation and redeployment of 'prefabricated signs' (de Certeau 1997, p. 133). The notion of reuse can be likened to that of *detournement* within art practice, where existing elements are used to create something new (Trier 2014, p. 2); thus the syntax of place serves as the raw material for a creative production. This creativity is of a particular type, being minority in status – not being sanctioned by the proper place – but majority in its proliferation – being everywhere all the time. De Certeau stressed the modesty of this creativity. It is not a creativity that results in 'a "cultural" object' and is therefore not marked by formal recognition. Instead, this is a common, ethereal creativity that is at once everywhere but unrecognised and unassailable: 'Far from being identified with what is rare, solid, costly, or "definitive" (the traits of a masterpiece, which is a patent), it aims to vanish in what it materializes' (de Certeau 1997, p. 141). De Certeau was clear that tactics are not a form of resistance – 'the actual order of things is precisely what "popular" tactics turn to their own ends, without any illusion that it is about to change' (de Certeau 1984, p. 26). Strategies and tactics are not oppositional. The effects of tactical operations are not a challenge to power, but by appropriating and redeploying place, they undermine the authority of place. In Buchanan's (2000, p. 89) analysis, he explains that while tactics do not subvert the status quo, they have a symbolic force: 'they offer daily proof of the partiality of strategic control and in doing so they hold out the token hope that however bad things get, they are not *necessarily* so'. Tactics do not challenge official structures and systems, but they reveal them as a fiction. This formulation of tactical operations reveals de Certeau's desire to elevate everyday practices as the true (but neglected) object of social and cultural inquiry and to posit that practices often characterised as passive (usage, consumption) are, in contrast, active productions characterised by far more complex power relations.

Practice is emergent

> We have a surfeit of knowledge and methods as far as structures are concerned, and we are impoverished as soon as we have to study operations, transformations, in short, movement.
>
> (de Certeau 1997, p. 145)

For de Certeau, practice is emergent – it unfolds as part of a dynamic, improvisational interplay of place, knowledge and time. Places are a precondition of practice, but they do not determine practices. The reuse of place is mediated by the invisible knowledge of practitioners. The operation of this invisible knowledge *in time* founds a 'rupture or break' (de Certeau 1984, p. 85) between two states. This is the interspace where tactics take place, pointing to de Certeau's distinction between *a state* (being) and an *operation* (becoming). A state is a fiction, existing out of time; practice takes place in the space in between fictional states of equilibrium. This location of practice in the interspace between fictional states is the foundation of de Certeau's ontological sense. Buchanan (2000, p. 15) suggested that de Certeau's conception of *tactics* is central to his theory of practice, pointing to an underlying ontology of emergence: 'it posits a flux in which all the old categories and ideas of social inquiry in any of its modes – history, sociology, anthropology, psychology, and so on – still clings to, can be dissolved'. De Certeau's tactics are the defining characteristic of a world in motion, of living and doing.

The location of tactical operations in time – in movement, in the interspace between states – means that practice eludes representation. Its locus is not the *proper* place, already mapped, but the dynamic interplay of many loci, of actions and circumstances that traverse places and that draw on secret knowledge that belong to occasions not places. A central complaint in de Certeau's best-known book, *The Practice of Everyday Life*, is that practices escape the mappings of social researchers and the framings of cultural theorists. This failure of research is the starting point of de Certeau's unfinished heterological project (Buchanan 2000), which seeks to outline a 'science of the singular' (de Certeau 1984, p. ix, preface to the English translation). De Certeau argued that an analysis that takes the *proper* place as its starting point can 'only catch hold of resistances' (de Certeau 1997, p. 138) – those movements and artefacts that make sense in relation to (and validate and are validated by) the logics of that place. For example, de Certeau (1984, p. 55) in discussing Bourdieu's early Kabylian research, critically describes Bourdieu's practices as dominated by an undisclosed 'economy of the proper place', involving strategies 'entirely peculiar to the close space in which Bourdieu examines them and to the way in which he observes them'[4]. By way of counter-example, in describing Freud and history, de Certeau (1986, p. 6) argues Freud rightly introduced 'the need for the analyst to mark his [sic] place . . . [as] a condition of possibility of a form of lucidity', thus substituting an open declaration of the place of production for any pretence of objectivity in scientific discourse.

The tactical practitioner

De Certeau emphasized the *artfulness* of everyday practice and also its *slipperiness* as doings unfold in time. In his analysis of de Certeau's metamethodology, Highmore provides a review of the adjectives used by de Certeau across his works to characterize everyday practice:

> First, these practices are 'hidden' ('dark', 'opaque', 'obscure', 'silent', 'invisible', 'surreptitious', 'unreadable', 'elusive'). Second, everyday practices are both heterogeneous ('singular' and 'plural') and extensive ('multiform', 'dispersed', 'scattered', 'swarming'). Third, they are 'devious' ('guileful', 'tricky', 'tactical', 'clandestine', 'insinuating', 'rueful', 'disguised', 'clever', 'cunning'). Fourth, they are 'stubborn' ('tenacious', 'obstinate', 'inert', 'persistent', 'ancient')
>
> (Highmore 2006, p. 108)

De Certeau's characterisation of everyday practice effects an explicit raising-up of the tactical practitioner as an anti-hero. Practices transform the objects and logics of place into new spaces through interplay of the rules of place and the practical know-how (knowledge/memory) of *walkers* who exploit particular situations or circumstances (the occasion). Tactical practitioners use their knowledge of (the proper) place and tune in to temporal opportunities (knowing the right moment) to effect under-the-radar productions of space. The *knowledge* that mediates spatial transformations is of a particular type – it is memory-in-action that brings together the 'treasure of past experiences' and an 'inventory of multiple possibilities' (de Certeau 1984, p. 83). This knowledge is invisible – it has no locus in place, only in time; it belongs to and defines *the occasion*. Like agents in game theory, the knowledge that mediates the production of space facilitates an optimisation of outcomes for the practitioner, but it is an agile undertaking that is not pre-planned or entirely rational, and it is not formalised as a strategy that can be decontextualized and reapplied – it belongs to the moment. Practices emerge in time as active productions of singularities, not as the implementation of some predetermined game plan. De Certeau draws on the Greek concept of *mētis* to think through elements of a practical intelligence that involves knowing the right moment and leaving no trace (de Certeau 1984, pp. 81–89). He cites Detienne and Vernant's description of *mētis*, a particular type of intelligence in which qualities such as flair, wisdom, deception, resourcefulness, vigilance and opportunism manifest in ways that are transient, shifting, ambiguous and not susceptible to exact measurements (Detienne & Vernant 1991, pp. 3–4).

Consistent with *mētis* is de Certeau's concept of *La perruque* (trans: the wig) (de Certeau 1984, p. 25) – de Certeau's modern-day equivalent of 'making do'. *La perruque* is an under-the-radar borrowing of resources (time, materials) whereby, in the guise of performing the work consistent with the official purpose of a particular place, practitioners make use of resources for their own purposes. These usages do not disrupt or seek to change the ordained structures of place, but instead are part of the everyday operations of people navigating the places available to them in order to achieve their own desires. De Certeau's emphasis on the temporal dimensions of practice, and also the harmless deception it enacts, is similarly evident in his use of the image of a tightrope dancer (citing Kant) to characterise the artfulness of everyday tactical operations:

> Dancing on a rope requires that one maintain an equilibrium from one moment to the next by recreating it at every step by means of new adjustments; it requires one to maintain a balance that is never permanently acquired; constant readjustment renews the balance while giving the impression of 'keeping' it. The art of operating is thus admirably defined, all the more so because in fact the practitioner himself [sic] is part of the equilibrium that he modifies without compromising it
>
> (de Certeau 1984, p. 74)

This description of the tightrope dancer points to the emergent nature of practice, and to the deception of any seeming equilibrium in a world where the appearance of a stable state belies the work that goes on to produce that appearance. The maintenance of a system is performative only – the performance can be seen but the practices involved in sustaining the deception cannot.

Strategic operations in research writing

A dancer disguised as an archivist

(de Certeau 1984, p. 80)

The recognition of research as an *everyday practice* may seem self-evident, but the epistemological and axiological implications of post-structural theories such as de Certeau's are complex and pose a challenge to the social science research establishment – in particular to orthodoxies around what the work of research is, ought to be and might be. This challenge has attracted much attention over the past decade as researchers grapple with what it means *in practice* to research and to write in post-modern times. Scholars influenced by continental theories challenging the discursive separation between the *in-here* and the *out-there* (Law 2004), and problematizing the presumption of writing in the ways that de Certeau does, provide strong critiques of the representational goals and assumptions of research traditions. This can be seen as a revival of ontologies of emergence and understandings of the performative, non-representational and more-than-representational work that research and research writing do (Anderson & Harrison 2010; Law 2004; Thrift 1996). De Certeau is one of a number of theorists – alongside other names that feature in this book, such as, Bourdieu, Deleuze and Latour – whose work in the latter half of last century has greatly influenced the thinking of social researchers by challenging and offering alternatives to binaries that previously characterised understandings of *the social* and approaches to social analysis, and whose diverse legacies currently support what has been dubbed a *turn to ontology* (Lather & St Pierre 2013).

In this section, we proceed from de Certeau's characterisation of everyday practice – as productive, emergent and enacted by a tactical practitioner – and apply this understanding to research writing practices. In de Certeau's terms, what are the *places* of research writing? What strategic operations seek to manage the uncertainties of this field of practice and in so doing obscure the micro-operations of practice in action, and how do these micro-operations tactically engage with authorised places? In the introductory chapter of Anderson and Harrison's (2010, p. 3) edited book on non-representational theories, they write, 'we keep within the recognised genre requirements of an introduction to an edited academic book; "storying" the emergence of non-representational theories as a successor "paradigm"'. This points to the meta-narrative of academic writing conventions, where a particular type of performance is expected and required. It is a recognition and admission of the artifice that is performed. One must create a warrant for the work being presented – its significance and its contribution – and the word 'create' is not used loosely here: de Certeau explicitly identified this type of discursive operation within scientific writing as a 'fabrication' (de Certeau 1988). Academic writing involves the manufacture of a range of normalised artefacts whose effect is to expunge the particularities of the author, the circumstances of production, the occasion of writing and the happenstance and messiness of research practices that the written text purports to represent. Recent work in post-qualitative research foregrounds the artifice of these discursive operations. For example, Lather and St Pierre (2013, p. 630) refer to 'the categories we have invented to organize and structure humanist qualitative methodology' and Petersen (2015, p. 158) refers to 'traditional academic storytelling practices'. From a Certeauian perspective, these research artefacts point to the *place* of research as seen from above: the fiction of research as an orderly, zoned undertaking, where the assumption is that the organisation of research writing reflects research practices. We don't attempt to list or map these categories here, but – before we move past them to ask what de Certeau can tell us about the hope for something different – we provide a discussion of some of the obvious heroes of social scientific writing – specifically, 'the context', 'the literature review', 'research methods' and 'the data' – arguing that these are some of the strategic place-making operations of research writing.

The front-ending of research papers with a statement about the *background* or *context* of the research is a standard research writing practice. The production of a *context* is effectively a *writing-out* of some entities – actors, events, movements, trends – as relevant, but as not explicitly treated as the matter of research manipulations. Some entities are the plasticine of the research machine – they are assembled, interrogated, processed, purified and then presented as the object of concern and the source of new knowledge. Other entities – the background, the context – are the fictional *given* of the project, of the research question, and of the research undertaking. They are the context that research findings will then speak back to. Petersen (2015) has noted this practice as a form of 'realist context-making' (p. 154), and as one of numerous 'ontologising practices' (p. 147) used in research writing. The boundary between 'context' and the substantive material of a research undertaking is actively produced through the discursive operations of research writing. By identifying a 'context', the writer both shows an awareness of its relevance and excises it from further engagements – it is acknowledged, bounded, gestured towards as the precondition of the enquiry, and possibly revisited in relation to the relevance and usefulness of research *findings* and *conclusions*. Non-representational theorists provide an explicit critique of the fictionalizing work of 'context' – as Thrift (1996, p. 5, citing Vattimo) explained it 'cannot be seen as "just a frill or a frame around social structures, a side-show to the 'real' business of existence"'. There is *work* involved in producing a context, in establishing and maintaining a centre and a periphery as though these are somehow pre-determined (Latour 1996). These boundaries and orderings are actively produced through our research-writing operations according to the rules of *place* that attempt to obscure onto-epistemological problematics.

The *literature review* is usually also found at the front-end of a piece of research writing – an artefact produced to perform at least two types of work in research. The literature review as process – supposedly undertaken prior to the commencement of project design and data collection – purports to identify the current state of knowledge and, following that, the next logical line of enquiry. In this way, the literature review speaks to the linear progression of conventional research design. In the text, the literature review is a section that ostensibly maps the boundaries of relevant knowledge, critically reviews that knowledge and positions the current contribution. Like the tightrope dance, the literature review presents the artifice of equilibrium, of a current *state* of affairs. It uses rhetorical turns of phrase to close off further interpretation and to recruit the observations and findings of others to the author's agenda. The writings of others are appropriated and redeployed – 'as can be seen in', 'as argued by', 'as demonstrated in' and so on. Performance of the literature review is an act of *closure*, similar to that noted by Law in relation to the knowledge production practices of science: 'Closure has been achieved. The object has been constructed. A single hinterland is in place. No more questions' (Law 2004, p. 56). The processes and materials that went into the production of a particular research 'finding' are hidden when presented as part of the body of accumulated evidence ('they found that . . . '). We deploy those strategies here when we call up names of currency within social research methods (the St Pierres, the Laws, the Lathers) and when we appropriate the words of others (and indeed of de Certeau) to add weight to our arguments. In our prose, the slippage from a St Pierre to a Law and then back to de Certeau strategically smooths out the differences in their accounts and erases the specificity of their situatedness in their own places and times. The production of a research grant application, a research report, a journal article, can be seen as an artful appropriation of these 'prefabricated signs' (de Certeau 1997, p. 133). Materials are assembled to produce the semblance of a topography ('names and a map': de Certeau 1986, p. 142) easily recognised by any practised academic writer or assessor – *here is the body of knowledge as already established, and here is the knowledge gap to be filled.* In this way, the research writer tactically bends the writings, findings and words of others in a redeployment of the conventions of genre and rhetoric, yet the product does not speak of the emergent nature of this work.

Convention suggests that we then move onto method and data, where the trappings of scientism stand in place of onto-epistemological engagements. In Petersen's (2015) analysis of research-writing practices, she notes that even within papers working with post-structural theory, most authors are careful to provide accounts of their instruments and processes 'as if to convince the reader that they had met the scientistic gold standard around systematicity and transparency' (Petersen 2015, p. 9). As the work of Latour and Woolgar (cited in Law 2004) demonstrates, even within the disciplines of 'science,' scientific method is neither systematic nor transparent. Aptly, Fish (2009) characterises the *in situ*, on-the-spot, unpredictable and uncertain nature of research practices with reference to the hero in picaresque literature, involving an 'openness towards what occurs, and generous response to what is found' and contrasts this with the vision of 'a traveller bent on his [sic] destination' (Fish 2009, p. 141). This contrast between the picaresque hero and the more linearly minded traveller captures some of the sense of the tactical practitioner researcher who, in going about his or her everyday research operations employs tactics that dialogue with the authorised *places* of research writing. These tactical research-writing operations meander behind the tidy representations found in the products of writing, but it is not just the emergent nature of research methods that are obscured by the scriptural operations of the research text; the otherness and othering of the object of study are also obscured through our dealings with 'data'.

The position of data is perhaps most contentious in contemporary post-qualitative research discussions (Lather & St Pierre 2013). The concept of data is troubled by materialist ontologies that, not only remind us of our imbrication with and implication in what we attempt to section off as the object of our enquiries, but also challenge the assumptions of ontological depth upon which attempts to analyse and to represent are based, assumptions that there is something essential that is hidden within our data sets and that can be found if our methods and instruments are up to the job. Writing about how the testimony of research participants has been engaged for the purposes of interpretation and theorisation, Harrison (2010, pp. 168–169) argues that testimony is treated in social research as flawed speech in need of repair: 'the basic methodological task which testimony poses to us, as social scientists, is to complete the semiotic circuit opened by the testimony in question *by providing the testimony's missing account of itself* and thereby recover the testimony's true but otherwise partial, embryonic, hidden or elided significance. . . [By insisting] that our informants make sense, knowing or not, we are insisting on the priority of our explanatory systems' (p. 169). De Certeau wrote of this methodological operation in his discussion of modern Western history writing, noting, 'It forces the silent body to speak. It assumes a gap to exist between the silent opacity of the "reality" that it seeks to express and the place where it produces its own speech, protected by the distance established between itself and its object' (de Certeau 1988, p. 3). In *The Writing of History*, de Certeau sees the establishment of this 'gap' or 'rupture' between the past and the present, between the analyst and her object, as the initial and necessary creative act of historiographic study and writing.

Thus, in research writing we engage in both strategic and tactical operations: we engage and reproduce writing and knowledge-production conventions which obscure the emergent, productive practices involved in creating a research text, and in this work we deploy representationalist rhetorical strategies in the service of our own authorial points of view, in attempt to establish our own position of power and to take readers to that place. De Certeau explicitly confronted these onto–episto–methodological challenges in several of his texts. He incites us to recognize the two faces of research writing – at once inadequate *and* generative – and its potential to go further than merely (feebly) seeking to represent the world, and instead to operate on the world by producing dissonance and discomfort through writing that reveals the problematics of research operations.

A productive, more-than-representational function for social research

> Within the frontiers, the alien is already there, an exorcism or Sabbath of the memory, a disquieting familiarity. It is as though delimitation itself were the bridge that opens the inside to its other.
>
> (de Certeau 1984, p. 129)

Amongst the many tropes employed by de Certeau in his writings are the ghosts that haunt historiographic work. Interpretation is doubly haunted: first, by the presuppositions that are linked to the occasion of writing – because the present always haunts the researcher's account;[5] second, by the object of inquiry, what we might call the 'real'. The former includes the narrativity discussed earlier – the 'mythic structure whose opaque presence haunts our scientific historical discipline' (de Certeau 1986, p. 203). The latter, while it cannot be summonsed via the symbolic order, seeps in all the same – a black cat troubling our peripheral awareness, challenging our belief in the rules of place. The everyday practices of reading and writing undermine attempts to represent and the presumptions of these attempts, suggesting an unknowable realm that is not present in the products of writing, but nor is it absent. The credibility of research texts and their presumption to represent the other, and to do nothing more, is always on shaky ground. Our work within and with research conventions is a Certeau-ian *reuse*, an appropriation and redeployment of the syntax available to us and of the circumstances that present, a practice of *mētis*. Research writers both appropriate and are subject to the logics of these conventions and our reuse of them has both representational and productive flows. Research-writing conventions provide a story (a representation) of the object of inquiry that necessarily reveals the place of writing, and through this revelation, produces effects in the authorised logics of knowledge production. Buchanan (2000, p. 18) argued that de Certeau positioned the work of his ghosts in the plane of belief – 'disrupt[ing] the fatality of the established order' (Buchanan 2000, p. 105). Our writing has the appearance of being founded upon realist ontologies, but we no longer believe it. We know that our words are inadequate to the real (de Certeau 1988, p. xxxvvii), but we persist in a production that is both obedient and broken, and through this brokenness, productive.

Research writing produces on at least two levels: it (re)produces the representational logics and structures of modern research writing, and it produces problematics that dialogue with these logics. Each of the research artefacts noted above – each a *place* that designates and corrals – is also a potential site for staging a rupture, for elevating the problematicity of research and research writing and for producing the new. We inhabit these places but through our inhabitation we can effect changes in the world of which they are a part. De Certeau deliberately sought to break away from traditional research meta-narratives and to take his own research and writing practices as an object warranting attention, as productive rather than representational practices. In the preface to *The Writing of History*, he wrote:

> Instead of proceeding with a chronological reconstruction overly obedient to the fiction of a linearity of time . . . it seemed preferable to bring into view the *present* site in which this investigation took its form, the *particularity* of the field, of the matter, and of the processes (those of "modern" historiography) allowing the scriptural operations to be analysed, and the *methodological deviations* (semiotic, psychoanalytic, etc.) that introduce other theoretical possibilities and practices into the Western function of writing. For this reason the book is a fragmented discourse fashioned from tactical investigations each obeying specific laws . . . Refusing the fiction of a metalanguage unifying the whole work clarifies the relation between *limited* scientific procedures and what they miss of the "real" with which they deal. I have avoided the illusion – necessarily dogmatizing – which belongs to discourse claiming to make us believe our words are "adequate" to the real.
>
> (de Certeau 1988, pp. xxxvi–xxxvii, Preface)

Within a Certeau-ian frame, the meta-narrative structures of research can be seen as *a place* – an architecture for tabulating the world, an attempt to domesticate unruly practices (both those of the researcher and those of the object of inquiry) and to represent them as something they are not. Following de Certeau's formulation, if these conventions are *a place*, then they are the raw material with which research writers must work, but they do not determine practice – 'The rules are always already put into play as soon as they are enunciated' (Buchanan 1997, p. 180). By implication, we have a repertoire of operations at our disposal that allow us to traverse this place in pursuit of other, productive agendas. De Certeau deliberately presented fragmented accounts and refused to reconcile the fragments as though there is some unifying hidden truth that could be brought forth through language. He brought a psychoanalytic sense to what is repressed through the rhetorical turns of language, and intentionally produced fissures in his texts where the repressed might stage a return: '[the text] is cracked from top to bottom . . . [and] each of its halves say what is missing from the other, rather than its truth' (de Certeau 1996, pp. 7–8). This is de Certeau's meta-methodology – his foregrounding of the inadequacy of his methods but also of the generative potential of a ruptured text: a text that does not seek to comfort through the presentation of a whole but instead provides space for trouble to emerge.

Meta-narrative research structures are part of the research writer's performance, but the audience is no longer deceived. The audience is part of the deception – through its complicity – and part of its rupture – through what it *makes of* the frisson of a broken text; through the productions of encounters with and between both normalising (strategic) and divergent (tactical) operations. The relationship between place and space – strategy and tactic – is dialogical. Places belong to us because our work performs their reproduction, but there are cracks that also belong to us – cracks in the credibility of these place-making structures, cracks that speak of and back to the traditional research edifice and that make traditional research logics an object for our attention, as we work in dialogue with normalising forces.

The logics of the traditional literature review are that of a geographical survey – over space and time: what is the lay of the land? What is the linear genesis of this current state of knowledge? Where are the uncharted territories? But close attention to the picaresque journeying of the reader/writer practitioner might suggest other logics, for example, a logic of *tracing* where the value of tracing an emergent chain of citation – from one idea to the next and to the next – might be substituted for an aggregation of 'results' and better support the production of the new. The treatment of data – traditionally also an aggregation, a determination of central tendency, an erasure of anomalies, and a smoothing away of the other – might be substituted for an amplification of alterity. There is an assumption in conventional social research methods and writing that participants' accounts are unproblematic in an onto-epistemological sense; that all researchers need do is present them more fully, or more openly, or more truthfully; that the real can be triangulated. A movement away from the (re)production of the same might involve attention to the limits of sense-making, an amplification of the outliers as the worthy object of inquiry, and a juxtaposing of the incommensurable and inconsistent without a need to produce an imagined missing piece. Harrison (2010) advocates in relation to informants' testimonies: instead of treating testimony as flawed speech in need of repair through an analyst's explanation and contextualization, researchers should treat it as *problematic*, disquieting speech. This is speech that, instead of representing some real, has an effect. As readers and reviewers of research writing, we are drawn to make assessments based on the degree of comfort and sense of recognition the text provides ('I understand that', 'It is consistent with what I know . . . with what I've read before', 'I recognise this form', 'It is internally consistent and complete'). Perhaps a better measure of the impact and contribution of research writing is the degree of discomfort, the dissonance produced, its failure to join up the dots – what might be termed its *problematicity*. Rather than inconsistency leading to an erasure or cancelling out, what do inconsistent accounts produce in dialogue? The production of 'findings' and 'conclusions' is conventionally a fictionizing undertaking – an attempt to produce a representation of a real, where the accuracy of representations is ostensibly improved incrementally. Instead of this fictionalizing work disguised as realist representation, research writing might be positioned as more openly akin to the writing of fiction. Rather than trying to advance understandings of social phenomena, social research could actively seek to progress the world of the social through its discursive operations – by producing texts that provide insights into possible futures, as glimpsed, for example, through the problematics of testimony, the pains of writing, our struggle with language and the gaps/contradictions in the representational text. This moves the research writing endeavor away from an account of what is happening, towards a sense of the limits of what happens and how these limits fail and shift, and what other might emerge. In this way, the products of research, rather than filling in the gaps of an unfinished drawing of the real, might effect a dissolving of the neat lines that conventionally mark a line between 'the context' and 'the study', and between the views of research subjects and those of an author, and instead draw attention to other lines – the connections and cracks, the resonances and silences – through which new practices can emerge.

In this chapter we set out to see how a Certeau-ian lens might render social research practices, asking: what do research writing practices look like when understood as everyday practices, and what might the work of social research be if we take on board de Certeau's conceptual framework and the ethic of minor transformations that it supports? In our embrace of de Certeau, we are drawn into the politics of his writing where alterity – framed as a shifting and multiple category – is celebrated. De Certeau's conceptualisation of everyday practice provokes us to see practices that might otherwise be conceived of as a passive consumption of available structures, instead, as a productive *reuse* that brings with it a proliferation of new spaces through dialogue with established orders. De Certeau's explicit project of amplifying alterity – coupled with an understanding of research as an everyday, productive practice – suggests a research ethic that goes further than merely investigating and explaining the social, and instead works towards interrupting the taken-for-granted and actively interfering in the world.

The reconceptualisation of practice offered by de Certeau's work opens up a space for other purposes. We might speculate that attention to research practices would unearth a repertoire of more-than-representational moves, where social research produces representations that also might be a form of advocacy; where conventional structures are interlaced with flows that interrupt our habituated responses and expose the illusion of research meta-narratives; where particular voices are explicitly amplified to particular effect; and, where the problematicity of research work and its objects is foregrounded. Instead of researchers operating as though the social research project ought to be the development of internally consistent descriptions of an *out there* that we recognise as familiar and complete, we can perform other types of work that speaks to the (also familiar) uncontainable, unsettled and emergent nature of social worlds and that owns the imbrication of our work in these worlds.

Notes

1 Accounts of criticism can be found in Ahearne (1995, p. 187), Buchanan (1996, p. 152), Buchanan (2000, pp. 39–42), Frow (1991, pp. 57–9) and Mitchell (2007).
2 Recent examples of the work found in diverse fields that take up de Certeau's ideas in generative ways include Saltmarsh (2014, p. 38) who, working within education policy studies, drew on de Certeau's ideas in her study of parent-school engagement policy to examine how policy and everyday practices 'work on' each other; Rinkinen et al. (2015) who, working within sociological studies of everyday life, analysed diary writings as 'random and haphazard documenting' and a way of 'being in the world . . . an essentially aesthetic form of expression'; and, Daskalaki et al. (2015, p. 420) who, working within entrepreneurship studies, were moved by de Certeau to embrace 'transformative insinuations' as they explored 'whether entrepreneurial initiatives nurture the emergence of bottom-up social transformations that are neither rigid nor bureaucratic'.
3 We draw upon each of: *Culture in the Plural* (1974/1998), *Heterologies: Discourse on the other* (1986), *The Writing of History* (1975/1988), *The Possession at Louden* (1970/1996) and *The Practice of Everyday Life: Volume 2* (with Giard) (1994/1998), but most central to our account of de Certeau's concepts is the experimental work he did in *The Practice of Everyday Life* (1980/1984). We also draw upon secondary texts by Ahearne (1995), Buchanan (2000) and Highmore (2006). We have a debt to each of these Certeau-ian scholars, but Buchanan's analysis (1997, 2000) has been the most influential on our thinking.
4 Bourdieu specifically took this issue up in his later work on the practice of research; for example, Wacquant (1989, p. 34).
5 Reekie (1996) writes about de Certeau's insistence that the present is the other of the historiographic text.

References

Ahearne, J 1995, *Michel de Certeau: Interpretation and its other*, Stanford University Press, Stanford, CA.

Anderson, B & Harrison, P 2010, 'The promise of non-representational theories', in *Takingplace: Non-representational theories and geography*, Ashgate, London, pp. 1–36.

Buchanan, I 1996, 'Review of Jeremy Ahearne Michel de Certeau: Interpretation and its other', *Social Semiotics*, vol. 6, no. 1, pp. 147–155.

Buchanan, I 2000, *Michel de Certeau: Cultural theorist*, Sage, London.

Buchanan, IM 1997, 'De Certeau and cultural studies', *New Formations*, vol. 1997, no. 31, pp. 175–188.

Daskalaki, M, Hjorth, D & Mair, J 2015, 'Are entrepreneurship, communities, and social transformation related?', *Journal of Management Inquiry*, vol. 24, no. 4, pp. 419–423.

de Certeau, M 1984, *The practice of everyday life*, University of California Press, Berkeley, CA (original work published in 1980).

de Certeau, M 1986, *Heterologies: Discourse on the other, vol. 17, Theory and history of literature*, University of Minnesota Press, Minneapolis, MN & London (This collection includes translations of previously published essays dating from 1978).

de Certeau, M 1988, *The writing of history*, Columbia University Press, New York (original work published in 1975).

de Certeau, M 1996, *The possession at Loudon*, University of Chicago Press, Chicago, IL (original work published in 1970).

de Certeau, M 1997, *Culture in the plural*, University of Minnesota Press, Minneapolis, MN & London (original work published in 1974).

de Certeau, M & Giard, L 1998, 'A practical science of the singular', in M de Certeau, L Giard & P Mayol (eds), *The practice of everyday life volume 2: Living & cooking*, University of Minnesota Press, Minneapolis, MN & London, pp. 251–256 (original work published in 1994).

Detienne, M & Vernant, J-P 1991, *Cunning intelligence in Greek culture and society*, University of Chicago Press, Chicago, IL (original work published in 1974).

Fish, D 2009, 'Research as a pragmatic practice: Unpredictable means, unforeseeable ends', in B Green (ed.), *Understanding and researching professional practice*, Sense Publishers, Rotterdam, pp. 19–38.

Frow, J 1991, 'Michel de Certeau and the practice of representation', *Cultural Studies*, vol. 5, no. 1, pp. 52–60.

Harrison, P 2010, 'Testimony and the truth of the other', in B Anderson & P Harrison (eds), *Taking-place: Non-representational theories and geography*, Ashgate, London, pp. 161–179.

Highmore, B 2006, *Michel de Certeau: Analysing culture*, Continuum, London.

Highmore, B 2007, 'An epistemological awakening: Michel de Certeau and the writing of culture', *Social anthropology*, vol. 15, no. 1, pp. 13–26.

Lather, P & St. Pierre, EA 2013, 'Post-qualitative research', *International Journal of Qualitative Studies in Education*, vol. 26, no. 6, pp. 629–633.

Latour, B 1996, *Aramis, or, the love of technology*, Harvard University Press, Cambridge, MA.

Law, J 2004, *After method: Mess in social science research*, Routledge, New York.

Mitchell, JP 2007, 'A fourth critic of the enlightenment: Michel de Certeau and the ethnography of subjectivity', *Social Anthropology*, vol. 15, no. 1, pp. 89–106.

Petersen, EB 2015, 'What crisis of representation? Challenging the realism of post-structuralist policy research in education', *Critical Studies in Education*, vol. 56, no. 1, pp. 146–160.

Reekie, G 1996, 'Michel de Certeau and the poststructuralist critique of history', *Social Semiotics*, vol. 6, no. 1, pp. 45–59.

Rinkinen, J, Jalas, M & Shove, E 2015, 'Object relations in accounts of everyday life', *Sociology*, vol. 49, no. 5, pp. 870–885.

Rothbauer, P 2010, 'Beyond a signpost for resistance: The promise of Michel de Certeau's practices of everyday life for LIS scholarship', in GJ Leckie, LM Given & JE Buschman (eds), *Critical theory for library and information science*, Libraries Unlimited, Santa Barbara, CA, pp. 53–62.

Saltmarsh, S 2014, 'Michel de Certeau, everyday life and policy cultures: The case of parent engagement in education policy', *Critical Studies in Education*, vol. 56, no. 1, pp. 38–54.

St Pierre, EA 2013, 'The posts continue: Becoming', *International Journal of Qualitative Studies in Education*, vol. 26, no. 6, pp. 646–657.

Thrift, N 1996, *Spatial formations*, Sage, London.

Trier, J 2014, *Detournement as pedagogical praxis*, Sense Publishers, Rotterdam.

Wacquant, LJD 1989, 'Towards a reflexive sociology a workshop with Pierre Bourdieu', *Sociological Theory*, vol. 7, no. 1, pp. 26–63.

Chapter 5

'Gestures towards'

Conceptualising literary practices for Crises of Ecologies

David Harris

In crises

We are entangled in Crises of Ecologies: global warming and climate change (IPCC 2013), mass extinction (Barnosky et al. 2011; Ceballos et al. 2015) and planetary degradation (Rockstrom et al. 2009; Steffen et al. 2011b). These crises are folded into, enfold and unfold from capitalism (Braidotti 2013; Guattari 2000; Hardt & Negri 2000). Capitalism exhibits a hyper-complex, devastating, anti-productive, eco-logic (Aryal & Massumi 2012; Guattari 2000, p. 44) – an eco-logic in that it traverses multiple existential registers, contracting subjective, social and environmental vitality[1]. We know that we are all implicated in potentially inerasable and overwhelming planetary transformations (Guattari 2000; Steffen et al. 2011b; Steffen et al. 2011a). We fear that our reliance upon science, technology, commercial ingenuity or political vision may not be enough to keep us from the worst of what may come. And, to some, there appear to be few bearable ways through or out (Collings 2014; Kolbert 2014; Rockstrom et al. 2009). In these terrifying circumstances it must seem something akin to madness to ask what literary practice might do to help (Collings 2014; Phillips 2003), and yet hasn't literature always expressed resistance and brought us to Life (Chambers 1991; Deleuze 1997)?

With the work of literary fiction in mind, I advocate for and explore here some of the modes of a literary practice for Crises of Ecologies. The approach taken here to conceptualise literary practices through which writing might cultivate ecological sense is shaped by conceptualisations of the work of art and literature, as well as onto-epistemological approaches to subjectivity, ecology and ethics associated with the thought of Deleuze, Guattari[2] and the new materialists[3]. Four modes of practice are outlined: literature as an affective technology of subjectivity (O'Sullivan 2006, 2012); writing vital matter; writing the posthuman; and minor literature. I contend that these modes of practice enable subjective resistance and renewal amidst Crises of Ecologies and I conceptualise the efficacy of these modes of practice in terms of their cultivating 'ecological sense', by which I mean: invigorating our 'affective athleticism' (Deleuze & Guattari 1994, p. 172); fostering a sense of those forces of Life that we often ignore, deny, or otherwise find imperceptible; improving our capacities to perceive the agency of the non-and-more-than-human world; radically reconfiguring our sense of our subjective interdependencies with all that is non-and-more-than-human, and thus of our potential agency amidst capitalism and ecological crises; attuning us to the ways in which we shape crises and, through them, denude Life and our lives; augmenting our capacities to perceive the harmful affective flows of both capitalism and ecological crises as well as the traumas associated with those flows; and gesturing toward the pursuit of unsanctioned affective trajectories and creative subjective renewal amidst these crises. I also raise some of the questions that arise from and complicate these arguments but which lie beyond this chapter's scope.

Problems of representation

In turning, first, to the problems with writing 'Nature', ecology and Crises of Ecologies, we find that we return to crises of representation (Phillips 2003, p. 8). Respectively, Deleuze (1994), Morton (2007, 2010b) and Phillips (1999, 2003, 2013) provide compelling critiques of representation, Nature writing and ecocriticism, and the problems writers face in cultivating attunement to Crises of Ecologies. Representations blind us to the world's complexity and to its unrepresentability, to its flows, to its vibrancy and to its chaos (Deleuze 1994). They also perpetuate dangerous fantasies of separable Nature and Humans. Nevertheless, writers continue literary practices that aim to compellingly (re)connect us to 'the world' and thereby transform how we think about the drastic impacts we Humans have upon it (Phillips 2003, p. 8). The passion put into these practices does not, however, effect a reconnection of writer or reader with the non-and-more-than-human. Art that re-inscribes the difference between things remains rooted in the idea of opposition, separation and alienation, even where it asserts a reconnection or bridging of that divide (Morton 2007, pp. 22–23). For Morton (2007), closer inspection of the world yields only greater complexity, strangeness and singularity; radical ontological enmeshment and intimacy; and our irreducible accountability to all those with whom we are enmeshed. Consequently, representational literary strategies, whatever we call them – ecomimesis, ambient poetics, eco-rhapsody, ecodidacticism (2007, pp. 61–62), metaphor, metonymy, Nature writing or eco-criticism (Garrard 2004) – remain highly problematic with regard to their influence on ecological sense. We cannot hope to literarily represent a fantasy – 'Nature' – that is not materially real beyond its cultural construction, and expect that representation to connect us more fully to it: it is not available for connection in the first place (Phillips 2003, p. 161; Morton 2007, p. 14). On the other hand, representational attempts to better attune us to the 'real' world's complexity risk 'unmaking' or dissolving literature in order to be true to that complexity. Perhaps, literature, if it is to 'work', needs to be approached *machinically* rather than mimetically: as carrying and participating in the world; as producing movement and transformation via relation, rather than as mirroring some fixed concept (Deleuze 1997, p. 78; Colebrook 2010, p. 96).

Literature as an affective technology of subjectivity

Literature expresses the material qualities and forces of the world absent the Human (Deleuze and Guattari 1994, p. 182), along with the forces of becoming that run between and are expressed by collisions between bodies: percepts and affects (Bourassa 2009)[4]. These forces are not reducible to communication or exemplification. Nor are they restricted to the prompting of feelings or emotions which then do nothing to produce a movement in the subjectivities they encounter (Bourassa 2009, p. 19). Affects produce becomings: breaks in habit; the drawing of bodies into compounds of sensation that did not exist prior to their encounter with the art work (Deleuze & Guattari 1994, p. 175). First, though not primarily, affects are the sensations one body provokes in another in a fictional narrative: the text operating as a conductor of the intensities transmitted. Second, literary works are vehicles of intensities (Deleuze & Guattari 1994) that, in collision with other bodies, always produce something entirely new. Via these relations we come to 'know' subjectivity 'in terms of what surpasses it, undermines it, fragments it, but also in terms of what simultaneously supports its, energizes it, and holds it together' (Bourassa 2009, p. 26). These becomings comprise the transformation of perceptual frames and boundaries and the catalysation of subjective lines of flight (Deleuze & Guattari 1987, p. 9).

Literature is not separated from Life; it carries Life and is involved in its 'perpetually moving, metamorphosing, or emigrating from one condition to another' (Deleuze 1993, p. xiv). For Deleuze, Guattari and new materialist thinkers on art practice, literature possesses a transformational material force – in both its initial production and in its subsequent interactions with other bodies – and it 'works' intensively, via the senses, to cultivate our perceptual capacities[5].

Our 'art practice can be understood as a form of thought and as a technology of subjectivity' (O'Sullivan 2006, p. 17). For Deleuze, Guattari and new materialists, subjectivity is multiple, polyphonic, always in process, always between, and not something that can be fixed or returned to 'normal'. It is ecological in its exteriority and multiplicity: renewed via our participations in the formation, expression and transformation of assemblages[6]. Art and literature are no less participants in these processes than other bodies (Human or non-and-more-than-human). The writer, in producing a text, introduces variation into self and world and works against forces that contract subjectivity. The self into which variation is introduced is neither singular nor plural but always collective (Braidotti 2010, p. 242). Even writing alone, the writer expresses a collective subjectivity and calls out to a people not yet in existence. In these ways, literary practice entails both material-discursive[7] expressions of collectivity and material-discursive collective expressions.

As escape/immersion/relation, literary practice releases desire from oppression – not desire for something we lack but desire for renewal through relation: to expand our affective capacities, to become more and to increase the intensities of our encounters (Spinoza 2009). If the capitalist subject's attunement to affect has been diminished and contracted, then literary encounters deliver an affective 'kick-start', attuning us to the infantilizing, stratifying, facialising and contractive affects employed to nourish capitalism[8]; enhancing our perception of the affects of ecological crises, of the intimate interconnection of these affects with us and of their traumatic effects; and offering access to affects other than those most common. By getting affect moving, literature can be a political instrument: a machine operating on and outside capitalism's power apparatus (Smith 2015); producing new machines whose own productions and enunciations remain indecipherable, unencodable, creative and liberatory.

Writing vital matter

Attachments to solely linguistic/deconstructive reconceptualisations of subjectivity, of the social and of ecology risk ignoring the material forces that traverse and shape these existential registers (Herzogenrath 2010, p. 5): forces carried, at least in part, by literature. New materialist theorists propose that literature has the potential to convey the vitality of matter or objects: the agency of things[9]. As Barad wrote of giving 'matter its due' (2003), so Jane Bennett writes of the political importance of giving 'the force of things more due' (2010, p.viii). Bennett references Deleuze and Guattari (1987), as well as Nietzsche's guidance in *Will to Power* that literature might connect us with Life: the 'monster of energy . . . that does not expend itself but only transforms itself. . . (entry 1067)' (2010, p. 54)[10]. Literature, Potter argues (2005), can convey a 'world in process' – an 'enchanted materialism' – that challenges anthropocentrism, widens our scope of attunement to the forces at work in the world, connects us intimately to them, and generates a sense of subjective instability, multiplicity and dynamism[11].

Still, with all literature written and read by Humans, and with the Human, in one form or another, always at the heart of literature (Bourassa 2002), can we avoid a literature of material agency returning us to the Human? An anthropomorphized literary evocation of material agency is to some degree acceptable to Bennett: 'We at first may see only a world in our own image, but what appears next is a swarm of "talented" and vibrant materialities (including the seeing self)' (2010, p. 99). Iovino and Opperman also argue, not unreasonably, that anthropomorphic patterns – as 'narrative expedient' (2012a, p. 82) – can be useful to convey material relations, kinships and connections that flow across the Human–nonhuman 'divide' (2012a, p. 83). But what is this divide? Do the benefits to ecological sense of such literary encounters with vital agencies – agencies occurring beyond us, flowing through us, but not us – outweigh the risks that the literary forms used to express those encounters will re-inscribe and privilege the humanisms already complicit in ecological crises? Posthuman materialists (Braidotti 2013) and deconstructive object-oriented ontologists (Morton 2007) might consider even a cautious acceptance of the Human-nonhuman divide in literary approaches to material agencies to be a regressive step. For example, Morton's assertion that the dissolution of the Human and the nonhuman (Nature) are potentially productive artistic modes of response to Crises of Ecologies (2007) seems at odds with literary modes that habitually subsume the material back into the Human, even if they express best intentions of coming out somewhere more illuminated on the 'other side'. The literary practices that we employ to encounter and engage with the material, matter.

Writing the posthuman

'In fact, the self is only a threshold, a door . . .'.

(Deleuze & Guattari 1987, p. 249)

It is, perhaps, by exploring the radical exteriority of subjectivity, that writers can access non-anthropocentric expressions of the non-and-more-than-human. For example, by losing the Human and turning toward the posthuman subject (Braidotti 2013), a writer might bring us (to) a new world of vital materiality. A posthuman-inspired literature might attune us to the dependence of our subjectivity upon nonhuman forces that we have a limited capacity to control (including 'vibrant matter' (Bennett 2010)); to our non-unitary existence in non-and-more-than-Human, material-discursive (Barad 2003, p. 822) assemblages; and to the flaws in our beliefs that we possess some prior essence or transcend the non-and-more-than-human. Such literature might populate the world with radically porous bodies; make the directions of flows indeterminate; blur distinctions and categories; and lose the individual in multiplicity. It might attune us to our posthuman subjectivities: to our radically relational onto-epistemological condition and, therein, to our becomings–nonhuman, revealing the rich, monstrous strangeness that is Life and our self. Such literary practices would entail and engender, in writer and reader, a degree of reorientation of our ethical frame: transforming contracted and limited *con*ceptions of sustainability into expansive/intensive *per*ceptions of sustainability; cultivating our sensitivity to our flourishing being dependent upon the flourishing of others. It is, for Deleuze, such injections of art into the everyday (1994, p. 293) that can make the chaos and difference of the world resonate with and deterritorialise the molar[12] capitalist individual, drawing us into becomings and greater perceptual intimacy with the Life we erroneously think we hold at a distance.

Literature can map the productions of posthuman subjectivities amidst Crises of Ecologies. It can tune us in: to the agency of matter; to the material reach of the intensities associated with capitalism; and to the psychical, social and environmental implications of our interconnectedness. Literary cartographies of our 'new earth' (Kingsolver 2012, p. 433) might, for example, express the unimaginable scope of the agency of hyperobjects like global warming (Morton 2013) – massively distributed in time and space, inescapably enveloping bodies, materially transformative, intimately revealed, their totality always withdrawn, at once sublimely large and invasively molecular – to shape and re-shape us[13]; or track the paths of discarded waste products and chemicals back to and through the Human[14]; or express the unavoidable and continuing intimacy we have with our abject matter – excrement, bodily fluids, animal byproducts and so on (Kristeva 1982, p. 3).

Literary becomings – occurring as we write the text, within the narrative, and as we read the text – are an embrace of immanence. They constitute sensuous openings-out to the world: to 'new levels, zones of liberated intensities where contents free themselves from their forms as well as from their expressions, from the signifier that formalized them' (Deleuze & Guattari 1986, p. 13). They entail the affirmative production of perceptual lines of flight and the cultivation of ecological sense[15]. They deterritorialise us from the molar of the Human, bore holes in anthropocentrism, break open the Oedipal family triangle (Deleuze & Guattari 1983) and resist the forces that work to reterritorialise the subject as capitalist individual. This is not a deletion of the subject but a reconfiguration of subjectivity. The creatures, subjects and bodies that we read about may move like familiar identities but their life occurs molecularly, through blocs of becomings. 'Real' Life is lived in-between the molar categories of subjectivity – man, woman, child, animal, other – and is produced by transversal encounters with the always radically other. Literary becomings-animal and becomings-imperceptible provide two instances of ways in which we might experiment transversally with subjectivity.

We need to engage differently with the animal; the beings that have been 'othered' and treated as resources – discursive and material, psychical and social (Braidotti 2002) – for the preservation of Humans and of capital; the beings whom we are unable to see and yet who exist already in us (Derrida & Mallet 2008). Becomings-animal – for example, Gregor's becoming-insect in Kafka's *Metamorphosis* (Deleuze & Guattari 1986, p. 22); Billy Parham's becoming-wolf in Cormac McCarthy's *The Crossing* (Bourassa 2009, p. 115); and Kai's becoming-bird in Tim Winton's *Eyrie* (2013) – express ways out of the perceptual poverty that shapes our destructive Human-animal relationships (Braidotti 2013, 2002). They involve the sensuous reconfigurations of subjectivities: the production of zones of indeterminacy in encounters between heterogeneous beings, within which categories, subjectivities, difference as negation, Human-animal dialectics and anthropocentric perceptions are lost.

Where literature embraces Life as *Zoe*[16] and the idea of the vitality of the non-and-more-than-human world, it might dissolve the subject and the object (Cohen 2006) and we might – as Deleuze (1987) finds in Virginia

Woolf[17]—'become progressively more molecular in a kind of cosmic lapping through which the inaudible makes itself heard and the imperceptible appears as such: no longer the songbird, but the sound molecule' (Deleuze & Guattari 1987, p. 248)[18]. Because such '[b]ecoming-imperceptible is the event for which there is no immediate representation' (Braidotti 2006a, p. 28) – which of course raises the question of how we write it – it affirms the uncontrollable, creative force of multiplicity that capitalism forever expands its boundaries to try and co-opt (Bell 2009), capital's prime objective being the production of the entirely predictable and therefore most profitable consumer. In this way, becomings-imperceptible offer escapes.

It may be that literary practice can attune us afresh to matters of sustainability (Braidotti 2006a), or the degree to which the vibrancy of our life depends upon the qualities of our affective encounters with the non-and-more-than-human: in particular, to the unfathomable diminution in energy, vibrancy and creative potential resulting from mass extinction, climate change and planetary degradation. Perversely, the contractions of Life that are Crises of Ecologies might well seed a literature of the contraction of becomings[19]: a practice that, perhaps, has kinships with Morton's dark ecology (2007, 2008, 2010a). Questions pertinent to literary practice arise when contemplating matters of finitude (Human and non-and-more-than-human) in this way[20]: what might be the literary practice for a failed Human project?; how might a literary practice for crises assist us to assimilate a 'broken world' without its spectre haunting us, or its actuality distressing us to such a degree that desire ceases to move?; conversely, how might such a literature fortify us to give up rather than retain hope of recovery, and to find composure in our destitution?; and how might literature engage with the 'nullity of our entire history' (Collings 2014, p. 154) if all that was once deemed progress of one sort or another can now be viewed, through the other end of the telescope, as a narrowing down to a self-inflicted absence? The discussion of a minor literature for Crises of Ecologies that follows, while it briefly acknowledges the importance of style (Deleuze & Guattari 1994, p. 170), focuses predominantly on fabulation as one mode of response to these melancholy questions.

Minor literature

As Bogue (2003) explains, minor literature is, for Deleuze and Guattari, a material pursuit. It 'catastrophises' with language, rupturing meaning and integrating catastrophe into the affective capacities of the work. It is a-signifying and intensive: 'nonrepresentative, nonillustrative, nonnarrative' (Deleuze 2003a, p. 100) and affective. Words operate physically, 'as lacerating, persecuting objects that rip into the flesh' (Bogue 2003, p. 27). Their traits are sensation and through sensation the writer breaks codes that are 'inevitably cerebral' and acts upon the nervous system (Deleuze 2003a, p. 109). Bogue notes that art becomes a schizophrenic experience[21], offering both a liberation and chaos. Syntactically and affectively, then, minor literature can disrupt majoritarian concepts, language and figurations that serve to perpetuate and deepen Crises of Ecologies: 'Nature'; the inevitability and irreplaceability of market capitalism; the continuity and primacy of the Human; the subordinated, subsumed animal; the pastoral and the bucolic as 'real' havens; environment as separate and in the background; that consumption brings individualism; that value is only measured in terms of capital accumulation; that technology, the government, innovators, social movements or God will save us; and that there is, indeed, some way out (Collings 2014).

Deleuze's reuse of Bergson's concept of fabulation[22] involves literary practice in the prospective and in offering access to worlds and futures beyond our rational expectations, and other than those produced by capitalism's material-discursive force. The writer 'diagrams' the forces shaping states of affairs[23], destabilises and points to cracks in the existing world (Bogue 2007, pp. 98–99), and catalyses new sense events, thoughts and visions in the reader. The visions of the writer (perhaps, a world beyond the extinction of the Human, or a ruined world in which the Human must persist?) may be intolerable but they are also a productive critique of received wisdoms – the true as well as the false (Bogue 2010, pp. 32, 226) – and a disruption to the sanctioned flow of history (Bogue 2007, p. 105). As with fabulation in cinematic science fiction (Braidotti 2002, p. 182), literary practices enable us to cope and come to terms with Crises of Ecologies, and renew our capacities to imagine worlds beyond the current state of affairs: even, beyond (though not redeemed from) the most dire existential prognoses (Collings 2014)[24].

A minor literature, for Deleuze and Guattari (1986), also operates as a future-oriented, intensive gesture away from structures of power and towards a collective that did not exist beforehand or that, perhaps, has been broken (Deleuze & Guattari 1987, p. 345). It issues a call to attunement, an invitation to a mutual inclusion, but it is not instructive, and it cannot lead or impose a program or an imperative. Its principle 'becomes', through performance or enactment, and can be as broad as desiring the counter to the current state of affairs and the augmentation of our powers of affirmative existence (Massumi 2002b). Literary fabulations can enact these gestures toward a collectivity: hallucinations of history[25] of such intensity that the writer's 'desiring-production in its positive function contributes to the formation of a group-subject, a self-determining, fluid and open collectivity' (p. 106)[26]. New myths are offered for those who do not recognise themselves in the ones that exist already and these are transformative: 'apocalyptic', O'Sullivan suggests (2006, p. 203). What might be the qualities of a collective for Crises of Ecologies? Aaltola's definition of 'person' (2008) – recognising the transversality of Life and incorporating all beings that can experience, not just Humans – might enable a more expansive (albeit speculative) response to this question.

We might speculate that the excluded – those most affected by, and those rendered powerless (O'Sullivan 2006, p. 78) by Crises of Ecologies – will (at least) include the oppressed, the poor, the non-Westerner, the colonised, those most exposed to the material forces of crises, dependants, and those still to be born: 'A people . . . created in abominable sufferings . . . They have resistance in common — their resistance to death, to servitude, to the intolerable, to shame, to the present' (Deleuze & Guattari 1994, p. 110). Of course, when it comes to the nonhuman, we might 'naturally' dismiss the prospects for animal, insect, plant, fungi, bacteria and single-celled organisms to be called into the collective. After all, the nonhuman cannot directly (or at least 'humanly') access and interpret the symbols and affects carried by a work of fiction. Nevertheless, from the darkness of this onto-epistemological abyss, perhaps a literary practice can call forth the non-and-more-than-human, precisely through the Human becoming-posthuman. We become a mutant collective, open to anyone and everyone, not only through the stuttering, stammering, breaking and failing of our human language but also through the material, incorporeal, transversal, species-less relations by which we all become. Deleuze suggests that minor literary practices fashion giants (1997, p. 118) and project images onto the real that express a life of their own. They create characters who embody collectives of oppressed and who produce their own 'empowering projective mythography' (Bogue 2010, p. 228). Might, then, the giants of a minor literary practice for Crises of Ecologies be the non-and-more-than-Human?

(In)conclusion

I conclude by attending to an Australian 'particularity' which has important consequences for literary practice[27], and which, I note, also has relevance to questions of literary practice amid Crises of Ecologies in other contexts entangled in capitalist exploitation, decolonisation and neo-colonialism (not least, North America, the Caribbean and the Global South). Since the colonisation of Australia began, Indigenous peoples and Country have been subjected to profound ecological devastation[28]. Ecological crises are, then, more than recent phenomena; for Indigenous peoples, they embody and perpetuate traumas spanning more than two hundred years. There have been appeals for non-Indigenous Australians to become more open to Indigenous onto-epistemologies and spirituality as ways by which we might embrace exteriority in our subjectivities and respond differently to aspects of Crises of Ecologies, including our impacts upon Indigenous peoples and Country[29]. There are of course deep problems with such exhortations, even though they may be voiced with good intent[30]. It may even be the case that an intensive attunement to the non-and-more-than-human is beyond us (the non-Indigenous) and that our own 'gap' is too large to close. If we settlers have not, so far, 'closed the gap' in our attunement to the non-and-more-than-human qualities of Life, and cannot hope to do so any time soon, what can we possibly expect to achieve with regard to finding responses to Crises of Ecologies? If settler history attests to our inability to care for Country, while those who possess different structures of thought and different knowledges relating to caring for Country remain disenfranchised, dispossessed and denied agency to make a difference (Patton 2001, 2002), then what are we to do next and who is capable of doing it?[31] If non-Indigenous 'solutions' are based upon an alien and limited 'knowledge' of Country, then will we do more damage than repair? How will these 'solutions' remain sensitive to and consistent with the knowledge of Country borne by the descendants of this continent's earliest human inhabitants (Wright 2011)?

Such questions as these should be profoundly discomforting for a non-Indigenous Australian considering the prospects for cultivating an Australian literary practice for Crises of Ecologies amidst our hardly 'post-colonial' state of affairs. And they are. What, if anything, can non-Indigenous literature do to cultivate ecological sense that Indigenous literature cannot always do better? As a settler, I concede that it is beyond my rights and capabilities, and I suggest a folly for Western thinking, to attempt to unilaterally theorise an Indigenous or non-Indigenous literary practice for Crises of Ecologies in the Australian context. However, I do want to note that there may be some affirmative resonances between certain Australian Indigenous practices/philosophies of Life – as non-Indigenous scholars understand them (Verran 1998, Rose 1996, 2004, Muecke 2004, Law 2004) – and new materialist notions of transversality, of the posthuman and of the agency of matter, and their implications for ecology. Law's work, after Verran, on Aboriginal onto-epistemology (2004) gestures towards these resonances. In his assessment, Aboriginal onto-epistemologies posit no reality independent of the subject: 'patterns of dualist separation are almost entirely absent from Aboriginal method assemblages' (p. 133). He observes that 'there is no universal or general, and instead everything is relatively specific, relatively "local", enacted at particular places on particular occasion ... there is no overall privilege' (pp. 137–138). Law alerts us to only a few of the potentially enriching ways in which Indigenous and new materialist onto-epistemologies might traverse each other. How such transversal relations might (and already do) affirmatively shape literary practices for Crises of Ecologies in varying post-colonial/neo-colonial contexts is a question that warrants further and urgent attention[32].

Notes

1 See Aryal and Massumi (2012), Braidotti (2013), Clough (2008a), Davis (2006), Guattari and Stivale (2009, p. 215), Piketty and Goldhammer (2014), Reber (2012, p. 84), Robinson (2013), Saunders (2011), Seymour (2013).

2 See Deleuze (1989, 1993, 1994, 1997, 2003a, 2003b, 2005), Deleuze and Guattari (1983, 1986, 1987, 1994) and Deleuze and Parnet (2007).

3 Writers include Alaimo (2010), Alaimo and Hekman (2008), Barad (2007, 2012, 2003), Bennett (2004, 2010), Braidotti (2006a, 2006b, 2002, 2013, 2005), Iovino and Oppermann (2012b, 2012a), Kirby (1997), Massumi (1995, 2002a, 2002b, 2011), Morton (2007, 2010a, 2010b, 2010c, 2013), Phillips (2013, 2003), Phillips and Sullivan (2012) and Pickering (1995).

4 That which Bourassa calls "all that lies outside of the scope of the human, but nonetheless makes it up" (cited in Uebel 2010, p. 20): difference rather than negation; the

not less-than-human; the organic, the inorganic, the anorganic; the corporeal and the incorporeal; the virtual and the actual; the impersonal, the apersonal, the pre-personal, the pre-individual; the affective and the intensive; desiring-machines, bodies, assemblages and their planes of existence.

5 See Bennett (2010), Braidotti (2002), Deleuze (1997), Deleuze and Guattari (1994), Iovino (2012), Iovino and Oppermann (2012a, 2012b) and Massumi (2002a, 2011).

6 Assemblages are dynamic, impermanent wholes constituted by corporeal and incorporeal bodies and characterised by relations of exteriority rather than interiority. See De Landa (2006) and Deleuze and Guattari (1983).

7 Barad explains: 'The relationship between the material and the discursive is one of mutual entailment . . . matter and meaning are mutually articulated . . . Neither has privileged status in determining the other' (2003, p. 822).

8 See Anderson (2012), Aryal and Massumi (2012), Clough (2008b), Deleuze and Guattari (1983, 1987, 2007), Negishi (2012), Reber (2012), Stiegler (2014) and Wendling (2012).

9 See Brown (2003), Cohen (2006), Deleuze and Parnet (2007, p. 39) and Iovino and Oppermann (2012a).

10 Bennett (2010, p. 45–45), suggests Kafka's Odradek as an example of literary engagement with the agential forces of matter, while Iovino and Oppermann (2012a, p. 81) suggest Conrad's river Congo.

11 However, the various perspectives on the proliferating scales at and registers across which the agencies of matter are expressed (see, for example, Phillips and Sullivan (2012, p. 447), Bennett (2010), Chakrabarty (2009), Morton (2013)), do not resolve questions of how to write these agencies.

12 Molar implies the notion of the unified, stable, solidified, fixed and rigid being, subject to dominating concepts that pre-shape it and constrain what a body might become (Deleuze and Guattari 1987).

13 See Tim Winton's *Eyrie* (2013) for an encounter with the hyperobject global warming. Also, see Barbara Kingsolver's *Flight Behaviour* (2012).

14 See Don DeLillo's treatment of waste in *Underworld* (1998).

15 See Bell (2009), Bogue (2010), Braidotti (2002, p. 149), Bruns (2007), Colebrook (2013), Danta (2007), Deleuze and Guattari (1987), Dillon (2011), Fullagar (2000), Goh (2009), Griggers (1997), Grosz (1999), Jarraway (2012), Knighton (2013), Lloyd (2010), Lorraine (2000), MacCormack (2010), Patton (2004), Vint (2005) and Žukauskait (2012).

16 Braidotti's proposal of *Zoe* (2006a) offers us 'the generative force of non-human life [which] rules through a trans-species and transgenic interconnection, or rather a chain of connections, which can best be described as an ecological philosophy of non-unitary, embodied subjects of multiple belongings' (2006b, p. 203). Dissolving nature and the human, without losing vital materialism, we look upon the subject always from the outside, as the 'echoing chamber of Zoe' (Braidotti 2006a, p. 8), as contingent upon the relations that comprise it and we look upon subjectivity as a production of *Zoe* but not the end goal of *Zoe*.

17 See also Braidotti's analysis of Woolf (2008).

18 Deleuze and Guattari suggest that becoming-imperceptible is to fall back into the world and become world; to return to the molecular flows that fold and refold Life: 'suppressed in oneself everything that prevents us from slipping between things and growing in the midst of things. One has combined "everything"' (1987, p. 280).

19 We might, for example, ask what becomings are possible in the ashen, sun-denied, cauterised waste of Cormac McCarthy's *The Road* (2006).

20 Colebrook (2014), Collings (2014) and Morton (2010a) offer perspectives on the ethical and aesthetic implications of the loss, decline and extinction of the human.

21 The word 'schizophrenic' is used here affirmatively, as a process of becoming and renewal (though such processes are not necessarily pain-free).

22 For Bergson (c1935, 1977), fabulation is a practice of social control to preserve stability.
23 Bryant (2013) offers a conceptualisation of these forces, via geopolitics, thermopolitics, infrapolitics and chronopolitics.
24 See Alexis Wright's *The Swan Book* (2013).
25 I note that Alexis Wright's *The Swan Book* (2013) suggests that such 'hallucinations' need not be of a past history but could be of a future one.
26 Deleuze references T. E. Lawrence as such a writer (1997, pp. 115–125).
27 Though there may be resonances to be found between the ideas proposed in this chapter and the ways in which Indigenous onto-epistemologies and practices shape and are shaped by Indigenous writing, I am not pursuing the question of what might be the qualities of an Indigenous literary practice for Crises of Ecologies.
28 See, for example, Flannery (1997), Griffiths and Robin (1997), Reynolds (1987, 1989, 2001, 2013, 2006), Rose (2004), Rose and Robin (2004).
29 See Brady (1999), Devlin-Glass (2008), Haraway (2011), Plumwood (1999), Rawlings (2009, p. 124), Rose (2004) and Rose and Robin (2004).
30 See Delrez (2007), Nick Rothwell (2007), Judith Wright (1999, pp. 295–296) and Judith Wright (Strauss 1995, pp. 49–50).
31 Protevi's works on political emotion (2014) and on political affect – embracing collective action, expression and the emergence of subjectivity (2009) – offer insights into potential somatic-social-semantic modes of resistance and renewal and raise questions as to how writers and literary practices contribute to emergent assemblages or bodies politic.
32 Although neither explores the entanglements of colonialism and Crises of Ecologies, collections by Bignall and Patton (2010; Burns and Kaiser (2012) address some of the challenges and potential pathways for critical and creative production arising from the interactions of Deleuzian and post-colonial thought. Rick Dolphijn's chapter, concerning the Deleuzian concept of 'Anotherness', and a new earth (2012) pursues some challenging ways in which literature might illuminate an ecophilosophy and inform our relations and orientations towards the earth.

References

Aaltola, E 2008, 'Personhood and animals', *Environmental Ethics*, vol. 30, no. 2, pp. 175–193.
Alaimo, S 2010, *Bodily natures: Science, environment, and the material self*, Indiana University Press, Bloomington.
Alaimo, S & Hekman, SJ 2008, *Material feminisms*, Indiana University Press, Bloomington.
Anderson, B 2012, 'Affect and biopower: Towards a politics of life', *Transactions of the Institute of British Geographers*, vol. 37, no. 1, pp. 28–43.
Aryal, Y & Massumi, B 2012, 'Beyond the "Techniques of Domination": Affect, capitalism and resistance', *Journal of Philosophy: A Cross-Disciplinary Inquiry*, vol. 7, no. 18, pp. 64–77.
Barad, K 2003, 'Posthumanist performativity: Toward an understanding of how matter comes to matter', *Signs*, vol. 28, no. 3, pp. 801–831.
Barad, K 2007, *Meeting the universe halfway: Quantum physics and the entanglement of matter and meaning*, Duke University Press, Durham.
Barad, K 2012, 'On touching – The inhuman that therefore I am', *differences*, vol. 23, no. 3, pp. 206–223.
Barnosky, A D, Matzke, N, Tomiya, S, Wogan, GOU, Swartz, B, Quental, TB, Marshall, C, McGuire, JL, Lindsey, EL, Maguire, KC, Mersey, B & Ferrer, EA 2011, 'Has the earth's sixth mass extinction already arrived?', *Nature*, vol. 471, no. 7336, pp. 51–57.
Bell, JA 2009, *Deleuze's Hume: Philosophy, culture and the Scottish enlightenment*, Edinburgh University Press, Edinburgh.

Bennett, J 2004, 'The force of things: Steps toward an ecology of matter', *Political Theory*, vol. 32, no. 3, pp. 347–372.

Bennett, J 2010, *Vibrant matter: A political ecology of things*, Duke University Press, Durham.

Bergson, H 1977, c1935, *The two sources of morality and religion*, University of Notre Dame Press, Notre Dame, IN.

Bignall, S & Patton, P 2010, *Deleuze and the postcolonial*, Edinburgh University Press, Edinburgh.

Bogue, R 2003, *Deleuze on literature*, Routledge, New York.

Bogue, R 2007, *Deleuze's way: Essays in transverse ethics and aesthetics*, Ashgate, Aldershot, UK.

Bogue, R 2010, *Deleuzian fabulation and the scars of history*, Edinburgh University Press, Edinburgh.

Bourassa, A 2002, 'Literature, language, and the non-human', in B Massumi (ed.), *A shock to thought: Expression after Deleuze and Guattari*, Routledge, London & New York.

Bourassa, A 2009, *Deleuze and American literature*, Palgrave Macmillan, New York.

Brady, V 1999, 'Towards an ecology of Australia: Land of the spirit', *Worldviews: Global Religions, Culture, and Ecology*, vol. 3, no. 2, pp. 139–155.

Braidotti, R 2002, *Metamorphoses: Towards a materialist theory of becoming*, Polity Press, Cambridge.

Braidotti, R 2005, 'Affirming the affirmative: On nomadic affectivity', *Rhizomes*, vol. 11/12, Fall 2005/Spring 2006, retrieved 8 April 2016, <http://www.rhizomes.net>.

Braidotti, R 2006a, 'The ethics of becoming imperceptible', in CV Boundas (ed.), *Deleuze and philosophy*, Edinburgh University Press, Edinburgh.

Braidotti, R 2006b, 'Posthuman, all too human: Towards a new process ontology', *Theory, Culture & Society*, vol. 23, no. 7/8, pp. 197–208.

Braidotti, R 2008, 'Intensive genre and the demise of gender', *Angelaki: Journal of the Theoretical Humanities*, vol. 13, no. 2, pp. 45–57.

Braidotti, R 2010, 'Schizophrenia' in A Parr (ed.), *The Deleuze dictionary* (revised ed.), Edinburgh University Press, Edinburgh.

Braidotti, R 2013, *The posthuman*, Polity Press, Cambridge, UK.

Brown, B 2003, *A sense of things: The object matter of American literature*, University of Chicago Press, Chicago.

Bruns, GL 2007, 'Becoming-animal (some simple ways)', *New Literary History*, vol. 38, no. 4, pp. 703–720.

Bryant, LR 2013, 'Politics and speculative realism', *Speculations IV*, pp. 15–21.

Burns, L & Kaiser, BM 2012, *Postcolonial literatures and Deleuze: Colonial pasts, differential futures*, Palgrave Macmillan, Houndmills, Basingstoke, Hampshire.

Ceballos, G, Ehrlich, PR, Barnosky, AD, García, A, Pringle, RM & Palmer, TM 2015, 'Accelerated modern human–induced species losses: Entering the sixth mass extinction', *Science Advances*, vol. 1, no. 5, e1400253, doi: 10.1126/sciadv.1400253.

Chakrabarty, D 2009, 'The climate of history: Four theses', *Critical Inquiry*, vol. 35, no. 2, pp. 197–222.

Chambers, R 1991, *Room for maneuver: Reading (the) oppositional (in) narrative*, University of Chicago Press, Chicago, IL & London.

Clough, PT 2008a, 'The affective turn: Political economy, biomedia and bodies', *Theory, Culture & Society*, vol. 25, no. 1, pp. 1–22.

Clough, PT 2008b, '(De)coding the subject-in-affect', *Subjectivity*, vol. 23, no. 1, pp. 140–155.

Cohen, WA 2006, 'Faciality and sensation in Hardy's "The Return of the Native"', *PMLA: Publications of the Modern Language Association of America*, vol. 121, no. 2, pp. 437–452.

Colebrook, C 2010, 'Expression', in A Parr (ed.), *The Deleuze dictionary*, (revised ed.), Edinburgh University Press, Edinburgh.

Colebrook, C 2013, 'Modernism without women: The refusal of becoming-woman (and post-feminism)', *Deleuze Studies*, vol. 7, no. 4, pp. 427–455.

Colebrook, C 2014, *Death of the posthuman – Essays on extinction*, Open Humanities Press with Michigan Publishing, Ann Arbor, MI.

Collings, DA 2014, *Stolen future, broken present: The human significance of climate change*, Open Humanities Press with Michigan Publishing, Ann Arbor, MI.

Danta, C 2007, "Like a dog . . . like a lamb': Becoming sacrificial animal in Kafka and Coetzee', *New Literary History*, vol. 38, no. 4, pp. 721–737.

Davis, M 2006, *Planet of slums*, Verso, London.

De Landa, M 2006, *A new philosophy of society: Assemblage theory and social complexity*, Continuum, London.

Deleuze, G 1989, *Masochism*, Zone Books, New York & Cambridge MA.

Deleuze, G 1993, *The fold: Leibniz and the Baroque*, Athlone Press, London.

Deleuze, G. 1994, *Difference and repetition*, Columbia University Press, New York.

Deleuze, G 1997, *Essays critical and clinical*, University of Minnesota Press, Minneapolis, MN.

Deleuze, G 2003a, *Francis Bacon: The logic of sensation*, Continuum, London & New York.

Deleuze, G 2003b, *The logic of sense*, Continuum, New York.

Deleuze, G 2005, *Cinéma 2: The time image*, Bloomsbury Publishing, London & New York.

Deleuze, G & Guattari, F 2007, 'Capitalism: A very special delirium', *Lectures by Gilles Deleuze*, weblog post, February 2007, retrieved 8 April 2016, <http://deleuzelectures. blogspot.com.au>.

Deleuze, G & Guattari, F 1983, *Anti-Oedipus: Capitalism and schizophrenia*, University of Minnesota Press, Minneapolis, MN.

Deleuze, G & Guattari, F 1986, *Kafka: Toward a minor literature*, University of Minnesota Press, Minneapolis, MN.

Deleuze, G & Guattari, F 1987, *A thousand plateaus: Capitalism and schizophrenia*, Continuum, Minneapolis, MN.

Deleuze, G & Guattari, F 1994, *What is philosophy?*, Columbia University Press, New York.

Deleuze, G & Parnet, C 2007, *Dialogues II*, Columbia University Press, New York.

DeLillo, D 1998, *Underworld*, Picador, London.

Delrez, M 2007, 'Nationalism, reconciliation, and the cultural genealogy of magic in Richard Flanagan's death of a river guide', *The Journal of Commonwealth Literature*, vol. 42, no. 1, pp. 117–129.

Derrida, J & Mallet, M-L 2008, *The animal that therefore I am*, D. Wills (trans), Fordham University Press, New York.

Devlin-Glass, F 2008, 'The eco-centric self and the sacred in Xavier Herbert's poor fellow my country', *Journal of the Association for the Study of Australian Literature*, vol. 8, pp. 45–63.

Dillon, S 2011, '"It's a Question of Words, Therefore": Becoming-animal in Michel Faber's "Under the Skin"', *Science Fiction Studies*, vol. 38, no. 1, pp. 134–154.

Dolphijn, R 2012, Undercurrents and the desert(ed), in L Burns & BM Kaiser (eds), *Postcolonial literatures and Deleuze*, Palgrave Macmillan, Houndmills, Basingstoke, Hampshire.

Flannery, TF 1997, *The future eaters: An ecological history of the Australasian lands and people*, New Holland Publishers, Sydney.

Fullagar, S 2000, 'Desiring nature: Identity and becoming in narratives of travel', *Journal for Cultural Research*, vol. 4, no. 1, pp. 58–76.

Garrard, G 2004, *Ecocriticism*, Routledge, London & New York.

Goh, I 2009, 'Becoming-animal: Transversal politics', *diacritics*, vol. 39, no. 2, pp. 37–57.

Griffiths, T & Robin, L 1997, *Ecology and empire: Environmental history of settler societies*, University of Washington Press, Seattle, WA.

Griggers, C 1997, *Becoming-woman*, University of Minnesota Press, Minneapolis, MN.

Grosz, E 1999, *Becomings. Explorations in time, memory and futures*, Cornell University, Ithaca.

Guattari, F 2000, *The three ecologies*, Athlone Press, London.

Guattari, F & Stivale, CJ 2009, *Soft subversions: Texts and interviews 1977–1985*, Semiotext(e), Los Angeles.

Haraway, DJ 2011, 'Speculative fabulations for technoculture's generations: Taking care of unexpected country', *Australian Humanities Review*, retrieved 8 April 2016, <http://www. australianhumanitiesreview.org>.

Hardt, M & Negri, A 2000, *Empire*, Harvard University Press, Cambridge, MA & London.

Herzogenrath, B 2010, 'Introduction', in B Herzogenrath (ed.), *Deleuze/Guattari and ecology*, Palgrave Macmillan, Basingstoke.

Iovino, S 2012, 'Ecocríticas: Literatura y medio ambiente. Edited by Carmen Flys Junquera, José Manuel Marrero Henríquez, and Julia Barella Vigal. Madrid: Iberoamericana, 2010 [book review]', *ISLE-Interdisciplinary Studies in Literature and Environment*, vol. 19, no. 1, pp. 206–207.

Iovino, S & Oppermann, S 2012a, 'Material ecocriticism: Materiality, agency, and models of narrativity', *Ecozon@: European Journal of Literature, Culture and Environment*, vol. 3, no. 1, pp. 75–91.

Iovino, S & Oppermann, S 2012b, 'Theorizing material ecocriticism: A diptych', *ISLE: Interdisciplinary Studies in Literature & Environment*, vol. 19, no. 3, pp. 448–475.

IPCC 2013, 'Summary for policymakers', in Stocker TF, Qin D, Plattner GK, Tignor M, Allen SK, Boschung J, Nauels A, Xia Y, Bex V & Midgley PM (eds), *Climate change 2013: The physical science basis. Contribution of working group I to the fifth assessment report of the intergovernmental panel on climate change*, Intergovernmental Panel on Climate Change, Cambridge, UK & New York, NY.

Jarraway, DR 2012, '"Becoming-Woman": Masculine "Emergency" After 9/11 in Cormac McCarthy', *Canadian Review of American Studies*, vol. 42, no. 1, pp. 49–64.

Kingsolver, B 2012, *Flight behaviour*, Faber, London.

Kirby, V 1997, *Telling flesh: The substance of the corporeal*, Routledge, New York, NY.

Knighton, MA 2013, '"Becoming-Insect Woman": Tezuka's feminist species', *Mechademia*, vol. 8, no. 1, pp. 3–24.

Kolbert, E 2014, *The sixth extinction: An unnatural history*, Henry Holt & Company, New York.

Kristeva, J 1982, *Powers of horror: An essay on abjection*, Columbia University Press, New York.

Law, J 2004, *After method: Mess in social science research*, Routledge, London & New York.

Lloyd, V 2010, 'Gilles Deleuze: Travels in literature. By Mary Bryden and Deleuze's Way: Essays in transverse ethics and aesthetics. By Ronald Bogue', *Heythrop Journal*, vol. 51, no. 1, pp. 166–167.

Lorraine, TE 2000, 'Becoming-imperceptible as a mode of self-presentation: A feminist model drawn from a Deleuzian line of flight', in D Olkowski (ed.), *Resistance, flight, creation: Feminist enactments with French philosophy*, Cornell University Press, Ithaca.

MacCormack, P 2010, 'Lovecraft through Deleuzio-Guattarian gates', *Postmodern Culture: An Electronic Journal of Interdisciplinary Criticism*, vol. 20, no. 2, retrieved 8 April 2016, <http:// muse.jhu.edu>.

Massumi, B 1995, 'The autonomy of affect', *Cultural Critique*, vol. 31, pp. 83–109.

Massumi, B 2002a, *Parables for the virtual: Movement, affect, sensation*, Duke University Press, Durham, NC.

Massumi, B 2002b, *A shock to thought: Expression after Deleuze and Guattari*, Routledge, London & New York.

Massumi, B 2011, *Semblance and event: Activist philosophy and the occurrent arts*, MIT Press, Cambridge, MA.

McCarthy, C 2006, *The road*, Picador, London.

Morton, T 2007, *Ecology without nature: Rethinking environmental aesthetics*, Harvard University Press, Cambridge, MA.

Morton, T 2008, 'John Clare's dark ecology', *Studies in Romanticism*, vol. 47, no. 2, pp. 179–193.

Morton, T 2010a, 'The dark ecology of elegy', in K Weisman (ed.), *The Oxford handbook of the elegy*, Oxford University Press, Oxford.

Morton, T 2010b, *The ecological thought*, Harvard University Press, Cambridge, MA.

Morton, T 2010c, 'Thinking ecology: The mesh, the strange stranger, and the beautiful soul', *Collapse*, vol. 6, pp. 265–293.

Morton, T 2013, *Hyperobjects: Philosophy and ecology after the end of the world*, University of Minnesota Press, Minneapolis, MN.

Muecke, S 2004, *Ancient & modern: Time, culture and Indigenous philosophy*, University of NSW, Sydney.

Negishi, K 2012, 'Smiling in the post-Fordist "Affective" economy', *Transformations (14443775)*, vol. 22, pp. 1–17.

O'Sullivan, S 2006, *Art encounters Deleuze and Guattari: Thought beyond representation* Palgrave Macmillan, Basingstoke and New York.

O'Sullivan, S 2012, *On the production of subjectivity: Five diagrams of the finite-infinite relation*, Palgrave Macmillan, Basingstoke.

Patton, P 2001, 'Reconciliation, aboriginal rights and constitutional paradox in Australia', *Australian Feminist Law Journal*, vol. 15, no. 1, pp. 25–40.

Patton, P 2002, 'Indigenous-becoming in the post-colonial polity', in J Cutting-Gray & JE Swearingen (eds), *Extreme beauty: Aesthetics, politics, death*, Continuum, London & New York.

Patton, P 2004, 'Becoming-animal and pure life in Coetzee's disgrace', *Ariel: A Review of International English Literature*, vol. 35, no. 1–2, pp. 101–119.

Phillips, D 1999, 'Ecocriticism, literary theory, and the truth of ecology', *New Literary History*, vol. 30, no. 3, pp. 577–602.

Phillips, D 2003, *The truth of ecology: Nature, culture, and literature in America*, Oxford University Press, Oxford & New York.

Phillips, D 2013, 'Ecocriticism's hard problems (its ironies, too)', *American Literary History*, doi 10.1093/alh/ajt017.

Phillips, D & Sullivan, HI 2012, 'Material ecocriticism: Dirt, waste, bodies, food, and other matter', *ISLE: Interdisciplinary Studies in Literature and Environment*, vol. 19, no. 3, pp. 445–447.

Pickering, A 1995, *The mangle of practice: Time, agency, and science*, University of Chicago Press, Chicago, IL.

Piketty, T & Goldhammer, A 2014, *Capital in the twenty-first century*, The Belknap Press of Harvard University Press, Cambridge, MA.

Plumwood, V 1999, 'The struggle for environmental philosophy in Australia', *Worldviews: Global Religions, Culture & Ecology*, vol. 3, no. 2, pp. 157–178.

Potter, E 2005, 'Ecological crisis and Australian literary representation', *Australian Humanities Review*, no. 37, December 2005, retrieved 8 April 2016, <http://www.australianhumanitiesreview.org>.

Protevi, J 2009, *Political affect: Connecting the social and the somatic*, University of Minnesota Press, Minneapolis, MN.

Protevi, J 2014, 'Political emotion', in C von Scheve & M Salmela (eds), *Collective emotions: Perspectives from psychology, philosophy, and sociology*, Oxford University Press, New York.

Rawlings, S 2009, 'Literature and environmental ethics: A dissensual ecosophy', PhD Communications and Creative Arts Thesis, Deakin University, retrieved 8 April 2016, DRO Deakin Research Repository database.

Reber, D 2012, 'Headless capitalism: Affect as free-market episteme', *Differences: A Journal of Feminist Cultural Studies*, vol. 23, no. 1, pp. 62–100.

Reynolds, H 1987, *Frontier: Aborigines, settlers and land*, Allen & Unwin, Sydney.

Reynolds, H 1989, *Dispossession: Black Australians and white invaders*, Allen & Unwin, Sydney.

Reynolds, H 2001, *An indelible stain?: The question of genocide in Australia's history*, Penguin, Ringwood, VIC.

Reynolds, H 2006, *The other side of the frontier: Aboriginal resistance to the European invasion of Australia*, University of New South Wales Press, Sydney.

Reynolds, H 2013, *Forgotten War*, NewSouth Publishing, Sydney.

Robinson, W 2013, 'Global capitalism and its anti-'Human Face': Organic intellectuals and interpretations of the crisis', *Globalizations*, vol. 10, no. 5, pp. 659–671.

Rockstrom. J, Steffen, W, Noone, K, Persson, A, Chapin, FS, Lambin, EF, Lenton, TM, Scheffer, M, Folke. C, Schellnhuber, HJ, Nykvist, B, de Wit, CA, Hughes, T, van der Leeuw, S, Rodhe, H, Sorlin, S, Snyder, PK, Costanza, R, Svedin, U, Falkenmark, M, Karlberg, L, Corell, RW, Fabry, VJ, Hansen, J, Walker, B, Liverman, D, Richardson, K, Crutzen, P & Foley, JA 2009, 'Planetary boundaries: Exploring the safe operating space for humanity', *Ecology and Society*, vol. 14, no. 2, retrieved 8 April 2016, <http://www.ecologyandsociety.org>.

Rose, DB 1996, *Nourishing terrains: Australian aboriginal views of landscape and wilderness*, Australian Heritage Commission, Canberra.

Rose, DB 2004, *Reports from a wild country: Ethics for decolonisation*, University of New South Wales Press, Sydney.

Rose, DB & Robin, L 2004, 'The ecological humanities in action: An invitation', *Australian Humanities Review*, no. 31/32 (April 2004), retrieved 8 April 2016, <http://www.australian humanitiesreview.org>.

Rothwell, N 2007, 'Lightweights on the landscape', *The Australian*, 7 November, retrieved 8 April 2016, <http://www.theaustralian.com.au/arts/lightweights-on-the-landscape/story-e6frg8px-1111114734533>.

Saunders, P 2011, *Down and Out: Poverty and exclusion in Australia*, Policy, Bristol.

Seymour, J 2013, *Poverty in plenty: A human development report for the UK*, Taylor and Francis, Hoboken.

Smith, RG 2015, *Affect and American literature in the age of neoliberalism*, Cambridge University Press, Cambridge, UK.

Spinoza, B 2009, *Ethics: Ethica Ordine Geometrico Demonstrata*, The Floating Press, Waiheke Island.

Steffen, W, Grinevald, J, Crutzen, P & McNeill, J 2011a, 'The Anthropocene: Conceptual and historical perspectives', *Philosophical Transactions of the Royal Society*, vol. 369, no. 1938, pp. 842–867.

Steffen, W, Persson, Å, Deutsch, L, Zalasiewicz, J, Williams, M, Richardson, K, Crumley, C, Crutzen, P, Folke, C, Gordon, L, Molina, M, Ramanathan, V, Rockström, J, Scheffer, M, Schellnhuber, H & Svedin, U 2011b, 'The Anthropocene: From global change to planetary stewardship', *AMBIO – A Journal of the Human Environment*, vol. 40, no. 7, pp. 739–761.

Stiegler, B 2014, *The re-enchantment of the world: The value of spirit against industrial populism*, Bloomsbury Academic, New York.

Strauss, J 1995, *Judith Wright*, Oxford University Press, Melbourne, AUS.

Uebel, M 2010, 'Deleuze and American literature: Affect and virtuality in Faulkner, Wharton, Ellison, and McCarthy by A. Bourassa [book review]', *Choice: Current Reviews for Academic Libraries*, vol. 47, p. 1473.

Verran, H 1998, 'Re-imagining land ownership in Australia', *Postcolonial Studies: Culture, Politics, Economy*, vol. 1, no. 2, pp. 237–254.

Vint, S 2005, 'Becoming other: Animals, kinship, and Butler's "Clay's Ark."', *Science Fiction*, vol. 32, no. 2, pp. 281–300.

Wendling, AE 2012, *The ruling ideas: Bourgeois political concepts*, Lexington Books, Lanham, MD.

Winton, T 2013, *Eyrie*, Hamish Hamilton, an imprint of Penguin Books, Melbourne, VIC.

Wright, J 1999, *Half a Lifetime*, Text Publishing, Melbourne.

Wright, A 2011, 'Deep weather', *Meanjin*, vol. 70, no. 2, p. 70.

Wright, A 2013, *The swan book*, Giramondo Publishing, Sydney.

Žukauskait, A 2012, 'Potentiality as a life: Deleuze, Agamben, Beckett', *Deleuze Studies*, vol. 6, no. 4, pp. 628–637.

Section 2

Practice, change and organisations

Chapter 6

Shaping and being shaped

Extending the relationship between habitus and practice

Julie Rowlands and Trevor Gale

Introduction

The focus of this chapter is on practice and what *informs* it – the influence that Pierre Bourdieu names as the 'habitus' – but also on how practice *forms* the habitus. In making explicit the potential influence of practice on habitus, we seek to extend Bourdieu's account of how the habitus is shaped and reshaped. We illustrate these issues within the context of prescribed approaches to accountability within academic research.

The chapter proceeds along three lines. First, it sets out a detailed account of Bourdieu's conception/s of practice, the relationship between habitus and practice, and the role of pedagogic work in the formation and reformation of the habitus within fields. Comparatively little attention has been given to these matters within higher education research literature. Second, the chapter aims to extend understandings of the role of practice in re/forming the habitus, in particular in response to an agent's own practices. Third, and in response to the first two, we explore what these concepts and their extension mean for the field of higher education, specifically in relation to academic workloads and how these determine the proportion of time allocated to research. Our intention here is to elucidate how we conceive of practice rather than to be definitive of academic workloads and their application.

What is Bourdieu's theory of practice?

Bourdieu did not offer a simple definition of practice, acknowledging that 'It is not easy to speak of practice other than negatively – especially those aspects of practice that are seemingly most mechanical, most opposed to the logic of thought and discourse' (1990b, p. 80). In a gesture towards specificity, Bourdieu's foundation text *Distinction* offers the formula: '[(habitus) (capital)] + field = practice' (1984, p. 101). However, its precise meaning is unclear beyond the rather general idea that 'it is through the workings of habitus that practice ... is linked with capital and field' (Reay 2004b, p. 432).

For Bourdieu, the field or 'social universe' is a space in which agents 'are defined by their relative positions' according to the amount and worth of the capital they hold (1985, p. 724). Fields are both 'identifiable and bounded' but they are also 'saturated with *interests*' and so are never neutral spaces (Grenfell 2012a, p. 30, original emphasis). Capital comprises valued resources of various types (social, economic, cultural) with the worth of the capital being determined within specific fields (Bourdieu 1986; Swartz 1997). Within a given field agents are in competition with one another for the largest share of the most highly prized capital and also in an effort to increase the comparative value of the capital or capitals they possess (Bourdieu 1986). Thus, fields comprise contested hierarchies of agents and capitals (Grenfell 2010) while it is practice that enables the accumulation of different kinds of capital in different fields (Rawolle & Lingard 2013, p. 126).

The meaning and purpose of practice is particular to fields. Even within specific fields, practice is not a unitary phenomenon but has a number of 'dimensions' (Bourdieu 1977, p. 163). Thus, Warde names three different but related ways in which Bourdieu refers to practice (2004, pp. 5–6).[1]

First, practice is juxtaposed to theory (see for example Wacquant 1989). A substantial theme of Bourdieu's work is theorising the 'distance' between the 'truth of the academic world and of the social world in general' or between what Bourdieu thought of as scientific knowledge and the practical experience of everyday life (Bourdieu & Wacquant 1992, p. 70), which he referred to as the difference between the 'logic of science' and the 'logic of practice'. In brief, the logic that informs practice is 'fuzzy': it 'can only be grasped in action, in the temporal movement that distinguishes it' (Bourdieu 1990b, p. 92).

Second, Bourdieu uses the notion of practice to describe a 'more or less coherent entity formed around a particular activity' or a 'coordinated, recognisable and institutionally supported practice' (Warde 2004, p. 6). Here, Bourdieu is referring to a recognisable domain of activity and examples might include a formally organised sporting activity (1984, p. 218), a doctor's practice or a specifically named policy or practice review (Rawolle & Lingard 2008), such as a state facilitated review of higher education.

Third, practice refers to undertaking some activity or other, alternatively described as 'manifest behaviours' (Warde 2004, p. 6). However, in Bourdieu's reckoning, such activity is only practice when it is purposeful and meaningful. Thus, action does not inevitably constitute practice and so 'it is necessary to abandon all theories which explicitly or implicitly treat practice as a mechanical reaction' (Bourdieu 1977, p. 73). Examples of this conception of practice include the act of giving of a gift (Bourdieu 1990b) or the doing of scientific research (Bourdieu & Wacquant 1992).

Warde argues that in the second half of his career Bourdieu allowed his 'theory of practice to fall into desuetude', displaced by the more 'fully developed concept of field' (2004, p. 3). Conversely, for Rawolle, Bourdieu's theory of practice 'foregrounds' and underpins his entire 'sociological approach'

(2010b, p. 26) where, in later work, practice serves not only as the 'underlying theme and problematic' but also as the 'object of research' (2010a, p. 125). That is, Bourdieu's concepts of habitus, field and capital were developed as a way of understanding and explaining practice, rather than to make up for some inadequacy or incommensurability within the theory of practice as Bourdieu had conceived it (Rawolle & Lingard 2013). Rawolle thus argues that Bourdieu's theory of practice is, at one and the same time, his theory of the social world.

Bourdieu understood practice as the outcome of internalised knowledge that is borne from history but which manifests as an agent's skills, proficiencies and competencies, enabling them to understand what is transpiring and what might transpire so as to achieve a particular goal or purpose (Webb 2012). He therefore likened practice to playing a game (Bourdieu 1990b). Games are temporal, played by agents with a 'sense of the history of the game' who at the same time have mastered 'in a practical way the future of the game', enabling them to anticipate the future 'flow of the game' (Bourdieu 1998, p. 81). By way of illustration:

> A player who is involved and caught up in the game adjusts not to what he [sic] sees but to what he fore-sees, sees in advance in the directly perceived present; he passes the ball not to the spot where his team-mate is but to the spot he will reach . . . a moment later, anticipating the anticipations of the other [the opponent] and . . . seeking to confound them. . . . And he does so 'on the spot', 'in the twinkling of an eye', 'in the heat of the moment' . . . He is launched into the impending future, present in the imminent moment.
>
> (Bourdieu 1990b, pp. 81–82)

A characteristic of most games, sporting or otherwise, is that they are competitive and this raises the question of whether practice is always associated with competition within a field. Warde (2004) argues that the use of game as a metaphor for practice is contentious because it works only in very specific circumstances and he provides examples of apparently non-competitive activities, such as solo swimming (for the purposes of relaxation) and home decorating, which exhibit fewer features of 'relationality and hierarchy' (2004, p. 20). But competition is not completely absent from these either. For example, in Warde's illustration of home decoration, while the practice might not be part of an organised sport or part of a formally organised competition (although sometimes that can be the case), it is nonetheless part of a competitive 'game' aimed at 'distinction and position taking' within a field (Warde 2004, p. 21). Bourdieu argues that not only do some games require participants 'to be "disinterested" in order to succeed', they may well be precluded from consciously understanding this paradox by both the rules of the game and the characteristics of the field in which it is played (1998, p. 83). Games are therefore social and field specific, played within a particular social space (Bourdieu 1990b).

Competition and game are so significant in Bourdieu's account of fields of practice that at times he uses the terms *field* and *game* interchangeably, although this does not necessarily mean that he always thought of games and fields as one and the same (Warde 2004, p. 9). It is more likely that a particular game, or a dominant game, may define a specific field (for example, its boundaries, its primary characteristics) rather than all games being fields and vice versa. It is the case that many practices are specific to certain fields and that fields can be defined and characterised by their specific logics of practice (Grenfell 2012a). For example, teaching practices take place in the field of education while research and scholarship take place within the subfield of higher education (albeit not exclusively). Thus, in considering what defines a field it is useful to identify the predominant practice evident therein.

It is the habitus that enables an agent to embody the game in what Bourdieu describes as being 'in the present in relation to a coming moment' (Bourdieu 1998, p. 82) or as a 'presence in the future' (Bourdieu 1990b, p. 82). So close is the relationship between habitus and practice that Rawolle and Lingard describe it as a 'couplet' (2013, p. 123). It is not only the case that habitus is reflected in practice (Bourdieu 1977) but that the concepts of habitus and practice share some of the same characteristics. For example, Bourdieu describes practice as organised strategy 'without being the product of genuine strategic intention' (1977, p. 73) or that which 'understands only in order to act' (1990b, p. 91). Bourdieu contrasts practice with 'reflexive attention to itself' and thus differentiates it from scientific or scholarly analysis which attempts to understand and explain, for its own sake (1990b, p. 91). In this way, Bourdieu's notion of practice goes beyond a 'conscious/unconscious' dichotomy (Grenfell 2012a, p. 29). The intuitive nature of practice is quite similar to that quality of the habitus that 'function[s] below the level of consciousness' (Bourdieu 1984, p. 466). It is these and other similarities that have led Crossley to describe Bourdieu's theory of habitus as 'a partial theory of practice' (2001, p. 95).

Habitus and its relationship to practice

Bourdieu's conception of habitus has been subject to substantial criticism, principally with regard to determinism (Jenkins 1982), that the habitus does not provide sufficient capacity for agency or self-transformation (Lukes 2005). Yet Bourdieu argued vigorously that charges of determinism reflect an inadequate understanding of his overall theoretical framework (Bourdieu 1977; Bourdieu & Wacquant 1992). Others have argued similarly that changed practices arise from the interaction between habitus and field (Swartz 1997).

Throughout his work Bourdieu sought to use the conceptual and methodological tool of habitus to resolve or transcend the dualisms of agency/structure and objectivity/subjectivity (Bourdieu 1990b), such that '[i]t is through the workings of habitus that practice (agency) is linked with capital and field (structure)' (Reay 2004b, p. 432). Bourdieu described habitus as 'an acquired system of generative schemes objectively adjusted to the particular conditions in which it is constituted' (1977, p. 95). Thus, habitus is produced by the social world and serves as a 'durable and transposable but not immutable' means through which agents perceive, understand and interact in that world (Grenfell 2012b, p. 52).Yet Bourdieu's concept of habitus is also complex, multifaceted and multilayered. Arising from his ethnographic work in a Chicago boxing gym, Wacquant discusses a number of specific properties of the habitus as Bourdieu conceived it.

First, habitus comprises dispositions that are developed rather than being innate (Wacquant 2011). For example, Bourdieu describes habitus as 'an acquired system of . . . schemes' (1977, p. 95), learnt not in a sentient, purposeful way, but more through a process of meaning making (Bourdieu 1984, p. 170). Thus Wacquant describes dispositions, which are both instilled and inscribed, as specific 'abilities, categories, and desires' (2011, p. 85).

A second and related principle is that the habitus operates below the '*level of consciousness and discourse*' (Wacquant 2011, p. 86, original emphasis). Agents are generally not aware of, do not actively engage with and do not explicate the habitus, which nonetheless shapes their thoughts, aspirations, perceptions, judgements, behaviours and interactions (Bourdieu & Passeron 1977).

Third, the dispositions that comprise an agent's habitus vary according to '*location and trajectory*' (Wacquant 2011, p. 86, original emphasis). For example, Bourdieu describes the habitus as being 'objectively adjusted to the particular conditions in which it is constituted' (1977, p. 95). Habitus arises out of, or is a product of, the physical and social conditions within which the agent operates. It does this not only by shaping how the field is comprised and how it should operate but also because the habitus expresses 'the social position in which it was constructed' (Bourdieu 1990a, p. 131), typically referring to an expression of social class.

A fourth and related characteristic of habitus is that it is inculcated through a process known as pedagogic work (Wacquant 2011, p. 86), which produces the primary habitus, characteristic of the earliest class or group to which the agent belongs as a child, and also any subsequent formation and reformation of the habitus (Bourdieu & Passeron 1977, p. 42). Habitus is therefore a product of history and leads to relatively consistent and predicable behaviour, but it is not unchanging or unresponsive to the present (Bourdieu 1990a, p. 77). For example, Crossley asserts that '[i]f users are acting, thinking and identifying themselves differently from how they used to, in a regularized way, then their habitus must have been transformed' (1999, p. 649).This results from what Reay describes as a 'complex interplay between past and present' (2004b, p. 434). The notion of pedagogic work and other means of habitus transformation are discussed further below.

In a similar vein to Wacquant, it is possible to identify additional ways in which Bourdieu characterises the habitus. For example, habitus is generated or produced but it is also generative (Bourdieu 1977, p. 95).This is what Swartz

Swartz

describes as the 'two faces of habitus' (2002, p. 635) and it is what Bourdieu means when he characterises habitus as 'structured structures predisposed to function as structuring structures' (Bourdieu 1977, p. 72). Second, habitus generates or produces practice together with an understanding of and desire for particular practices organised in particular ways and within particular limits. Reay argues that this means habitus not only 'allows for individual agency, it also predisposes individuals towards certain ways of behaving' (2004b, p. 433). That is, while Bourdieu's concept of habitus suggests that agents are less likely to engage in culturally unfamiliar practices, habitus is also not a synonym for rules and prescriptive behaviours. Third, the relationship between habitus and the social world is both metaphysical and physical in that through habitus agents carry the structures of their social world within them, in internalised, embodied form (Bourdieu 1990a). This is what Bourdieu means when he notes that '[t]he body is in the social world but the social world is also in the body' (1990a, p. 190). The habitus becomes the means through which the social world is expressed such as through practices related to accent, manners, styles of dress and modes of deportment (Reay 2004b).

A further characteristic of habitus is that it can also be collective (Bourdieu & Wacquant 1992), operating as 'a system of shared social dispositions and cognitive structures which generates perceptions, appreciations and actions' (Bourdieu 1988, p. 279). The issue here is not so much that habitus is either individual or collective. Instead, dispositions that constitute the habitus and are held individually can also be shared across a group or community by virtue of common or homologous conditions or circumstances, or shared history (Bourdieu 1990b). This, in turn, can lead to common or shared practices and beliefs without those practices and beliefs being subject to any formal organisation or co-ordination. Thus, Bourdieu described a 'linguistic habitus' (1991, p. 21) and a professorial habitus (1988). It is also habitus that enables the transfer of certain practices from one field to another (Bourdieu 1984, p. 173).

Pedagogic work and formation/reformation of the habitus

As noted above, Bourdieu describes the process by which habitus is produced as involving pedagogic work (PW) within which the social conditions of the field are internalised as habitus and misrecognised as natural and desirable. Pedagogic work legitimates the culture of the dominant group while representing the culture of those on the periphery as illegitimate (Bourdieu & Passeron 1977).

Pedagogic work comprises a series of prolonged actions that may or may not be consciously purposeful (Gale & Mills 2013). Its foundation is what Bourdieu describes as pedagogic action (PA): a practice that operates by exerting symbolic violence, defined as 'power which manages to impose meanings and to impose them as legitimate by concealing the power relations which are the basis of its force' (Bourdieu & Passeron 1977, p. 4). The effect of this concealment is that agents are complicit in the exercise of the domination to which they are subject (Bourdieu & Wacquant 1992). Thus pedagogic work helps to maintain the 'broader social system' by authenticating and defining cultural goods and by creating and legitimising consumers of those goods (Bredo & Feinberg 2006, p. 319). Pedagogic actions involve more than passive transmission because they 'stamp' the cultural message, and the 'consequences of receiving it or not, as valid and important' (Robbins 2004, p. 318).

Bourdieu refers to pedagogic action as the practice of education but he means education in its broadest sense rather than only that exercised by formally designated educational institutions such as schools and universities (Bourdieu & Passeron 1977). Thus, the first site where pedagogic work takes effect – *primary pedagogic work* – is within the family or 'domestic group' (Bourdieu & Passeron 1977, p. 6). The primary habitus that it produces is long-lasting insofar as it is 'capable of perpetuating itself after the PA has ceased' (Bourdieu & Passeron 1977, p. 31). It is also transposable, in that it is 'capable of generating practices conforming with the principles of the inculcated arbitrary in a greater number of different fields' (Bourdieu & Passeron 1977, p. 33). Other sites in which primary pedagogic work takes place include one's extended family and wider community. Primary pedagogic work forms the basis for any subsequent habitus formation or reformation. Indeed, Bourdieu states that '[t]he success of all school education, and more generally of all secondary PW, depends fundamentally on the education previously accomplished in the earliest years of life' (Bourdieu & Passeron 1977, p. 43). Thus, secondary pedagogic work takes place in the context of formal educational institutions and schooling (Gale & Mills 2013) and beyond, such as in the workplace.

Case exemplar

In part, the value of Bourdieu's account of practice and habitus lies in the strength of the explanation it provides of empirical contexts. However, our intent in presenting the case exemplar that follows is not so much to test the explanatory power of Bourdieu's concepts but to extend them. The exemplar is focused on an academic workload model and draws on data from one of Australia's newer teaching and research universities. Academic workload models are not new although the application of standardised formulae for allocating workload to teaching, research and administration or service activities for individual academics is becoming more widespread across the UK, Australia and Europe, in particular. The exemplar seeks to highlight a prescribed approach to an aspect of academic work, with a specific focus on research analysed through the lens of Bourdieu's theory of practice. We consider whether, in response to the demands of the situation, an agent's own practices play a role in shaping or reshaping the academic habitus within the field. That is, is it possible for an agent to engage in pedagogic work on their own habitus, even though it is largely unconscious?

Exemplar: Research output as a contributor to academic workload calculations

In many universities the proportion of an academic's workload allocated to research is determined on the basis of their research output in preceding years – usually over a rolling three-year period. In making such determinations, it is common for numerical targets to be set as a measure of research output, taking into account such indicators as the number of publications of varying types, the number of PhD students supervised to completion, and the monetary value of external research grants. While these models vary in detail, they are common across similar institutions and national boundaries (Barrett & Barrett 2008). They represent examples of a numerical approach to quality assurance and form part of what Lingard (2011) describes as a 'policy as numbers' approach to the global governance of educational research.

We recognise that in addition to numerical indicators of research output, measurement and assessment of research impact or utility are also a significant focus, both in other models and in other parts of the higher education field (Colley 2013). However, in our analysis, we specifically focus on the targets for publications in our case-institution, in which one point is allocated for each sole-authored journal article published in a journal recognised by the national research assessment scheme (ERA: Excellence in Research, Australia), five points are allocated for a research-based book or monograph published with a recognised academic publisher, and so on. To be designated as research active in our case institution and thereby achieve the standard 40% teaching, 40% research and 20% service workload allocation, academics must meet or exceed designated thresholds for research points according to their level of appointment. For academics at lecturer level, the threshold standard for research output points is somewhat lower than for senior lecturers, which is lower than the points required of associate professors/readers, and so on. However, for all academics at this university, publication point thresholds are increasing year-on-year. Specifically, within academic units covering the humanities, arts, social sciences and education, thresholds in our case-institution increased by 50% between 2014 and 2015.

Although the stated aim of the research program at this university is to achieve research outputs of the highest quality, the model appears to focus primarily on the *number* of books or journal articles published. In short, there is significant contradiction between the specified aims of the research program to produce quality outputs and the publication practices rewarded by the model. However, as is also the case elsewhere, the university's academic promotion process appears to reward publication quality over quantity. Thus, a smaller number of journal articles published in top-ranked international journals are often more highly regarded for promotion purposes than a larger number of journal articles published in local, low-status journals. This recognition within the academic promotions process of the quality of research output reflects its role in building a high-status, research-based career over the longer term (Blackmore 2010).

For early career researchers in particular, the tension between these two conflicting measures of success is palpable and often results in some form of trade-off. For example, the effect of not meeting research active publication output thresholds is potentially more immediately concerning for many than the prospect of promotion some years down the track. Under the model, being designated as 'non-research active' results in a research time allowance of 20% or less and a corresponding substantial increase in teaching allocation. In turn, this makes devoting time to research more difficult and so the prospect of being non-research active is more likely to continue.

Our analysis of these matters focuses on the effect of the research output targets on the practices of academics attempting to comply with the requirements of the model as they strive to achieve or retain research active status. For very early career researchers, who are unlikely to have been an academic long enough to have supervised a higher-degree research student to completion or to have secured a large external research grant, the most feasible way of obtaining research points is through publication. Thus, the practices under consideration are not only those involved with the calculation of research points but also the practices of conducting, writing and publishing research itself.

Can practice have a role in shaping and reshaping the habitus?

Above we noted that within Bourdieu's theory of practice, it is habitus that generates or produces practice within fields. For this reason, it is commonly understood that an agent's habitus can be read from their practice, at least partially. In fact, Bourdieu says as much (Bourdieu & Wacquant 1992). Although an agent's habitus sits beneath their level of consciousness, the practices in which they engage can provide a window through which the habitus can be seen and understood. However, Bourdieu also indicates that this relationship between habitus and practice is not one-way. In *Outline of a Theory of Practice* he notes that the habitus is 'determined by the past conditions which have produced the principle of their production, that is, by the actual outcome of identical or interchangeable past practices' (Bourdieu 1977, pp. 72–73). This suggests that an agent's habitus not only influences their practice but that the things agents have done in the past also contribute to shaping their habitus.

On the face of it, this seems a relatively obvious and straightforward idea. It was noted earlier that a key link between practice and habitus is the notion of pedagogic work. It is through the pedagogic work of others that the habitus is formed, shaped and reshaped. However, it is also possible to interpret Bourdieu's theory of practice as suggesting that agents' practices, the things they have done previously, may have contributed to shaping and reshaping their own habitus; that they are, in fact, engaged in pedagogic work on themselves. This is implied in Swartz's examples of pedagogic work as including 'imitation, repetition, role-play, and game participation' (2002, p. 635). These are all activities in which individuals engage themselves – within whichever field they may be located at the time. The link between practice, habitus and the past is important here because habitus is somewhat more inclined to reflect the past than the present (Bourdieu 1990a, p. 77). If an agent's own practices contribute to shaping the habitus, then it is very likely to be the practices of the past involved in that shaping. By extension, the practices of the present shape the habitus of the future.

Many of the practices undertaken by academics seeking to comply with research output measures, as part of workload allocation models, are an agent's own. While individual academics do not generally contribute to determining the publication targets they must meet in order to be considered research active – although they may have some opportunity to comment during a consultation process – they do have agency to determine how they wish to respond to the model and to tailor their practices accordingly. For some, the choices are relatively easy. They can mobilise their intellectual capital to produce sufficiently large numbers of high-quality publications to both meet institutional targets and establish or retain their position within their global disciplinary field. For others, the new academic 'game' is more difficult. Some may choose to submit large numbers of articles to low-status journals with high acceptance rates simply to meet institutional targets, with little regard for future promotion prospects. Others might seek inclusion as an author on publications in which they have had little or no input. In both cases, the research practices of academics change in response to the research output calculation model.

The Bourdieuian concepts of a collective academic habitus (Reay 2004a) and of intellectual capital within disciplinary fields (Bourdieu 1988) are well known. Intellectual capital represents scholarly reputation and is primarily accumulated through research output, exemplified by the central and dominant place of research within global university ranking scales (Rowlands 2013). It follows, then, that practices that constitute secondary pedagogic work and thus contribute to any reshaping of the academic habitus will be research practices. Research practice has a particular logic that is specific to traditionally autonomous disciplinary fields (Henkel 2007). For example, research within the physical sciences has a different logic of practice – a different way of conceiving, theorising and undertaking research – to that of the social sciences. In turn, it is these different logics of practice that contribute to defining academic disciplines as separate, global, fields. Moreover, the global communities of scholars that comprise these fields define these fields in a way that is traditionally independent of the university at which they are each employed (Macfarlane 2012).

At the same time, universities sit within a global field of higher education (Marginson 2010). In contrast to the disciplinary fields within which intellectual capital dominates, academic capital currently dominates the higher education field and is accumulated through position taking within the organisational hierarchy (Kloot 2009). The prevailing logic of practice within this field is corporate managerialism, defined as the adoption within public sector entities of ideologies and practices drawn from the private or business sector

(Deem & Brehony 2005). Key foci of this practice are efficiency, accountability, value-for-money and executive-dominated corporate and entrepreneurial-style governance practices. The research output model described within our case exemplar is a clear instance of managerial practice, influenced by external research assessment exercises such as the Research Evaluation Framework (REF) in the UK and Excellence for Research in Australia (ERA). Both the academic and managerial habitus are examples of what Bourdieu describes as 'specific habitus': dispositions required within a particular field or fields (2000, p. 99).

Academics working within universities straddle both their disciplinary field and the management-dominated institutional field of higher education. As a result, they commonly undertake both disciplinary-based research practice and managerial practices aimed at complying with internal and external reporting and accountability requirements. And while much research is undertaken in disciplinary fields, research on higher education itself – in areas such as teaching, learning and higher education systems – is increasingly common (Altbach 2014). That is, the two fields (of higher education and specific disciplines) do not operate as unrelated, isolated social spaces. Moreover, the habitus is transposable, 'capable of generating practices conforming with the principles of the inculcated arbitrary in a greater number of different fields' (Bourdieu & Passeron 1977, p. 33). Indeed, the phenomena of cross-field effects, where practices from one field impact on practices or are taken up in another, is now well established (Rawolle 2010a). Although, Maton (2005) argues that the autonomy of higher education as a field is far more resistant to influences from outside the field (i.e., challenges to 'relational' autonomy) than it is to the influences of outside actors installed into positions of power within the field (i.e., challenges to 'positional' autonomy).

A key issue, then, is the extent to which practices from one of these fields might potentially impact on the shaping or reshaping of the specific habitus associated with the other. While this is a subject for future research, two existing studies do provide some insight. First, Cheng (2011) examined the impact of external quality audits conducted within the UK on the teaching practices of academics. She found that because the audits were initiated by an external body, academics felt that the audit had symbolic rather than actual control over their work – there was little, if any, impact on their day-to-day practice (Cheng 2010). Staff were able to make strategic decisions to comply with the requirements of the audit process on the surface while continuing to teach in their preferred manner within the classroom and elsewhere (Cheng 2011). This is consistent with Bourdieu's argument that in response to the specific demands of the field at a given moment in time, agents can make 'a strategic calculation tending to carry on quasi-consciously the operation [while] the habitus carries on in quite a different way' (Bourdieu 1977, p. 76; 1990b, p. 108).

Unlike Cheng's study, the research output metrics within our case exemplar have a direct and unequivocal impact on academics' day-to-day work because the outcome determines the proportion of their workload allocated to teaching, research and service, respectively. This is not symbolic but actual and direct control. In a study of four New Zealand academics, Waitere and others found that research output calculation models – which classified staff in one of four categories from highly research active to not research active for the purposes of workload allocation – had a significant impact not only on research practices but also on how these academics conceived of themselves as researchers 'playing an elaborate game' (Waitere et al. 2011, p. 206). The metaphor of a game is used here to describe not only performative practices required to comply with the requirement to count research output but also the way research is now being conceived and conducted:

> ... short-term outcomes are now embraced with the oppressive knowledge of the need to publish in the window that will allow your article to see the light of day before the next PBRF round.
>
> (Waitere et al. 2011, p. 206)

While Bourdieu is careful to point out that habitus is not the only driver of practice (1977), he also asserts that primary pedagogic work and, therefore the primary habitus, are not necessarily fixed or absolute. Secondary pedagogic work can bring about what Bourdieu and Passeron describe as a 'radical conversion' by 'killing off' the old habitus and 'engendering the new habitus ex nihilo' (1977, p. 44). The 'deculturating and reculturating' techniques required to achieve this are not everyday occurrences but are extreme, found in what Bourdieu and Passeron describe as 'total' institutions [such as] barracks, convents, prisons, asylums, boarding schools' (1977, p. 44). In general terms, the efficiency of secondary pedagogic work is determined by the level of similarity between the habitus it is seeking to produce and the pre-existing primary habitus (Bourdieu & Passeron 1977). The greater the difference, the more pedagogic work is required to bring the secondary habitus into line with the field. The process that Bourdieu describes as 'hysteresis' arises from a substantial discrepancy between the habitus of an agent and the field in which they are situated (Bourdieu 1977, 1984, 2000). Responding to this discrepency in such a way as to 'to recognize, grasp and occupy . . . new field positions', can result in a significant transformation of the habitus, especially for agents who hold sufficient capital to recognise and take advantage of this as an opportunity (Grenfell 2012b, p. 135). A more minor discrepancy may result in what is described by Bourdieu as 'adaptation' (Bourdieu 2000, p. 161), where the habitus *adjusts* to the demands of the field.

Thus, where the gap between the habitus of an agent and the demands or requirements of the field is substantial, secondary pedagogic work may transform the habitus to produce a closer alignment. However, this is not the only possible response. Agents may also withdraw from the field in an act of self-selection (Swartz 2002) or experience 'inertia in the habitus' resulting in an inability to take advantage of the prospects a transformation of the field may provide (Grenfell 2012b, p. 135). Less common, but evident in examples of social dissent, is when agents choose to remain present so as to protest against (and therefore seek to change) those conditions of the field that have produced the discrepancy. In this they oppose what Bourdieu described as the doxa of the field, 'the point of view of the dominant' (1998, p. 57). Bourdieu's concept of 'illusio' is also useful here because it describes the value of the game being played in the field (Bourdieu 1993), regardless of whether all agents consider that game to be something they want to play (Colley & Guery 2015; Rowlands & Rawolle 2013). Bourdieu gives the example of agents 'wanting to undertake a revolution in a field' as evidence of illusio, that the game being played in that field is of sufficient importance to make a revolution both imaginable and desirable (1998, p. 78).

Conclusion

In this chapter we have sought to convey a sense of Bourdieu's account of practice and of its sophistication. Bourdieu argues that one's practices are informed by one's habitus and are produced in interaction with the field in which one is located; practice is the product of habitus-field interactions. Further, one's habitus is the result of pedagogic work, which conforms the habitus (and, therefore, future practice) to the logic of the field. The habitus is thus the embodiment of the cultural capital of the field. In providing this account, we have also sought to extend it – albeit in keeping with Bourdieu's own inclinations, arguing that one's own practices also constitute pedagogic work on one's own habitus. That is, past practice has played a role in shaping the habitus of the present and current practice can play a role in shaping the habitus of the future. In bringing Bourdieu's theory of practice to bear on academic workload models, we suggest that practices required of academics to comply with publication output targets have a substantial impact not only on academic practice but potentially contribute to a reshaping of the academic habitus and, in turn, to a redefinition of what it means to be a researcher and to actually do research.

Further, the analysis allows us to speculate that academics may respond to research output targets within academic workload models in different ways, depending in part on the respective amounts of academic, intellectual and other capitals they possess. For academics with high levels of intellectual capital and research outputs that easily meet the designated targets, no change to academic practice might be required at all. But at least two other responses are also possible. A second group, with relatively lower levels of intellectual capital, might be disposed to opt out of the game altogether, giving up before even attempting to meet their publication output target, given the extent of the gap between the schemes of the habitus and the demands of the field. For many, this would mean a significantly increased teaching allocation and changed academic practice, by virtue of less time allocated to research. For a third group, disposed to engage in the game and with somewhat higher levels of academic capital, a performative approach might result in changed academic practice. In this instance, there could be a tendency to 'pump out the pubs' at whatever standard is required to 'get over the line' and worry about building a high-status research career 'down the track', if at all. For groups two and three, if this changed academic practice continued over the longer term, it could take the form of secondary pedagogic work and potentially impact on a reshaping of the habitus, including the collective academic habitus, reducing the size of the gap between these and the higher education field. In turn, there might be corresponding increases in the size of the gap between these modified academic habitus and the demands of the disciplinary field.

While these are speculative accounts of the effects of academic workload models that include metrics-based research outputs and clearly require further research to validate, they are nonetheless a logical outworking of Bourdieu's theory of practice. In the same way, we suggest that one's own practice is at work on the habitus to inform future practice. For this reason, we are concerned by the potential longer-term impact of the practices required of academics to comply with these models on both the nature of research practice itself and on their identities as academics and researchers. However, it is also possible to envisage a fourth response to the demands of numerically based research output targets described in this chapter that have become doxa within the field in Australia and elsewhere. This would see academics attempting to change not only the dominant game but also the field in which it is being played; that is, where their illusio, or recognition of the stakes of the game that comprises academic workload models based on numerical targets for research output, results in participation in that game so as to achieve a transformation of it (see Bourdieu & Wacquant 1992, p. 99). The extent to which this fourth response is possible turns on whether academic publication practices are scientific, or ordinary in nature. As noted earlier, agents are largely unaware of the logic governing everyday or ordinary practice (Bourdieu 1990b), in contrast to the reflexivity associated with scientific research practices (James 2014).

In Bourdieu's terms, what is needed here are strategies to discredit the value of the ordinary practice of counting research outputs on a numerical basis as a proxy for quality and to increase the value of new knowledge for its own sake as an outcome of scientific practice. Thus, while 'impact' is a central interest of education research which is traditionally close to education practice, measurement of this research impact is also not necessarily the answer (Colley 2013). Similarly, we cannot achieve transformation of the rules of the game if we have exited the field or disengaged from it to the extent that our research becomes merely a performative exercise. If the goals of critical sociology include not only critiquing what is current but also making way for what is yet to come, then it is incumbent upon each of us to shape the collective academic habitus of the future through reflexive and disruptive individual research practices in the present.

Note

1 Rawolle (2010a) suggests that Bourdieu also uses the notion of practice in a fourth way, referring to products or outcomes of practice, such as a policy text or a piece of scholarly work (Bourdieu 1988), although we think this could also be conceived as an aspect of Warde's second practice category.

References

Altbach, PG 2014, 'The emergence of a field: Research and training in higher education', *Studies in Higher Education*, vol. 39, no. 8, pp. 1306–1320.

Barrett, L & Barrett, P 2008, *Management of academic workloads: Full report on findings*, Leadership Foundation for Higher Education, London.

Blackmore, J 2010, 'Research assessment: A calculative technology governing quality, accountability and equity', in J Blackmore, M Brennan & L Zipin (eds), *Re-positioning university governance and academic work*, Sense, Rotterdam, pp. 67–84.

Bourdieu, P 1977, *Outline of a theory of practice*, Cambridge University Press, Cambridge.

Bourdieu, P 1984, *Distinction: A social critique of the judgement of taste*, Routledge & Keegan Paul, London.

Bourdieu, P 1985, 'The social space and the genesis of groups', *Theory and Society*, vol. 14, no. 6, pp. 723–744.

Bourdieu, P 1986, 'The forms of capital', in JG Richardson (ed.), *Handbook of theory and research for the sociology of education*, Greenwood, New York, pp. 241–258.

Bourdieu, P 1988, *Homo academicus*, Polity, Cambridge.

Bourdieu, P 1990a, *In other words: Essays towards a reflexive sociology*, Polity, Cambridge.

Bourdieu, P 1990b, *The logic of practice*, Polity, Cambridge.

Bourdieu, P 1991, *Language and symbolic power*, Policy, Cambridge.

Bourdieu, P 1993, *The field of cultural production*, Polity, Cambridge.

Bourdieu, P 1998, *Practical reason: On the theory of action*, Polity, Cambridge.

Bourdieu, P 2000, *Pascalian meditations*, Polity, Cambridge.

Bourdieu, P & Passeron, J-C 1977, *Reproduction: In education, society and culture*, Sage, London.

Bourdieu, P & Wacquant, LJD 1992, *An invitation to reflexive sociology*, Polity Press in association with Blackwell Publishers, Cambridge.

Bredo, E & Feinberg, W 2006, 'Meaning, power and pedagogy: Pierre Bourdieu and Jean-Claude Passeron, *'Reproduction: In education, society and Culture"*, vol. 11, no. 4, pp. 315–332.

Cheng, M 2010, 'Audit cultures and quality assurance mechanisms in England: A study of their perceived impact on the work of academics', *Teaching in Higher Education*, vol. 15, no. 3, pp. 259–271.

Cheng, M 2011, 'The perceived impact of quality audit on the work of academics', *Higher Education Research & Development*, vol. 30, no. 2, pp. 179–191.

Colley, H 2013, 'What (a) to do about 'impact': A Bourdieusian critique', *British Educational Research Journal*, vol. 40, no. 4, pp. 660–681, doi: 10.1002/berj.3112.

Colley, H & Guery, F 2015, 'Understanding new hybrid professions: Bourdieu, illusio and the case of public servant interpreters', *Cambridge Journal of Education*, vol. 45, no. 1, pp. 113–131.

Crossley, N 1999, 'Fish, field, habitus and madness: The first wave mental health users movement in Great Britain', *British Journal of Sociology*, vol. 50, no. 4, pp. 647–670.

Crossley, N 2001, *The social body: Habit, identity and desire*, Sage, London.

Deem, R & Brehony, K 2005, 'Management as ideology: The case of 'new managerialism' in higher education', *Oxford Review of Education*, vol. 31, no. 2, pp. 217–235.

Gale, T & Mills, C 2013, 'Creating spaces in higher education for marginalised Australians: principles for socially inclusive pedagogies', *ELiSS*, vol. 5, no. 2, pp. 7–19.

Grenfell, M 2010, 'Being critical: The practical logic of Bourdieu's metanoia', *Critical Studies in Education*, vol. 51, no. 1, pp. 85–99.

Grenfell, M 2012a, *Bourdieu, language and linguistics*, Bloomsbury, London.

Grenfell, M 2012b, *Pierre Bourdieu: Key concepts*, Acumen, Stocksfield, UK.

Henkel, M 2007, 'Can academic autonomy survive in the knowledge society? A perspective from Britain', *Higher Education Research & Development*, vol. 26, no. 1, pp. 87–99.

James, D 2014, 'Investigating the curriculum through assessment practice in higher education: The value of a learning cultures' approach', *Higher Education*, vol. 67, no. 2, pp. 155–169.

Jenkins, R 1982, 'Pierre Bourdieu and the reproduction of determinism', *Sociology*, vol. 16, no. 2, pp. 270–281.

Kloot, B 2009, 'Exploring the value of Bourdieu's framework in the context of institutional change', *Studies in Higher Education*, vol. 34, no. 4 pp. 469–481.

Lingard, B 2011, 'Policy as numbers: Ac/counting for educational research', *Australian Educational Researcher*, vol. 38, no. 4, pp. 355–382.

Lukes, S 2005, *Political Power: A radical view* (2nd ed.), Palgrave Macmillan, Hampshire & New York.

Macfarlane, B 2012, *Intellectual leadership in higher education: Renewing the role of the university professor*, Routledge, London.

Marginson, S 2010, 'Higher education as a global field', in S Marginson, P Murphy & M Peters (eds), *Global creation: Space, mobility and synchrony in the age of the knowledge economy*, Peter Lang, New York, pp. 201–228.

Maton, K 2005, 'A question of autonomy: Bourdieu's field approach and higher education policy', *Journal of Education Policy*, vol. 20, no. 6, pp. 687–704.

Rawolle, S 2010a, 'Practice chains of production and consumption: Mediatized practices across social fields', *Discourse: Studies in the Cultural Politics of Education*, vol. 31, no. 1, pp. 121–135.

Rawolle, S 2010b, 'Understanding the mediatisation of educational policy as practice', *Critical Studies in Education*, vol. 51, no. 1, pp. 21–39.

Rawolle, S & Lingard, B 2008, 'The sociology of Pierre Bourdieu and researching education policy', *Journal of Education Policy*, vol. 23, no. 6, pp. 729–741.

Rawolle, S & Lingard, B 2013, 'Bourdieu and educational research: Thinking tools, relational thinking, beyond epistemological innocence', in M Murphy (ed.), *Social theory and education research: Understanding Foucault, Habermas, Bourdieu and Derrida*, Routledge, New York, pp. 117–137.

Reay, D 2004a, 'Cultural capitalists and academic habitus: Classed and gendered labour in UK higher education', *Women's Studies International Forum*, vol. 27, no. 1, pp. 31–39.

Reay, D 2004b, '"It's all becoming a habitus": Beyond the habitual use of habitus in educational research' *British Journal of Sociology of Education*, vol. 25, no. 4, pp. 431–444.

Robbins, D 2004, 'The transcultural transferability of Bourdieu's sociology of education', *British Journal of Sociology of Education*, vol. 25, no. 4, pp. 416–428.

Rowlands, J 2013, 'Academic boards: Less intellectual and more academic capital in higher education governance?', *Studies in Higher Education*, vol. 38, no. 9, pp. 1274–1289.

Rowlands, J & Rawolle, S 2013, 'Neoliberalism is not a theory of everything: A Bourdieuian analysis of illusio in educational research', *Critical Studies in Education*, vol. 54, no. 3, pp. 260–272.

Swartz, D 1997, *Culture and power: The sociology of Pierre Bourdieu*, The University of Chicago Press, Chicago, IL.

Swartz, D 2002, 'The sociology of habit: The perspective of Pierre Bourdieu', *The Occupational Therapy Journal of Research*, vol. 22, Winter 2002 Supplement, pp. 615–695.

Wacquant, L 1989, 'Towards a reflexive sociology: A workshop with Pierre Bourdieu', *Sociological Theory*, vol. 7, no. 1, pp. 26–63.

Wacquant, L 2011, 'Habitus as topic and tool: Reflections on becoming a prize fighter', *Qualitative Research in Psychology*, vol. 8, no. 1, pp. 81–92.

Waitere, HJ, Wright, J, Tremaine, M, Brown, S & Pause, CJ 2011, 'Choosing whether to resist or reinforce the new managerialism: The impact of performance-based research funding on academic identity', *Higher Education Research & Development*, vol. 30, no. 2, pp. 205–217.

Warde, A 2004, *Practice and field: Revising Bourdieusian concepts, CRIC Discussion Paper No. 65*, University of Manchester, Manchester, retrieved 10 March 2010, <http://www.cric.ac.uk/cric/Pdfs/DP65.pdf>.

Webb, J 2012, 'The logic of practice? Art, the academy, and fish out of water', *Text*, vol. 14, special issue website series: Beyond practice–led research, pp. 1–15.

Chapter 7

Practicing policy networks

Using organisational field theory to examine philanthropic involvement in education policy

Joseph J. Ferrare and Michael W. Apple

Introduction

In recent years there has been a growing body of work that has sought to ana-
lyze the complex webs of individuals and organisations that are collectively
working to transform the processes by which educational policies are conceived, challenged and implemented. Researchers have been drawn to these
questions as it has become clear that these webs – or policy networks – both
mediate and circumnavigate the institutional contexts of policy-making processes (Rhodes 2006). At the most general level, policy networks are self-
organising sets of interconnected actors (organisations, individuals, agencies,
etc.) who exchange a variety of resources to achieve desired policy outcomes
(Davies 2005). The proliferation of policy networks in education has, in part,
been an outcome of the shifting political and economic landscapes that have
fundamentally changed the ways states and markets work to shape educational institutions around the world (Apple 2010, 2006; Ball 2012). Policy
networks have come to play an influential role in multiple domains as social
democratic contracts have eroded in the context of advanced deregulation,
trade liberalisation and other neoliberal reforms (Harvey 2005; Stedman
Jones 2012). Thus, the focus on policy networks is strongly linked to the
broader project of understanding and rethinking the ways politics, markets
and culture shape educational and social change (Apple 2013).

While policy network analysis (PNA) is an established (though relatively
young) field in political science, its application in education has only recently
begun to gain momentum. Scholars in education have used PNA to interrogate the relationships between traditional actors and jurisdictional challengers,
and to raise critical questions about the democratic functioning of education
systems within these contexts (Au & Ferrare 2015; Ball & Junemann 2012).
The use of PNA in education constitutes an important recognition that hierarchical bureaucratic structures and grassroots mobilisations are not the only
social structures through which educational policy is transformed. Indeed, policy networks have become a crucial context through which actors successfully

navigate the institutional terrain shaping formal policy making while simultaneously appealing to grassroots sensibilities in modern democratic nations (see, e.g., Au & Ferrare 2014).

A central component of policy network analysis in education is examining the role of philanthropic foundations in brokering relations between disconnected actors (Burt 1992; Obstfeld 2005). Although ostensibly foundations' primary task is funding initiatives and organisations; when done strategically the effect is to create, sustain and transform policy networks. Indeed, it has been demonstrated that the power of foundations is less about their financial capital than leveraging the networks and knowledge that are formed through funding (especially convergent funding) practices (Reckhow & Snyder 2014; Scott & Jabbar 2013). In this sense, the work of philanthropic foundations in education (e.g., brokering, leveraging and converging) must be viewed as forms of organisational practice. As such, understanding the role of philanthropic foundations in education policy requires that we develop an organisational practice theory of their role in policy networks.

The present chapter introduces a field theory of organisational practice that accounts for the ways that philanthropic foundations construct education policy networks through a combination of organisational and ideological work. That is, in the practice of building policy networks, philanthropic actors attempt to create organisational network structures to influence education in ways that reflect their policy objectives. In the process, however, foundations must navigate existing institutional rules and bureaucratic structures, and thus confront uncertainty, risk and the potential for contradictory outcomes. Our objective is to develop a theoretical model of these practices, demonstrate the basic components of the model through an empirical case study, and to generate questions for future work in the realm of education policy network analysis.

Philanthropic practices in education policy networks

The research literature focusing on philanthropic involvement in education policy networks has been very productive in recent years. While the active role of philanthropists in education is not a new phenomenon, their objective of building network capacity through strategic forms of giving are relatively novel. Most notably, policy analysts have argued that venture (or 'strategic') philanthropy has become a dominant practice within the philanthropic field (Reckhow 2013; Scott 2009). Venture philanthropy – often contrasted with scientific philanthropy (Saltman 2010) – is an approach to philanthropic giving that closely follows the principles of venture capital investment. Similar to the latter, venture philanthropists seek to leverage returns on investments, broker relations to expand educational markets, and co-fund advocacy organisations that promote a market-oriented policy agenda (Cohen 2007; Lipman 2015, 2011; Scott 2009). Of course, organisations actively seek out philanthropic foundations for their financial and social capital, so there must be a certain degree of ideological alignment between grantees and the foundations that support their objectives.

Philanthropic foundations have found policy networks to be an efficient means of influencing education policy since these networks offer an alternative route to change than the traditional democratic institutions that have long been perceived as the fundamental barriers toward such change (Chubb & Moe 1990). Indeed, scholars have argued that a key philanthropic practice is to broker relations between disconnected organisations such as think tanks, media, charter management organisations and advocacy groups in order to leverage strategic advantages toward their policy objectives (Scott & Jabbar 2014). At the same time, the relatively informal nature of policy networks allows foundations to maintain a cautious and incremental stance toward their potentially risky engagement in policy (Ferris et al. 2008).

In addition to brokering relations and leveraging advantages, coalitions of major philanthropic foundations have used convergent grant-making (i.e., co-funding) practices to advance a relatively homogeneous policy agenda that emphasises market-based interventions (Ball & Junemann 2012; Saltman 2010; Scott 2009) through discourses of entrepreneurship, innovation and enterprise (Anderson & Donchik 2014; Ball & Exley 2010; Bell 2015; see also McShane & Hess 2015). For example, recent policy network analyses in the United States have found that major foundations are central actors in a policy network working to shape reform through the proliferation of school choice and alternative teacher and leadership certification (Kretchmar et al. 2014). These same foundations have converged in state-level charter policy by co-funding non-profit organisations working to influence school choice campaigns directly through in-kind contributions and the dissemination of research (Au & Ferrare 2014). Observation of similar structures in many other countries (see Au & Ferrare 2015) suggests a degree of global isomorphism in the ways major philanthropic foundations practice policy networks (Ball 2012; Olmedo 2014; Rizvi & Lingard 2010).

The most pervasive illustration of the philanthropic practice of convergence in education policy networks can be found in the work of Reckhow and Snyder (2014; see also Reckhow 2013). In their longitudinal study, Reckhow and Snyder demonstrate that between 2000 and 2010 the top fifteen philanthropic donors in education had doubled the amount of money donated to national advocacy and research organisations and dramatically shifted their giving patterns away from traditional institutions (e.g., public school districts) toward jurisdictional challengers such as charter schools, alternative teacher training (e.g., Teach For America) and venture capital (Reckhow and Snyder 2014). A similar analysis found that non-major foundations had converged on many of the same organisations but are also working to construct more varied networks by focusing on the arts, curricular support services and other forms of student enrichment (Ferrare & Reynolds 2016).

Theorising philanthropic involvement in education policy networks

In this section we discuss two theoretical perspectives that have been used to analyse the practices of philanthropic foundations in education policy networks: the concept of heterarchy that has been developed across the social sciences and recently applied to education policy, and new institutional theory from organisational studies. Following our explication, we suggest how organisational field theory complements the latter theoretical perspectives and gives us additional tools to analyse the practices constituting philanthropic involvement in policy networks.

From hierarchies to heterarchies

A key feature of network governance is the shift away from the bureaucratic structures of the state to heterarchical structures of interpersonal networking, negotiation and navigation through (and around) traditional bureaucratic organisations (Hedlund 1986; Jessop 2002). To be clear, heterarchical structures do not replace traditional hierarchies of the state, but rather constitute organisational structures through which the latter can be influenced and, if necessary, circumnavigated. Whereas bureaucracies are the embodiment of hierarchies, policy networks are the operationalisation of governance within heterarchical structures of policy making.

The concept of heterarchy has been quite illustrative in the literature on education policy network analysis and, in particular, elite philanthropic involvement in this form of governance. For instance, Ball and Junemann (2011) demonstrated how elite philanthropic foundations working within heterarchical structures become 'a vehicle for processes of destatization but also [offer] a degree of public legitimacy not yet available to for-profit providers wanting to access core areas of education delivery' (p. 659). In this sense, elite philanthropists and their foundations utilise heterarchies to mobilise both material and ideological resources to influence policy landscapes and, ultimately, outcomes (see also Au & Ferrare 2014).

Olmedo (2014) builds on this perspective by illustrating the ways that venture philanthropists mobilise discourses of creative capitalism through policy networks to expand market-oriented practices and meanings into new policy terrain. As political spaces become increasingly heterarchical, he argues, elite philanthropic actors are well positioned to have a pervasive impact on virtually every aspect of social life. In education, this takes shape by creating competitive markets, utilising punitive measures in the name of accountability, and blurring the lines between public and private. The common thread across all of the these practices 'is the fact that "new" philanthropy is a strategic component and leverage tool for the redefinition of what has been referred to . . . as the state' (Olmedo 2014, p. 582). Thus, elite philanthropists work effectively through heterarchies to generate markets while simultaneously working within traditional hierarchical boundaries. As Jessop quipped, 'the invisible hand [is] combined with the invisible handshake' (1998, p. 43, cited in Olmedo 2014; see also Clarke & Newman 1997 on concomitant changes in the state itself).

The concept of heterarchy is a powerful tool for conceptualising the ways that philanthropic actors work in and through policy networks to redefine and transform education and social policy. Heterarchical concepts help scholars model the ways that these network governance structures interact with markets and bureaucracies and mobilise material and ideological power to move toward desired outcomes. Yet, an important piece of the puzzle remains. Namely, why is it that, despite the push for diversification and competition, research consistently shows a strong degree of homogeneity in the policy network funding strategies utilised by philanthropic actors?

New institutional theory and isomorphism

To deepen our theoretical understanding of philanthropic involvement in policy networks we turn to the concept of institutional isomorphism as developed by new institutional theorists in organisational studies (e.g., DiMaggio & Powell 1983). The central premise of new institutional theory is that, in the face of uncertainty, organisations tend toward similarity through three processes of isomorphism: mimetic, coercive and normative pressures. For instance, a philanthropic organisation looking to award grants in education may follow the funding patterns of an established and respected organisation such as the Bill & Melinda Gates Foundation as a strategy to minimise uncertainty related to engaging in a policy domain (i.e., mimetic isomorphism). Alternatively, a foundation may follow certain patterns due to political pressure from a coalition of other foundations and policy actors (coercive). Finally, a philanthropic organisation may implicitly follow funding patterns because they tend to hire senior staff that have recognisable experiences and/or affiliations with other foundation executives (normative).

Institutional theory has proven to be a productive line of research in organisational studies in general and in the realm of education in particular (Meyer 1977; Meyer & Rowen 1978). In the present context, Reckhow (2010) used this perspective to help explain how philanthropic foundations use strategic (or venture) giving practices to introduce jurisdictional challengers (see Mehta & Teles 2012) into traditional public school districts in order to diversify service providers and legitimate those providers from the private sector. That is, these foundations utilise strategic giving to engage in network construction and simultaneously work to normalise the positions of these network actors within traditionally public spaces. The concept of institutional isomorphism would further suggest that over time foundations would tend to converge their funding practices on similar organisations (i.e., mimetic isomorphism) given the degree of political uncertainty and contentiousness involved with integrating private actors into public spaces in education. This is, in fact, precisely what Reckhow and Snyder (2014) found in their longitudinal analysis.

The success of new institutional theory in predicting the gradual convergence of venture philanthropic practices in education is impressive. The extent of ideological alignment among major foundations is difficult to deny in the face of extensive empirical evidence (Au & Ferrare 2014; Kretchmar et al. 2014; Olmedo 2014; Reckhow 2013; Reckhow & Snyder 2014). Yet, it would be a mistake to conclude that new institutional theory tells the whole story of philanthropic involvement in policy networks. Indeed, while new institutional theory has been successful at explaining conformity in educational organisations, it has not been able to adequately explain the emergence and transformation of organisational fields and the extent to which even stable fields are shaped by power relations (Fligstein & McAdam 2012, 2011). To bridge this gap, we now turn to organisational field theory.

Bridging the gaps: Organisational field theory

To this point we have argued that the concepts of heterarchy and institutional isomorphism each generate insights into how and why philanthropic foundations have utilised policy networks as a space of practice to shape education policy. At the same time, we have seen that these theoretical perspectives leave some important questions to be resolved. In particular, how do we conceptualise periods of stability and transformation concerning philanthropic involvement in network governance? And how do we adequately account for the differentiated positions occupied by these network(ing) actors? To address these questions we introduce organisational field theory. Field theory has a rich history that spans the social sciences, from social psychology and sociology to organisational studies (for a comprehensive review, see Martin 2003). In the present context, our goal is to show how the organisational component of field theory builds upon previous insights into the meso-level realm where philanthropic foundations practice policy networking.

At its core, organisational field theory is a theory of practice (Bourdieu 2005; Emirbayer & Johnson 2008; Mohr 2013) that shares much in common with new institutional theory in the assumptions that 'strategic action fields are the fundamental units of collective action in society' (Fligstein & McAdam 2011, p. 3). However, whereas institutional theory emphasises stability and conformity among actors in organisational fields, organisational field theory understands these fundamental units as constituted by positions of incumbents (i.e., those who wield disproportionate influence), challengers (i.e., those who wield little influence but may have alternative visions), and, in some cases, governance units (i.e., those who oversee rule compliance in the field) through which field emergence, contention, innovation, appropriation and settlement are possible (Fligstein & McAdams 2012). The extent to which organisations are successful at maintaining their incumbent status or challenging established norms hinges on their social skill – the ability to frame strategic actions and simultaneously mobilise the cooperation of other actors (Fligstein 2001).

Many readers will recognise that organisational field theory is an extension of Bourdieu's more general theory of fields (Bourdieu 1993). Indeed, the space of positions through which incumbents and challengers vie for power is inherently connected to a space of meanings that frame social action germane to an organisational field. Bourdieu referred to these meanings as position-takings that 'derive their semiotic significance in relational fashion from their difference vis-à-vis other such position-takings within a *space of position-takings*' (Emirbayer & Johnson 2008, p. 14, original emphasis). The space of position-takings is thus the feature of organisational fields where the practices constituting the space of positions become intricately woven together with meaning. This duality of practice and meaning is the foundation of all social action, whether at the level of individuals, groups or organisations (Breiger 1974; Mohr & Duquenne 1997).

Organisational field theory contributes multiple insights into philanthropic involvement in policy networks. First, the faction of the philanthropic field concerned with education policy is constituted by incumbents and challengers who occupy a differentiated space of positions. This means that the philanthropic practice of building policy networks is always a tenuous endeavor given the power dynamics that shape the funding strategies pursued by incumbents and challengers. For example, education policy analysts often cite the perceived failure of the Annenberg Challenge as a rupture in the philanthropic field (Colvin 2005; Fleishman 2009; Reckhow 2010) that effectively created space for challenger organisations to try new forms of action. One such challenger at the time was the newly formed Bill & Melinda Gates Foundation, who went on to redefine philanthropic involvement in education and subsequently rose to incumbent status in the field. Not only does organisational field theory anticipate this change in field structure, it assumes that such action is always a possibility given the right conditions.

A second and related insight is that philanthropic practices in policy networks can take on both hierarchical and cooperative forms. The nature of this organisation is dependent on the distribution of capital among actors in the field. Where the distribution of capital is highly unequal we can expect a hierarchical structure, and where there exists a number of organisations of similar resource capacities we can expect more co-operative action and coalition building (Fligstein & McAdam 2011, p. 12). The stability of policy networks mobilised by philanthropic organisations is thus dependent on the structure of the field. Fligstein's and McAdams' (2011) proposition suggests that philanthropic power in education policy will be stable when there is either a clear hierarchical (i.e., incumbent/challenger) order or strong coalitions between relatively equal-resourced foundations. Note that this proposition allows for heterarchical structures but does not assume that such structures will always constitute philanthropic involvement in policy networks.

Finally, organisational field theory assumes that philanthropic practices of creating and sustaining education policy networks always include ideological work. Much of this ideological work takes place through patterns of giving to advocacy organisations, think tanks and research centers in the private sector and academic institutions. Yet, in this space of position-takings there is room for contradictions to emerge, especially in the current climate of advancing non-traditional organisations (i.e., jurisdictional challengers) into terrain that has long been occupied by public institutions. Thus, while the literature is clear that philanthropic foundations rely heavily on funding advocacy organisations to advance their ideological and policy agendas through network structures, organisational field theory anticipates that it is through this work that challenger organisations and coalitions will seek to disrupt incumbent funding strategies and cultivate alternative visions of education policy and networks of action toward those visions.

The model of philanthropic practice in education policy that we have advanced synthesises existing theoretical insights while contributing additional propositions. Namely, organisational field theory accepts the premise of isomorphism advanced by new institutional theory, but also provides a basis for conceptualising the power relations that lead to instability and transformation. Further, the perspective we have presented acknowledges the heterarchical structure of philanthropic network governance, while allowing for these governance structures to assume hierarchical forms given the right conditions of resource allocation. Finally, organisational field theory assumes that periods of stability and change are not only determined by the flow of material resources, but also through contentious ideological work performed by organisations in these networks. We now turn to a case study of philanthropic funding practices in policy networks in the United States to illustrate certain features of this model in action and to raise questions for future scholarship.

Building networks in fields: A case study of philanthropic involvement in US education policy networks

Our case study unfolds in two sections. In the first section we provide a bird's eye view of the philanthropic field in US primary and secondary education by illustrating funding patterns from foundations to a variety of education policy domains. This representation demonstrates the overall gravity of the field via the relative positions of foundations and the domains of policy they are working to transform. In the second section we zoom in on six foundations and construct select components of their education policy networks to illustrate the organisational and ideological strategies they use to influence education policy from their particular position within the broader philanthropic field.

Data and methods

The first step in the analysis draws from the Foundation Center's 2010[1] Top 50 Foundation Funding lists for eleven different domains of elementary and secondary education policy: accountability, arts education, college and career preparation, early learning, standards, literacy/reading skills, low-performing schools, out-of-school/summer, rural education, STEM and teacher quailty. These lists produced a total of 230 unique philanthropic foundations. A foundation-by-policy domain matrix was then created in which each cell illustrates the percentage of total dollar awards that foundation i contributed to policy domain j. We then used correspondence analysis (CA) to position the 230 foundations in relation to the eleven policy domains. The goal of CA in this context is to represent the (dis)similarity between foundations and policy domains in the contingency table as distances in a low dimensional space (Greenacre & Blasius 2006). In CA, distance refers to the χ^2-distance, which for two points (x, y) is simply a form of weighted Euclidean distance:

$$d_{x,y} = \sqrt{\sum_{j=1}^{P} w_j (x_j - y_j)^2}$$

where w_j refers to the specific weight of the jth dimension.

The next step in the analysis looks to six foundations' 990 tax forms from 2010 as provided by the Foundation Center's 990 Finder.[2] Our subset of foundations includes: Bill and Melinda Gates Foundation, Bradley Foundation, Open Society Foundations, Altman Foundation, Barr Foundation and Kauffman Foundation. These six foundations were selected based upon their varying prominence in the field, diverse ideological leanings (neoconservative, neoliberal, etc.) and range of education policy interests. Using the 990s, each foundation's contributions to educational organisations were recorded in a matrix. We also coded each recipient organisation type (e.g., public school/district, national advocacy, testing organisation) following Reckhow's & Snyder's thematic scheme (see 2014, Appendix B). In the end, our subset of six foundations awarded $261.1 million to 641 organisations in 2010. In the field theoretic lexicon, Gates is the most dominant incumbent actor among this subset both in terms of the number and amount of grants awarded to education, as well as the media attention and perception of policy influence in the public sphere. The remaining five foundations, on the other hand, constitute a variety of challenger foundations that in some cases align with Gates and in others diverge substantially.

We again used correspondence analysis to map the organisational network funding strategies utilised by our subset of philanthropic foundations to influence education policy. In this case the input matrix was the set of six philanthropic foundations and the set of organisational codes applied to each recipient organisation (see above). In addition, we used a directed graph to focus on the specific research and advocacy networks that these foundations helped to create and sustain through strategic grants. In a matrix of directed relations, actor i may direct a relation (e.g., gives money) to actor j, but this does not necessarily mean that the relation is reciprocated (i.e., $n_j \rightarrow n_i$). When combined with the correspondence analysis, this approach allows us to illustrate how an organisational field theory of philanthropic practices in policy networks illuminates the coalitions and contradictions inherent in this domain of education policy.

The philanthropic field in US education policy

Figure 7.1 illustrates the first two dimensions – representing 17.4% and 16.9% of the total variance in the matrix, respectively – of the correspondence analysis of foundations and policy domains. For the sake of clarity, the only object labels included in the figure are those that represent the top ten funders from 2010 (see Reckhow & Snyder 2014), the subset of six foundations selected for the network analysis, and the eleven policy domains that the foundations are attempting to influence through direct grants and network building. Intuitively, philanthropic foundations that are positioned in close proximity to one another in the plot tended to distribute their awards more similarly across policy domains than those that are positioned farther apart. On the other hand, the policy domains that are clustered together tended to share the same funders in common relative to the policy domains that are farther away.

Figure 7.1 provides a bird's eye view of the organisational positions and policy objectives among 230 philanthropic foundations in the United States. It is clear that the gravity of the philanthropic field in 2010 was to converge on policies related to curriculum standards, teacher quality, low-performing schools, college and career readiness, and science education (STEM). We know from the existing literature (see above) that the major (i.e., incumbent) foundations seek to leverage their influence over these policy domains by converging around organisations that advance teacher deregulation and charter school proliferation. At the periphery of the philanthropic field, on the other hand, were those domains of policy that include the arts, rural education, early childhood education, literacy and out-of-school programs.

It is also clear from Figure 7.1 that the incumbent (i.e., top ten) foundations were relatively united in their policy emphasis – with the lone exception being the W. K. Kellogg Foundation who made up a disproportionate amount of the funding that was aimed at influencing rural education. Thus, the philanthropic field in 2010 was organised into a relatively clear core/periphery structure. The periphery of the philanthropic field was occupied almost entirely by non-major (challenger) foundations. Meanwhile, at the center of this structure

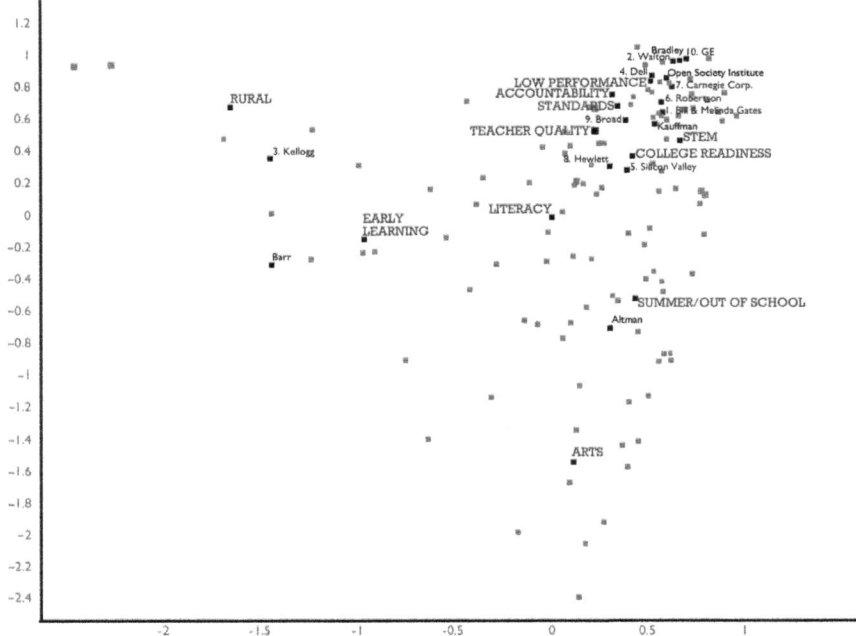

Figure 7.1 Correspondence Plot of Foundations by Policy Domains, 2010

(Note: All gray dots are foundations whose labels have been suppressed for the sake of clarity. Further, the values along the X- and Y- axes are coordinates used to position the foundations and policy domains based upon their (dis)similarity in funding and receiving patterns, respectively.)

was a coalition of incumbent foundations emphasising market-based reforms. Note, though, that a significant number of non-major (challenger) foundations were also working to influence these domains of policy. As noted above, previous research suggests that these latter foundations did display many of the market-driven funding and convergence practices used by their incumbent counterparts, but they also pursued non-market-oriented objectives (e.g., arts education) falling outside the purview of the incumbent foundation agenda. Thus, as anticipated in field theory, incumbents tended toward similarity (i.e., isomorphism and heterarchical coalitions) while the set of challengers worked to influence policies that both aligned and diverged from the objectives of incumbents.

Building organisational networks

We now take a closer look at the divergent and overlapping organisational network pratices used by a subset of foundations in the philanthropic field. In particular, we examine the funding patterns of the most dominant incumbent actor, Bill & Melinda Gates Foundation, in relation to a variety of less prominent foundations occupying challenger positions in the field. Figure 7.2 illustrates the first two dimensions – representing 37.2% and 29.4% of the total variance, respectively – of the correspondence analysis of our subset of foundations and the types of organisations to which they awarded money to advance their policy agendas.

In relation to the types of organisations funded in 2010, this subset of foundations can be differentiated into four factions. At the top of the space is the conservative Bradley Foundation located in Milwaukee, Wisconsin. Relative to the other five foundations, Bradley focused heavily on building networks of national and state advocacy organisations, media organisations, religious and student groups, alternative leadership training, private schools, among others. In the lower right corner of the space are the New England-based Barr (Boston) and Altman (New York) Foundations. In contrast to Bradley, these foundations focused on funding networks of organisations working in the realms of local advocacy, race relations, early childhood education, civics and community

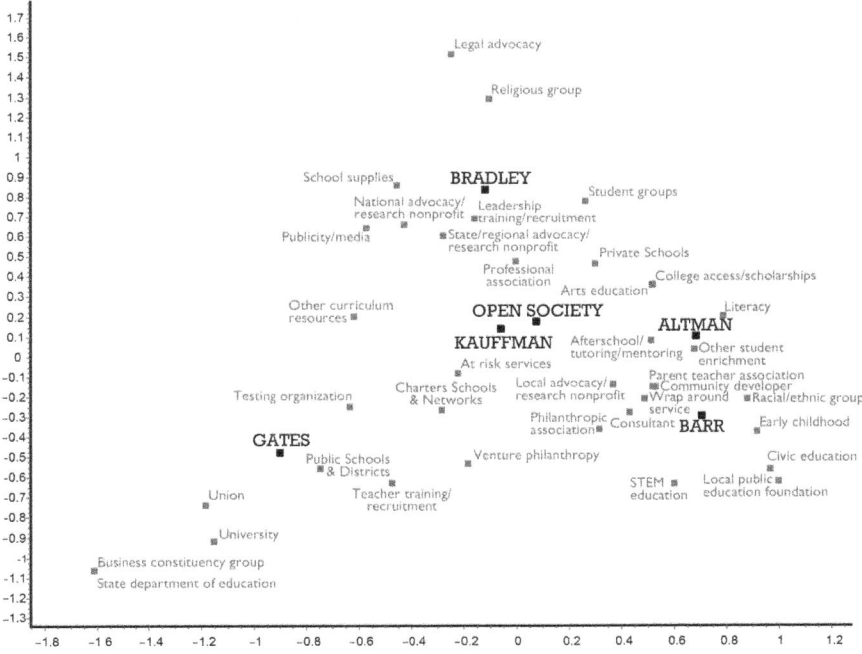

Figure 7.2 Correspondence Plot of Foundations by Grantee Type, 2010

(Note: The values along the X- and Y- axes are coordinates used to position the foundations and policy domains based upon their (dis)similarity in funding and receiving patterns, respectively.)

development. Positioned in the center of the space are the Kauffman Foundation and Open Society Foundations, whose organisational giving profiles similarly reflected the average profiles across all foundations in the subset.

The incumbent actor, Bill & Melinda Gates Foundation, occupies an interesting position in the lower left corner of the space. Here we can see that, relative to the other five foundations in 2010, Gates' funding practices focused on both traditional institutions (universities, state departments of education, public schools and teachers unions) and mobilising networks of venture philanthropists, teacher training organisations, charter schools and networks, and business constituency groups. However, the largest of the grants given to public school districts – $10 million to Denver Public Schools and $9.6 million to Atlanta Public Schools – were designed to accelerate teacher value-added and evaluation models that constitute a major foundation of the market-based reform strategy. Similarly, a substantial portion of the funding to state departments of education were strategically targeted to advance the Common Core State Standards ($1.9 million to Georgia and $1 million to Kentucky). Thus, while Gates did pursue seemingly contradictory policy network funding strategies at the organisational level, it is clear that these strategies were generally aligned with the broader market-based ideology that guides their support of non-traditional organisations.

Building ideological support through advocacy

So far we have illustrated how organisational field theory directs us to relationally examine the policy stances and organisational network funding practices that foundations pursue as they construct and mobilise policy networks to influence education. Organisational field theory assumes these policy networks are held together by relational ties that experience periods of stability and, if the conditions are right, instability or transformation. The degree of stability depends, in part, upon the extent to which the field is organised by hierarchical incumbent/challenger structures and/or strong coalitions. The analysis above, in conjunction with previous literature, demonsrates that in 2010 there was a strong coalition of incumbent foundations situated within a broader core/periphery structure. In this final section of our case study we highlight the organisational network funding strategies that foundations practiced to perform the crucial ideological work necessary to advance their reform agenda.

Figure 7.3 represents a directed bi-partite graph of the funding flows from our subset of foundations to the advocacy and research organisations they funded in 2010. The recipient nodes are shaded to differentiate the scale of advocacy and research that each organisation emphasises: local, state/regional and national. The graph consists of multiple clusters centered around each of the foundations. While Barr, Altman and Open Society funded sets of advocacy and research organisations that were disconected from the other foundations in the subset, Gates, Bradley and Kauffman converged upon (i.e., co-funded) a

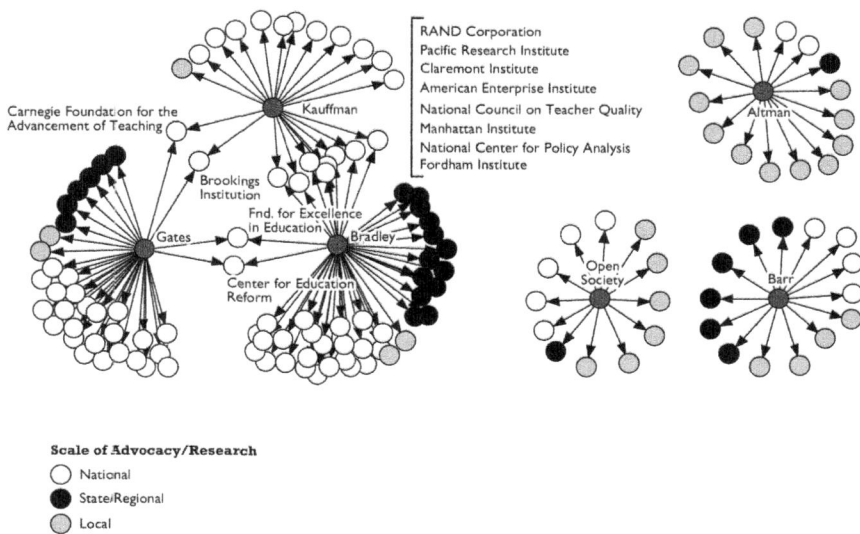

Scale of Advocacy/Research
○ National
● State/Regional
◐ Local

Figure 7.3 Directed Bipartite Graph of Funding Flows to Advocacy and Research Organisations, 2010

(Note: Only foundations and co-funded organizations are labeled.)

number of advocacy and research organisations (see labels) and were thus connected into a larger structure.

Looking across the full range of organisations who received funds from our subset of foundations gives the impression that, at least in 2010, funding advocacy and research organisations was a central strategy in the ways that foundations practiced policy networks. In fact, a quarter (25.5%) of all funds awarded by these six foundations were to think tanks, advocacy and research organisations. No other type of organisation even comes close to this level of funding. This is not surprising when viewed from the perspective of organisational field theory since the work of practicing policy networks is always constituted by a duality of material strategies (funding flows in this case) and the ideological work of framing how policy is imagined and contested. These research and advocacy organisations thus serve as the meaning-making and framing arms of the policy networks cultivated by philanthropic foundations.

Our subset of foundations follow some discernable patterns when it comes to the ways they sought to advance the ideological work of policy networks through the funding of think tanks and advocacy organisations. Altman, for instance, almost exclusively funded local advocacy organisations while Barr and Open Society funded across all scales. The larger cluster consisting of Gates, Bradley and Kauffman, however, was strongly oriented toward funding and co-funding national organisations. It is evident that Kauffman and Bradley shared similar ideological visions through their convergence around conservative think tanks such as the Fordham Institute, Manhattan Institute and American Enterprise Institute. Kauffman and Gates, meanwhile, converged around more centrist advocacy and research organisations (Brookings Institution and Carnegie Foundation for the Advancement of Teaching), and Gates and Bradley co-funded two market-friendly organisations, Foundation for Excellence in Education (founded by Jeb Bush) and the Center for Education Reform.

Next steps in practicing policy networks

In this chapter we have sought to theorise how philanthropic organisations engage in the practice of building policy networks. To do so we have built upon the insights generated in previous work, especially through the concepts of heterarchy and institutional isomorphism. We have suggested that organisational field theory allows us to integrate the latter insights while addressing crucial features of philanthropic network governance. In particular, we have argued that organisational field theory pushes us to simultaneously focus on the different forms of power relations (material and ideological) and social structures (heterarchical and hierarchical) that shape processes of stability and change in the philanthropic field. Accounting for change is a particular strength of organisational field theory. Although our case study focused on a single year, in practice the philanthropic field is constantly in motion as foundations' priorities shift in relation to political, cultural and economic contexts (e.g., see Reckhow & Snyder 2014). Thus, future work should pay close attention to the dynamic temporal positionings of the philanthropic field in education.

At the most general level, our case study illustrates many of the core features of the field theoretical perspective at work. We saw that the philanthropic field is a highly differentiated space of incumbents and challengers organised into both hierarchical 'core/periphery' structures and heterarchical coalitions. Depending on how they are positioned in this differentiated space, foundations utilised different funding practices to build policy networks aligned with their objectives. A key aspect of this work was the funding of advocacy and research organisations that generate and disseminate the ideological content used to support policy outcomes. Indeed, it is clear from our case study and previous literature that many foundations perceive that the success or failure of their reform movements hinge on changing the common sense understandings of education policy (Apple 2006, 2013). The reliance on think tanks, in particular, has long been a strategy in the push to proliferate market-based reforms in the realm of social policy (Stedman Jones 2012).

The extraordinary range of advocacy and research organisations that are linked into education policy networks through philanthropic funding has the dual effect of creating ideological alignment and discontinuity. On the one hand, foundations often converge their funding around think tanks and advocacy organisations that share similar visions of how to reform the education system, and the latter organisations also seek out foundations in a similar fashion. It is inevitable, then, that a certain degree of ideological redundancy will circulate through the social closure of policy networks. On the other hand, the sheer breadth of organisations that receive funding will always create 'structural holes' (Burt 1992) that leave open the potential for the introduction of novel information. This is especially true among those organisations that do not adhere to a rigid ideological foundation. Future work should focus on these structural holes and how the specific brokerage practices of foundations can result in contradictory outcomes.

A practice-based theory of philanthropic involvement in education policy networks suggests these networks take form through conflicts and coalitions that emerge through tenuous political maneuvers and ideological work. That is, in the practice of building policy networks, philanthropic foundations and other organisational actors attempt to structure policy actions and meanings in ways that create ideological alignment and contradiction. It is through these contradictions, we argue, that there is space for challengers to interrupt dominant understandings of education reform and put forward alternatives. Philanthropic practices in policy networks are not homogenous, but instead represent competing visions over what the education system should be and who should have a voice in the process. As such, we suggest that future work focus on the cracks and contradictions that are inherent to education policy networks. Through this work education policy scholars can identify spaces where grassroots network mobilisations are currently happening and areas of possibility in the future. We believe that organisational field theory provides a useful point of departure, though not an end, for this work.

Notes

1 The Foundation Center is a non-profit organisation that, among other things, collects and distributes information about philanthropy in the United States and abroad. The 2010 Top 50 Foundation Funding lists are the most recent publicly available lists from the Foundation Center http://foundationcenter.org/educationexcellence/top_lists.html, retrieved on June 15, 2014.
2 990 tax forms must be filed by most tax-exempt organisations in the United States (including philanthropic foundations). These forms, among other things, detail the financial gifts awarded by philanthropic foundations. The 990s for this analysis were retrieved from http://foundationcenter.org/findfunders/990finder/ on June 15, 2014.

References

Anderson, GL & Donchik, LM 2014, 'Privatizing schooling and policy making: The American legislative exchange council and new political and discursive strategies of education governance', *Educational Policy*, vol. 30, no. 2, pp. 322–364.

Apple, MW 2006, *Educating the 'right' way: Markets, standards, god, and inequality*, Routledge, New York, NY.

Apple, MW (ed.) 2010, *Global crises, social justice, and education*, Routledge, New York, NY.

Apple, MW 2013, *Can education change society?*, Routledge, New York & London.

Au, W & Ferrare, JJ 2014, 'Sponsors of policy: A network analysis of wealthy elites, their affiliated philanthropies, and charter school reform in Washington State', *Teachers College Record*, vol. 116, no. 8, pp. 1–24, retrieved 8 April 2016, <http://www.tcrecord.org ID Number: 17387>.

Au, W & Ferrare, JJ (eds) 2015, *Mapping corporate education reform: Power and policy networks in the neoliberal state*, Routledge, New York, NY.

Ball, SJ 2012, *Global education Inc.: New policy networks and the neoliberal imaginary*, Routledge, New York, NY.

Ball, SJ & Exley, S 2010, 'Making policy with "Good Ideas": Policy networks and the "Intellectuals" of new labour', *Journal of Education Policy*, vol. 25, no. 2, pp. 151–169.

Ball, SJ & Junemann, C 2011, 'Education policy and philanthropy – The changing landscape of English educational governance', *International Journal of Public Administration*, vol. 34, no. 10, pp. 646–661.

Ball, SJ & Junemann, C 2012, *Networks, new governance and education*, Policy Press, Bristol, UK.

Bell, S 2015, 'Mapping the discourse of neoliberal education reform: Space, power, and access in Chicago's renaissance 2010 debate', in W Au & JJ Ferrare (eds), *Mapping corporate education reform: Power and policy networks in the neoliberal state*, Routledge, New York, NY, pp. 126–146.Bourdieu, P 1993, 'Some properties of fields', in *Sociology in Question*, Thousand Oaks, London.

Bourdieu, P 2005, *The social structures of the economy*, Polity Press, Cambridge.

Breiger, R 1974, 'The duality of persons and groups', *Social Forces*, vol. 53, no. 2, pp. 181–190.

Burt, RS 1992, *Structural holes: The social structure of competition*, Harvard University Press, Cambridge, MA.

Chubb, JE & Moe, TM 1990, *Politics, markets, and America's schools*, Brookings Institution Press, New York.

Clarke, J & Newman, J 1997, *The managerial state: Power, politics and ideology in the remaking of social welfare*, Sage, London.

Cohen, R 2007, *Strategic grantmaking: Foundations and the school privatization movement*, National Committee for Responsive Philanthropy, Washington, DC.

Colvin, RL 2005, 'A new generation of philanthropists and their great ambitions', in FM Hess (ed.), *With the best of intentions: How philanthropy is reshaping K-12 education*, Harvard Education Press, Cambridge, MA, pp. 21–48.

Davies, JS 2005, 'Local governance and the dialectics of Hierarchy, market and network', *Policy Studies*, vol. 26, no. 3/4, pp. 311–335.

DiMaggio, P & Powell, WW 1983, 'The iron cage revisited: Institutional isomorphism and collective rationality in organizational fields' *American Sociological Review*, vol. 48, pp. 147–160.

Emirbayer, M & Johnson, V 2008, 'Bourdieu and organizational analysis', *Theory & Society*, vol. 37, no. 1, pp. 1–44.

Ferrare, JJ & Reynolds K 2016, 'Has the elite foundation agenda spread beyond the gates? An organizational network analysis of non-major philanthropic giving in K12 education', *American Journal of Education*, vol. 123, no. 1.

Ferris, JM, Hentschke, GC & Harmssen, HJ 2008, 'Philanthropic strategies for school reform: An analysis of foundation choices', *Educational Policy*, vol. 22, no. 5, pp. 705–730.

Fleishman, JL 2009, *The foundation: How private wealth is changing the world*, Public Affairs, New York, NY.

Fligstein, N 2001, 'Social skill and the theory of fields', *Sociological Theory*, vol. 19, no. 2, pp. 105–125.

Fligstein, N & McAdam, D 2011, 'Toward a general theory of strategic action fields', *Sociological Theory*, vol. 29, no. 1, pp. 1–26.

Fligstein, N & McAdam, D 2012, *A theory of fields*, Oxford University Press, Oxford, UK.

Greenacre, M & Blasius, J (eds) 2006, *Multiple correspondence analysis and related methods, Statistics in the social and behavioral sciences series*, Chapman & Hall/CRC, Boca Raton, FL.

Harvey, D 2005, *A brief history of neoliberalism*, Oxford University Press, Oxford, UK.

Hedlund, G 1986, 'The hypermodern MNC – A heterarchy? *Human Resource Management*, vol. 25, no. 1, pp. 9–35.

Jessop, B 1998, 'The rise of governance and the risks of failure: The case of economic development', *International Social Science Journal*, vol. 50, no. 155, pp. 29–45.

Jessop, B 2002, *The future of the capitalist state*, Polity Press, Cambridge, UK.

Kretchmar, K, Sondel, B & Ferrare, JJ 2014, 'Mapping the terrain: Teach for America, charter school reform, and corporate sponsorship', *Journal of Education Policy*, vol. 29, no. 6, pp. 742–759.

Lipman, P 2011, *The new political economy of urban education: Neoliberalism, race, and the right to the city*, Routledge, New York.

Lipman, P 2015, 'Capitalizing on crisis: Venture philanthropy's colonial project to remake urban education', *Critical Studies in Education*, vol. 56, no. 2, pp. 241–258.

Martin, JL 2003, 'What is field theory?', *American Journal of Sociology*, vol. 109, no. 1, pp. 1–49.

McShane, MQ & Hess, FM 2015, 'The politics of entrepreneurship and innovation', in BS Cooper, JB Cibulka, LD Fusarelli (eds), *Handbook of education politics and policy*, Routledge, New York, NY, pp. 304–321.

Mehta, J & Teles, S 2012, 'Jurisdictional politics: A new federal role in education', in FM Hess & AP Kelly (eds), *Carrots, sticks, and the bully pulpit: Lessons from a half-century of federal efforts to improve America's schools*, Harvard Education Press, Cambridge, MA, pp. 197–216.

Meyer, JW 1977, 'The effects of education as an institution', *American Journal of Sociology*, vol. 83, no. 1, pp. 55–77.

Meyer, JW & Rowen, B 1978, 'The structure of educational organizations', in M Meyer (ed.), *Environments and organizations*, Jossey-Bass, San Francisco, CA, pp. 233–263.

Mohr, JW 2013, 'Bourdieu's relational method in theory and practice: From fields and capitals to networks and institutions (and back again)', in F Depelteau & C Powell (eds), *Applying relational sociology: Relations, networks, and society*, Palgrave Macmillan, New York, NY, pp. 101–136.

Mohr, JW & Duquenne, V 1997, 'The duality of culture and practice: Poverty relief in New York City, 1888–1917', *Theory & Society*, vol. 26, no. 2, pp. 305–356.

Obstfeld, D 2005, 'Social networks, the Tertius Iungens orientation, and involvement in innovation', *Administrative Science Quarterly*, vol. 50, no. 1, pp. 100–130.

Olmedo, A 2014, 'From England with love . . . ARK, heterarchies and global "Philanthropic Governance"', *Journal of Education Policy*, vol. 29, no. 5, pp. 575–597.

Reckhow, S 2010, 'Disseminating and legitimating a new approach: The role of foundations', in KE Bulkley, JR Henig & HM Levin (eds), *Between public and private: Politics, governance, and the new portfolio models for urban school reform*, Harvard Education Press, Cambridge, MA, pp. 277–304.

Reckhow, S 2013, *Follow the money: How foundation dollars change public school politics*, Oxford University Press, Oxford, UK.

Reckhow, S & Snyder, JW 2014, 'The expanding role of philanthropy in education politics', *Educational Researcher*, vol. 43, no. 4, pp. 186–195.

Rhodes, RAW 2006, 'Policy network analysis' in M Moran, M Rein & RE Goodin (eds), *The Oxford handbook of public policy*, Oxford University Press, Oxford, UK, pp. 423–445.

Rizvi, F & Lingard, B 2010, *Globalizing education policy*, Routledge, New York, NY.

Saltman, KJ 2010, *The gift of education: Public education and venture philanthropy*, Palgrave Mac-Millan, New York, NY.

Scott, J 2009, 'The politics of venture philanthropy in charter school policy and advocacy' *Educational Policy*, vol. 23, no. 1, pp. 106–136. Scott, J & Jabbar, H 2013, 'Money and measures: Foundations as knowledge brokers', in D Anagnostopoulos, SA Rutledge & R Jacobson (eds), *The infrastructure of accountability: Data use and the transformation of American education*, Harvard Education Press, Cambridge, MA, pp. 75–92.

Scott, J & Jabbar, H 2014, 'The hub and the spokes: Foundations, intermediary organizations, incentivist reforms, and the politics of research evidence', *Educational Policy*, vol. 28, no. 2, pp. 233–257.

Stedman Jones, D 2012, *Masters of the universe: Hayek, Friedman, and the birth of neoliberal politics*, Princeton University Press, Princeton, NJ.

Chapter 8

A Cultural-historical approach to practice

Working within and across practices

Anne Edwards

Introduction

> While *context* and *situation* continue to appear in discussion of culture in mind, in recent years there has been an increasing use of the terms *activity* and *practice* in their place.
>
> (Cole 1996, pp. 137, original emphases)

In the twenty or so years since Cole's observations, cultural–historical approaches to learning and development have become more widely understood and the limitations of the dualism found in terms such as context and situation have been increasingly acknowledged. As a result, we are now clearer about what these shifts in terminology mean and can see that that are not simply a matter of substituting one word for another. In this chapter I examine how cultural–historical theory employs the ideas of activity and practice and consider the implications of this approach for how we might think about: transitions between practices; changing practices and creating new ones; and collaboration across practices on complex problems. In working through these examples, what is fore-grounded is the constant dynamic of agency with the historically formed, yet future-oriented, demands in the practices.

The key features of cultural–historical approaches, which will therefore underpin these discussions, are the recognition of: (1) the historicity of practices; and (2) the dialectical nature of the relation between person and practice. Together these features acknowledge that people usually enter practices that have already been configured by others, but work intentionally in and on them, in turn contributing to them. People therefore are shaped by practices, but may also shape them.

It is clear, from this perspective, that practices are inhabited and not a set of actions that one carries out. The following definition of practices attempts to capture the features central to a cultural–historical view: '. . . practices are knowledge-laden, imbued with cultural values and emotionally freighted by the motives of those who already act in them' (Edwards 2010, pp. 5). It follows that people enter historically constructed practices with intentions, which are shaped by and shape what matters to participants in the practice. As participants approach, interpret and engage in the activities that make up a practice, they exercise a personal agency, which they learn to align with the motives that shape the practice while also impacting on the practice with their actions.

This definition of practice and the dialectic with personal agency indicates how the non-dualist cultural-historical approach to practice overcomes the problem of transfer between practices that bedevils so many accounts of practice. It works well for examining, for example, how a child learns at home and school; how new employees are inducted into work practices; and how people make transitions between practices. At the same time it points to the challenges involved in creating new practices or radically changing old ones in order to meet new demands; such as collaborating across professional practices or building strong links between researchers and potential research users. The discussions that follow unpack the theoretical underpinnings of this dialectic and examine the implications of how cultural-historical theory addresses these challenges for research and practice.

A cultural-historical view of practice

The work of Vygotsky in Russia in the late 1920s until his death in 1934, and of his colleague A. N. Leont'ev from the 1920s until the 1970s, aimed at teasing out the inter-penetration of culture and mind, the societal and the individual. This was no idle intellectual exercise; the intention was to identify and explain a psychology which could support agentic action on the world, to make it a better place. It was in essence an interventionist psychology which reflected the dialectic of person and practice and located it within the affordances and constraints of societal conditions (Vygotsky 1997). The dialectic therefore also recognised the connections between institutional practice and society. Leont'ev summarised the iterative relationship of person and societal conditions as follows: '. . . society produces the activity of the individuals forming it' (Leont'ev 1978, pp. 7). Human agency is accordingly evidenced in our ability to work on and change the conditions in which we act, a view which is echoed by, for example, Taylor (Taylor 1977). Where the exercise of agency can be accomplished, practices are not static but responsive and emergent, as fresh demands are recognised, new knowledge brought into play and values and motives questioned and reconfigured.

But if practices are the responsive architecture in which we act out our lives, how do we conceptualise what we do and connect our actions with these practices? There are two linked answers to this question. The first comes from Vygotsky, for whom learning involved a process of both internalisation and externalisation (Vygotsky 1997). The dialectic arises when we externalise our understandings by interpreting demands and responding to them by taking action. Actions in activities therefore involve people in using conceptual tools as they interpret and act on with the world.

The second and related response was given by Leont'ev, who offered activity as the link between action and practice. It is worth noting at this point that I use the term cultural-historical and not CHAT (Cultural Historical Activity Theory) (Roth & Lee 2007). Discussions in this chapter draw on Leont'ev and his development of a theory of activity, but they do not examine the activity systems and systemic change that mark Engeström's seminal work on these topics (Engeström 1999, 2007). The focus of the present chapter is a cultural-historical account of actions in activities in practices and the implications for research and practice.

People's actions may at times be routine but they will all involve a process of interpretation and response. Routine action in activities in practices include actions such as grinding coffee beans and putting them in a pot with hot water as part of the activity of making breakfast in the practice of family life. Non-routine actions, may call for what Taylor sees as deliberative agency (Taylor 1989), where attention is given to the demands presented by a task and effort is made to respond to them. For example, if a child suddenly asks for American pancakes at breakfast, this UK-based writer would need to find a recipe, check ingredients and learn how to make them. She would know that Scottish drop scones or French crêpes would not meet the demand being made. That is, her interpretation of the demand would recognise the challenge in it and she would have the resources at hand to help her meet it and she would learn as she worked to do so.

This example points to the important relationship between what people bring to an activity and the demands to be found in an activity. Actions in activities involve actors in recognising the demands in them. But the actions we take in activities also involve motive. In the practice of family life and the activity of breakfast-making, my motive is that people have a good start to the day and – as the child is likely to be a visiting grandchild – there is the motive of a little extra care to be given to him as I work on the task of providing breakfast. In cultural-historical theory practices, activities and actions are connected by a notion of motive. This view of motive differs from most psychological accounts because it starts from what is important within a particular practice, whether family life or social work, rather than from individual need.

The cultural-historical approach to motive originated in the work of Leont'ev. The terminology he used when discussing motive, object of activity and object motive were important elements in his efforts to overcome what he saw as a dualistic psychology, which separated motives and societal conditions. His argument was that the dialectic of person in activity in practices in society gives rise to the object motive, which in turn directs the participation of the actors in activities. He explained object motive, somewhat opaquely, as follows: 'The main thing that distinguishes one activity from another, however, is the difference in their objects. It is exactly the object of activity that gives it a determined direction. According to the terminology I have proposed, the object of activity is its true motive' (Leont'ev 1978, p. 17).

Let's unpack this statement using the breakfast example. The object of activity for this indulgent grandmother is the breakfast food she is working on: toast, coffee, pancakes. The outcome is a well-fed and cared-for family. While working on the food, the object motive for her is giving pleasure to a grandchild; hence she deviates from her plans, finds a recipe and makes pancakes. Giving pleasure to a visiting grandchild matters to her and she sees in the pancakes a way of giving it. The object motive (giving pleasure) is therefore both embedded in the object of activity (breakfast food) and in what she brings to the activity (being a grandmother involves indulging grandchildren).

In a more serious example, a social worker might have a child's trajectory of social exclusion as an object of activity, something she is working on and trying to reconfigure. While interpreting the object of activity, her expertise as a social worker will lead her to see the trajectory in terms of what matters to her professionally, such as the strength of the family network. The object motive for her will then lead her to strengthening the family network to put support around the child. Her actions, as she works on the object of activity, are given direction by the object motive, i.e., what she recognises as important in the object of activity. A teacher, on the other hand, might read the trajectory differently, with the child's educational success as the object motive, leading her to focus on school attendance in her actions in response to the problem of social exclusion.

While Leont'ev's view of motive helps us connect action to practice through the idea of object motive, there are considerable analytic challenges in the dialectic emphasis on how mind and action arise in and may also shape societal conditions in both his and Vygotsky's work. One useful response to the challenge comes from Hedegaard, who has been refining a conceptual framework consisting of interconnected planes of analysis, which emphasise the motives to be found at each plane and offers a way of designing research to attend to the dialectic. Table 8.1 shows a slight adaptation of this framework (Hedegaard 2012).

Table 8.1 allows us to see how activities are located in practices which are imbued with motives which may, for example, mediate national or regional

Table 8.1 Planes of Analysis (after Hedegaard, 2012)

Entity	Process	Dynamic
Society	Political economy	Societal needs/conditions
Institution (e.g., a school, department, team, family …)	Practice	Values/motives/objectives
Activity setting (e.g., a lesson, meeting, evening meal …)	Activity/situation (with potential for individual learning)	Motivation/demands
Person	Actions in an activity (which may or may not give rise to learning)	Motive/intentions

policies and provide constraints and affordances for individual actions within activities. For example, government policies might require social workers to offer quick solutions rather than undertake long-term work with families. But the practices within a social work team may still value family work and hence mediate and downplay the emphasis on quick solutions, to allow actions which focus on strengthening the family. Equally, an individual social worker may want to emphasise family work but finds herself in a team which follows government demands. There therefore may be a difference in motives at the institutional and personal planes, which will mean that the researcher will be alerted to how the social worker navigates institutional expectations to take forward what matters for her as a professional.

Hedegaard developed this framework while studying young children's transitions between home and school (Hedegaard & Fleer 2008) and how they learnt in each activity setting. A key Vygotskian concept in her analysis was the social situation of development (Vygotsky 1998). I will not elaborate on its implications for human development, but simply explain three features which are relevant to this discussion of practices. First, the social situation of development offered by an activity is always potential, whether learning or development occurs depends on what demands are recognised by the actor and how she responds to them. Second, the actor therefore creates her own social situation of development as she agentically approaches the object of activity, engages with demands and propels herself forward. Third, the object motive that arises in the interaction of person in activity is likely to be mediated by the motives in the practices in which the activity is located.

Table 8.1 therefore helps the analyst recognise how historical practices may mediate external demands and in turn place demands on actors in activities within the practices. But the interlinking of societal conditions, institutional motives and interpretations of and responses to activities in Table 8.1 also points to the challenges involved in making transitions between practice; radically changing practices, or creating new ones; and collaborating across practice boundaries. In the sections that follow, each of these processes are discussed from the perspective of the cultural-historical framings I have outlined.

Transitions across practice boundaries

Because of the dialectic between person and activity in practice it is impossible for a cultural-historical analyst to work with a notion of transfer, where knowledge acquired in one setting is simply applied in another. Instead the cultural-historical researcher follows sense-making actors as they move between practices and attempt to interpret the opportunities and demands within them. Three researchers who have particularly contributed to accounts of these transitions are Holland, Dreier and Beach. I shall look at each in turn moving from Holland's account of practice landscapes and their navigation, to Dreier's attention to how practices differ and are negotiated when people move between them, and finally to Beach's attention to the individual as they make transitions which are of consequence to them.

Holland's work (Holland et al. 1998) does not overtly tackle transitions; but her notion of how practices in institutions form a 'figured world' which is interpreted and navigated with varying degrees of expertise is extremely helpful when following trajectories that move across practices. The team define figured world as follows: '. . . a socially and culturally constructed realm of interpretation in which particular characters ad actors are recognized, significance is attached to certain acts, and particular outcomes are valued over others' (Holland et al. 1998, p. 52). Holland's own work has focused on single institutions, such as the life of romance in a US college and alcoholics anonymous. With a direct focus on transitions, Lundsteen used this framing to study how Oxford University undergraduate interns interpreted and navigated the new-to-them figured world of the trading floor at an international bank (Lundsteen 2011), while Tan is currently drawing on it in a doctoral study to raise questions about how student teachers are supported as they move between different school placements during their one year teacher education programme. Using the concept of figured worlds, he has found that when student teachers moved between schools, they needed to start from scratch in identifying what is significant, what outcomes are valued and so on in their new school placements, in ways that impede their expected progress through course requirements (Tan in progress).

Holland's concept of figured worlds, in part, addresses Dreier's concern that a study of transition needs to start with an analysis of the practices to be encountered (Dreier 1999). His premise is that the psychological aspects of human action should be studied as part of practices and therefore analyses benefit from starting with attention to practices. His background is in psychotherapy, where he noticed the efforts made by clients as they took forward their life trajectories and moved between different contexts (Dreier 2000). His concern is therefore primarily the individual subject and their transitions across different configurations of social practices as they take part in everyday life. In discussing how individuals position themselves and take different stances in different practices, he calls for more attention to how contexts are structured and inter-related within wider societal configurations. From a therapy perspective, he suggests that attention should be paid to the structuring of what he terms contextual practices, to enable the participation of people in activities within them. This point is also relevant to the experiences of interns and student teachers as they move into new practices in which they are expected to learn very quickly.

While Dreier argues for the need to start from an analysis of practices in order to get to grips with the subjective aspects of transitions, Beach returns us to a cultural-historical focus on motives to give insight into the dialectical nature of engagement with practices and its implications for individuals as they make transitions. His seminal paper (Beach 1999) is a strong argument against notions of transfer in education, replacing them with the idea of consequential transitions. This is a concept that focuses simultaneously on learners and social organisations that aims at capturing '. . . the recursive and mutually constitutive relationship to one another across time' (Beach 1999, pp. 111). Central to the idea of consequential transition is that there is 'a developmental change in the relation between an individual and one or more social activities . . . Transitions are consequential when they are consciously reflected on, often struggled with, and the eventual outcome changes one's sense of self and social positioning' (Beach 1999, pp. 114).

A consequential transition may therefore involve repositioning oneself in a practice, such as succeeding in maths after years of failure. But they can also apply to movements between practices such as from school to work. The 1999 paper offers a tentative typology of transitions and points to the implications of these for research design. A key element here is the idea of 'developmental coupling', which 'encompasses aspects of both changing individuals and changing social activity' (Beach 1999, pp. 120). This is a rich line of argument which Beach extends by drawing on Leont'ev to explain how these developmental couplings are also located in the broader themes of cultural conditions. Therefore, like Dreier, but with an educational focus, he suggests there is much to be gained from paying attention to examining similarities of practices inside and outside schools and in particular by 'expanding the boundaries of school activities in to culturally productive activities that are beyond its current purview. . . .' in order to aid these transitions (Beach 1999, p. 132).

Radically changing or creating new practices

A cultural-historical notion of practices, by acknowledging both their historicity and the agency of actors in them, points to how practices may operate as stabilising forces, which call for strong agency on the part of actors if they are to be changed. Indeed, Table 8.1 indicates how practices are constructed in a recursive relationship between societal conditions and individual actions in activities and therefore how difficult it is to change historically constructed institutional practices simply through shifts in what people do in activities. As Lave observed, practices enable us to have an ordered life: 'People are engaged in on-going activity far more than they are paralyzed into suspended action' (Lave 1988, p. 176).

Lave's starting point was practice and the knowledge embedded in it. Yet she concludes, like Hedegaard, that 'the activity of persons-acting in setting' (p. 177) is the most useful unit of analysis for examining the crucial iteration between person and practice. This analytic focus, she suggests, allows attention to cognition within a theory of practice. She goes on to argue, like so many of the cultural-historical theorists discussed here, that this complex unit of analysis also requires attention to 'relations between sociocultural structure and social practice' (Lave 1988, p. 177).

This unit of analysis, embedded within these relations, was taken into her influential work with Wenger (Lave & Wenger 1991), where they examined the processes of apprenticeships into existing practices, coining the term 'community of practice'. In their 1991 book, the focus on the practices called for by Dreier is found in descriptions such as: 'To take decentred view of master-apprentice leads to an understanding that mastery lies not in the master but in the organization of the community of practice of which the master is a part . . .' (Lave & Wenger 1991, p. 94). Lave's work quite clearly indicates that her understanding of the cognitive aspects of coming to know and act do not lie entirely outside the mind of actor, but the idea of community of practice appears, as I have argued elsewhere (Edwards 2005a, 2007), to have played to a widely felt need for an ordered view of sustained practice for many researchers. What the notion of community of practice does offer, however, is a reminder of how difficult it is to accomplish radical change in practices. At the very least change involves shifts in motive at each of the analytic planes found in Table 8.1, together with an alignment of the new motives. These changes cannot easily be imposed, but need to espoused and integrated into the actions of actors in activities in practices that provide the wherewithal for them to be taken forward.

One example of where this change has recently been accomplished is the implementation of a new form of pupil assessment, introduced through government policy, in secondary schools in Norway. Hermansen followed teacher teams in three schools while they engaged in what she called 'knowledge work', which she defined in cultural-historical terms as 'the actions that teachers carry out as they work with and upon the knowledge that informs their professional practice' (Hermansen 2014, pp. 470). Their knowledge work in relation to pupil assessment allowed the teachers to recognise the histories and motives in the different schools' practices in relation to assessment and its purposes, and to move forward to a jointly produced and co-owned revised version of future assessment practice in each school.

Hermansen's study indicates the need for motives at each plane of analysis to be broadly aligned and therefore the value of allowing institutions to allocate time for knowledge work. Knowledge work of the kind identified in the teacher team study included attention to motives in institutional practices: how they are played out in the way activities are approached, and in the actions in the activities. Time is therefore needed to ensure that new ideas are worked with and on both cognitively and affectively to create the opportunities for changes in 'mental landscape [which] make new thoughts possible' (Bazerman 2012, p. 260). These changes may, as in Hermansen's research, produce tailored responses to policy demands that fit school values; but they may also lead to strong resistance to policies that do not align with the motives of participants and the practices they inhabit.

Studies of the creation of new practices are less common than accounts of adaptations of existing practices. Software engineering is one example of a newly formed practice. It is particularly marked by being responsive to technical innovations and to new demands from clients. It is therefore open to constant change and lacks the stabilising forces of historicity. Several software engineers were studied in the University of Oslo ProLearn project, and were found to be making efforts to create stable practices by devising their own very explicit professional standards. The motive in their creation of their practice in that way appeared to be to keep abreast of changing technologies, without compromising the quality of their work (Nerland 2008).

The attention the engineers gave to standards in order to ensure consistency in quality points to the importance of the dialectic between person and practice found in cultural-historical accounts of practice. Without the demands in the practice, the practitioner is in danger of becoming the kind of overweening self, the product of modernity discussed by Taylor (Taylor 1991). There is therefore an argument to be made for the role of practice in sustaining ordered lives.

Collaborating across practice boundaries

The third set of challenges offered by the cultural-historical dialectical account of practices shown in Table 8.1 is collaboration across practice boundaries, whether inter-professional or professional and client. I have elaborated these challenges and responses to them in some detail elsewhere (Edwards 2005b, 2010, 2011, 2012) and here simply discuss some of the key concepts offered by a cultural-historical analysis.

First, the definition of practice given at the beginning of this chapter (Edwards 2010) reveals how central the notion of knowledge is to cultural-historical accounts; knowledge is embedded in resources, ways of interpreting and acting as well as in the mental categorisations of practitioners in the practices. This knowledge, these ways of knowing and ways of interpreting and responding, comprise the expertise that enables an actor to take their intentions forward in a practice. In inter-professional collaborations and in working with clients, this expertise is what each person brings to the exchange. Consequently I have come to recognise the importance of the work that occurs at the boundaries of practices, where the expertise from different practices is brought to bear on a complex problem, such as the developmental trajectory of a vulnerable child. In my own research I have found that collaborations of this kind are more effective when they occur in 'sites of intersecting practices' (Edwards 2010, p. 41) than when a practitioner from one practice is parachuted into another practice and expected to make a difference. The dialectic discussed in this chapter would explain why the parachuting model is doomed.

In analysing the work that occurs at these sites of intersecting practices I have identified three concepts that appear to explain successful collabora-tions: relational expertise, common knowledge and relational agency (Edwards 2010, 2012, 2016). These are the labels I have given to aspects of the expertise exercised by the practitioners who accomplished effective inter-professional work. The labels reflect practitioners' capacity to recognise and work with the motives in the professional practice of collaborators.

The first and super-ordinate concept, relational expertise, is a capacity to work relationally with others on complex problems. It involves collaboration in the interpretation of the problem as well as in the response, so that the object of activity is jointly expanded to reveal its complexity. It involves being professionally multi-lingual, recognising the meanings that different practices give to words and their importance in each practice discourse. From a cultural-historical perspective, it is a capability that can be broken down into being able to: (1) recognise the standpoints and motives of those who inhabit other practices, and (2) mutually align motives in interpreting and responding to a problem.

Relational expertise is therefore an extra form of expertise, which is in addition to specialist expertise as a social worker or teacher and focuses on responsive collaborations. But these collaborations needed to be mediated, and this is where the idea of motive in practice comes to the fore in the concept of common knowledge. The common knowledge that was relevant to, for example, inter-professional collaboration was not knowledge of how to do each other's jobs. Instead, common knowledge, as the concept has been developed in my work, consists of the professional motives for each practitioner, i.e., what matters in each profession, the motives that shape and take forward their professional practice.

Common knowledge, once we see it as a respectful understanding of different professional motives, can then become a resource, which can mediate responsive collaborations on complex problems such as a child's trajectory towards social exclusion. For example, knowledge of each other's motives allows the teacher to recognise why the social worker needs time to strengthen the family before key decisions are made. At the same time, the social worker can recognise why school attendance, attainment and social inclusion are important for the teacher.

Common knowledge needs to be created. My analyses have shown that it is built over time in interactions in sites of intersecting practices, which overtly emphasise the following:

- Recognising similar long-term goals, such as children's wellbeing, as some kind of affective or value-laden glue that holds all motives together;
- Revealing specific professional values and motives in discussions, by legitimising asking for and giving reasons for interpretations and suggestions; and
- Listening to, recognising and engaging with the values and motives of others.

Elsewhere I have argued that sites of intersecting practices, where reasons are given and considered seriously, are places where common knowledge, the knowledge of the motives in the potentially collaborating practices, can be made visible (Edwards 2016).

Common knowledge is of course important when planning support for a family over time, but it is perhaps most crucially important when action needs to be taken quickly. The third concept, relational agency, is a way of explaining what happens in those circumstances. I first recognised it as a conceptual tool, able to explain joint action, while observing how family workers supported vulnerable women in a drop-in centre for women with mild mental health problems (Edwards 2005b). The joint agency that ensued, for example when the workers helped the service users to negotiate payments of arrears in their utility bills, meant the service users were powerful in these negotiations. The concept was later tested in analyses in other studies of inter-professional work where it explained how responses in the heat of action were strengthened through joint action, which drew on common knowledge (Edwards 2010, 2011, 2012). Understanding of each other's motives enabled quick calibrations of responses, based on an awareness of what mattered in the practices inhabited by each collaborator.

These three concepts have now been taken up and their explanatory power tested in a number of projects where collaboration between different practices is crucial. These include sites as varied as family work and inter-professional collaboration in early education in Australia, school leadership in Chile, how commercial sales strategies interact with those aimed at poverty reduction in Kenya, and networked collaborations based in Finland (Edwards 2016).

Two of the chapters recounting these projects in the 2016 collection have also reflected on how these concepts may inform the negotiation of relationships between researchers and participants in the practices they are studying or intervening in (Hasse 2016; Hedegaard 2016). Researchers who take a cultural-historical approach need to be attuned to how their own presence may disrupt activities and the practices in which they are located. Indeed, at times they intend to be disruptive in order to elicit tacitly held meanings. There is therefore a pressing need to reflect on researcher-research participant relationships.

I have also tested the three concepts in a study of knowledge exchange in the social sciences (Edwards & Stamou 2016). In that study, participants, who were successful in achieving high impact for their research, were asked to explain what they do to ensure their impact on policy, practice or both. Data collection focused on their actions in activities in and across academic and research user practices, such as academic geography and urban planning. We found that every participant had created sites for two-way knowledge exchange between researchers and potential users of the research. In these sites what mattered, the motives for researchers and for participants in the research sites, was made visible and discussed. The common knowledge that arose in these discussions became a resource for the researchers as they planned and took forward their projects. The researchers recognised that knowledge exchange aimed at research impact called for a relational form of expertise which was in play throughout the research process, in addition to their specialist knowledge as statisticians or sociologists.

In summary, practices and the expertise located in them are necessarily highly boundaried. Consequently ways of understanding how the expertise can be brought into play when needed are required. Collaborations of the kind just outlined attempt to respect the history, ways of knowing and stabilising functions of practices, while recognising that new problems may call for fresh interpretations and new responses which benefit from a mix of expertise.

Final reflections

In pulling together the threads of this account of Vygotsky and Leont'ev's legacies for an understanding of practice, I have almost entirely ignored the vast literature on discourse and practice within the cultural-historical field. Here I can only acknowledge the gap, pointing the reader towards Bazerman on genre and research writing within the tradition (Bazerman 2012) and to the interesting work at the Linnaeus Research Centre at Gothenburg carried out by Mäkitalo and Säljö and their colleagues (Hjörne & Säljö 2004; Mäkitalo 2006; Mäkitalo & Säljö 2002).

Instead, the chapter has focused on the implications of a strong and fruitful dialectic between potentially agentic actors and the demands they encounter as they interpret and engage with the problems of practice. In the three strands of work examined here – transitions across practice boundaries, changing or creating practices, and collaboration across boundaries – I have indicated how this dialectic manages to overcome problems such as transfer, which more dualistic accounts of practice find difficult to handle.

But the cultural-historical approach also creates new challenges for researchers. Not the least of these is the need to combine attention to societal conditions, institutional practices, the activities that occur in them and the intentional actions carried out in them. The solution, as so many of the studies mentioned have recognised, is to follow actions in activities, while recognising how institutional practices may mediate societal demands and so limit the possibilities for action within an activity. Here the dialectic and attention to the motivated agency of the actor becomes a crucial aspect of cultural-historical theory's non-dualistic understanding of practice.

References

Bazerman, C 2012, 'Writing with concepts: Communal, internalized, and externalized', *Mind, Culture, and Activity*, vol. 19, no. 3, pp. 259–272.

Beach, K 1999, 'Consequential transitions: A sociocultural expedition beyond transfer in education' *Review of Research in Education*, vol. 24, pp. 101–139.

Cole, M 1996, *Cultural psychology: A once and future discipline*, Harvard University Press, Cambridge, MA.

Dreier, O 1999, 'Personal trajectories of participation across contexts of social practice', *Outlines*, vol. 1, no. 1, pp. 5–32.

Dreier, O 2000, 'Psychotherapy in clients' trajectories across contexts', in C Mattingly & L Garro (eds), *Narratives and the cultural construction of illness and healing*, University of California Press, Berkeley CA, pp. 237–258.

Edwards, A 2005a, 'Let's get beyond community and practice: The many meanings of learning by participating', *The Curriculum Journal*, vol. 16, no. 1, pp. 53–69.

Edwards, A 2005b, 'Relational agency: Learning to be a resourceful practitioner', *International Journal of Educational Research*, vol. 43, no. 3, pp. 168–182.

Edwards, A 2007 'An interesting resemblance: Vygotsky, mead and American pragmatism', in H Daniels, M Cole & J Wertsch (eds), *The Cambridge companion to Vygotsky*, Cambridge University Press, Cambridge, pp. 77–100.

Edwards, A 2010, *Being an expert professional practitioner: The relational turn in expertise*, Springer, Dordrecht.

Edwards, A 2011, 'Building common knowledge at boundaries between professional practices', *International Journal of Educational Research*, vol. 50, no. 1, pp. 33–39.

Edwards, A 2012, 'The role of common knowledge in achieving collaboration across practices', *Learning, Culture and Social Interaction*, vol. 1, no. 1, pp. 22–32.

Edwards, A (ed.) 2016, *Working relationally in and across practices: Cultural-historical approaches to collaboration*, Cambridge University Press, New York.

Edwards, A. & Stamou, E forthcoming, 'Knowledge exchange in the social sciences: The role of relational expertise', in A Edwards (ed.), *Working relationally in and across practices: Cultural-historical approaches to collaboration*, Cambridge University Press, New York.

Engeström, Y 1999, 'Activity theory and individual and social transformation', in Y Engeström, R Miettinen & R-L Punamäki (eds), *Perspectives on Activity Theory*, Cambridge University Press, Cambridge, pp. 19–38.

Engeström, Y 2007, 'Putting Vygotsky to work: The change laboratory as an application of double stimulation', in H Daniels, M Cole & J Wertsch (eds), *The Cambridge Companion to Vygotsky*, Cambridge University Press, Cambridge, pp. 363–382.

Hasse, C forthcoming, 'Research as relational agency: Expert ethnographers and the cultural force of technologies', in A Edwards (ed.), *Working relationally in and across practices: Cultural-historical approaches to collaboration*, Cambridge University Press, New York.

Hedegaard, M 2012, 'The dynamic aspects in children's learning and development', in M Hedegaard, A Edwards & M Fleer (eds), *Motives in children's development: Cultural-historical approaches*, Cambridge University Press, New York, pp. 9–27.

Hedegaard, M forthcoming, 'When day-care professionals' values for transition to school do not align with the educational demands from society and school', in A Edwards (ed.), *Working relationally in and across practices: Cultural-historical approaches to collaboration*, Cambridge University Press, New York.

Hedegaard, M & Fleer, M 2008, *Studying children: A cultural-historical approach*, Open University Press, Buckingham.

Hermansen, H 2014, 'Recontextualising assessment resources for use in local settings: Opening up the black box of teachers' knowledge work', *The Curriculum Journal*, vol. 25, no. 4, pp. 470–494.

Hjörne, E & Säljö, R 2004, '"There is something about Julia": Symptoms, categories, and the process of invoking attention deficit hyperactivity disorder in the Swedish school: A case study', *Language, Identity and Education*, vol. 3, no. 1, pp. 1–24.

Holland, D, Lachicotte, W, Skinner, D & Cain, C 1998, *Identity and agency in cultural worlds*, Harvard University Press, Cambridge, MA.

Lave, J 1988, *Cognition in practice*, Cambridge University Press, Cambridge, MA.

Lave, J & Wenger, E 1991, *Situated Learning: Legitimate peripheral participation*, Cambridge University Press, Cambridge, MA.

Leont'ev, AN 1978, 'The problem of activity in psychology', in *Activity, consciousness and personality*, Prentice Hall, Upper Saddle River, NJ, retrieved 21 April 2016, <http://marxists. anu.edu.au/archive/leontev/works/1978>.

Lundsteen, N 2011, 'Learning between university and the world of work', PhD Social Sciences Thesis, University of Oxford, retrieved 21 April 2016, University of Oxford Research Archive, <http://ora.ox.ac.uk/objects/uuid:f2686c18–4133–4561–9835–ae0e3f6ab8d9>.

Mäkitalo, Å 2006, 'Effort on display: Unemployment and interactional management of moral accountability', *Symbolic Interaction*, vol. 29, no. 4, pp. 531–556.

Mäkitalo, Å & Säljö, R 2002, 'Invisible people: Institutional reasoning and reflexivity in the production of services and "social facts" in public employment agencies', *Mind, Culture, and Activity*, vol. 9, no. 3, pp. 160–178.

Nerland, M 2008, 'Knowledge cultures and the shaping of work-based learning: The case of computer engineering', *Vocations and Learning: Studies in vocational and professional education*, vol. 1, no. 1, pp. 49–69.

Roth, M & Lee, Y-J 2007, '"Vygotsky's neglected legacy" cultural historical activity theory', *Review of Educational Research*, vol. 77, no. 2, pp. 186–232.

Tan, D (in progress), 'How student teachers learn to use AfL as a pedagogic tool', PhD thesis in progress, University of Oxford.

Taylor, C 1977, 'What is human agency?', in T Mischel (ed.), *The self: Psychological and philosophical issues*, Oxford University Press, Oxford, pp. 103–135.

Taylor, C 1989, *Sources of the self: The making of modern identity*, Cambridge University Press, Cambridge, MA.

Taylor, C 1991, *The ethics of authenticity*, Harvard University Press, Cambridge, MA.

Vygotsky, LS 1997, *The collected work of LS Vygotsky. Vol. 3 the problem of the theory and history of psychology*, Plenum Press, New York.

Vygotsky, LS 1998, *The collected work of LS Vygotsky. Vol. 5 child psychology*, Plenum Press, New York.

Chapter 9

The development of a text counselling practice

An actor-network theory account

Ailsa Haxell

Introduction

> 'Cn I js txt, coz I don wanna b hrd'

To not be seen, to not be heard: to interact silently and at a distance seems an oddity for the practice of counselling. Counselling has been so aligned with what has been collectively referred to as talking therapies and to a client 'feeling heard', that counselling by text would seem an absurdity. However, with the advent of text-capable mobile phones, text messaging has become a preferred option for young people in New Zealand when communicating at a distance (Thompson & Cupples 2008) and this shift has had significant impact for Youthline (NZ), a youth-oriented counselling helpline[1]. At Youthline, the helpline phones hardly ring anymore. Young people still have problems, and Youthline's volunteers still provide assistance, but this now occurs in the near-silent spaces of text or SMS messaging. This chapter therefore considers just how a practice so strongly aligned with talking evolves when it is silenced.

In this chapter, the question of whether a change to Youthline's counselling practice is good or bad is not addressed. Such evaluative concerns are unable to be addressed in the abstract. In the abstract we cannot know if talking to strangers is good or bad, or talking loudly or quietly, or whether long sentences are more effective than short ones, or if counselling verbally or by texted SMS messaging is better. To each of these statements, the answer has to be 'it depends'. This chapter focuses instead on articulating the relationships negotiated that have lead to, and sustain, a change in practice, and in so doing opens up possibilities: for things might also, always be done otherwise.

At Youthline, altering commonly held conceptions of what counselling involves places the organisation in a difficult situation. The organisation, being a charitable trust, is dependent on goodwill and philanthropy for funding. Funding bodies want to know that the practice is valid, or at least that it does no harm. A dilemma emerges: there is no evidence base for this practice – for new practice there never is. This brings forward a further conundrum: how do practices evolve when tied to measures developed in a past? In wanting to be responsive to current demands, how is this space of past and present traversed?

This chapter addresses questions such as these by drawing on actor-network theory (ANT). ANT puts to work a range of interrelated concepts that together might be considered as providing a sensibility, an interruption or an intervention, for drawing nearer a phenomenon (Fenwick & Edwards 2010); and, thus, an ANT account serves quite a different purpose to more conventional research accounts of innovation and change. In providing a rich descriptive account of the relations involved, an ANT-informed analysis focuses not on the design, implementation and diffusion of a particular practice, but on the mutual shaping of things *in relation*.

A heterogeneous array of actors

An ANT-informed analysis involves the recognition of heterogeneous actors – human and otherwise. The defining feature of an actor is that it *acts upon* or changes another – it is a *mediator*, not an *intermediary* (Latour 2005). Actors are also made in association, and the use of the term actor-network – with the hyphen – points to this, where a network is what is traced in the researcher's account of what actors make one another do (see Latour 2005, p. 108). Given the view that actors are made in association, the boundaries between things human and other, or social and technical, dissolve. This is a foundational aspect of ANT and is reflected in the seminal writings of ANT theorists, who proposed a radical democratising of things social and technical, invoking what has come to be known as a principle of generalised symmetry (Callon 1986; Latour 1987). Given that entities of all kinds are effects of network relations, these theorists assert that all entities human or non-human, technical or social, need to be discussed on the same terms.

When thinking of counselling we would likely imagine a counsellor and a client, and most probably imagine these two beings as situated within the same room. When considering why someone initiates counselling, it is perhaps too easy to see this as individually located with some personal inadequacy to be addressed. In turn we tend to imagine a counselling scenario as involving just the client and a counsellor. However, for many people it is because relationships are a concern that they are seeking counselling. Therefore brought into the counselling space are memories from prior relationships as well as hopes for future ones. In what is talked of, the numbers of actors therefore grows. For the counsellor also, the past is brought into the present. Influences on the counsellor will include theorists and prior working relationships, and so it goes on. Have those involved slept and eaten well? Does the state of the building provide against the elements? Might the chairs sat upon add or detract from a sense of comfort, or even add or detract from the effectiveness of a counselling session? The influences of non-human actors – such as seating arrangements – seem less evident in current times although the symbolic counselling and therapy cliché of Freud's couch persists to this day. Those that would influence a counselling relationship extend then to actors – human and otherwise – those physically present as well as distant, and where such distance might be spatial or temporal.

The socio-technical interactions are multi-layered. Youthline's telephone counselling could not occur without phones. In making a telephone, humans are involved. In addition, humans are not left unmoved by their associations with such technologies. I can speak to the other side of the world when my voice is carried by a phone call; and to a similar scale my hearing is amplified. That this becomes possible is an outcome of a network of hundreds and thousands of actors, dispersed around the world and even beyond. For telephony to be operational there is a network of people and things involved. For example, this includes copper wires as well as the people involved in mining for copper and industrial processes of smelting raw copper and creating wire. In addition is a plastics industry that contributes to the manufacturing of phones. Needed also are staff employed by Telecom service providers, and the associated technologies enabling every connection to be traced and billed. In addition are people who generate further customers in advertising and customer relations, through to those involved in a space programme that made it possible to have satellites through which telephone signals might pass, and so it goes on. The assemblage of actors would seem never-ending[2].

However, to view actors as separate entities is also problematic. Law (2012) explores how associations do not just occur at the borders between entities but permeate our very being. In taking the unusual example of salmon in a pond, he points out that the water around the salmon, and the water in the salmon, co-evolve. One does not exist without the other. Were we to consider actors in the network of associations leading to text counselling at Youthline, similar arbitrary divisions between actors might also be shown to be more permeable than might at first be assumed. In this discussion of how practice is shaped, those who counsel, and those who need counselling, co-evolve.

Tracing associations

In accepting actors as beings made in association, it follows that agency does not reside individually but is distributed. ANT therefore provides for a distinctive understanding of innovation and change, where humans are not privileged as having 'world making' capacity. Instead, a relational view of agency is supported. Latour notes that the role of an ANT account is to deploy diverse actors in their full by tracing the agencies that are making them act (see Latour 2005, p. 184). In tracing agencies, each connection in a network is seen as providing an alteration or 'translation' on what occurred previously. A 'theory of change' is therefore a 'theory of translation' (Latour 1996, 2005) and describing the relationships and the negotiations involved becomes integral to an ANT account.

Deploying the myriad actors is one part of an ANT account, but it is the movements between them, and the minutiae of detail involved in such relationships, that provides challenge. With increasing alliances and associations, the durability of a particular practice might be enhanced, and the converse is also true. Where associations flounder, a given practice is unlikely to be sustained. However, if such attachments and changes occur continuously across a network, where then does one start or stop? And where might tracing the threads of such associations be cut? Strathern (1996) notes that networks do not cut themselves and that, in reality, one cannot trace connections forever. Networks do not have definitive edges, neither spatially nor temporally, and being 'in the middle of things' (Latour 2005, p. 196), with vibrant things (Bennet 2010), is a particularly difficult space. The actors do not stay still when gazed upon, and similarly, the person gazing is not unmoved.

In explicating, we too are implicated: layer upon layer, 'fold upon fold' (Latour 2003, p. 6). This research position is not unique to ANT, but is also evident in the work of feminist writers such as Haraway (1992), who argued there is no 'view from nowhere'. In discussing agential realism, Barad (2007) takes this further. She argues, not only is there no clear line between subject and object, but there is also no possible demarcation between a knower and what is known. She argues that nothing is inherently seperate, but the act of observing makes a cut of inclusion and exclusion. For the researcher there is then no neutrality. A cut is made; a point of interest is brought into focus; certain practices are deemed more and less relevant; certain aspects of a network are made more and less visible with what is written in and written out. The network brought forward in this account is selected for a reader to appreciate the heterogeneity of actors involved, how they shape each other, the ways alliances form, and the agency of the non-human in this. This brings forward an unusual account of change that unsettles conventional notions of human agency and organisational change with respect to practice.

My own experience with Youthline began almost thirty years ago. I have been a Youthline volunteer providing telephone and face-to-face counselling, teaching their volunteers basic counselling skills, and providing clinical supervision for counselling. The account I present relates to conversations I had when interviewing staff and volunteers at Youthline involved in the provision of text counselling, interviews with young people who have initiated text counselling conversations with Youthline, as well as an analysis of documents, media releases and digital traces of some 6000 text messages sent and received by Youthline[3]. I start my account at a point marked in time by the gift of a personal digital assitant (PDA) to Youthline in 2004, and I cut the threads of tracing the agencies involved at a point in time when the new practice of text counselling is – at least for a moment – stabilised. I stop at a time in 2008 when the phones at Youthline hardly rang anymore as the near silence of text messaging had replaced the hum of phones ringing and audible conversations occurring.

Tracing associations

A shift from verbal counselling conversations to counselling by text was not planned. In 2004, a law company with which Youthline had long been associated, deployed the costs usually associated with sending out Christmas cards toward the gift of a hand-held PDA that was given to, and gratefully received by, Youthline. Gift giving and receiving involves carefully choreographed movements. There is a hint of a question and subtlety in suggesting mutual benefit. Who initiates the idea? Who selects the gift? These questions are gauche; they place gifting and generosity at risk. The supposition shared was 'If a company were to look at alternative ways of demonstrating generosity at Christmas, Youthline could work with this, right?' and further, 'Might not corporate social responsibility be channeled into good will of an enduring kind?' As discussed by Titmuss (1971) gift giving involves negotiated relationships of accountabilities and responsibilities. In this instance, conspicuous charitability involves a gift that is tangible, novel and attracts media attention. An advertisement – aesthetically presented as a Christmas card – is placed in New Zealand's largest circulating newspaper. In this advertisement the law firm challenges business associates and competitors to contribute with a 'gift that keeps on giving'. This challenge is accepted by one of New Zealand's largest Telecom providers, which agrees to meet the costs of young people texting Youthline.

Costs are important. Youthline is a charitable trust. Philanthropy, volunteerism and goodwill provide for much of Youthline's services. Costs are also a concern for those with mobile phones. When Youthline's text service begins, a five-minute mobile call through either of New Zealand's largest Telecom providers on a prepay plan (the commonest form of mobile phone contract at that time) would cost NZ$4.45, and the New Zealand adult minimal wage at that time was NZ$8.26 per hour after tax. A person would have to work 32 minutes to pay for a five-minute call. The cost of a mobile phone call on Vodafone prepay 'Anytime Plan' or Telecom's 'Anytime Go Prepaid Plan' was NZ$0.89 per minute, in contrast with NZ$0.20 for sending a text message (Haxell 2013). In subsequent years these sustained high costs were described as unacceptable (New Zealand Commerce Commission 2011). It might have been anticipated that young people – whose financial situation is likely to be restricted – would opt to text a helpline, but it was not.

Talking with Jasmine (pseudonym) – who was thirteen when she initiated text contact with Youthline – the impact of financial costs as an actor are confimed. Jasmine shows me her mobile telephone. It is decorated with flowers and words drawn in nail polish and twink (whiteout). A hair-tie keeps the flip-top of this mobile phone attached. Without the flip-top this phone would have the functionality of a paper weight. 'It's a Telecom prepay', she tells me. I told her mine's prepay too but with Vodafone. Jasmine says, 'Where I live everyone's with Telecom but Auckland's mostly Vodafone. It's a pain, it costs more when you text them.' The Telecom companies charge more when calls are sent from a mobile phone to one of their competitors, and so she minimises the costs where possible. On her Telecom prepay plan she selects the 'text extra' option of 1500 texts for $18.00 each month. As she explains, 'When this maxes out, I can top up for a further $5.00'. For Jasmin to need a 'top-up', she would need to have sent more than fifty texts a day. This seems a lot, but I review my assumption when she tells me it's how she keeps in contact with her boyfriend, who her parents dislike.

Jasmine's texting Youthline occurred following a disagreement with her family regarding the relationship she had her boyfriend. She had left home late at night, in winter, in a rugged rural area where there was no street lighting and where houses were several kilometres apart. The ruggedness and isolation of this environment brings forward further actors. For the transmitting of messages, a mobile phone needs to be within range of a cell phone tower. There is continual work undertaken by these non-human actors as mobile phones and cell towers seek out each other's presence. The hidden work of technological entities talking to other technological entities, as towers and phones continually search for each other, is rarely attended to by human actors. The invisibility of such work is well described by Farman (2015), who notes that with or without our knowledge or consent, our cell phones continually track our movements, connecting with global positioning system (GPS) satellites orbiting the earth. Such relating occurs at levels far outside of our human perceptive capabilities. What is attended to is when such work fails. It fails in areas where there are no towers, or where insufficient towers are available for the number of calls or messages occurring at the time; it fails in the 'dead zones' where valleys and mountains cause mobile phone coverage to be patchy. Even without such obvious topographical features, connectivity can fail in spaces between tall buildings, or even within such buildings dependent on the materials used in either interior or exterior walls.

Materiality shapes Jasmine's actions: her phone is always with her; it provides her a means of connecting when she needs it. She does not need to reflect on an event as with a face-to-face appointment; help can be provided in real time addressing concerns of safety. In this instance, her story tells of mountains and valleys as actors that might intrude on connectivity. Being not only cheap and therefore convenient, Jasmine has learnt, whether consciously or not, that the smallness of a text message traverses such barriers as mountains. Her text message can get through when a phone call can not.

Recruiting allies; Strengthening alliances

Jasmine's story is also told to me by her uncle – Stephen – who happens to work at Youthline:

> I have lots of texts with my nieces, and Jasmine's just 13 going on 30 and she lives in the back of beyond. She's having angsty stuff with her parents about boys and relationships and stuff. And she's often texting me, and

sometimes she gives me a call, but there's also me saying try out the Youthline texting thing.

Anyway she took off from home, it's middle of nowhere, and I wasn't available for some reason and anyway she texts Youthline. And she said that she got through it, but she said she felt like she'd done something wrong. She thought she was doing it wrong because they replied back with 'give us a ring here's our number' and she thought they don't really want to text. What she felt was that somehow she'd got it wrong to text; that texting was wrong, and that she was wrong. She got that kind of a message.

Stephen also tells this story at the Youthline annual conference, and with minor variations he repeats it at the Auckland Youthline weekend away for staff and volunteers. And so the story becomes a further actor contributing to the shaping of text counselling. Stephen emphasises how hard it can be for a young person to reach out. He points to the immediate risk to safety and of the damage done to a young person learning that there is no one there for them. He brings the focus of attention to 'being there' for young people in the places of their choosing, asserting 'Youthline has always been about that'. He invokes the language of the World Health Organisation through the Ottawa Charter (World Health Organization 1986) describing effective health services as appropriate, affordable, accessible and *acceptable*. His measure of acceptability is that young people – as users of the service – decide this, and that they will make use of what they experience as being of value.

A counter-narrative regarding the value of text counselling is shared by an experienced counsellor within this organisation. She asks, 'How would a Youthline counsellor respond to a young person nervous of their first sexual relationship? What harm might we (Youthline) cause? Without any cues of age that might be inferred form someone's voice, might Youthline be implicated in condoning a sexual relationship for an underage minor? And also, might a condoning reponse stay in a digital trace and end up in the news doing damage to Youthline?' Those willing to support a text counselling service minimise the concern. They explain that verbal counselling through the helpline similarly provides no assurance of knowing someone's age; even with face-to-face counselling there may be wrong assumptions made. They argue that in texting, just as with other forms of counselling, one can always ask more about the situation before responding.

Both stories prompt the imagination for where the presence or absence of a text counselling service might lead, and hopes and fears are evident in both accounts. The invocation to consider Youthline's reason for being, and aligning this purpose and the activities undertaken with the World Health Organisation is a deft movement of persuasion. There is little room for dispute. There is then a convergence of reason and authority, and an outcome that supports what has been stated by Latour: 'the strongest reason always yields to reasons of the strongest' (Latour 1998). With more counsellors aligning on a pro-texting stance – because there is always an option to ask for more information – internal dissent toward texting is reduced.

Concurrently, a wider community of stakeholders who have supported Youthline historically – including philanthropists as well as external counsellors and psychotherapists – also needs to be maintained. The CEO of Youthline develops a response to challenges. He positions a text message, a phone call and face-to-face meeting as part of a continuum. He places text counselling at one end, face-to-face counselling in the middle ground, and psychotherapy at the far end. The metaphorical spacing means the modalities of counselling need not conflict; those who perceive texting as a 'thin' medium might still align with a services identified as an entry level to further services.

Nonetheless, the boundaries to what is or isn't counselling remain contested. Debate as to who provides counselling or any therapeutic 'talking therapy' is not new in the arena of counselling. Corsini et al. (2008) identify there is nothing that a psychotherapist does that a counsellor does not do, stating 'counselling and psychotherapy are the same qualitatively: they differ only quantitatively' (p. 1). With respect to telephone counselling, Rosenfield (2013) suggests that telephone counselling is different to the emotional support provided by a crisis helpline, as the latter predominantly involves crisis intervention work. In contrast, Tudor (2008) argues the length of counselling interactions, or the number of sessions, are not definitive. Naming this new modality as text counselling, Youthline becomes embroiled in a broader political field of naming and framing that brings forward issues of power and control. While Youthline has provided both telephone and face-to-face counselling since 1975, from 2008 the professional bodies associated with psychotherapy and counselling in New Zealand seek government regulation to become registering boards. The result is a heightened sensitivity to the naming of this particular novel practice.

The differing realities of those who would make use of a service, various counsellors within the organisation, and professional associations that include counselling and psychotherapy, are played off one against the other. This voluntary organisation is keen to sustain a service responsive to young people, whilst also maintaining the willing services of volunteers who provide the service. This occurs concurrently with a need to stay in good standing with the professional organisations whose judgements may impact on funding decisions, both governmental and charitable. Similar contestations are evident in other actor-network theory accounts: Mulcahy (2010) demonstrates this in regard to policy formation within education; similarly Verran (2011) points to the power plays and negotiations undertaken within the arena of environmental politics. Within healthcare also, Mol (2002) describes the conflicting realities espoused by a variety of healthcare professionals and their approach to the treatment of arteriosclerosis. In Mol's account, attention is drawn to how the tension associated with conflicting realities is reduced when there is a geographical separation of the various health professionals; they do not clash when distributed in departments that rarely come together.

Youthline's CEO provides a metaphorical distribution similar to that described by Mol. He positions the text service as a portal — as an entrance to services of greater depth — the wider professional community of counsellors and psychotherapy practitioners remain as allies. He alters his references to the text counselling service when resistance is met, naming the service a provider of emotional support. The service might then continue to be provided regardless of what it is called.

The agency of matter

Much of human behaviour has long been shown to be unconscious (see for example Freud 2005; Jung 2012). Intentions do not necessarily materialise into actions (Armitage & Conner 2001), and explanations for behaviour may not be available on reflection (Blank et al. 2007). As summarised by Bennett (2010), 'in the face of every analysis, human agency remains something of a mystery' (p. 34).

Taking the example of telephone counselling, the impact of a non-human actor becomes apparent. The core skills used in counselling — active listening, conveying empathy, sensitive confrontation — alter when mediated by a phone call. With the absence of nonverbal cues such as body language and eye movements, counsellors become more attuned to the paralinguistic cues of tone, volume, pitch and speed of voice (see for example Rosenfield [2013]). Active listening is altered when attentiveness cannot be demonstrated by nodding or facial responses, and is conveyed instead through an increased use in minimal encouragers (aha, mmm), reflection (restating parts of what was said) and paraphrasing. In the use of 'sensitive confrontation', Rosenfield suggests counsellors should be more cautious in the delivery of probing questions so that empathy is not compromised. Demonstrated in these examples is practice being (re)shaped in and through socio-technical associations.

With text counselling, the texting capacity of the mobile phone places constraints on message size favouring brevity and so texted conversations initiated by young people with Youthline tend to go straight to the heart of the matter. The following opening sentence is received by Youthline, 'Heh. I dont wanna cut anymor. I dnt kno wat 2 do. HELP!!!' The digital traces of text counselling received by Youthline are marked by an absence of social niceties. The sequence of 'troubles talk' (Jefferson 1988) — where a person is talked into talking about their troubles — is disrupted. There is no 'small talk' about unimportant matters while building up to what is really important. There is no discernible phase of rapport or trust building. The dissembodiment of a text message characterised by invisibility, inaudability and seemingly increased anonymity, alongside brevity, allows for leaving the counselling relationship with no 'loss of face'. Being able to leave a session without explanation is also suggestive of having control within the interaction.

The text-capable mobile phone alters how the human actors engage. The act of writing, reading and constructing a brief response makes for a slower conversation than could be had were talking involved. The slowing down of responses is not just in generating a message, but also in making sense of what is seen. Working out what to say when restricted to 160 characters is an unusual imposition on conversations, let alone counselling conversations. When text-capable mobile phones were developed there was no expectation that these would be used for conversations. Texting was not, at least initially, intended such that customers of service providers would be texting each other at all (McVeigh 2012). It was not meant to evolve into the preferred means of communications for young people in New Zealand, or elsewhere. And it certainly was never anticipated that texting would become a preferred means through which young people initiate counselling conversations. The shape of a mobile phone was not made for this; not the small screen; not the 160 character message limit; not the numeric keyboard that multitasks to perform an alphabet. Such changes occur nevertheless, and re/design does occur, but only 'in the middle of things'.

The technology has not compelled particular uses be made of it. That a mobile is even mobile is dependent on its aligning with other actors. There is no technical determinism at play. Instead what is portrayed are movements – negotiations, an enrolment of actors – and just as some alliances develop and are strengthened, others weaken, fail to develop, or even end. And within such relational processes, the actors – human and otherwise – are altered. In ANT terminology, translation is occurring.

Youthline enlists the assistance of a computer technician so that the texted messages can be read on a computer screen that automatically counts the length of any message sent. While Youthline negotiated with Telecom companies not to charge young people making use of their service, there is still a cost to the organisation for each outgoing message. At the time, to exceed the standard length of one SMS message (160 characters) by even one character doubles the costs involved. Migrating the received messages to a computer programme also allows for 'nesting' of the texted messages received, so they can be read as a conversation. Whenever a text message is received, the unique identifier of that person's mobile phone number provides the computerised system with information to cluster all conversations from that phone number together in dated order. As a counselling session may progress across hours, even across days, this introduces a significant alteration to previous forms of counselling; just who is involved becomes so much less easy to discern[4].

Having nested conversations not only removes the need for repetition, but also provides opportunity for clarification or 'sensitive confrontation' as the following response from a counsellor indicates, 'I'm a bit confused. B4 you said "she" but now it's "I". Tell me more about what's going on 4 u.' In the young person's response they explain they had handed the phone over to their friend. Being able to text alongside a friend had made the process of seeking counselling less difficult.

The digital trace remaining on a young person's phone also allows for the young person texting Youthline to reflect on what is written. This is demonstrated in the following interview with Megalyn (pseudonym).

> I liked texting [Youthline]. With a text I can read it and reread it, even the next day. Texting stopped me going round and round in circles, which would have been more distressing. It allowed me to think. Texting made it clearer for me: I could see what I had written, and it became clearer. I solved my own problem, but I don't think I would have if I hadn't texted them.
>
> The best message I got I still remember, it wasn't a suggestion, although it was good to get those too. They're still there. I wanted to keep them, they felt good. I deleted what I texted in, I didn't need my own words. Also I had said things about my Dad. I wondered about what if my boyfriend looked at them so I deleted those.

The written trace stopped Megalyn from going round in circles and retraumatising herself. That a conversation was written allowed for messages to be available for future reference, though this is identified as occurring with both benefit and risk[5]. The materiality of texting allows things that other material arrangements might not, demonstrating agency enacted inside of particular material relations.

Re/assembling practice

I have not described a change in practice as the result of something problematized and solved. This text counselling service is not the result of practitioners actively seeking a solution to problems they identify in their work by reflecting on their practice and deciding to change it[6]. Similarly, what evolves is not the result of any rational planning approach on change involving managerial planning. ANT provides an alternative to both bottom-up and top-down approaches to understanding change. This is quite distinct from how Rogers (2003) characterises innovation; there was neither design nor diffusion. This was not a lineal process moving forward in anticipated steps. In critiquing Roger's diffusion of innovation theory, Bigum (2000) argues there are no essential qualities that inhere to actors in any stable way. Nor are labels such as change champions, early adopters, late adopters and laggards useful in this description of change. Neither human nor non-human actors can be easily typecast. Within every interaction between actors, human or otherwise, are moments of translation as accommodations occur.

What I have described here is practice as it is made and done. Practices are performed moment by moment. That a particular practice becomes more or less stable is a function of multiple alliances formed and maintained, and of the capacity for multiple realities to co-exist. Any of these negotiated relationships might flounder: a phone battery may lose charge; a power cut could prevent the computers at Youthline from working; a change in funding models might influence the preferred means of communication. The stability of a particular practice takes work. There are no identical repetitions. Every occurrence involves different configurations. ANT is therefore not a predictive theory for change; variance is unavoidable. What occurs in one time and place does not travel easily and therefore could not be assumed to be something that might be rolled out elsewhere. The capacity for generalising based on what occurs in one setting is limited in every instance as a different range of actors is involved and their relationships and negotiations will vary.

Law and Singleton (2000) note, 'things don't come to rest in a single form once agreement – or what is called 'closure' – is achieved. They rumble on and on, as it were, noisy and noisome' (p. 775). With changes to telephony enabling Internet connectivity and with increasingly available free Wi-Fi zones, text counselling at Youthline (NZ) is already undergoing change. For new practices to survive, let alone to flourish, there needs to be fluidity in professional practice. While fluidity may appear 'sub-optimal, unregulated, even sloppy' (Law 2002), longevity requires adaptability. In providing a rich descriptive account, identifying heterogeneous actors and their agencies, there is an opportunity to see how practice is being configured also to see that practice might also, always, be configured otherwise.

Conclusion

In this chapter I have sought to invoke an appreciation for practice as involving a network of contingent and precarious relationships. Such relationships are demonstrated as being both more extensive but also more fluid than might first be supposed. Inside of an ANT analysis I have demonstrated text counselling as having evolved through a series of negotiations between heteroneous actors. While providing descriptive accounts of what is, rather than suggesting what should, or could, be done elsewhere, ANT nonetheless provides a means through which possibilities might be considered. While describing what is, it becomes possible to anticipate that the removal or addition of particular actors will have impact. As Youthline positions itself as meeting with young people in the spaces of their choosing, such spaces are already relocating. While future gazing remains an imprecise art, ANT at least prompts consideration for the complexity of practice and of the work undertaken in keeping things the same, as well as work that might be involved in effecting change. By recognising the agency of matter, ANT allows for consideration of how changes in networks might make a difference. More importantly, such considerations matter because some people's realities are difficult enough without being made worse. How then do we negotiate such responsibilities when we do not know with confidence where such activity leads? Suchman (2007) addresses this arguing that our inability to see ourselves within a history of relations derives from a tendency to construct boundaries between others and ourselves. As portrayed here, we are made in association and therefore such boundaries can be renegotiated. To see practices as formed in association opens up questions not only about who and what is involved in the here and now, but about future possibilities also. If we are to hold hope for improving professional practice, for professional practice development that strengthens particular realities over others, then ANT provides enormous potential for deliberations in enacting change in ways that consider how change occurs. In looking for the non-coherence between the accounts of different actors, a range of realities are uncovered, and in moving toward the ontological politics of how accounts of practice might make a difference, we may hope to make a difference. As Law (2009) has stated, 'reality is not destiny'.

Notes

1   Youthline (NZ) is named with permission.
2   A detailed tracing of telephone networks is provided by Spinuzzi (2008)
3   This chapter draws on a larger study undertaken into change and the use of emergent technologies. Two University ethics committees, Deakin University in Melbourne and the Auckland University of Technology approved this research. Identifying information has been removed and the content altered where needed to protect the anonymity of those involved.
4   A subsequent study by Gibson and Cartwright (2014) notes that those making use of the service tend to gloss over this aspect; their experience is one of continuity.
5   While writing within therapeutic interventions has been validated within counselling (see for example Bolton et al. 2006), the practice of text messaging for counselling is not yet so settled as to be written into such texts.
6   As seen for example in Argyris (1997), Argyris (2004), Schön (1990) and Schön and Rein (1994).

References

Argyris, C 1997, 'Initiating change that perseveres', *American Behavioral Scientist*, vol. 40, no. 3, pp. 299–309.
Argyris, C 2004, *Reasons and rationalizations. The limits to organizational knowledge*, Oxford University Press, Oxford, UK.
Armitage, CJ & Conner, M 2001, 'Efficacy of the theory of planned behaviour: A meta-analytic review', *British Journal of Social Psychology*, vol. 40, no. 4, pp. 471–499.
Barad, K 2007, *Meeting the universe halfway: Quantum physics and the entanglement of matter and meaning*, Duke University Press, Durham, NC.
Bennett, J 2010, *Vibrant matter: A political ecology of things*, Duke University Press Durham, NC.
Bigum, C 2000, 'Actor-network theory and online university teaching: Translation versus diffusion', in BA Knight & L Rowan (eds), *Researching futures oriented pedagogies*, Post-Pressed, Flaxton, QLD, pp. 7–22.
Blank, H, Musch, J & Pohl, RF 2007, 'Hindsight bias: On being wise after the event', *Social Cognition*, vol. 25, no. 1, pp. 1–9.
Bolton, G, Howlett, S, Lago, C & Wright, J (eds) 2006, *Writing cures: An introductory handbook of writing in counselling and therapy*, Brunner-Routledge, New York, NY.

Callon, M 1986, 'Some elements of a sociology of translation: Domestication of the scallops and the fishermen of St Brieuc Bay', in J Law (ed.), *Power, action and belief: a new sociology of knowledge?*, Routledge, London, UK, pp. 196–223.

Corsini, RJ, Wedding, D & Dumont, F (eds) 2008, *Current psychotherapies*, Thomson, Belmont, CA.

Farman, J 2015, 'The materiality of locative media: On the invisible infrastructure of mobile networks', in A Herman, J Hadlaw & T Swiss (eds), *Theories of the mobile internet: Mobilities, assemblages, materialities and imaginaries.* Routledge, New York, NY, pp. 45–59.

Fenwick, T & Edwards, R 2010, *Actor-network theory in education*, Routledge, New York, NY.

Freud, S 2005, *The unconscious*, Penguin Books, London, UK.

Gibson, K & Cartwright, C 2014, 'Young people's experiences of mobile phone text counselling: Balancing connection and control', *Children and Youth Services Review*, vol. 43, pp. 96–104.

Haraway, D 1992, 'The promises of monsters. A regenerated politics for inappropriate/d others', in L Grossberg, G Nelson & P Treichler (eds), *Cultural studies*, Routledge, New York, NY, pp. 295–337.

Haxell, A 2013, 'Enactments of change: Becoming textually active at Youthline NZ', Unpublished Doctoral Dissertation, Deakin University, Melbourne, AUS, <http://dro.deakin.edu.au/view/DU:30061580>.

Jefferson, G 1988, 'On the sequential organisation of troublesome talk in ordinary conversation', *Social Problems*, vol. 35, no. 4, pp. 418–441.

Jung, C 2012, *Psychology of the unconscious*, Courier Corporation, North Chelmsford, MA.

Latour, B 1987, *Science in action*, Harvard University Press, Cambridge, MA.

Latour, B 1996, *Aramis: Or the love of technology*, Harvard University Press, Cambridge, MA.

Latour, B 1998, *The pasteurization of France*, Harvard University Press, Cambridge, MA.

Latour, B 2003, *An imaginary dialogue on modernity*, Bruno Latour personal homepage, retrieved 14 April 2016, <http://www.bruno-latour.fr>.

Latour, B 2005, *Reassembling the social*, Oxford University Press, Oxford, UK.

Law, J 2002, 'Objects and spaces', *Theory, Culture and Society*, vol. 19, no. 5–6, pp. 91–105.

Law, J 2009, 'Seeing like a survey', *Cultural Sociology*, vol. 3, no. 2, pp. 239–256.

Law, J 2012, 'Notes on fish, ponds and theory', *Norsk antropologisk tidsskrift*, vol. 23, no. 3–4, pp. 225–236.

Law, J & Singleton, V 2000, 'Performing technology's stories. On social constructivism, performance, and performativity', *Technology and Culture*, vol. 41. no. 4, pp. 765–775.

McVeigh, T 2012, 'Text messaging turns 20', *The Guardian*, 1 December, retrieved 14 April 2016, <https://www.theguardian.com/technology/2012/dec/01/text-messaging-20-years>.

Mol, A 2002, *The body multiple: Ontology in medical practice*, Duke University Press, London, UK.

Mulcahy, D 2010, 'Assembling the "accomplished" teacher: The performativity and politics of professional teaching standards', *Educational Philosophy and Theory*, vol. 43, no. s1, pp. 94–113.

New Zealand Commerce Commission 2011, *Standard terms determination for the designated services of the mobile termination access services (MTAS) fixed-to-mobile voice (FTM), mobile-to-mobile voice (MTM) and short messaging services (SMS). Decision 724*, retrieved 5 May 2011, <http://www.comcom.govt.nz/dmsdocument/7902>.

Rogers, E 2003, *Diffusion of innovation* (5th ed.), Free Press, New York, NY.

Rosenfield, M 2013, *Telephone counselling: A handbook for practitioners*, Palgrave MacMillan, New York, NY.

Schön, D 1990, *Educating the reflective practitioner*, Jossey-Bass, San Francisco, CA.

Schön, D & Rein, M 1994, *Frame reflection. Towards the resolution of intractable policy controversies*, Basic Books, New York, NY.

Spinuzzi, C 2008, *Network: Theorizing knowledge work in telecommunications*, Cambridge University Press, Cambridge, MA.

Strathern, M 1996, 'Cutting the network', *Journal of the Anthropological Institute*, vol. 2, no. 3, pp. 517–535.

Suchman, L 2007, *Human-machine reconfigurations. Plans and situated actions*, Cambridge University Press, Cambridge, UK.

Thompson, L & Cupples, J 2008, 'Seen and not heard? Text messaging and digital sociality', *Social & Cultural Geography*, vol. 9, no. 1, pp. 95–108.

Titmuss, R 1971, *The gift relationship: From human blood to social policy*, Vintage Books, New York, NY.

Tudor, K 2008, *Brief person-centred therapies*, Sage, London, UK.

Verran, H 2011, 'Imagining nature politics in the era of Australia's emerging market in environmental services interventions', *The Sociological Review*, vol. 59, no.3, pp. 411–431.

World Health Organization 1986, 'The Ottawa charter for health promotion', *First international conference on health promotion*, Ottawa, Canada.

Section 3

Practising subjectivity

Chapter 10

Parsing and re-constituting human practice as mind-in-activity

Peter H. Sawchuk

Introduction

There are two main premises that will likely have to be granted for the argument about the value of exploring human practices in the way I recommend below to carry any weight. As we will see, the first premise revolves around dialectics. Specifically, the idea that reality really does depend – ontologically and epistemologically – on the inter-penetrating connections of parts and whole summarized by such notions as a philosophy of internal relations (e.g., Ollman 1993). The second premise involves granting the existence of the thinking, feeling, knowing, choice-making and acting subject who can and does play a role – within and beyond itself vis-à-vis a philosophy of internal relations – in change. Praxis, in any formulation one could imagine, could not be meaningfully entertained otherwise. And, it is in this way that we are faced with the choice of whether or not to take the expanded notions of mind and learning seriously in our concern for human practice. Taken together, I argue these two main premises suggest the need for a theory of mind-in-activity; a substantive, systematic-categorial series of concepts reconstructed from empirical reality with a concern for understanding the practices of human development under the auspices of dialectical methodologies.

Building from these premises, I will argue that what later on in the chapter is referred to as the dialectical 'Humpty Dumpty problem' (Ollman 1998) deserves to be a relevant going concern within critical studies of practice. However, I will also argue that just as concerning should be the tendency to presume, caricature, ignore or otherwise not take seriously those very dimensions of human practice – those connected to our learning and capacity to change ourselves and our world – so central in the successes and failures of our practices, and change, over time. Thus, what follows is a rationale for and explanation of an expansive material dialectics in the study of human practice as a matter of mind-in-activity in the course of two sections. Specifically, the first section provides a discussion of dialectical philosophy that I argue is an essential starting point for an effective theory of practice. In the second section I outline the relationship of dialectical philosophy to Cultural Historical Activity Theory (CHAT), and the notion of mind-in-activity, as exemplar expressions of what Stetsenko (2009) refers to more broadly as the Vygotskian project.

A dialectical foundation for an alternative appreciation of human practice

If there is a case to be made that in the course of the better part of the twentieth century an interest in dialectical thought suffered a decline, then it may be equally fair to say that dialectical thought is making a comeback. Over the last two decades, echoing from various quarters, the clues are detectable: from questions posed in Marxist Human geography (Harvey 2008), in discussions of critical realism (Bhaskar 1993; Roberts 2014), feminism (Hartsock 2008) and perhaps even systems theory (Levins 2008), all the way through to the standing projects of recovery and explication (e.g., Arthur 2002; Ollman 1993; Smith 1993). Concern for an understanding of inherently contradictory non-causal relationships as a system of internal relations in motion appears to be re-assembling.

The decision to forefront the argument for human practice as a matter of mind-in-activity rooted in a recovery of dialectical methodologies is not an arbitrary one. This is because several themes expressed by these methodologies are already partially embedded in many critical perspectives that (as noted in the introduction of this volume) question the reified, mainstream conceptions of practice that have begun to propagate. Exposing such reifications, in fact, is a task for which dialectics is designed. As Zanetti (2003), paraphrasing Herbert Marcuse, summarizes: 'the function of dialectical thought is to break down the self-assurance and self-contentment of common sense, to undermine the sinister confidence in the power and language of facts' (p. 262). In this context, it becomes relevant to not only think about the difference between non-dialectical and dialectical methodologies, but also the difference between oblique, partial or uneven applications of dialectics as opposed to a more *intentional* and *systematic-categorial* approach as well.

Before going further, however, a pre-emptive word of clarification is in order in terms what I have just referred to as intentional and systematic-categorial dialectics. In the following pages the notion of an *intentional* dialectics, drawing on the work of Bertell Ollman, is used primarily as a series of insights into how dialectical methodologies may relate to empirical material. It speaks to techniques that allow us to be dialectical in our analyses. By contrast, the notion of *systematic-categorial* dialectics, drawing on the work of Tony Smith, is used primarily to emphasize an epistemological contribution of a dialectic methodology. It supports the verification of the reconstructed intelligibility of a substantive theory (i.e., a theory dealing with a particular topic of interest) in terms of a totality of relationships. Qualified in these ways, here a dialectical systematic–categorial approach serves as a check on any piecemeal (oblique, partial or uneven) applications of dialectical empirical–analytic procedures. The term I use to represent this combination of emphases is expansive material dialectics.

With these qualifications out of the way, I begin by addressing a basic question. What is the problem to which an expansive material dialectics purports to respond? Beyond Zanetti's general sentiment quoted earlier, we can turn to the work of Ollman.

> No one will deny, of course, that everything in society is related in some way and that the whole of this is changing, again in some way and at some pace. Yet, most people try to make sense of what is going on by viewing one part of society at a time, isolating and separating it from the rest, and treating it as static. [. . .] As a result, looking for these connections and their history becomes much more difficult than it has to be. They are left for last or left out completely, and important aspects of them are missed, distorted, or trivialized. It's what might be called the Humpty Dumpty problem. After the fall, it was not only extremely hard to put the pieces of poor Humpty together again, but even to see where they fit.
>
> (Ollman 1998, pp. 339–340)

Extending this point, for researchers grappling with the potentially bewildering overdeterminations of concrete human practice, dialectical methodologies begin to make sense all the more because the analytic use of formal logic alone is not helpful. As Meikle (1979) notes: 'To the extent that one operates exclusively with ordinary formal logic as it exists, and it exists in a form that centrally builds around timeless, untensed propositions, attention will be directed away from questions of time and change' (p. 8). Following this, a concern for a rich, systematic conceptualization of human practice as a matter of the concrete, overdeterminations of lived reality is antithetical to the exclusive use of formal logic.

In *Dialectical Investigations* (1993) Ollman explains that, at its very heart, formal logic argues that everything in reality is what it is. Drawing on Marx and Hegel, he describes an alternative:

> Marx, on the other hand, following Hegel's lead in this matter, rejects what is, in essence, a logical dichotomy. For him [X] is itself a relation, in which the ties of [Y and Z], etc., are interiorized as parts of what [X] is. Marx refers to "things themselves" as "their interconnections" (Marx & Engels 1950, p. 488). Moreover, these relations extend backward and forward in time, so that [X's] conditions of existence as they have evolved over the years and its potential for future development are also viewed as

parts of what it is. On the common sense view, any element related to [X] can change without [X] itself changing. [. . .] In the history of ideas, the view that we have been developing is known as the *philosophy of internal relations*.

(Ollman 1993, pp. 35–36; emphasis added)

That is, in the classic philosophical notation this is what is meant by X is X, and X cannot be Y or Z; and thus such things (X, Y and Z) may interact with each other, but in the end their identities (as X, Y and Z) remain one thing and their relationships are another.

To be clear, a dialectical philosophy of internal relations does not mean that researching any problem needs to go on forever (i.e. tracing the identity-constitutive relations of everything to everything else) with no points of reference. Abstractions (concepts/categories) we adopt to consider a research problem are not arbitrary. As Ollman says, 'to say that boundaries are artificial is not to deny them an existence, and, practically speaking, it is simply not necessary to understand everything in order to understand anything' (1993, p. 34). Objective distinctions found in material reality (through a body of empirical research) play a definitive role: 'abstractions do not substitute for the facts, but give them a form, an order and a relative value; [they] determine, albeit in a weak sense, what [we] will look for, even see, and of course emphasize' (Ollman 1993, p. 39). Thus, our selection of the topic of interest and all the facts pertaining to it continues to matter a great deal.

Understood as an intentional application of dialectics, we can note that Ollman (1993) goes on to specify a series of procedures directly relevant to the handling of empirical materials (cf. Roberts 2014; Roth 2007; Sawchuk 2003, 2013, 2015). These include the need for the procedures of 'extension' (seeing the past, present and potential/future) of abstractions vis-à-vis empirical materials; and, the need for recognizing standpoints within analysis (e.g., gendered, racialized, classed and so on). Particularly noteworthy for us here are Ollman's discussions of (1) level of generality and (2) contradiction. The former 'enables us to see the unique qualities of any part, or the qualities associated with its function in [a social system], or the qualities that belong to it as part of the human condition' by setting 'a boundary around and bring[ing] into focus a particular level of generality for treating not only the part but the whole system to which it belongs' (Ollman 1993, p. 40). In terms of the latter, he addresses five interpenetrating movements,

[. . .] the two most important ones are the movements of *mutual support* and *mutual undermining*. Pulling in opposite directions, each of these movements exercises a constant, if not even or always evident, pressure on events. The uneasy equilibrium that results lasts until one or the other of these movements predominates. [. . .] A third movement present in contradictions is the *immanent unfolding* of the processes that make up the "legs" of any contradiction. In this way, a contradiction becomes bigger, sharper, more explosive; both supporting and undermining movements become more intense, though not necessarily to the same degree. [. . .] A fourth movement found in contradictions is the *change in overall form* that many undergo through their interaction with other process in the larger system of which they are part. [. . .] The fifth and final movement contained in contradiction occurs in its *resolution* when one side overwhelms what has hitherto been holding it in check, transforming both itself and all its relationships in the process. The resolution of a contradiction can be of two sorts, either temporary and partial or permanent and total.

(Ollman 1993, pp. 51–52; emphasis added)

Through the intentional application of such procedures Ollman makes it clear that dialectics improves our ability as analysts to undertake more complete and less reified conceptualisations of a topic of interest. He emphasizes that 'it is not a matter of [dialectics] making such procedures possible – since everybody abstracts – but of making them easier, and enabling [us] to acquire greater control over the process' (1993, p. 39). And as such, the potential for a more expansive understanding of the nature of contradiction-driven change, from particular standpoints, at multiple levels of generality, extended over space as well as time begins to emerge making the way in which things *cohere* (materially and relationally) a defining attribute.

It is here that Tony Smith's recovery of Hegel and Marx's *systematic-categorial* perspective on dialectics in *Dialectical Social Theory and Its Critics* (1993) makes an additional, overlapping contribution (cf. Arthur 2002). Recovering the methodological goals of Hegel directly, Smith explains:

If we wish to grasp a reality in its full complexity and concreteness we cannot simply take it as made up of immediately given beings. Nor can we simply take it as made up of isolated existences with their own unique grounds. Nor can we simply see it in terms of actualities externally mediated with other actualities through various correlations.

(1993, p. 13)

Indeed, these types of limitations of analysis are those regularly seen in even many of the most sensitive treatments of human practice (including some offered by those studying the dynamics of mind–in–activity specifically). What Smith confirms in response is as follows:

Instead we must employ a framework in which objects are united in difference with other objects through the essential particularities *and* universalities that make these objects what they are. This cannot be done through a single assertion or through a series of isolated assertions. It can be done *only* through a theory in which a number of different sorts of arguments are *systemically connected*.

(p. 13; emphasis added)

In summarizing Hegel's culminating discussion (in *Science of Logic*), Smith explains a triadic system of *syllogisms* (forms of reasoning): specifically, three circuits of multi-directional mediations involving at least three levels of generality.

As a principle the syllogism connects three moments: universality (*U*), particularity (*P*), and individuality (*I*). As principled [abstracted], objects are individuals mediated by particularities that are essential to them *qua* individuals, and these particularities in turn are mediated through a universal that is essential to the particularities. As a principle no single syllogism is sufficient to capture the intelligibility of its object. Any attempt to conclude that there is a connection between *I* and *U* through premises asserting a connection between *I-P* and *P-U* leaves these latter assertions unjustified. Likewise any attempt to derive *P-U* from *P-I* and *I-U* leave the latter two premises unmediated; and any attempt to derive *P-U* from *P-I* and *I-U* leave the latter two premises unmediated; and any attempt to connect *I-P* through *I-U* and *U-P* treats those premises as imply given immediately. For syllogisms to operate as principles, a system of all three sorts of syllogism is required *I-P-U*, *P-I-U*, and *I-U-P*. Only the system of syllogisms as a whole serves as the principle of explanation on this level of the theory. There are two key points here. First, each determination is thoroughly mediated with the other two. Second, each determination takes in turn the role of the middle term, whose function is to mediate the extremes into a single totality.

(pp. 11–12; original emphasis)

For those less familiar with Hegelian terminology, I note that the three levels Smith highlights are likely not as alien as they might seem at first. Given a philosophy of internal relations perspective is retained, it likely does not hurt to think of them provisionally as micro/meso/macro distinctions for example. Likewise, the often-provocative term 'universality' might be interpreted provisionally as simply the social and material culture of a society (e.g., in the same way one might refer to a contemporary Western society as 'neoliberal', 'capitalist', 'neo-colonial', 'patriarchal' and so on). Whether these suggestions are provisionally helpful or not, the overall point here is that it is a systematic application of syllogisms in conjunction with each of the procedures identified earlier in Ollman (1993) that constitute the distinctiveness of the expansive material dialectic approach recommended. Together they support the realization of a fully situated, relational account of human practice in motion that could intelligibly consider how thinking, feeling and acting, people *and* their environment are *both* the subject and object of change over time (rather than simply being in interaction with one another).

And yet, as we move forward still the following must be noted, as Smith does in his review of Hegel's and Marx's method(s) (referring once again to Hegel's *Science of Logic*):

> The *Logic* consists in an ordering of progressively more complex structures of principles [abstractions/concepts] and what is principled [abstracted/conceptualized]. As such it provides a set of canons to follow in theoretical work rather than some magic formula automatically churning out theoretical pronouncements like sausages in a factory.
>
> (Smith 1993, p. 13)

In other words, dialectics, both intentional and systematic-categorial, can only take us so far on our journey. What is still required is a series of substantive concepts and sub-concepts uniquely suited to a dialectical consideration, in time and place, of human practice as the specified topic of interest.

Human practice as mind-in-activity: The contribution of the Vygotskian project

Up to this point I have tried to establish the basic need and suitable meta-considerations for an appreciation of human practice as mind-in-activity. This centred on the meaning of an expansive material dialectic. However, what I have yet to do is speak directly to the origins and meaning of the notion of mind-in-activity. In doing so let me begin with a half-step backwards.

As opposed to other leading considerations of human practice, why embark on a consideration of a dialectical theory of mind-in-activity and the Vygotskian project? There are many theoretical traditions in the human sciences – and in particular across those taking seriously the concept of human practice – that orient to people, their capacities and agency as culturally, politically, economically, historically and materially shaped. However, despite sometimes evoking notions of creativity, rarely do these approaches offer a convincing account of anything more than an *adaptive* view of human learning and transformations as well. Alternatively, when relatively textured accounts of learning *are* to be found, such accounts regularly turn flat in relation to political, economic or historical significance. In this sense the aspirations of the Vygotskian project come to appear as quite distinct. And, if as Edwards (2007) put it, the devil is in the details when it comes to formation of mind, a consideration of Vygotsky's 'continuous dialectic between mind and a world' (p. 84), may be useful.

Building on these possible gaps it seems useful, as in the previous section, to start off by asking and answering another question in the course of moving forward: What does the Vygotskian project and its leading contemporary form, Cultural Historical Activity Theory (CHAT), seek to do?

> Activity theory seeks to analyze development within practical social activities. Activities organize our lives. In activities, humans develop their skills, personalities and consciousness. Through activities, we also transform our social conditions, resolve contradictions, generate new cultural artefacts, and create new forms of life and the self.
>
> (Sannino et al. 2009, p. 1)

In this we can note that CHAT is a theory of human learning and development that conceives of 'activity' as the minimal, meaningful unit of analysis for understanding the mutually constituting, yet contradictory, dimensions of practice as they unfold *and* become transformed over time through the dynamics internalization and externalization. In parallel with the goals of many critical theories of practice, it becomes impossible to understand the moments and dimensions of practice in isolation from the patterns of social, political, economic and historical relationships that constitute them, *and become, each, transformed* over time. What is more, fully in keeping with the type of expansive material dialectical treatment I outlined earlier, the notion of mind-in-activity is *not* just a conceptual tool to increase understanding amongst analysts. As the phrasing in the excerpt from Sannino et al. above suggests, activity also represents the concrete form that practice actually takes on as you and I, live, learn and, in short, carry out our lives. Thus, in the context of our selection of human practice as our topic of interest, we discover that as both the minimal, meaningful unit of analysis *and* the minimal, meaningful unit of concrete human agency, mind-in-activity may offer a distinctive epistemological and ontological opening to consider.

It is important to note, of course, that despite its potential the Vygotskian project and CHAT specifically are hardly immune to (diverse) questions of concern (e.g.,; Avis 2009; Bakhurst 2009; Langemeyer & Roth 2006; Martin & Peim 2009; Niewolny & Wilson 2009; Sawchuk & Stetsenko 2008; Smith 2005). While some of these concerns are more warranted than others, in the case of questions directly involving the relationship between mind-in-activity and dialectical thought, explanations of varying types, achieving varying degrees of success, can be found (e.g.,Blunden 2010; Engeström 1987; Ilyenkov 1982; Sawchuk 2003, 2013; Roth 2007).

In the context of these debates, I suggest that were we to be forced to seek only a single statement on how an approach to mind-in-activity and dialectical thought have been – *and could be* – more effectively integrated, we could consider looking no further than an article by Stetsenko: *Standing on the Shoulders of Giants: A Balancing Act of Dialectically Theorizing Conceptual Understanding on the Grounds of Vygotsky's Project* (2009). It is here that the Vygotskian project as predicated upon the ideas of contradiction, infinite movement and inter-penetration of all aspects of reality is made particularly clear.

> Vygotsky's project can be seen as one of the earliest and most articulate attempts (though not a fully-fledged account) to address the issues of human development and learning within the dialectical worldview and while focusing on the organisms' continuous ongoing engagements (i.e., activities, practices) with the world as the core foundation for these processes. Explicitly grounded in Marxist philosophy (for political historical reasons being among the first to be in affinity with its ideological under-pinnings and to have access to relevant works) and profoundly saturated with the goals of radical social transformation, this theory stands out even today in terms of its conceptual breadth, its clear commitment to social justice, and its pursuit to provide an account of human development and learning on fully relational, dialectical premises while not excluding the phenomena at the individual level from this account. Moreover, Vygotsky's project can be said to pursue and implement key principles of the dialectical methodology and outlook on reality because, whereas many other theories within the sociocultural framework pursue descriptions at the level of the totality of social systems and activities (such as community practices), Vygotsky's project also directly and centrally focuses on this level of analysis yet also breaks down this totality into interconnected deriva-tive parts and tracks down their historical contradictions and connections, while never leaving sight of their unity in difference.
>
> (pp. 81–82)

These are themes that echo many of the comments made above regarding modes of abstraction, or procedures, necessary for an expansive material dia-lectics. Indeed, it is a perspective likewise echoed by Marx and Engels (1978) when in *The German Ideology* (and elsewhere) they spoke clearly about the centrality of life's concrete 'activity' in their theorizing overall:

> [t]he premises from which we begin are not arbitrary ones, not dogmas, but real premises from which abstraction can only be made in the imagination. They are the real individuals, their activity and their material conditions of their life, both those which they find already existing and those produced by their own activity.
>
> (Marx & Engels 2004, p. 42)

Based on these premises, the attractiveness of a systematic–categorial form of an expansive material dialectical theory of mind-in-activity emerges. This is an expansive materialist dialectical approach that, in the first instance, can be traced to the triadic structure of Hegel's integrated syllogisms as but one support for coherently parsing and re-constituting the full complexity of human practice – extended through time, from particular standpoints across multiple levels of generality (*I, P, U*) – in terms of a transformative series of engagements of people and the world around them. Beginning with the work of Vygotsky himself, this substantive conceptual system takes as its inherent starting point the notion that Hegelian and Marxist dialectical methods likewise privileged: *mediation*.

Evincing notions of multi-mediating levels of generality and the syllogisms outlined earlier, for L. S. Vygotsky (e.g., 1978, 1987) and his colleague A. N. Leontiev (e.g., 1978), the principle of *mediation* directs our attention to some very concrete facts. People always act on (and are acted upon), think about, feel, perceive and know the world as mediated by artefacts or tools of some kind. These tools/artefacts include an enormous range of items: from physical objects and technologies to spatial or temporal properties of the environment; from language, narrative and non-narrative aspects of discourse or ideology to organizational rules, divisions of labour or norms; from specific cognitive or affective schema to desires, fears or other elements commonly associated with personality, subjectivity or identity. At the same time, CHAT analysis makes additional demands of this concept of tool/artefact mediation. It requires the procedures of extension and attention to the history of things (e.g., their history of design, production, reproduction and alteration in use) in order to understand effective tendencies – the affordances, inhibitions and prohibitions – of mediation. And it is in this way, tool/artefact mediation places human thought, feeling and action in constant symbolic and material communion with the both the past and the future and the limits and pressures of our given time, place, culture, economy and so on. Artefacts, tools and their various mediational configurations in practice represent the history we encounter, reconfigure and otherwise make, but not simply as we please.

Likewise mirroring the general dialectical observations we reviewed earlier, central to understanding the Vygotskian project was the claim that human practice, learning and development unfold *not from part to whole but rather from whole to part* (Vygotsky 1987). Indeed, it is this principle of practice as constituted by a *mediated wholeness* that, I argue, is a direct methodological descendent of dialectical thought as explicated by, for example, Ollman's (1993) philosophy of internal relations and Smith's (1993) discussion of Hegel's inter-penetrating triad of syllogisms. Perhaps most important in this regard is that, following these types of observations, Vygotsky quickly arrived at the realization that a theory of symbolic and material mediation was, on its own, inadequate to the task of providing a proper account of practice that could make intelligible the concrete dynamics of practice, learning, knowledge formation and transformation. A further reconstruction was required. A new abstraction/category, one that preserved and synthesized – or in Hegelian terminology *sublated* – earlier conclusions, was necessary for this analytic task. As Vygotsky (1987) put it, what was needed was a 'unit' that could possess '*all the basic characteristics of the whole*

[as] a vital and irreducible part of the whole' (p. 46; emphasis original). And, as Leontiev clarifies, what emerged was a theory of 'activity':

> [a]ctivity is a molar, not an additive unit of the life of the physical, material subject. In a narrower sense, that is, at the psychological level, it is a unit of life, mediated by psychic reflection, the real function of which is that it orients the subject in the objective world. In other words, activity is not a reaction and not a totality of reactions but a system that has structure, its own internal transitions and transformations, its own development.
>
> (Leontiev 1978, p. 50)

Thus, as it regards this 'structure' – placed within Vygotsky's aspirations for a broader dialectic appreciation (e.g., Stetsenko 2009)—I claim a philosophy of internal relations and a systematic-categorial ordering helps us better appreciate a theory practice as mind-in-activity. Parsed dialectically, below we see that the notion of mind-in-activity is constituted by a series of *sublations*; that is, constituted by an order through which the more abstract/generalized concepts preserve and synthesize the more overdetermined and concrete ones. Thus, in what follows I am moving from the abstract to the concrete in my description of constituent concepts (epistemologically) and moments/dimensions (ontologically) of mind-in-activity – namely, object/motive, goal-directed action and operations.

In a CHAT theory of practice, the term *object* as it relates to the concept of *object/motive* is meant to refer to the concept/moment in which the learning subject's 'minimal, meaningful unit of concrete agency' (see above) is synthesised and preserved within the intelligibility of a more generalised set of institutions, economies and societies. In other words, in carrying out its practices vis-à-vis the particularities of some zone of proximal development we find that need becomes a motive capable of directing actions only at the moments when it finds its object (Leontiev 1978). It is in this context that what CHAT refers to as the *object-relatedness* of activity can be said to seek to assure attention to, for example, the syllogism Smith (1993) identified with the *I-U-P* circuit in which the societal (or political, or cultural, or economic) object *mediates* a series of more overdetermined and concrete instances of practice; attention/dis-attention, meaning-making, problem-solving, choice-making as inherent dimensions of the object/motive of some unavoidably contradictory praxis. Recalling the multi-directionality of the entire triadic system of syllogism again, we likewise discover the CHAT concept of *double stimulation*, (i.e., the world-changing the practices of the (individual and/or collective) subject, and the subject changing the world). Understood as a substantive theoretical expression of a philosophy of internal relations, we therefore see here a dialectically (categorially) ordered set of conceptual resources that permit us to address human practice in terms of the mediations of mind and the learning subject at a broader level of generality.

Parsing the notion of mind-in-activity further, we can in turn come to see how CHAT analysis distinguishes, first, between *goal-direct action* and *activity*. Human practice, in this approach, is *not* reducible to an action. Rather, an action is understood as conducted by an individual (or a collective) subject to fulfil some self-consciously held goal. We are speaking directly here of the realm of reflexive awareness, intentionality, or what people explicitly understand themselves to be doing at any particular juncture. Indeed, a point made by CHAT analysis is that an exclusive concern for self-conscious, reflexive awareness and intentionality cannot generate an adequate understanding of transpiring practices. In fact, nor is it the case that subject's themselves rely exclusively on these in the course of their practice, learning and development. Rather from the perspective of a systematic-categorial dialectics, goal-directed action within a zone of proximal development is a more concrete, overdetermined concept sublated by that of participation in activity.

Parsing the notion of human practice as mind-in-activity still further, at this point we arrive at another key CHAT concept: *operation*. As a concept that is likewise sublated (this time by both activity and goal-directed action), an operation refers to un-self-conscious responses to immediate symbolic and material conditions of activity. In relation to their execution, operations cannot be self-consciously, or reflexively/declaratively, formulated. They are subject to tacit awareness only. They involve responses to the entirely overdetermined simultaneity and concreteness that is, in effect, seen but unnoticed.

In bringing each of these abstractions together we find a characterization of both the technical and the social divisions of labour inextricably and simultaneously implicated at multiple levels of generality in the notion of human practice as mind-in-activity. In empirical analysis, the task of interpretation can then, carefully, be unfolded by noting the following for example:

> An analysis leading to an actual disclosure of sense cannot be limited to superficial observation. [...] After all, from the process itself it is not evident what kind of process it is — action or activity. Often in order to explain this, active investigation is required: substantiating observation, hypothesis, effective verification. That to which the given process is directed may seem to be inducing it, embodying its motives; if this is so, then it is activity. But this same process may be induced by a completely different motive not at all coinciding with that to which it is directed as its results; then it is an action. [...] In spite of what it seems to be from the superficial point of view, this is a way that confirms the objectivity of its bases to a high degree inasmuch as this way leads to an understanding of the consciousness of man [*sic*] derived from life, from concrete beginnings, and not from the laws of consciousness of surrounding people, not from knowledge.
>
> (Leontiev 1978, pp. 173–174)

We see, therefore, that from this perspective the idea of atomised practice (certainly those in keeping with the basic definitions offered by mainstream perspectives on practice theory) is epistemologically unintelligible and onto-logically impossible without reference to all the contradictory, mediated dimensions and moments of mind–in–activity.

It is in these ways that CHAT revolves around practices, but practice as parsed and reconstituted in relation to both the concrete and more generalized whole which permits the recognition of the contradictory moments of praxis implicated in (it could be said following Marx) social *being over consciousness*. The approach is dialectical, expansive as well as materialist in this way. Indeed, as Blunden (2010) noted in reference to the *Theses on Feuerbach*: 'When Marx [says] that "The question whether objective truth can be attributed to human thinking is not a question of theory but is a practical question", he is making *practice* the subject-matter, not just the criterion of truth' (p. 97; emphasis added). It is in keeping with an expansive material dialectical methodology that we attend to activity as a whole – the principle of wholeness – as well as the mutuality among concepts, dimensions and moments that define the intelligibility (for subject and analyst) of practice. It is in keeping with a philosophy of internal relations that at the heart of effective analysis of practice is *not* simply a grasp of individual concepts or dialectical procedures but also their systematic-categorial integration. And, this is what another of Vygotsky's talented colleagues (P. Y. Galperin) referred to artfully as the elusive 'blue bird' of analysis (see Arievitch 2003, p. 283): that is, the intellectual aspiration that recognises human practice vis-a-vis the internally related ways that object/motives, action, operation express a series of contradictory, changing and yet intelligible forms of mind–in–activity.

Conclusions

> To William Faulkner's supposed remark, "The past is not dead – it is not even in the past," Marx could have added, "And the future is not unborn – it is not even in the future." Potential is the form in which the future exists inside the present [. . .]
>
> (Ollman 1998, p. 354).

The complexity of a study of human practice should be challenging. And as with every study that dares to entertain this complexity, there is always the danger of reification that loses sight of interconnectedness – or totality – of concepts/moments and, in so doing misplaces what is likely definitively human about it. In this regard, I have emphasized a concern for losing sight of the dynamics of learning and transformation. Misplacing such a thing means misplacing the potential that exists within the present forms of agency we exercise. Thus, a central point in this chapter has been analysis of the dynamism of human practice that appreciates the notion of *mind-in-activity*, a notion of learning disabused of its caricature as merely individualized, cognitive, adaptive and so on. It is a notion that specifically requires us to face up to the difficulties of providing an historicized account of contradiction-driven processes of practice, always in motion, unfolding the future that exists inside the totality of the present.

I have argued that it is in its championing of the relevance of the concrete human practices of daily life as fully situated in its (institutional, societal, political, economic and historical) specificities, and its unending – hidden and pronounced – dynamics of individual as well as collective transformations over time that the potential of the dialectical synthesis offered by the concept of mind-in-activity is found.

> [. . .] human *Being* needs to be understood as an indivisible and seamless, unitary (not composite) process of humans engaging with their world – the totality of life – that cannot be meaningfully broken into disconnected parts such as, for example, a putatively self-sufficient endeavours of a conceptual understanding on the one hand, and of perceiving the world, memorizing facts about it, tackling moral dilemmas, or solving practical tasks and so on – on the other. Instead, all of these endeavours and acts need to be seen as forming one continuously unfolding stream, one whole seamless flow of life where various facets and moments mutually interpenetrate and define each other, are represented in each other, and thus are not reducible to a chain of single discrete episodes or disconnected levels and dimensions.
>
> (Stetsenko 2009, p. 83)

With its treatment of the epistemological and ontological gaps that serve to keep notions of human mind separate from the internally related cultural, political, economic and historical dimensions of practice – I argue we arrive at a distinctive opportunity to seize on the fundamental contradictions that, in turn, power the transformational dimensions of the learning that should be inherent to a critical theory of human practice. Through this, unearthed is the potential for a range of more specified (and creative) analytical paths and practices: e.g., the notion of consolidating/expansive *as well as* fractionating/repressive trajectories of practice; the notion of learning dynamics that lead to *both* the creation and disappearance of knowledge forms in practice; the notion of not simply the generic mind-in-activity *but also*, for example, mind-in-political-economy, mind-in-patriarchy, mind-in-colonialism and so on (cf. Sawchuk 2013).

In this context we see that there are a series of analytic procedures that, when ignored, disadvantage researchers seeking to make *both* immediate empirical sense of the particulars of human practice *while also* allowing the development of an explanation of how these particulars cohere in the broader ways that ultimately account for their (historical, political, economic) significance. Venturing into the potentially challenging analytic realm that characterises this approach has, at the very least, brought to light a series of worthy concerns for our understanding of human practice. And, these are concerns to which the expansive material dialectics of the Vygotskian project may be uniquely responsive.

References

Arievitch, I 2003, 'A potential for an integrated view of development and learning: Galperin's contribution to sociocultural psychology', *Mind, Culture & Activity*, vol. 10, no. 4, pp. 278–288.

Arthur, C 2002, *The new dialectic and Marx's Capital*, Brill, Leiden.

Avis, J 2009, 'Transformation or transformism: Engeström's version of activity theory', *Educational Review*, vol. 61, no. 2, pp. 151–165.

Bakhurst, D 2009, 'Reflections on activity theory', *Educational Review*, vol. 61, no. 2, pp. 197–210.

Bhaskar, R 1993, *Dialectic: The pulse of freedom*, Verso, London.

Blunden, A 2010, *An interdisciplinary theory of activity*, Brill, Boston.

Edwards, A 2007, 'An interesting resemblance: Vygotsky, mead and American pragmatism', in H Daniels, M Cole & J Wertsch (eds), *The Cambridge companion to Vygotsky*, Cambridge University Press, New York, pp. 77–100.

Engeström, Y 1987, *Learning by expanding: An activity-theoretical approach to development research*, Orienta-Konsultit, Helsinki.

Hartsock, N 2008 'Marxist feminist dialectics for the twenty-first century', in B Ollman & T Smith (eds), *Dialectics for a new century*, Palgrave MacMillan, New York, pp. 222–234.

Harvey, D 2008, 'The dialectics of spacetime', in B Ollman & T Smith (eds) *Dialectics for a New Century*, Palgrave MacMillan, New York, pp. 98–117.

Ilyenkov, EV 1982, *The dialectics of the abstract and concrete in Marx's capital*, Progress, Moscow.

Langemeyer, I & Roth, W-M 2006, 'Is cultural-historical activity theory threatened to fall short of its own principles and possibilities in empirical research?', *Outlines. Critical Social Studies*, vol. 8, no. 2, pp. 20–42.

Leontiev, AN 1978, *Activity, consciousness, and personality*, Prentice Hall, Englewood Cliffs, NJ.

Levins, R 2008, 'Dialectics and systems theory', in B Ollman & T Smith (eds), *Dialectics for a New Century*, Palgrave MacMillan, New York, pp. 26–49.

Martin, D & Peim, N 2009, 'Critical perspectives on activity theory', *Educational Review*, vol. 61, no. 2, pp. 131–138.

Marx, K & Engels, F 2004, *The German ideology*, CJ Arthur (ed.), Lawrence & Wishart, London.

Meikle, S 1979, 'Dialectical contradiction and necessity', in J Mepham & D-H Ruben (eds), *Issues in Marxist philosophy: Volume one – Dialectics and method*, Humanities Press, New Jersey, pp. 5–35.

Niewolny, K & Wilson, A 2009, 'What happened to the promise? A critical (re)orientation of two sociocultural learning traditions', *Adult Education Quarterly*, vol. 60, no. 1, pp. 26–45.

Ollman, B 1993, *Dialectical investigations*, Routledge, New York.

Ollman, B 1998, 'Why dialectics? Why now?', *Science and Society*, vol. 62, no. 3, pp. 338–357.

Roberts, J 2014, 'Critical realism, dialectics, and qualitative research methods', *Journal for the Theory of Social Behaviour*, vol. 44, no. 1, pp. 1–23.

Roth, W-M 2007, 'Emotion at work: A contribution to third-generation Cultural-Historical Activity Theory,' *Mind, Culture and Activity*, vol. 14, no. 1–2, pp. 40–63.

Sannino, A, Daniels, H & Gutiérrez, K (eds) 2009, *Learning and expanding with activity theory*, Cambridge University Press, New York.

Sawchuk, P 2003, *Adult learning and technology in working-class life*, Cambridge University Press, New York.

Sawchuk, P 2013, *Contested learning in welfare work: A study of mind, political economy and the labour process*, Cambridge University Press, New York.

Sawchuk, P 2015, 'Informal learning as dialectics of activity', in O Mejiuni, P Cranton & O Taiwo (eds), *Measuring and analyzing informal learning in the digital age*, IGI Global, Amsterdam.

Sawchuk, P & Stetsenko, A 2008, 'Sociological understandings of conduct for a non-canonical activity theory: Exploring intersections and complementarities', *Mind Culture and Activity*, vol. 15, no. 4, pp. 339–360.

Smith, D 2005, *Institutional ethnography: A sociology for people*, Rowman & Littlefield, Landham, MD.

Smith, T 1993, *Dialectical social theory and its critics: From Hegel to analytical Marxism and postmodernism*, SUNY Press, Albany, NY.

Stetsenko, A 2009, 'Standing on the shoulders of giants: A balancing act of dialectically theorizing conceptual understanding on the grounds of Vygotsky's project', in W-M Roth (ed.), *Re/structuring science education: Re-uniting psychological and sociological perspectives*, Springer, New York, pp. 69–88.

Vygotsky, LS 1978, *Mind in society: The development of higher psychological processes*, Harvard University Press, Cambridge, MA.

Vygotsky, LS 1987, *The collected works of L. S. Vygotsky (volume 1: Problems of general psychology)*, Plenum Press, New York.

Zanetti, L 2003, 'Holding contradictions: Marcuse and the idea of refusal', *Administrative Theory & Praxis*, vol. 25, no. 2, pp. 261–276.

Chapter 11

Boobs and Barbie

Feminist posthuman perspectives on gender, bodies and practice

Julia Coffey and Jessica Ringrose

Introduction

In this chapter our aim is to look at the complex relational assemblages by which young people's bodies are engaged in 'gendered becomings' to show a feminist posthuman perspective. We draw on conceptual tools from Deleuze and Guattari in combination with Barad to re-think practice. From this perspective, gendered embodiments are not simply the reproductions of dualist gender formations; rather, gender is engaged, negotiated and produced continually through affects and micro-relations. We show this by exploring the territorialisations and micro-relations involved in the practice of cosmetic surgery (breast implants), and examples of transversality in a feminist school-based project that aimed to produce different gendered assemblages through research practice. A focus on the 'doings' of gender enables the ambiguities and complexities of gender to be explored, including, the discursive, bodily, sensate, affective and material dimensions of practice. In particular, this approach can assist in developing alternative understandings of the ways the conditions of possibility for gendered embodiments and social change emerge through practice.

Posthuman feminist ethology: What can a (gendered) body do?

While some practice theories are influenced by the phenomenology of Merleau-Ponty in their emphasis on ontologies where experience is the foundation of knowledge, new material and posthuman practice theories are differentiated by their refusals of singular foundations (Lenz Taguchi 2013). Indeed, Deleuze and Guattari argued that it is impossible to secure any foundation for knowledge in human experience, and as a result, there is the possibility for invention and creativity without reference to an underlying human subject. Accordingly, it has been suggested that Deleuze's work is a 'radicalisation of phenomenology' (Colebrook 2002, p. 2). A humanist, phenomenological perspective of practice

(Simonsen 2012, p. 221) would ask how (human) bodily doings and sayings constitute meanings, identities and social orders. In contrast, a posthumanist, ethological perspective of practice would ask how the social is composed by the arrangements of (human and non-human) entities. 'Ethology' approaches the body as a complex relation, which is defined by the affects it is capable of: 'what can a body do?' (Deleuze 1992, p. 626).

This focus on a body's 'doings' rather than a body's unity is part of a wider move towards posthumanist perspectives, particularly through the work of Karen Barad. Barad's (2007) work on posthuman performativity aims to retheorise human agency as constituted in dynamic intra-action with time, space and matter. Barad argues:

> an agential realist notion of dynamics [. . .] is not marked by an exterior parameter called time, nor does it take place in a container called space, but rather iterative intra-actions are the dynamics through which temporality and spatiality are produced and reconfigured in the (re)making of material-discursive boundaries and their constitutive exclusions.
>
> (in van der Tuin & Dolphijn 2010, p. 10)

Rather than approaching human bodies as separate unities, bodies are understood as composed through the intra-actions of a range of discursive, spatial and temporal 'matterings' that make up more than human power relations. We suggest that *intra-action* – which considers the relationality between bodies, things, objects, space and time – can be set in useful dialogue with the Deleuzo-Guattarian concepts of *assemblage, territorialisation* and *transversality* to develop a different perspective of practice as assembled relations of power. We use these aligned concepts to consider the different pieces of data and recollections together, which enable us to explore the discursive, sensory, affective and material aspects of bodily practice and relations which comprise 'what a body can do', and might be able to do differently.

Barad's focus on phenomena as products of ongoing intra-actions is similar to Deleuze and Guattari's theories of agencement and assemblage. An assemblage 'designates something which happens between two terms which are not subjects, but agents, elements' (Deleuze & Parnet 2002, p. 51). An assemblage is *'always collective*, [and] brings into play within us and outside us populations, multiplicities, territories, becomings, affects, events' (Deleuze & Parnet 2002, p. 51). Thus assemblages are functional, active collections of connections (Currier 2003) that are more than human, trans-human and posthuman. Our interest here is specifically in the implications this has for the category of gender, as assemblages are not 'transcendent structures' which can be traced to an essence or mapped back onto social orders. Instead, they are 'continually in flux' (Currier 2003, p. 321). Current formations of gender can thus be reframed as an active collection of connections, which operates as only a temporary articulation rather than an essential identity category. This also shifts the key orientation of discursive regulation – as found for instance in Foucauldian analytics – to a more open questioning and to a cartography of mapping flatter or more dispersed power *relations* (Grosz 1994).

The Deleuzo-Guattarian concept of *territorialisation* further assists in explaining the process by which social categories and hierarchies, such as gender, class, ability and ethnicity, can function to regulate and produce bodies (Fox 2002, p. 353)[1]. Territorialization can be understood as a key dimension of a body's continual process of assembling, in tension with the 'forces of the social', such as gender, and the 'experimenting body as it becomes-other' (Fox 2002, p. 360). A Deleuzo-Guattarian perspective offers a radical view of practice as composing a body alongside territorialisations of space and objects (bodies) and with potential for experimentation (Budgeon 2003; Coleman 2009; Grosz 1994). Therefore, in addition to mapping out the familiar repetitions of power relations (territorialisations), Deleuze and Guattari (1984) offer a language for examining the complexity of relations and affects between bodies and the world, including ruptures, 'resistances' and interruptions of territorialisation (Renold & Ringrose 2008). There is a concern for not only what the body is or has been constituted as – for example in theorisations of subjectivisation qua Butler – but also for what these relations and affects enable bodies to *do*.

We use the concept of *transversality* to assist in analysis and critique of gender from a Deleuzo-Guattarian perspective on practice. This concept was developed by Felix Guattari to theorise institutional and cultural change in assemblages through his experiments at the clinic La Borde. According to Genosko (2009, p. 51), one of Guattari's most significant contributions is 'the political idea of (nonhierarchical) transversal relationships'. This was based on micro-practices, so Guattari re-routed the daily tasks performed by patients, staff and doctors at the clinic with a new circulating '*la grille*' or 'grid' of tasks and activities that challenged vertical power relations, for instance the patient becoming cook for the day. Transversality operates between hierarchy and accommodation within the power relations of assemblages, where openness is introduced through variations in relationships and practices that disrupt, rework but also productively inhabit hierarchies. Guattari showed how specific and tangible differences (at the level of the micro) can foster institutional changes that enable 'mutually enriching encounters . . . so that individual did not fall back into old roles and the repressive fantasies attached to them or succumb to retrogressive habits of how to respond to authority and fixed ways of communicating' (Genosko 2009, p. 56). Importantly, changing social relations was only deemed possible when subjects were psychically contained enough (they felt safe) to engage in the experiments (Walkerdine 2013). In this case the experiments are new configurations that enable a changed set of relations to and within a body. But how did this actually work? What material conditions and objects enabled change in particular time/space parameters? How can this contribute to understanding not only how gender assembles, but also how it could be assembled differently?

In what follows, we first investigate how objects and matter work to assemble and territorialise gendered bodies with different outcomes in relation to the practice of breast implant surgery. Next we consider how transversal relations can be generated in research and how transitional, material objects may enable relational change.

The research studies: Diffractive entanglements

The first example is drawn from a study of young people's body work practices in Melbourne, Australia. The study was comprised of twenty-two in-depth semi-structured interviews with men and women aged 18–33 in Melbourne, Australia, which explored participants' experiences of body work and broader understandings of health and gender. Participants were recruited through asking personal contacts to forward electronic advertisements to their friends (not known to the researcher) through Facebook and email, which enabled participants to self-select to be involved in this research. Participants were mainly white, middle-class and heterosexual, and had a range of professions and education levels. Participants discussed a variety of body work practices such as exercising through jogging, attending classes at a gym or weights training, as well as diet, wearing make-up, tattooing and cosmetic surgery (Coffey 2013a; Coffey 2013b; Coffey 2016). Exploring body work practices provided a means of addressing the bodily aspects of gender assemblages and dynamics of territorialisation.

The second example is drawn from a research project, *Feminism in Schools: Mapping impact in practice*, funded by Cardiff University in 2014. Feminist clubs were set up or researched in seven highly diverse secondary schools across England and Wales, including mixed, single-sex and fee-paying institutions and participants from a range of religious, ethnic and socio-economic backgrounds. Schools participated for at least six weeks, with some continuing to the present day. To date the project has generated qualitative data with approximately eighty-five young people (girls and boys), as well as the teachers and academics involved in each of the feminist groups. Students participated in a range of semi-structured group and individual interviews, as well as creative arts-based methodologies from which a range of material 'intra-activisms' and artefacts were documented or collected (e.g., poems, writings, blogs, sculptures and online posts from sites like Facebook, Tumblr and Twitter)[2].

In bringing different data from different projects together we aim to contribute a theoretically rich analysis of the different ways gender is produced and potentially transformed through sensory, affective, discursive and material aspects of bodily practice. Of course our writing up of these data together is also an assemblage, and we 'plug in' (Jackson & Mazzei 2011) and out of our data as researchers. The idea of the research process and writing up data as an assemblage resonates with Taguchi and Palmer's (2013) use of Barad's (2007) idea of diffraction, where diverse elements blend, intra-act and entangle. Diffraction rather than mimetic reflection allows for different data to be brought together and re-assembled to create something new.

Study 1. Breast implants and micro-relations of gender

In the study of young people's body work practices, two participants, Kate and Isabelle, both aged 24, had undergone breast implant surgery. Narrowly defined feminine bodily norms were important dimensions framing both surgeries. Where Kate described the practice of surgery as enabling her to live more fully, Isabelle describes feeling locked into a cycle of continuing surgeries ('when will it stop?'). Because they engaged differently with the regulative, territorialising gender norms which informed their body work, the ways their bodies assemble (what their bodies can do) is different. Rather than seeing these norms as providing a simple explanation for the practice of cosmetic surgery however, approaching gender as something that must be actively assembled (and intra-acts with the numerous other entities, objects and materials in spaces), assists in making sense of why Kate and Isabelle had different possibilities available to them following the surgery. Their examples shed light on the ways micro-relations of gender assemble through practice and the dynamics of territorialisation – including relations between other people (friends, mum, boyfriends); affects (fear, shame, humiliation); materials (silicone implants); environment and spaces (the pool, the shower) and objects (items of clothing such as bikinis).

Kate: 'If I'd had any boobs, I wouldn't have done it'

Throughout the interview, Kate described wanting to be 'curvy' and admiring 'womanly' bodies. She described the pain she suffered related to having a 'stick' figure with 'no boobs' throughout her adolescence. She insisted that her breasts were not just small but were 'non-existent'. She explains it was this desire to have 'womanly curves' that led her to have breast implant surgery when she was twenty.

> If I'd had any boobs, I wouldn't have done it. Just any boobs, an A cup, I would have been happy with that. . . . I would always hide them from everyone. And I remember, this was the saddest thing, this is what I remember, I'd be in the shower and I'd freak out about someone coming in and going 'oh my god you have no boobs!' And then it would be winter and I'd be freaking out, worrying about summer coming around, and thinking about all my friends going to the beach, and I'd always just be stuck on the sand with this big towel wrapped around me wearing a big T shirt afraid to go

in the water. And at school my friend lived really close to the school and he had a pool so in summer everyone would go there at lunchtime to swim, and all the girls would sit around the pool in their bikinis, and I would have to make up an excuse every lunchtime as to why I couldn't go. And when I say no boobs, I mean like, nothing, flat. [After I'd made the decision to have the surgery] my two very best friends were like, Kate, you have to show us your boobs! And I remember lifting up my top and both of them go, 'man, we'd get a boob job too' [laughing] It was so, so, oh – in summer I just wouldn't go to the beach, I wasn't living my life because I was so self-conscious about it. But when I went and saw the surgeon, I said, I just want to go a size A, I just want to have an 'A'. And he was like 'an A cup? I think that would be a waste of your money Kate!' and my mum said 'I think you should go bigger than an A' and I was like, I just wanted boobs, any boobs, and no one understands that, except for you going through it, and other women that are in your position, but it's about anything, any complex you have about your body. People think, oh, you should just get over it but you don't.

Kate's description is interlaced with examples of the ways shame and embarrassment about her breasts permeated her life and delimited her from 'normal' social activities. This includes specific seasons such as summer, which for young women living on the coast in Australia often denotes social activities of going to the beach or pool with friends and wearing bikinis. Kate's body concerns, which stem from narrow gendered body norms which emphasise the importance of breasts in producing a liveable feminine subjectivity, prevented her from fully 'living her life', proscribing the parameters of what her body can do. This gender territorialisation contextualises the intensity of the affects of 'fear', shame and sadness in the summer spaces of the beach and friend's pool which close down her potential for 'living', and help to explain why Kate was drawn to the procedure of breast implant surgery and the resulting breast-object relation.

Stemming from Barad's concept of bodies as comprised through intra-active relations between other objects, bodies and materials, the materiality of the object of the silicone-gel filled implant becomes important to understanding the way gender assembles through the practice of breast implant surgery. Objects in the environment (silicone-gel implants) and practices of surgery and alteration are drawn upon as the 'remedy' to her 'complex' about her breasts. The bringing of silicone into the body – the body becoming in some part plastic – is important in demonstrating the 'measures' that have become normative to reach the impossible ideals of feminine bodily perfection (Bordo 2003). These are not just discourses of bodily perfection but endless regimes of bodily practice that make up the beauty, health and image industries of pharmacology and plastic surgery – a world that is more than human in its biological and material manifestations of becoming someone newer and better.

The cosmetic surgeon and Kate's mother – who convinced her to have C-cup implants rather than the A-cups Kate originally requested – were also crucial actors in the micro-relations of Kate's breast-implant assemblage. This 'advice' connects the micro-relations of the encounter with the broader political terrain of body politics, in which decades of feminist research has drawn attention to the ways in which the female body is regulated and territorialised by restrictive, heterosexist and patriarchal gender norms relating to appearance across the fields of medicine, cosmetic surgery and popular culture. The relations and affects described above can be seen as territorialisations that comprise Kate's capacities in relation to her body and led her to undergo cosmetic surgery.

The surgery has a distinct impact on Kate's life. She describes that since having the surgery she is able to 'enjoy [her] life, just really live it':

> [Since the surgery] I've had so many moments where I just feel . . . like I don't have this feeling in my stomach where I'm worried about wearing bathers . . . Like going to Hawaii, if I wanna wear bathers, or going to China and going shopping in the silk markets, going 'oh I could wear this, it would fit me!' You know, dresses are designed for women with boobs. And just, everything. Not stressing about summer, and enjoying your life, and just really living it.

The altered materiality of Kate's body through the object-relations of the breast implants has expanded the affective potentials available to her. That these expanded capacities occur in the context of normative feminine bodily presentations does not detract from their significance in understanding the complex ways in which gender is intra-actively engaged through the practice of cosmetic surgery and produces what a body can do.

Isabelle: '[My boobs] looked a bit funny'

Like Kate, Isabelle also described 'boobs' as crucial to an ideal feminine bodily appearance. However the dynamics of this ideal are more intensive for Isabelle as she works in a cosmetic surgery centre. She says, 'It's in my face every day!'

[INTERVIEWER]: I've been asking people to describe the characteristics of a supposedly ideal body . . .

ISABELLE: For me personally, in my job, doing beauty therapy and because we work in cosmetic surgery – [pauses while server delivers coffees] – a female who is like a slender, athletic female, um, clear complexion, symmetrical face, this is like perfection – nice hair, things like that.

[INTERVIEWER]: So in terms of like body shape, is there . . . ?

ISABELLE: Yeah, just like a slim athletic build I think is nice. Like, we have a lot of body shapes at our work, like we have apples and pears, but they come to our work to change that, so . . .

[INTERVIEWER]: What about other physical characteristics . . . like boobs, or . . .

ISABELLE: Yeah, I think boobs and arse. I've got fake boobs, I got them last year. Cos I had one [breast] that was a C and one was an A [cup], so I had to have reconstructive surgery, but they made them a D anyway because they had to put 2 implants in each to make them look normal. And they had to move one of my nipples, so, I think that's important too. Just to feel comfortable, to feel normal, because they looked a bit funny. Um . . . yeah that's important too I suppose, nice skin, body image . . .

[INTERVIEWER]: Yeah, so what was it like having the operation? Was it everything you wanted, was it more difficult than you thought, or?

ISABELLE: It wasn't that painful actually, it's made me a lot more confident with my boyfriend especially, like I didn't like to wear bathers and stuff like that cos they looked funny. But now I'm a lot happier. And people . . . you can't tell they're fake because I had the natural tear-shaped [implants], not round, so they look nice. Yeah.

The space and context of Isabelle's employment as a beauty therapist hooks her into the broader assemblage of the consumer culture-fashion-beauty complex (Bartky 1990; Featherstone 2010) which trades on being able to surgically 'correct' (mostly women's) bodies in line with extremely narrow gendered norms of 'perfection'. Where Kate described her surgery as necessary because she had 'no boobs', Isabelle similarly emphasises the need for 'reconstructive surgery' to correct an imbalance in breast sizes. Similar to those in Davis' (1995) study, Kate and Isabelle describe their breast implant surgery as aimed at looking 'normal' rather than for vanity or advantage. Like Kate, Isabelle describes being previously self-conscious being naked with boyfriends or in wearing bikinis because she felt her breasts 'looked funny'. She emphasises the benefit of having the surgery in enabling her to feel 'comfortable', 'normal', 'happier' and 'more confident', playing down the pain and invasiveness of the surgery which she said involved inserting two implants in each breast and moving one of her nipples. Clearly, normative heterosexual gendered ideals related to the body's appearance are critical for understanding the dynamics by which Isabelle's body is assembled through the practice of breast implant surgery. This example illustrates how gendered body norms territorialise and compose Isabelle's body through practice and a body's engagements. At each turn, a body is actively produced through activities, practices and connections rather than understood as passively inscribed. The extensive relations between her body and those of her patients at work, her boyfriend and the broader cultural norms rewarding efforts towards physical perfection (and emphasising the importance of symmetrical, 'nice, 'natural-looking' breasts in heterosexual relations of desire) compose what

Isabelle's body can do, in her case, leading to breast implant surgery and further cosmetic procedures to follow.

Unlike Kate, who felt more able to 'fully live' following surgery, Isabelle describes wondering almost immediately, 'Right, what can I do next?' She has continued to have further cosmetic surgical procedures, including Botox and liposuction, which she receives for free at work ('the nurses needed someone to practice on'). Where Kate's assembled relations through gendered territorialisations, other actors and the implant itself led to expanded capacities for living, Isabelle can see no end to the number of procedures she will have: 'I'll have everything done . . . but you think, when will it stop?'

A feminist posthuman perspective can assist in making sense of the different outcomes of Isabelle and Kate's breast implant surgeries, which produce a different range of bodily potentials. The practice or enactment of cosmetic surgery is implicated in a broader material-discursive enactment of gender. Performative entanglements between actors – such as socio-historical aspects of gender, alongside various environments of bodily display (the beach, the pool), and heterosexual, peer and family relationships – are important features through which Kate and Isabelle's cosmetic surgeries are produced. The materiality of the objects of the silicone implants are also themselves important actors in this context. The size of the implant (A or C cup?) and shape (round or tear-shaped) are important dimensions of the object, which align to very specific and narrow cultural idealisations of women's breasts. They are the 'objects' that communicate the ideal dimensions, shape and size of this highly sexualised female body part, available for purchase. Purchase of these objects positions Kate and Isabelle as consumers. These objects are sold as solutions to 'deformities' such as 'tuberous breast deformity' (meaning simply breasts which are 'asymmetrical', a term invented by surgeons themselves) (Haikem 1997). Cosmetic surgery is a highly commodified market in which 'medicine' and 'beauty' intersect, and the profitability of which has been likened to a 'modern gold rush' benefitting surgeons (Taylor 2012). The power of surgeons to define body parts as being 'deformed' if they are not symmetrical is key to the enormous economic success of cosmetic surgery as a market. The materialities of the implants literally alter Kate and Isabelle's bodies, and play an important role in mediating their bodily capacities that follow.

The conditions of *what their bodies can do* are produced through the specific entanglements of the cosmetic surgery assemblage, which are different for Kate and Isabelle. Though the factors themselves are relatively similar (both discuss being affected by discourses of feminine bodily perfection and wanting to change their breasts to become 'more confident' in social situations, including sexual relationships with boyfriends), the material-discursive agents intra-act differently and can therefore be understood to produce different bodily potentials for both women. The differing experiences and bodily possibilities resulting from cosmetic surgery can thus be understood as being produced by differing entanglements (intra-actions between) of similar material-discursive arrangements. Such an approach assists in making sense of the active and unpredictable processes by which bodily practices and phenomena are co-constituted. We suggest this is useful in assisting better understandings of the highly complex and contentious phenomenon of cosmetic surgery, highlighting the import of conceptual frameworks that move us beyond reductive readings of such practices through constructionist lenses of structure/agency for example. Both bodies are produced in intra-action with the gendered phenomenon of cosmetic surgery, but they are produced and lived differently.[3] This suggests the contingent, rather than predetermined, embodiment of gender produced through a broader palette of intra-actions between myriad material-discursive elements. Such a reading suggests that the specificities of micro-context is a productive way in which to explore complex phenomena, and – more than this – neglecting micro-contexts risks reductive readings that perpetuate non-productive understandings of bodies and how they are practiced.

A feminist posthuman perspective lends detail to understanding how gender currently assembles through cosmetic surgical procedures such as breast implants and why such bodily practices are undertaken. Approaching Kate and Isabelle's bodies as passively inscribed by unequal gender relations would miss the significant detail relating to how their bodies are actively composed in this context. Through territorialisation we can understand how social forces 'impinge on individuals', but this occurs through a process of engagement rather than being simply imposed on a passive body. As Fox (2002, p. 360) describes, '... for anyone, the social may impinge to territorialize (a body) to establish limits from which it is hard to fly. But these limits can be redrawn, especially if one has a little help'. This connects to the concept of transversality, explored in the following examples, which specifically attempts to redraw the social relations in assemblages to alter or extend what a body can do.

Study 2. Body image, Barbie and transversality

In the following examples we focus on the feminist group at West End High – a small, fee-paying, prestigious co-educational performing arts school in London for students aged 10 to 16 – where three days of the week are based around their academic education and two days are focused on training in drama, dance and singing.

As noted earlier, this school was one of several schools studied as part of a larger project, which involved researchers working with feminist group, clubs or societies in secondary schools. The project was framed as an explicit attempt to impact the school community through a feminist 'intra-activist' research assemblage to enable transversal relations between students, teachers, school management and academics (Ringrose & Renold 2016). In this school, twelve year 9 and 10 girls at the school met through weekly 'fem club' – as they became known – meetings that were facilitated by a committed self-defined feminist teacher.

The school operates as a professional agency and, despite the school's admission policy stating that it makes decisions free of any discrimination, the children appear to be given a place on the basis of their marketability for professional work (a striking number of students are slim, able-bodied and white). Market values and commodification are central as students become constituted in 'economic terms' as competitors for uptake in London's entertainment industry (Retallack et al. 2016). Such social forces can be thought of as territorialisations or modes of discursive, material and affective 'capture' (Ringrose 2013) that shape the potentialities of the students' embodiment. Unsurprisingly given this context, discussion was largely oriented around body image, sexual objectification and self-esteem, which emerged as significant issues in the context of the school's dramatic and performing arts focus. These issues came up at nearly every meeting and were captured in the interview talk about body shaming, including even of women that are 'too skinny':

DEMI: Like people who are kind of curvy go to skinny people, 'God you are just anorexic'.

ROBYN: And they go 'Real women have curves' stuff like that, and every woman is a real woman. It doesn't matter what they look like.

APRIL: That is on social media so much.

DEMI: It's ridiculous.

INTERVIEWER: Social media?

DEMI: Yes skinny models saying, 'Is this what sexy is?' and then they do like –

APRIL: This is what a real woman looks like. But some people are just naturally skinny and they see that and they think . . . That is skinny shaming and there is a shaming for everything and there really shouldn't be.

ROBYN: People should stop focusing on how people's bodies look and more on what their personality is because that is what means more than how someone looks or their body shape and everything.

INTERVIEWER: So what if you don't fit these ideals at all?

ROBYN: Then you are going to have really poor self-esteem.

DEMI: You are not going to feel comfortable with your own body.

ROBYN: We go on and on saying oh people who look like that should just feel happy . . . but I just feel that no one likes their own body . . . your own shape . . .

INTERVIEWER: How did you become critical of these images?

ROBYN: When I looked in the mirror and didn't see that . . . If other people put you down for the way you look then you are going to put yourself down for the way you look later on in life . . . It really depends on who is around you.

Looking 'in the mirror' here is discussed as an element of lack in relation to ideals of femininity. The practices of power, in this case are explicitly contextualised by Robyn as depending on the material relations of 'who is around you' – in this case the repressive theatre school where star grooming has led to a difficult context of bodily perfectionism. However, the group was convinced that talking about it with each other was key:

DEMI: The only way that we can get to that point is that if we get rid of the discomfort we have talking about these issues.

In order to tackle their discomfort the group worked on various projects, including art and blog entries to discuss body objectification, and using social media to challenge the sexist bodily relations. Here we want to focus on one participant Robyn who had a particularly difficult time of things as she was the only 'over-weight' (as she termed it) girl, not only in the feminist group, but also in the entire school. In the discussion that follows, we consider the possibilities of the affirmation of difference in practices that resist and transform the norm. Part of Deleuze and Guattari's ontology is micro-political in its recognition that the capacity to be otherwise is implicit in the assemblage because of the ways it is continually in process. But an activist-research assemblage can also enable difference and transversal relations through the creation of conditions whereby subjects and objects in assemblages can enter into power relations differently to challenge binaries (e.g., male/female, fat/fit, pretty/ugly, confident/low self-esteem, etc.). Below we consider how Robyn uses her criticality with her feminist group to materially reconfigure 'fat' through her relationship with an object – a Barbie doll.

Robyn's 'talent' was singing and opera, and she noted her 'ultimate goal is to be an opera singer at *La Scalla* . . . or as a starring part to play Christine in *Phantom of the Opera* or Mimi from *La Boheme*'. While becoming an opera singer could accommodate her size somewhat better than other theatrical ambitions (like dancing/drama), she was nonetheless deeply concerned about the fat shaming that went on at school, particularly by the boys at school. For one of her blog entries Robyn undertook a research interview on 'male image of women and what they expect us to be' with a friend in her peer group – a boy Ian – who had previously attended the school, and then told a story about being called 'fatsuma' at school:

ROBYN: What is your idealistic woman?
IAN: Thin, smaller than me. She has to be talkative and fun but she has to be pretty. Blonde hair and blue eyes . . .
ROBYN: What do you think is more important in a girl, their appearance or their personality?
IAN: Looks over personality cause their face is what I see every day . . .
ROBYN: Would you date a girl who is wider than most others?
IAN: She would have to be super nice and have a pretty face but no bigger than, say, you.

We discussed the interview in a feminist group session with the researchers in particular expressing some shock/horror that Ian would openly suggest that he couldn't possibly date anyone 'bigger' than Robyn, to her face. The callousness of Ian's sense of entitlement struck a chord with all of the girls, but Robyn seemed to face it with a stony sense of resignation about that being how boys are. Indeed she seemed to imply that being able to get this type of frank response was part of the very criticality needed to then confront these power relations. She continued to debate these issues in the blog entry that accompanied the interview extracts.

ROBYN: I find it really annoying when girls think they need to change themselves for a boy. All my life I've been friends with boys and after a few years to develop a hard skin when it comes to insults or 'jokes' as they call it. I've been called so many things . . . I just cry for ten minutes and get over it. I did have a friend in my old school who used to love playing sports-football especially we used to always meet up with the boys in our class for a game but then one day one of our friends called out to her on the field that she should stop playing because her fat distracts them flopping about when she was running. And she cried for about a week, mostly glued to my shoulder, and I tried to comfort her saying that your body doesn't matter and that what he said was just a malicious comment that had no meaning but the damage was already done. Comments like that just confuse me because I just can't decipher their thought process and how someone can think something like that won't hurt a girl. I did talk to him later and he was sorry for what he said, he claimed that he wasn't thinking and an insult like that would just bounce off someone else . . . let's just say he wouldn't be upsetting any of the girls in our class like that after I had talked to him!

However, because we are in a theatre school I do think that the boys in this school are kinder than that but still a few comments can sting. For example when I was in year seven a boy in my class started spreading rumours about my weight and used a particularly unbecoming word (fatsuma) to highlight how fat he thought I really was. It went around the whole school and I was one of the last people to find out, not even from him. And he still denied what he had said. I knew I wasn't (and still aren't) the skinniest or prettiest or bubbliest person and I think knowing that for years at my old school gave me a defence but when I came here I didn't know anyone and that guard kind of slipped and that's why a comment like that which probably wouldn't have affected me in my old school really upset me. I do think that generally boys don't really understand how some of their comments can affect a girl as it wouldn't affect them themselves because in my opinion, boys have a lot more confidence and can push away a comment a lot easier than a girl can because we are made by the media especially to be very self-conscious and to take pride in our appearance.

This blog entry was accompanied by four images: first an image of 'all women are real, all bodies are beautiful' featuring differently shaped models from the Tumblr site 'All bodies are beautiful'; second a photo of Julia Lawrence saying 'it should be illegal to call somebody fat on TV'. There were also two images of Barbie: the first of a woman holding Barbie with plastic surgery lines drawn all

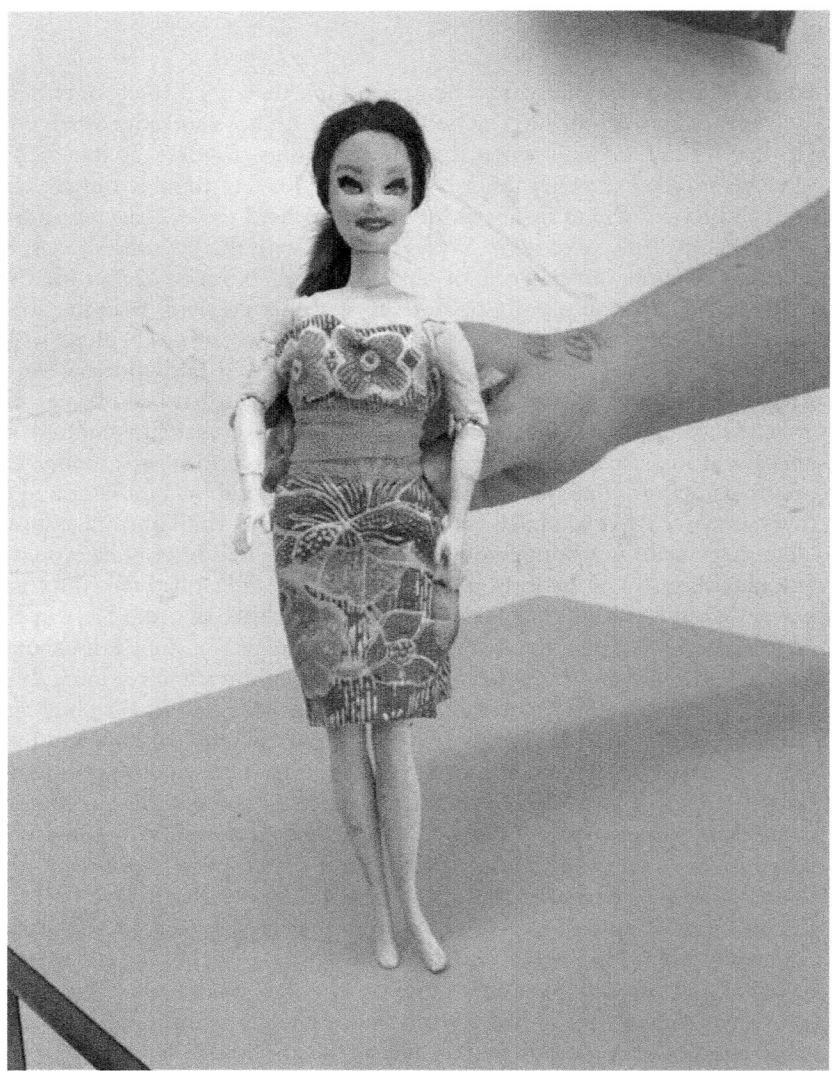

Figure 11.1 'Curvy Barbie'

over her body to slim her to Barbie proportions and the second of Barbie on the cover of *Sports Illustrated*. During the session discussion we also decided to try to think further about Barbie and what her body could not and could do. We had the usual discussions of her top-heavy body and high-heeled feet, so she would always be on her tippy toes. Afterwards at home Robyn constructed what she coined a 'curvy Barbie' who was 'more like her' (See Figure 11.1). Robyn adapted Barbie's body by adding plaster to her arms and middle, she dyed her hair brown and changed the eye colour to green and also created a new outfit of looser clothing, bar the sash pulling in the waist.

Curvy Barbie was met with much discussion in the feminist group. The girls took pictures of it and it led to a discussion of how a range of material artefacts from childhood – such as Barbie underpants – were both loved and despised at the same time. These are more than human object relations. The materiality of engaging with and altering Barbie's material form and proportions (engaging Barbie's plasticity) are significant. In our analysis, curvy Barbie is a more than human transitional object, which is part of how Robyn works to challenge the territorialising relations around fatness at her school and in her peer group.

The data we have explored above – from Kate but particularly from Isabelle – demonstrated a form of internalised and externalised set of practices undertaken to reach the ideal proportions of objects like Barbie as part of a much wider global assemblage of consumer-based norms of feminine beauty, where participants brought silicone into their bodies to materially change their shape. In contrast, we see Robyn's creation of curvy Barbie as a remarkable example of girls' practices that work to change the material object itself. Refusing the fixity of the plastic form they adapt the material object. Robyn makes Barbie more like her, rather than adapting to fit the prototype. This practice is discussed as helping girls feel better about their bodies.

In this example it is obvious that gender is not simply discursive. Gendered and sexualised matter is worked upon and in important ways. Also crucial to foreground was how it was the assembled relations and practices of the feminist group that allows for conditions of possibility for something different to emerge together. 'Fem Club' is the spatial and temporal pedagogical-research assemblage that enables a transversal disruption of hierarchical power relations (much like Guattari's clinic) and possible practices of positive transformation. We suggest that the repeated territorialisation through normative feminine bodily norms is disrupted through the transversal relations that occur in the group, as well as through the 'thing power' of curvy Barbie (Bennet 2010).

Conclusion

We have drawn on conceptual tools from Deleuze and Guattari in combination with Barad to re-think practice. Deleuze and Guattari's call to move from representationalism to a topographical mapping or cartography has been welcomed by qualitative researchers who wish to incorporate more than ideological notions of axiomatics of power (van der Tuin 2014) and instead, to consider power relations organised spatially, temporally and through the multi-modalities of sound, touch, feel *and look* (Ringrose & Coleman 2013). Karen Barad's work – specifically her theorisation of human agency as constituted via material intra-actions – enabled a revaluing of matter and an exploration of how agency is distributed beyond a human subject to a more than human set of intra-active relationships and practices.

The empirical examples explored in this chapter show how such Deleuzo-Guattarian and Baradian posthuman perspectives contribute to our under-standings of how gender assembles through the body and informs what a body can do (or not do), and how these assembled relations may enable dis-ruptions to oppressive norms (in this case the idealised forms of embodied femininity) or not. The examples of Kate and Isabelle's breast implant surgeries drew on this feminist posthuman approach and used concepts of assemblage, territorialisation and intra-action to understand the complex ways gender materialises differently to inform 'what a body can do'. From this perspective, the practice or enactment of cosmetic surgery occurs in a broader material-discursive enactment of gender. Performative entanglements between actors such as socio-historical aspects of gender, alongside various environments of bodily display (the beach, the pool), heterosexual, peer and family relation-ships and the material-object relations of the implants are important aspects through which Kate and Isabelle's cosmetic surgeries were produced. Nar-rowly defined feminine bodily norms were of course also important dimen-sions framing both surgeries. However rather than seeing these norms as providing a simple explanation for the practice of cosmetic surgery, a posthu-man feminist perspective reframes gender as an intra-active assemblage which composes a body's possibilities (what a body can do). This perspective assists in making sense of why Kate and Isabelle had different possibilities available to them following their surgeries. This approach aims to sketch a more complex picture of the way gender is intra-actively assembled through myriad contex-tual factors such as the 'problematic' practices of cosmetic surgical procedures and highlights the micro-relations through which such bodily practices are undertaken.

In our second examples we drew on the idea of transversality to show how changing the social relations of power in and around school may be possible via feminist politics and practices. We suggest that the re-assembling of subjectivity that occurred through the girls' intra-actions in the feminist group – through their discussions, practices and object relations – enabled transversal relations that disrupted normative hierarchies of pupil/teacher and toy industry/con-sumer. The concepts and examples we drew on aimed to show 'what a body can do' through gender as a process produced in continual tension between the potential for territorialisation and transversality. This contributes to under-standings of both how gender currently assembles, and how it could also be assembled differently.

Overall we have shown how the toolkit from this posthuman concern with matter disturbs notions of discrete human-centred subjective agency as well as re-staging the onto-epistemlogical logics of social and ecological change. A focus on the more than human 'doings' of gender enables the ambiguities and complexities of gender practices to be explored, including the bodily and sensate dimensions, beyond the discursive and including consideration of materiality and objects. We have also shown what transversal relations can look like, particularly those that interfere with normative contexts of idealised femininity organised through competition, comparison, shaming and self-hatred. Our configuration and deployment of the concepts of assemblage, territorialisation, intra-action and transversality offered us useful explanations for the ways the conditions of possibility for gendered embodiments are relational, constantly in motion, and are sometimes open to transformative change depending upon the types of practice in play.

Notes

1 The concept of affect is also crucial to Deleuze and Guattari's understanding of bodies and the process of territorialisation. For a useful overview and discussion, see Fox (2002). The concept of territorialisation is prioritised in this chapter as it denotes the 'capturing' of affect that occurs through gender as a (current) hierarchical social category.
2 The ethical protocol involved getting informed consent from parents and students to participate in interviews and to document and share some of the group productions, including social media posts and messages through screen shots. Please see Ringrose and Renold (2016) for further methodological and ethical details about the process of working in this way with schools – what we call creating intra-active feminist research assemblages.
3 The different outcomes and bodily potentials stemming from Kate and Isabelle's cosmetic surgeries are explored in more detail elsewhere (Coffey 2013a, 2016).

References

Barad, K 2007, *Meeting the universe halfway: Quantum physics and the entanglement of matter and meaning*, Duke University Press, Durham, NC & London.

Bartky, S 1990, *Femininity and domination: Studies in the phenomenology of oppression*, Routledge, New York.

Bennett, 2010, *Vibrant matter: A political ecology of things*, Duke University Press Durham, NC.

Bordo, S 2003, *Unbearable weight: Feminism, Western culture and the body*, University of California Press, California.

Budgeon, S 2003, 'Identity as an embodied event', *Body and Society*, vol. 9, no. 1, pp. 35–55.

Coffey, J 2013a, 'Bodies, body work and gender: Exploring a Deleuzian approach', *Journal of Gender Studies*, vol. 22, no. 1, pp. 3–16.

Coffey, J 2013b, "Body pressure': Negotiating gender through body work practices', *Youth Studies Australia*, vol. 32, no. 2, pp. 39–48.

Coffey, J forthcoming, 'What can I do next?' Cosmetic Surgery, femininities and affect', *Women: A Cultural Review*.

Colebrook, C 2002, *Gilles Deleuze*, Routledge, London.

Coleman, R 2009, *The becoming of bodies: Girls, images, experience*, Manchester University Press, Manchester & New York.

Currier, D 2003, 'Feminist technological futures', *Feminist Theory*, vol. 4, no. 3, pp. 321–338.

Davis, K 1995, *Reshaping the female body*, Routledge, New York.

Deleuze, G 1992, 'Ethology: Spinoza and Us', in J Crary & S K Winter (eds), *Incorporations*, Zone, New York, pp. 625–633.

Deleuze, G & Guattari, F 1984, *Anti-Oedipus: Capitalism and schizophrenia*, Athlone Press, London.

Deleuze, G & Parnet, C 2002, *Dialogues II*, Columbia University Press, New York.

Featherstone, M 2010, 'Body, image and affect in consumer culture', *Body and Society*, vol. 16, no. 1, pp. 193–221.

Fox, NJ 2002, 'Refracting "Health": Deleuze, Guattari and body-self', *Health*, vol. 6, no. 3, pp. 347–363.

Genosko, G 2009, *Felix Guattari: A critical introduction*, Pluto Press, London.

Grosz, E 1994, *Volatile bodies: Towards a corporeal feminism*, Allen & Unwin, St Leonards.

Haikem, E 1997, *Venus envy: A history of cosmetic surgery*, Johns Hopkins University Press, Maryland.

Jackson, AY & Mazzei, LA 2011, *Thinking with theory in qualitative research: Viewing data across multiple perspectives*, Routledge, London.

Lenz Taguchi, H 2013, 'Images of thinking in feminist materialisms: Ontological divergences and the production of researcher subjectivities', *International Journal of Qualitative Studies in Education*, vol. 26, no. 6, pp. 706–716.

Renold, E & Ringrose, J 2008, 'Regulation and rupture: Mapping tween and teenage girls' resistance to the Heterosexual Matrix', *Feminist Theory*, vol. 9, no. 3, pp. 314–339.

Retallack, H, Ringrose, J & Lawrence, E 2016, '"Fuck your body image!" Teen girls, twitter feminism and networked affect in a London school', in J Coffey, S Budgeon & H Cahill (eds), *Learning bodies: The body in youth and childhood studies*, Springer, New York, pp 85–103.

Ringrose, J 2013, *Postfeminist education?: Girls and the sexual politics of schooling*, Routledge, London.

Ringrose, J & Coleman, R 2013, 'Looking and desiring machines: A feminist Deleuzian mapping of affect and bodies', in R Coleman & J Ringrose (eds), *Deleuze and research methodologies*, Edinburgh University Press, Edinburgh, UK, pp. 125–144.

Ringrose, J & Renold, E 2016, 'Cows, cabins and tweets: Posthuman intra-acting affect and feminist fires in secondary school', in CA Taylor & C Hughes (eds), *Posthuman research practices in education*, Palgrave, London, pp. 220–241.

Simonsen K, 2012, Encountering other bodies: Practice, emotion and ethics, in P Harrison & B Anderson (eds), *Taking-place: Non-representational theories and geography*, Ashgate Publishing, Ltd, London, pp. 221–239.

Taylor, JS 2012, 'Buying and selling breasts: Cosmetic surgery, beauty treatments and risk', *The Sociological Review*, vol. 60, no. 4, pp. 635–653.

van der Tuin, I 2014, *Generational feminism: New materialist introduction to a generative approach*, Lexington Books, Lanham, MD.

van der Tuin, I & Dolphijn, R 2010, 'The transversality of new materialism', *Women: A Cultural Review*, vol. 21, no. 2, pp. 153–171.

Walkerdine, V 2013, 'Using the work of Felix Guattari to understand space, place, social justice, and education', *Qualitative Inquiry*, vol. 19, no. 10, pp. 756–764.

Chapter 12

The practice of survival

Reflexivity and transformation of contract-employed beginning teachers' professional practice

Michelle Ludecke

The 'problem'

This chapter explores the 'problem' of contract employment in teaching, within beginning teaching in particular, as the difficulty of retaining beginning teachers continues to prevail in practice, the literature and the media. The problem is explored through a practice approach as a way of grasping the conditions of human action and social order (Reckwitz 2002). Through an investigation of twelve beginning teachers' experiences of contractual employment conditions an understanding of symbolic structures of knowledge, such as the transmission of tacit knowledge, was sought. The investigation revealed how systems such as contract employment can enable and constrain individuals to interpret the world according to certain forms, and to behave in corresponding ways, impacting on their commitment to remain in the teaching profession.

Context

Beginning teacher attrition in relation to employment conditions remains a global concern, and the negative consequences of high teacher turnover have great implications for the future of quality education and educational reform. Such issues are reflected in the Australian context. The 'Kennett Revolution' (1992 to 1999), as then-Premier Jeff Kennett himself described it (Costar & Economou 1999), was largely responsible for the casualisation of the teaching profession in the state of Victoria, Australia. The decentralisation of public schools, culminating in the *Education (Self-Governing Schools) Act 1998* (Vic), resulted in individual schools bearing the responsibility of managing their own funds and hiring their own staff. In this climate, employing more teachers on contracts was economically rationalised. Government funding for the public school system was substantially reduced, with 350 government schools closed, and 7000 teaching jobs removed between 1992 and 1995. New teaching jobs were advertised as contract positions during this period (Costar & Economou 1999).

Today the Australian Education Union (AEU) reports that 45–50% of beginning teachers are employed on short-term contracts (Australian Education Union [AEU] 2013). They contend that contract employment discourages people from entering and staying in the profession, and report that teachers on contracts say the lack of job security is very stressful. Staffing decisions in Victorian government schools (which constitute upwards of 70% of schools in Victoria) are made in the context of the school's preferred staffing profile, which takes into account the school's strategic plan, legislative requirements, curriculum, funding available and projected student enrolments. While the Department of Education and Training (DE&T) states a commitment to the standard mode of employment in schools being ongoing, they also recognise that for some positions fixed-term or casual employment is necessary such as when replacing short-term absences or responding to predicted staff excess (DE&T 2015b).

To apply for a teaching position in Victoria, beginning teachers are required to complete a two-fold process of registration with the Victorian Institute of Teaching (VIT) and demonstrate evidence of 'initiatives' such as Principles of Learning and Teaching (PoLT) and the Australian Professional Standards for Teachers (APST) in their practice. The APST outline 'what teachers should know and be able to do' (AITSL 2015). The PoLT are self-described as 'a range of audit instruments, professional development modules and support materials to support teachers to examine their pedagogical practices and establish a plan of action in their schools' (DE&T 2015a). White contends that PoLT 'permeates official documentation and, disturbingly, all new teachers in Victoria as well as those seeking promotion must demonstrate their knowledge of and fidelity to PoLT' (2010, p. 280). A practice of survival aligns with White's contention that providing 'competency standards for how teachers should measure up, or specifications of how teaching should be performed ... serves to reduce teachers rather than improve teaching' (2010, p. 293). A performative agenda is also apparent in the VIT process for provisional and full registration.

> Provisional registration with the VIT is granted to teachers who have yet to demonstrate that they have met the APST at the proficient level. Provisional registration is granted for a period of two years. During this period it is expected that teachers will be eligible to apply for full registration.
>
> (VIT 2015)

These few examples are some of the systems that graduate teachers work in their transition to beginning teaching in Victoria, Australia. These conditions are representative of conditions of employment in other Australian states, and in various countries around the world, such as the casualisation of teaching in Ireland and Canada, which have the potential to contribute to the phenomenon of beginning teacher attrition. Correa et al. (2014) link similar performative agendas to beginning teachers' reality shock (Kim & Cho 2014). In the context of this research, such systems reinforce to graduate and beginning teachers the perception that others are in control of their professional trajectory.

Theoretical framework

To investigate the reflexive relationship between contract employment and beginning teachers' experiences, including how individuals and agents carry, reproduce and transform practices, I take a practice approach drawing from the theoretical influences of Reckwitz, Schatzki and Kemmis. Practice theories and approaches are quite varied. Of the many theorists working in the practice field, the works of these theorists have been selected to frame this chapter as they treat practices as a way of understanding the interconnected conditions of human action and social order in large social phenomena such as educational establishments. Specifically Reckwitz's consideration that a practice is a 'routinized way in which bodies are moved, objects are handled, subjects are treated, things are described and the world is understood' (2002, p. 250) provides an overarching framework. Within this framework the 'field of practice', the place to study the nature and transformation of the subject matter (Schatzki 2001a), is contract employment of beginning teachers. The subject matter is the experiences of beginning teachers, the symbolic structures of knowledge they develop and ascribe to, and how their practice is reflexively transformed as a result of these experiences. In addition Kemmis (2010) articulates the necessity of moving towards a more encompassing view of practice that recognises extra-individual features such as material-economic features of practice. Different participants in a practice enact it in different ways, using their bodies in different ways, having profound effects on practices and the practitioner. The individuals in this research enacted their practice differently while under contract employment conditions, a material-economic feature of their practice. What emerges through framing the research within these practice approaches is a practice of survival.

Beginning teachers' practice is conceived as embodied, materially mediated arrays of human activity centrally organised around shared practical understanding (Schatzki 2001a). Within practices there is a transformative aspect that involves 'changing existing states of affairs in the components of semantic space ("sayings"), physical and material space and circumstances ("doings"), and social space ("relatings")' (Kemmis 2009, pp. 22–23). The maintenance of practices, and the persistence and transformation of social life, rests centrally on the development of shared embodied know-how (Schatzki 2001a), through which practitioners' sayings, doings and relatings transform, and are transformed by, their practice as individuals and agents. Reckwitz posits that practice theorists have hardly treated the question of the specific place for the 'individual', as distinguished from the agent, in practice theory (2002, p. 256). As every agent carries out a multitude of different social practices, the 'individual is the unique crossing point of practices, of bodily-mental routines' (Reckwitz 2002, p. 256). The various practices that comprise this practice of survival, discussed further in this chapter, include sayings that revealed denial of status, perceptions of being under surveillance, and engaging in strategies for increasing visibility; doings such as creating an appearance of being in control (swimming), showing signs of struggling (sinking), and periodic activities of job seeking; and relatings including participation in, and perpetuation of, survival discourses, and comparisons of employment conditions and workload. The practice of survival also encompasses transmission of tacit knowledge among agents – in this case beginning teachers employed on a contract.

Contract teaching as a field of practice creates a system within a system. Agents acting within a system employ know-how, emotion and motivational knowledge according to the particular practice (Reckwitz 2002, p. 249). These formal and informal forms of knowledge and expectations shape agents to learn how to 'be a body' in a certain way and 'carry, reproduce and transform' practices (Reckwitz 2002, p. 249). In a survival state, agents will cling to security in any form. As such they will ascribe to myths and rumors and attribute off-hand comments with more weight than they are intended. They attempt to make sense of their practice while in a state of survival, and their attempts to rationalise their practice are revealed in what they say, what they do and those they relate to. The embodiment of a practice of survival transforms beginning teachers' entrance, induction and commitment to the teaching profession. Beginning teachers speak of 'this bloody contract. If I was permanent it would be great. They've got you by the neck – they've got you by the throat!' Such teachers are expected to demonstrate ongoing commitment to the profession while experiencing ongoing uncertainty regarding the conditions of their employment. The contract, as a material-economic feature of practice, positions the beginning teacher as if in a lifeboat, where they cannot feel like a 'real' teacher until they can operate with certainty. Such positioning impacts on the practice of beginning teaching and the broader practice of teaching.

The participants

This chapter draws from a larger qualitative study (Ludecke 2013) investigating beginning teachers' experiences through an examination of the differences between and within individuals, allowing categories of description to emerge from the data. Data was collected from participants through individual semi-structured interviews and written communication over three years. The aim was to unearth questions that have been clouded by perceived 'problems' of beginning teachers such as reality shock, attrition, stress and lack of status.

Table 12.1 Overview of Participants and Employment Conditions

Teacher, Teaching Category, Age bracket	Sector & Region	Previous practicum at employed school	Condition of employment 1st year	Condition of employment 2nd year	Condition of employment 3rd year
Janet Primary 26–29	Government Melbourne Metropolitan	Yes 1 year prior to 1st year	6-month short-term contract, rolled over	1 year fixed-term contract	Family leave replacement (between 6 months and 7 years)
Maggie Primary >25	Government Melbourne Metropolitan	Yes 1 year prior to 1st year	6-month short-term contract, rolled over	New school, 1-year fixed-term contract	1-year fixed-term contract, rolled over
Lachy Secondary >25	Government Melbourne Metropolitan	No	6-month short-term contract, rolled over	1-year fixed-term contract, rolled over	1-year fixed-term contract
Lara Primary >25	Government Melbourne Metropolitan	No	6-month short-term contract, rolled over	Family leave replacement (between 6 months and 7 years)	Ongoing
Amelia Secondary >25	Catholic Melbourne Metropolitan	Yes 4 years prior to 1st year	1-year maternity leave replacement contract	1-year maternity leave replacement contract	Ongoing – on unpaid leave, teaching in the UK, 2-term contract
Cassidy Secondary >25	Government Regional Victoria	No	6-month contract, successfully applied for 2-year fixed-term in April	2-year fixed-term contract	2-year fixed-term contract, rolled over for another 2 years

(Continued)

Table 12.1 (Continued)

Teacher, Teaching Category, Age bracket	Sector & Region	Previous practicum at employed school	Condition of employment 1st year	Condition of employment 2nd year	Condition of employment 3rd year
Richard Primary >25	Government Melbourne Metropolitan	No	6-month short-term contract, rolled over	6-month short-term contract, rolled over	1-year fixed-term contract
Sari Secondary >25	Catholic Melbourne Metropolitan	Yes 1 year prior to 1st year	1-year fixed-term contract	1-year fixed-term contract	Ongoing
Beth Secondary >25	Government Melbourne Metropolitan	Yes 1 year prior to 1st year	6-month short-term contract, rolled over	6-month short-term contract, rolled over	1-year fixed-term contract
Sandra Secondary >25	Government Melbourne Metropolitan	No	6-month short-term contract, rolled over	6-month short-term contract, ongoing semester 2	Ongoing
Tash Primary >25	Government Melbourne Metropolitan	Yes 2 years prior to 1st year	6-month short-term contract, rolled over	1-year fixed-term contract	Rolled over to ongoing
Sebastian Primary >25	Government Melbourne Metropolitan	Yes 3 years prior to 1st year	1-year fixed-term contract, rolled over	1-year fixed-term contract, rolled over	Rolled over to ongoing

A practice of survival

In this chapter a practice of survival is revealed through sayings, doings and relatings. Sayings include hegemonic discourses of 'just a grad' and 'only a first-year', denial of status, perceptions of being under surveillance, and employment of strategies for increasing visibility. Doings incorporated creating an appearance of being in control, showing signs of struggling and periodic activities of job seeking. Relatings comprised of participation in, and perpetuation of, survival discourses, and comparisons of employment conditions and workload. The participants in this study are part of a collective with shared understandings of what it means to be a beginning teacher and to be employed on a contract. They constitute their own truths in order to understand the incomprehensible, creating and perpetuating myths that allow them to make sense of the perceived injustices they experience. The contract as the material-economic feature of these beginning teachers' practice is rationalised in a variety of ways, viewed as an external inhuman oppression, or an object for manipulation in order to reach the goal of ongoing employment.

Through the way the participants make sense of their world, an evolution of the survival discourse is evident. Discourse, in this sense, is being, while practice is the becoming from which discourses result, and to which they eventually accede (Schatzki 2001b, p. 53). If, as Schatzki posits, social order is established within the sway of social practices, and that mind is a central dimension of this 'process', a practice of survival has developed from, and subsequently contributes to survival discourses (2001b, p. 50). In addition the main extra-individual feature recognised in relation to this context is the contractual nature of beginning teachers' work (Kemmis 2010, p. 3). Schatzki asserts that contexts can prefigure – enable or constrain – what occurs in them (2002, p. 62). These teachers' perceptions of their own multi-faceted practice affect their efficacy and their ability and willingness to cope with educational change. As these beginning teachers' understanding of the system grew, so did their ability to act as agents within the system. A causality dilemma arises where the teachers' practice shapes the employment climate, which reflexively aids the transformation of beginning teachers' practice of survival. Part of their practice of survival has little to do with the day-to-day work of teaching and the development of their pedagogical practices. Rather, their 'work' involves getting and maintaining employment through collecting evidence of their professional practice, negotiation of contracts, job seeking, applications and interviews.

Situated work involves active participation in the material world in the material here-and-now, times, places and physical conditions, and frequently involves systematically structured material interactions such as role-related functions (Kemmis 2010). There has been much discussion in Victoria in the material here-and-now regarding the function of teacher contracts in relation to issues of attrition. The convoluted and often context-specific nature of employment in Victorian schools is rarely fully understood by beginning teachers applying for their first teaching position. The participants in this study report a variety of complicated employment conditions that impact on their role as a teacher throughout their first year and beyond. For many of the participants, their tacit knowledge of the nature of their work under such conditions shape the way they perceive their commitment to their school and the profession. Ongoing job uncertainty contributes to the feeling that their practices are under surveillance.

Beginning teachers are unable to view their future with as much perspective (through the benefit of hindsight) as their more experienced colleagues, therefore they are less likely to see how their situation may change or improve. This research reveals that things have become much worse for beginning teachers than in the past. Certainly there has been much research into, and tacit understanding surrounding, the plight of the beginning teacher, and not much has changed in at least forty years with respect to the emotional toll the first year in particular takes on a beginning teacher. Since Lortie (1975) recognised the teaching profession is an isolated one, survival themes in the literature continue to emerge. For example, collegial isolation (Renard 2003; Schlichte et al. 2005), the wash-out effect (Feiman-Nemser 1990; Shoval et al. 2010; Veenman 1984; Wideen et al. 1998; Zeichner & Tabachnik 1981), burnout such as stress-related dropout (Friedman 2000; Goddard et al. 2006; Høigaard et al. 2011; Maslach 2003), 'initiation' (Berman 1994, p. 49; Maslach 2003); (Schempp et al. 1993), liminality (Pierce 2007) and shock (Kim & Cho 2014; Shoval et al. 2010; Stokking et al. 2003). Despite this wealth of literature, there is a lack of empirical research on the understanding and impact of contract teaching positions in Australian contexts.

The participants in casualised positions after three years (Table 12.1) report their experiences with more negativity than those with ongoing employment. Negativity is expressed through a perceived surveillance of their practices, shaping the way they survived their transition to teaching. Their negative perceptions, feelings of surveillance and the embodiment of dispositions particular to this group reveal a manifestation of a practice of survival. The beginning teachers in this research practice survival in a variety of ways – having both negative and positive outcomes, depending on whether they experience a sense of agency in their practice. Their practice of survival is expressed through denial of status, increasing visibility (perceived and enacted) and ascribing to and perpetuating myths.

Sayings as indicators of status and identity – 'just a grad' and 'only a first year'

The participants in this study often call themselves 'just a grad' or 'only a first-year', separating themselves from their more experienced colleagues. One of the most telling phrases that emerged from the interviews is Janet's: 'Part of me still sees myself as just a grad, just because I don't have years of experience under my belt'. Janet's anxiety comes from feeling like she was asking a lot of questions, having someone else in the classroom with her 'watching me', worrying about 'looking like an idiot', being perceived by others as inexperienced, and having to 'perform', particularly when employed in a contractual position. Similarly Amelia uses the term 'grad' in a non-pejorative sense when describing the way her colleagues place higher expectations on her because they know she is familiar with the school – she says, 'they forget I'm just a grad'. Cassidy also reports a lack of status through the mismatch between her expectations and the reality of the conditions of her employment. This mismatch led to feelings of confusion and isolation, causing her to feel less like a 'real teacher'. These discourses are a form of othering themselves. Gee contends:

> [that] nonelites are 'encouraged' to accept the inferior identities elites ascribe to them in talk and interaction . . . as if they were the actual achieved identities of these nonelite people, achieved on the basis of their lack of skill, intelligence, morality, or sufficient effort in comparison with the elites.
>
> (Gee 2000, p. 113)

The participants here ascribe and accept inferior identities that distinguish them from 'elites'.

When employing such sayings, beginning teachers indicate an absence of status, their low positioning in the social hierarchy within their school, and their affiliation with other beginning teachers in the wider teaching community. While the term 'grad' likely began as a pejorative term, the teachers in this study use the term in a non-pejorative sense, to define who they are at this moment in time; that they are who they are because of the experiences they have had within their affinity group (Gee 2000). Similarly, the beginning teachers in this study use the term 'real' teacher to indicate a similar lack of status as well as a lack of access to what they perceive are the tools of the profession. These are tangible tools such as keys, technical knowledge, learned skills and techniques that develop over time, and tools in the form of employment conditions that symbolise status and belonging. Lack of access to, or understanding of, such tools of the teaching profession heightens the difference in status between beginning teachers and their more experienced or tenured colleagues. Feelings of being 'on the outer' contribute to the shaping of a collective practice of survival that is outside the realm of the 'real' teacher. 'Real' work is still perceived as located in the face-to-face interactions with students. However, most reported that the main focus of their work became about the conditions of their employment.

Hinchliffe and Jolly encourage moving away from thinking about graduates in regards to skills and more towards an examination of the conditions of performance (2011, p. 546). They stress the importance of an individual being able to understand how a particular practice is enacted (the language and vocabulary, the goals and purposes, and the broader environment in which a practice takes place) and to be able to construct a legitimate identity. A practice of survival forms the basis of these beginning teachers' identity, which is articulated through sayings. For these teachers, the main aspect of the practice of survival is reflected in the connections between such sayings and the way beginning teachers perceive themselves as under surveillance, and how perceptions shape their doings.

'Doings': Increasing visibility versus feeling under surveillance

Beginning teachers on short-term contracts are working under conditions of performance that include lack of control combined with mixed messages from colleagues and administration regarding expectations of commitment. In order to demonstrate commitment, these teachers increase their visibility, alongside creating the appearance of being in control. Many describe undertaking co- and extra-curricular involvement outside their areas of expertise, refraining from sharing their struggles with mentors, working late nights and early mornings, and over-committing to day-to-day aspects of teaching such as testing, assessment and reporting. They object to constantly feeling under surveillance, while at the same time attempt to increase their visibility. Such feelings contribute to a climate of performativity.

Many of these teachers are strongly encouraged, and often expected, to become involved in a number of extra-curricular activities within their school. Lachy was told that all first-year teachers at his school are expected to help run the weekly Writing Club from 4.00 pm to 9.00 pm, and that it is the responsibility of the first-year teachers to stay until the very end as they are 'young, and don't have families to get home to'. Such activities are often deemed a rite of passage. Within social processes, and through interactions constituting and constituted by social practices, beginning teachers' colleagues 'apprentice' new members via their attentions (Gee & Green 1998) and the ways they enact and embody the practice of teaching. Drama teacher Beth was naturally expected to be involved in extra-curricular performances. However, in addition, she was expected to assist with sport and the Year 9 Experience program run off-site all day every Friday. The expectation that beginning teachers are seen to be 'performing' was is apparent at Lara's school where she became aware that other beginning teachers had developed and were involved in more extra-curricular programs for students than she was. She felt compelled to be involved but was caught between wanting to be 'seen' and developing something authentic in her area of expertise for the benefit of the students. As such Lara was also apprenticed by other beginning teachers.

Lara ultimately increased her visibility most effectively by applying for other jobs. She was promised the opportunity to apply for an ongoing position at the end of her first year. According to the (then) Department of Education and Early Childhood Development (DEECD):

> Where an ongoing position becomes available in a school, the principal should determine if the position is a suitable position for any eligible fixed term employee(s) in the school. Where the position is suitable the eligible fixed term employee should be offered ongoing employment. Where the position is not suitable the principal is to inform all eligible fixed term employees of that decision before proceeding to advertise the position.
>
> (DEECD 2012)

Later Lara was informed there were no ongoing positions available for her at the school for the following year, despite an ongoing position being advertised a short time after. She was offered a maternity leave replacement position for anywhere between six months to seven years, on the condition that if the person she was replacing wanted to come back, Lara's position would be terminated, but she would 'most certainly' be offered ongoing before then or at that time. Lara decided to begin applying for other jobs three months prior to the end of the school year, and soon after reported that she got an interview at another school for a more permanent position. When she told her current principal this, Lara was immediately offered a larger role within the school if she stayed at the school on a contract. Lara told the principal she would think about it, and still go along to the scheduled interview. A couple of days later Lara was offered an ongoing position at her current school, without that position being advertised. The inconsistent and unpredictable practices of some administration teams can contribute to beginning teachers' practice of survival through the impact of the nature of teachers' employment conditions and their commitment to remain at the school or in the profession.

'Relatings': Perpetuation of myths

The 'sink or swim' myth is one of a variety of survival discourses still prevalent in beginning teaching. Such discourses shape and are shaped by systemic attitudes preserved and maintained by beginning teachers, their colleagues and the wider teaching profession. Survival discourses assist to produce a structure of learned dispositions towards beginning teaching. Participants such as Lachy and Sandra were left to their own devices in the early stages of their first year, as they appeared to be 'swimming'. In contrast, other beginning teachers at their respective schools appeared to be 'sinking', demonstrated by visibly high levels of anxiety, crying and frequent absences. Visible signs of struggle have their pros and cons. They raise awareness of the problem but also, as Sandra states, 'they make you look incompetent.' A very emotional beginning teacher prompts others to provide support. Such a reactive type of support is like throwing a much-needed lifeline, yet it is not only the sinking teacher that requires such support. However, many beginning teachers are hesitant to increase their visibility in such a way for fear their contract will not be renewed. The embodiment of such attitudes has distinct effects on practices as the physical performance of a practice also shapes their willingness to ascribe to myths within the profession.

Maggie's experience of contract employment perpetuates the myth of 'last in, first out'; that the most recent person to be employed, usually on a short-term contract, would be the first teacher the administration team considered most expendable. Often, and unfortunately, retention of teachers comes down to number crunching and economics rather than merit. Despite their highly visible enactment of professional practice and commitment, some contract-employed beginning teachers have limited control over whether there will be a position at the school for them in the future. Declining student enrolments over a number of years impacted on Maggie's ability to remain at her first school. Conversely, Cassidy gained a two-year contract after only two months of employment as her school experienced increased student enrolments. Schools such as Amelia's with greater staffing flexibility and stable student enrolments seemed in a better position to offer longer contracts and ongoing employment. Such a variety of approaches to staffing among this group of beginning teachers reflect how confusing it can be to understand the complexities of employment conditions. Comparisons between graduates regarding their tenure contribute to an ongoing uncertainty regarding the conditions of their employment, and therefore uncertainty with regards to their ability to reap the personal benefits of being a professional.

Differences between contract-employed beginning teachers and their ongoing colleagues continue to shape the survival discourses. One emergent theme is the imagined removal of surveillance if granted a continuing appointment. Contract-employed beginning teachers desire an ongoing position not only for its stability, but also because they believe it will signify the end of the surveillance of their practice. The timing of advertised positions contributes to periods of heightened stress, while the process of applying and being interviewed for their 'own job' detracts such teachers from what should be a period of development and consolidation of practice. The additional element of competition for positions, often among friends, increases their anxiety. These aspects contribute to the development of a shared understanding among contract-employed beginning teachers that concerns the development and transmission of tacit knowledge in relation to status and belonging.

The 'body-activity-society complex'

The participants' sayings, doings, and relatings act in conjunction with each other, as a 'body-activity-society complex', in the enactment of a practice of survival: a 'routinized type of behaviour which consists of several elements, interconnected to one other', including forms of bodily activities such as increasing visibility, forms of mental activities such as feelings of exclusion, a background knowledge in the form of technical knowledge, shared embodied know-how and states of emotion (Schatzki 2002, p. 12). A practice of survival, a way of working as a beginning teacher under contract employment conditions, forms a collective whole whose existence necessarily depends on the existence and specific interconnectedness of these elements, and which cannot be reduced to any single element.

The combination of such sayings, doings and relatings create a dense, oppressive environment within which these teachers practice, and to which they often become acclimatised. The development of their tacit knowledge involves access to, and the use and transfer of, resources available to the agent. These resources take the form of strategies chosen in response to the situation. Power and positioning are ascertained from expectations developed during pre-service teaching experiences and shaped within the present context of contract employment. For the participants in this study, teaching was their first professional job. They were so excited to get a job offer, they rarely discussed the contractual nature of their employment offer with their employers at the time and remained relatively unaware of the implications of a short- or fixed-term position. Beth, for example, thought she was offered an ongoing position, without fully understanding what the term 'ongoing' meant. The nature of the conversation in her interview and after, when she was offered the position, contained phrases implying that there was a position at the school for her well into the future, leading Beth to interpret the job offer as long term and therefore ongoing. It was not until a few weeks into the start of the school year that Beth developed a tacit understanding of the nature of contract employment at this particular school.

Many beginning teachers have a theoretical understanding of the nature of employment, though misconceptions can come about in the process of applying for an advertised position for an extended or ongoing period where the position is offered to another applicant. Most beginning teachers in this study were second-choice applicants where the interview panel, having filled the advertised vacancy, offered short-term contracts to these applicants to fill other existing or anticipated temporary vacancies. In doing so, school administrators contribute to the collective understanding that these teachers are of a lower status in being given more tenuous employment conditions. While short-term contracts are effective in schools where predicting future staffing depends on anticipating changes in student enrolments, the overuse of short-term contracts for beginning teachers reminds these teachers that they are mere newcomers (Pierce 2007). Their misconceptions evolve to form a tacit understanding of the nature of employment placing them in survival mode. The convoluted and context-relevant nature of employment means that only a tacit, rather than explicit, understanding is developed, causing yet another barrier to job security and retention of beginning teachers. In such situations the school principal needs to bear some of the responsibility for fully alerting the beginning teacher to the realities of entering the profession on a short-term contract at their specific school.

Many of the participants in this study described the contradiction between their expectations following pre-service teaching and the realities of beginning teaching. Gravett et al. (2011) suggest that teachers should be recruited with realistic expectations, which may lead to their retention in the profession. Cassidy bemoans that 'no one told me', and 'No one prepares you. This is what they don't tell you at uni! They neglect to tell you this part!' Her comments serve to draw attention to pre-service and beginning teachers' expectations of themselves: believing they should be a 'real' teacher like their colleagues in their first year. Yet the additional challenges in regards to their tenure and the uncertainty short-term contracts bring cause many to question whether they should focus their energies to the extent that ongoing staff do, when their future at the school is uncertain. While these teachers found themselves swimming in relation to their work, they discovered they were sinking when their contracts came to an end.

Extra-individual features of practice such as the material-economic category heighten the devastating impact uncertainty can have on teachers' work that is shaped by school reform and political contexts (Lasky 2005). Within a climate of job uncertainty and performativity, these teachers found their work physically and emotionally draining. Having to adapt to teaching with all its challenges is difficult enough for the beginning teacher without having these difficulties compounded by reapplying for their (or other) jobs half way through the school year, only to face the same uncertainty in another five months. Many participants were unable to reach financial independence and had to remain, or return to, living in the family home. Often participants were advised by their administration teams to 'hold off' applying for other jobs as there 'might be something coming up', which sometimes did not eventuate. In such cases, participants reported looking for 'any job' or moving from school to school without having the opportunity to consolidate their practice in an established context. Other participants considered further study, a different profession or unskilled work as alternatives. While many of the teachers in this study practice survival in different ways, at the end of their first year they were all still 'in a lifeboat', not considered by others or themselves to be a 'real' teacher until they could operate with certainty. These teachers were being a certain type of person within a specific context, thus a reflexive relationship between contract employment and beginning teaching develops. Beginning teachers in survival mode affiliate with each other and see themselves as different to their ongoing-employed colleagues, despite being expected to do essentially the same job as such colleagues.

Thus it appears that the contract itself is not the only problem. The resulting practice of survival also becomes a significant problem in and of itself. Beginning teachers employed on a contract speak, enact and relate to others in survival mode. They feel as though they are putting on a show, presenting a persona that is not indicative of the type of teacher they thought they would be, or believe they will be when employed in an ongoing capacity. It also raises the question of what happens to the practice of survival when agents gain ongoing positions? Anecdotal evidence, from some of the more fortunate participants such as Amelia and Sari who were employed in the private Catholic system, shows that upon being granted an ongoing position they cease to ascribe to a practice of survival and begin to enact practices that are afforded to permanent staff. Both teachers took leave without pay in order to travel and later return to the security of their job. In the government system, upon gaining an ongoing position, Sandra took leave without pay in order to explore a different career path. She remained disillusioned with her school and the numerous other issues that are reported to impact on beginning teachers' attrition. Maggie is currently teaching overseas, tired of having to apply for jobs after yet another termination of her contract. The solution for teachers who practice survival seems to be ongoing employment. As long as contracts remain typical of the contemporary economic system, the Holy Grail will be gaining ongoing employment.

Conclusion

While the contract remains an unexpected obstacle imposed by the teaching environment, it will compound the other issues beginning teachers continue to face on entrance to the profession. Kim and Cho (2014) posit that future investigations into, and attention to the possibility of, reality shock may help pre-service teachers develop and maintain a high sense of teaching efficacy and intrinsic motivation so that more quality teachers remain in the teaching profession. Thus, more investigation into the additional layer of job insecurity could assist to retain efficacious and motivated beginning teachers. These teachers, as agents and individuals, are in a position to transform the current practice of survival; however, they cannot do this alone. To increase their agency, beginning teachers need to ensure they understand the terms of their employment and discuss with their employers the context-specific opportunities for gaining job security. Teacher educators can also contribute to a reduction in practices of survival, through drawing attention to the prospective discrepancies between what pre-service teachers envision and what they may experience upon entrance to the teaching profession. Teacher educators need to make clear connections between pre-service teachers' practice and policy, such as the APST and PoLT in Australia, in order to demystify the performative climate of beginning teaching in schools. However, this is a short-term solution to the continued problem of reality shock and related attrition in beginning teachers' transition to the profession. The additional layer of the contract as an extra-individual feature of practice ensures that reality shock continues in more contemporary forms, resulting in a practice of survival.

Others complicit in the practice of survival include school principals and policy makers. When making staffing decisions in the context of the school's preferred staffing profile and on the basis of projected student enrolments, principals and school leaders need to weigh up the potential impact of attrition against long-term school-based reform. Effective induction and mentoring of beginning teachers employed on a contract needs to be more robust at the local school level as well as at the broader policy level. A commitment to the continuation of teacher education through the transition to in-service teaching at both levels can transform the practice of survival. This needs to begin by changing the perception that employing beginning teachers to fill staffing gaps is standard practice based on financial justification. Reducing contract employment of beginning teachers will assist in reducing the practice of survival, reducing attrition of beginning teachers, and will allow those teachers greater agency. The transformative aspect within practices that involves changing existing states of affairs in the areas of sayings, doings and relatings has the potential to transform the practice of survival through the development of shared embodied know-how among agents, who, as individuals are both subject to and agents of practices. These agents have the capacity to not only ascribe to the existing state of affairs but to transform practices for the promotion of quality teaching and learning.

References

Australian Education Union [AEU] 2013, *Contract employment*, retrieved 1 March 2013, <http://keepthepromise.com.au/the-issues/contract-employment/>.

Australian Institute of Teaching and School Leadership [AITSL] 2015, *National professional standards for teachers*, Australian Institute of Teaching and School Leadership, Carlton, VIC.

Berman, DM 1994, 'Becoming a teacher: The teaching internship as a rite of passage', *Teaching Education*, vol. 6, no. 1, pp. 41–56.

Correa, JM, Martínez-Arbelaiz, A & Aberasturi-Apraiz, E 2014, 'Post-modern reality shock: Beginning teachers as sojourners in communities of practice', *Teaching and Teacher Education*, vol. 48, pp. 66–74.

Costar, BJ & Economou, NM 1999, *The Kennett revolution: Victorian politics in the 1990s*, UNSW Press, Sydney.

Department of Education and Early Childhood Development [DEECD] 2012, *Recruitment in schools*, Department of Education and Early Childhood Development & State Government of Victoria.

Department of Education & Training [DE&T] 2015a, *Principles of learning and teaching [PoLT]*, Department of Education & Training, retrieved 3 July 2015, <http://www.education.vic.gov.au/school/teachers/support/Pages/bgresearch.aspx>.

Department of Education & Training [DE&T] 2015b, *Recruitment in schools*, retrieved 1 September 2015, <http://www.education.vic.gov.au/hrweb/careers/Pages/recruitinsch.aspx>.

Feiman-Nemser, S 1990, 'Teacher preparation: Structural and conceptual', in W Houston (ed.), *Handbook of research on teacher education*, Macmillan, New York, pp. 212–233.

Friedman, IA 2000, 'Burnout in teachers: Shattered dreams of impeccable professional performance', *Journal of Clinical Psychology*, vol. 56, no. 5, pp. 595–606.

Gee, JP 2000, 'Identity as an analytic lens for research in education', *Review of Research in Education*, vol. 25, pp. 99–125.

Gee, JP & Green, JL 1998, 'Discourse analysis, learning, and social practice: A methodological study', *Review of Research in Education*, vol. 23, pp. 119–169.

Goddard, R, O'Brien, P & Goddard, M 2006, 'Work environment predictors of beginning teacher burnout', *British Educational Research Journal*, vol. 32, no. 6, pp. 857–874.

Gravett, S, Henning, E & Eiselen, R 2011, 'New teachers look back on their university education: Prepared for teaching, but not for life in the classroom', *Education as Change*, vol. 15, no. Supplement, pp. S123–S142.

Hinchliffe, GW & Jolly, A 2011, 'Graduate identity and employability', *British Educational Research Journal*, vol. 37, no. 4, pp. 563–584.

Høigaard, R, Giske, R & Sundsli, K 2011, 'Newly qualified teachers' work engagement and teacher efficacy influences on job satisfaction, burnout, and the intention to quit', *European Journal of Teacher Education*, vol. iFirst article, pp. 1–11.

Kemmis, S 2009, 'Understanding professional practice: A synoptic framework', in B Green (ed.), *Understanding and researching professional practice*, Sense Publishers, Rotterdam, pp. 19–38.

Kemmis, S 2010, 'What is professional practice? Recognising and respecting diversity in understandings of practice', in C Kanes (ed.), *Elaborating professionalism: Studies in practice and theory*, Springer, London, pp. 139–165.

Kim, H & Cho, Y 2014, 'Pre-service teachers' motivation, sense of teaching efficacy, and expectation of reality shock', *Asia-Pacific Journal of Teacher Education*, vol. 42, no. 1, pp. 67–81.

Lasky, S 2005, 'A sociocultural approach to understanding teacher identity, agency and professional vulnerability in a context of secondary school reform', *Teaching and Teacher Education*, vol. 21, no. 8, pp. 899–916.

Lortie, DC 1975, *Schoolteacher: A sociological study* (1 ed.), University of Chicago Press, Chicago, IL.

Ludecke, M 2013, 'Firsts: Performing ways first year teachers experience identity transformation', Research Doctorate thesis, Deakin University.

Maslach, C 2003, 'Job burnout', *Current Directions in Psychological Science*, vol. 12, no. 5, p. 189.

Pierce, KM 2007, 'Betwixt and between: Liminality in beginning teaching', *The New Educator*, vol. 3, no. 1, pp. 31–49.

Reckwitz, A 2002, 'Toward a theory of social practices: A development in culturalist theorizing', *European Journal of Social Theory*, vol. 5, no. 2, pp. 243–263.

Renard, L 2003, 'Setting new teachers up for failure or success', *Educational Leadership*, May, pp. 62–64.

Schatzki, TR 2001a, 'Introduction: Practice theory', in TR Schatzki, K Knorr-Cetina & E Savigny (eds), *Practice turn in contemporary theory*, Routledge Florence, KY, pp. 10–23.

Schatzki, TR 2001b, 'Practice minded orders', in TR Schatzki, K Knorr-Cetina & E Savigny (eds), *Practice turn in contemporary theory*, Routledge New York, pp. 50–63.

Schatzki, TR 2002, *The site of the social: A philosophical account of the constitution of social life and change*, The Pennsylvania State University Press, University Park, PA.

Schempp, PG, Sparkes, AC & Templin, TJ 1993, 'The micropolitics of teacher induction', *American Educational Research Journal*, vol. 30, no. 3, pp. 447–472.

Schlichte, J, Yssel, N & Merbler, J 2005, 'Pathways to burnout: Case studies in teacher isolation and alienation', *Preventing School Failure*, vol. 50, no. 1, p. 35.

Shoval, E, Erlich, I & Fejgin, N 2010, 'Mapping and interpreting novice physical education teachers' self-perceptions of strengths and difficulties', *Physical Education & Sport Pedagogy*, vol. 15, no. 1, pp. 85–101.

Stokking, K, Leenders, F, de Jong, J & van Tartwijk, J 2003, 'From student to teacher: Reducing practice shock and early dropout in the teaching profession', *European Journal of Teacher Education*, vol. 26, no. 3, pp. 329–350.

Veenman, S 1984, 'Perceived problems of beginning teachers', *Review of Educational Research*, vol. 54, no. 2, pp. 143–178.

Victorian Institute of Teaching [VIT] 2015, *Categories of registration*, retrieved 3 July 2015, <http://www.vit.vic.edu.au/registration/categories-of-registration/Pages/provisional-registration.aspx>.

White, J 2010, 'Speaking "over" performativity', *Journal of Educational Administration and History*, vol. 42, no. 3, pp. 275–294.

Wideen, M, Mayer-Smith, J & Moon, B 1998, 'A critical analysis of the research on learning to teach: Making the case for an ecological perspective on inquiry', *Review of Educational Research*, vol. 68, no. 2, pp. 130–178.

Zeichner, KM & Tabachnik, BR 1981, 'Are the effects of university teacher education 'washed out' by school experience?', *Journal of Teacher Education*, vol. 32, no. 3, pp. 7–11.

Legislation

Education (Self-Governing Schools) Act 1998 (Vic).

Chapter 13

Classroom activity systems and practices of care

Catherine Smith and Russell Cross

Introduction

This chapter investigates the practice of care as it relates to the pedagogic work of teachers in schools, with a focus on the methodological affordances offered by cultural historical activity theory. To do so, we consider a subset of data from a larger project on the social justice dispositions of teachers in classrooms at the extremes of advantage and disadvantage in Australian secondary schools. This chapter examines the teaching practices of Mary[1], an early career teacher in a disadvantaged school in the outer suburbs of Melbourne, Sutton Community School, with particular attention to how practices of care 'come to be' in the context of her work as a teacher in that setting.

For the purposes of our study, we acknowledge the broad and oft-referenced[2] 'Marxian and Feurbachian' (Tronto 2013, p. 216) definition of caring from the work of Joan Tronto in her early collaboration with Bernice Fisher; namely, that caring is:

> a species activity that includes everything that we do to maintain, continue, and repair our 'world' so that we can live in it as well as possible. That world includes our bodies, ourselves and our environment, all of which we seek to interweave in a complex, life-sustaining web.
>
> (Fisher & Tronto 1990, p. 41)

Tronto (1993) calls for a recognition that all practices, and those related to care in particular, ought to be seen in relation to their cultural and historical contexts. Practice, as she puts it, is 'the embodiment of our abstract ideas' (1993, p. 124), with a 'theory of practice' allowing us to relate practical action with social change (Tronto 1993). In studying the practices outlined in the following case study, an activity theory framework allows us to analyse and deconstruct how they have come to be. In doing so, we are able to identify the contradictions which emerge in teachers' practices of care, to understand why these contradictions are able to persist, and to identify possibilities for social change in classroom practices of care.

The chapter opens with a brief overview of care and care practices within the literature as it relates to the 'ethics of care' tradition, arguing that one important way to understand care from such a perspective is the extent to which 'caring practices' lead to more socially just outcomes for members of society. The chapter then explains the context for Sutton Community School and how it is situated against the broader backdrop of Australian secondary schooling, before outlining the three-phase methodology used to generate the data we consider for analysis. This includes an explanation of Engström's (1987) second generation of activity theory and an application of his construct of activity as 'system' as a way of identifying contradictions between what might be considered the ideal, against what is ultimately being realised as practice. Illustrating this through an analysis of empirical data, we conclude by arguing that the strength of this approach for researching the practices of care is its power to reveal how things might be done differently through the interplay of teacher and learners, within the constraints and affordances of the settings in which they come to realise and take up those roles.

The ethic of care

To understand care and care practices in teaching, this chapter draws on the work of theorists who write about the 'ethics of care'. Ethics of care is a normative theory of ethics; that is, instead of asking 'What is just?' as most theories of ethics do, it asks, 'How *should* people respond to socially unjust situations?' (Held 2005; Tronto 1993). Therein, this approach to care further provides a relational theory of social justice. Taking a predominantly feminist approach to research, the work of those who write from an 'ethics of care' perspective argues that an *ethic of care* guides resistance to the internalisation of power imbalance experienced in gender, race and class relations. For example, Gilligan identifies moments in childhood and adolescent development in which young people learn to 'repress' their instinctual caring and relating behaviours to meet their perception of societal expectations (Gilligan & Wiggins 1987; Gilligan et al. 1982a, 1982b; Gilligan et al. 1989). In our study, the teacher refers to moments and events in her own life with respect to current instantiations of teaching practice as it relates to care.

In addition to being seen as an instantiation of meeting a person's needs, care should also be seen as a process (Tronto 1993) and a practice (Tronto 2013). Care cannot be reduced to a binary – as the work of the carer towards the cared-for (Tronto 1993) – but as relational work involving dialogue and exchange (Noddings 2002, 2013). Recognition of the care-receiver – of their voices and choices – is thus central in the 'ethics of care' literature (Held 2005; Gilligan 2008; Walker & Unterhalter 2007). In Tronto's work, she addresses this by including both the giving and receiving of care as phases, thus the giver and receiver have roles and responsibilities (Tronto 1993, 2013). In particular, she asserts that caregiving should necessarily involve direct contact with the care-receiver: 'care-giving involves the direct meeting of needs for care. It involves physical work, and almost always requires that care-givers come in contact with the objects of care' (Tronto 1993, p. 107). Tronto explains that the simple act of giving money for the care of others (for charity, social causes, child or aged care), for example, is not caregiving. Such practices express that the cause or person is significant, but do not 'do the work'. In public policy this point is of utmost importance as care is often seen as accomplished by directing public funds to a particular portion of society, as is the case in the funding for schools for the care and education of young people. The problem with identifying this as care is that there is no measure of whether the care has been received, and ultimately if the needs of the care-receiver have been met. If the measure of success is merely that a service has been provided, then the voice of the 'care-receiver' becomes irrelevant (Folbre 2008; Tronto 1993, 2013). By way of contrast, in recognising one's needs and the needs of others, it is important for one to recognise when the person's needs are met (Zemblylas et al. 2014) and, wherever possible and reasonable, to empower the care-receiver to be the one to make this decision. The 'voice' of the care-receiver is therefore the most important in an 'ethic of care' (Bozalek & Lambert 2008; Gilligan 1982a). In classroom learning, these points on care translate into a requirement for ways in which the student (and where appropriate, their families) can enter into dialogue with the teacher on their progress and whether their needs are met.

To summarise, 'practice of care', from the perspective of ethics of care, are understood as situated within cultural and historical contexts. At various times in everyone's lives, people require care. Care cannot therefore be seen as a binary relationship of care-giver and care-receiver, but as a larger societal practice that expands over our lifetimes and an understanding that we build up relationally through our ongoing interaction with others. For this reason, the work of teachers in caring, and in teaching students to care, can be seen as part of a broader act towards a democratically established social justice. As we highlight in the analysis that follows, caring as it relates to the practices of teaching is mediated within and by contexts for teacher's pedagogic work, including the challenges in realising those caregiving and receiving roles and responsibilities. Through activity theory, we are able to reveal contradictions at work within this teacher's context for practice while caring for her students, and in turn identify what possibilities might exist to support alternative, positive transformations of practice.

Activity as a unit of analysis to research practice

The dialectic between the care-giver and care-receiver, and the attention to dialogue and exchange that should be evident in models of good 'care practice', make activity theory particularly suited to a critical and relational analysis of care in teaching. Activity theory has developed as an extention of Vygotsky's sociocultural theory of mind, which rejected Cartesian dualism in the sense of there being any direct relationship between mind/body, or the subject and the world within which they exist (Blunden 2009). Activity theory attempts to explain institutional learning and change by focusing on dynamics between collective social relationships, in context, and as practice. In this chapter, we use Engeström's (1987, 1999) most recent formulation of activity theory which conceptualises these dynamics through his construct of an 'activity system' (Figure 13.1).

Within activity theory the *subject* refers to the 'human do-er' (Hasan & Kazlauskas 2014; or do-*ers*, if a collective perspective is taken (Ashwin 2012)) which provides the lens through which the system is being interpreted as the basis for their (re)action. The subject is situated in relation to the *object* – the 'problem space' towards which the subject's action is directed (Center for Activity Theory and Developmental Work Research 2005). In our case, the subject is the teacher and the object is the students, particularly the characteristics, qualities, needs and interests that the children in this space present, as perceived by the teacher. This framing positions the children relationally as students. The subject draws on cultural artefacts to mediate the relationship with the object, whether material/physical artefacts (e.g., *tools*, such as technology, books, but even the less obvious, such as clothing that designates levels of formality, etc.) or symbolic/ideational artefacts (*signs*, such as language, strategies and routines, concepts and knowledge, etc.). This relationship between subject and object is manifested as instances of observable, concrete practice (Engeström 1987) that are set against the sociocultural context of the *rules* that sanction and regulate

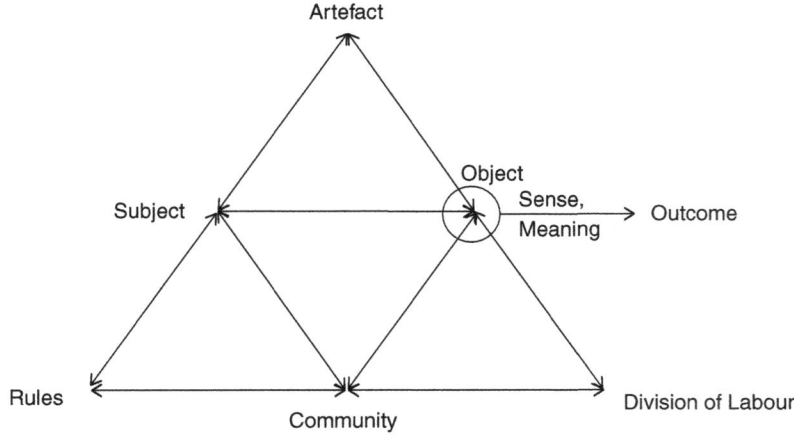

Figure 13.1 Structure of a Human Activity System (Engeström 1999, p. 29)

certain possibilities of behaviour (both implicit and explicit), the interests of the wider *community* also invested in that activity, and the *division of labour* in terms of the distribution of roles, responsibilities and power within the system (Engeström 1987, 1999).

This system, within activity theory, provides the basic unit of analysis (Bozalek 2014). The system reveals an 'instantiation' (Nicolini 2012, p. 112) of practice and, through this, tensions and contradictions in the activity emerge. In addition to being emergent, practice is understood in activity theory as fragmented because the object is not 'visible in its entirety to any one of the participants' (p. 112), but all may hold different interpretations and interests. Finally, the object (the student) is constantly evolving as a 'moving target' (Engeström 2001, p. 136). The mediation of the object is itself transformational, not simply facilitating practice, but shaping and transforming it. Nicolini (2012), in reviewing the central role of mediation in activity, summarises that 'mediation makes practice, all practices, even those carried out in isolation, a historically situated and profoundly social phenomenon' (p. 107).

Within the classroom, there are many activity systems which are 'knot-worked' (Engestrom 2008). Activity, as activity lived in the concrete moment-by-moment unfolding of real time, is dynamic, fluid, constantly changing and evolving. It is multi-layered, depending on the object identified to frame any one particular focus. As an object of research, the unit of analysis – the activity system – is identified by an observable manifestation of activity or practice. The object motivates, defines and characterises the response of the subject. To study the 'practice of teaching', it is therefore necessary to adopt a lens whereby the subject is the position from which one studies the activity system. As an analytic framework for making sense of the data we explore below, we identify, 'teacher practice', as activity (Cross 2010) which is intentionally more comprehensive than a specific targeted 'action' (for example, the pedagogic approach to literacy development). This allows us to investigate how, and to what extent (if at all), an ethic of care is evident within the broader set of collective actions that make up that practice of 'being a teacher', given the conditions against which this teacher–student relationship is set (i.e., the rules, division of labour and community interests).

Stetsenko and Arievitch argue that activity theory provides a 'major avenue for exploring human life and development' (2004, p. 478) by enabling a conceptual analysis of social devices and conventions at their 'unfolding'; that is, a way into examining what comes to constrain and enable different acts of practice. Beyond what we see in the observable (immediate, concrete) present, however, Vygotsky also argued that 'behavior can *only* be understood as the history of behavior' (Blonsky in Vygotksy et al. 1992, p. 70, emphasis added). Historicity is thus central to any activity theoretical analysis (Engeström 2001), with the past always necessarily present in what we see being shaped and reshaped in the now: the histories, backgrounds and presumptions brought into the system by each constituent node on the basis of what has gone before. This includes assumptions around how a certain artefact 'should' be used, the extent to which a rule might have been flexible based on past precedents and the subject's own personal experience of having been in a perceived similar situation in the past as a different member of the community. The past shapes the way that the subject comprehends the object in the present.

Engeström's (1987) formulation of activity as a system also allows us to understand not only how and why practices come to take the form that they do in a particular setting, but also the 'inherently conflictual, dialectic and developmental nature' of interactions between actors within that system, which continue to maintain and/or drive new transformations of the activity itself (Niccolini 2012, p. 112). These conflicts and tensions are inherent and necessary qualities of every system, propelling the activity forward as old disturbances are resolved and new ones are introduced as different forms of practice. These contradictions exist within activity systems and are historically cumulative, sometimes over large scales of time, which can make them hard to see as they become 'sedimented' as part of a taken-for-granted structure for activity (Daniels & Edwards 2013, p. 7). Engeström and Sannino (2011) explain that we have no direct access to contradictions so they 'must [instead] be approached through their manifestations' (p. 373).

By conceptualising practice within an activity system and understanding where contradictions lie – and how they come to be – activity theory makes possible to see what other alternatives exist to rework historical tensions to enable new forms of practice given the conditions within which the actors are situated. We argue that an activity theoretical analysis helps identify the tensions experienced by the teacher in her practice as it relates to care and the sources of those contradictions, as well as possibilities for how things might be done differently to empower her as a practitioner with different forms of practice.

Research design

As noted above, central to activity theory is understanding the system from the subject's perspective, necessitating an emic approach to data collection and analysis (Hennink et al. 2011). Our analysis draws on data generated with one teacher as part of a larger project involving sixteen teachers from ten schools. The project involved a three-phase methodology which included an interview with the principal of the school (Phase One), three 'scaffolded reflective interviews' (Anderson et al., 2015) using film clips of the teachers own practice (Phase Two), and one scaffolded reflective interview using film clips of the practice of other teachers in the study (Phase Three). Each of the interviews lasted between sixty to ninety minutes. The technique in the second and third phases is an extension of established stimulated recall procedures (Gass & Mackey 2000) in which video recordings of a lesson that had just been taught are played back as stimulus to generate the teacher's account of what just happened – their 'unique insider perspective' (Rowe 2009, p. 432). However, scaffolded reflective interviews also take into account the impact this process has on shaping the teacher's approach to each subsequent lesson (and reflection), even if not intended as a deliberate intervention into changing practice. A variation on this process was the fourth teacher interview (Phase Three), which took place the following semester after the first three interviews and involved teachers responding to a selection of video excerpts taken from *other* schools participating in the larger study. The aim of this fourth interview was to provoke an even deeper reflection on practice by asking teachers to draw on their experiences and assumptions to 'read' the practices evident in each video as a point of comparison and contrast from their own settings for activity.

Interviews were transcribed and analysed qualitatively through a process of *a priori* coding based on each node of activity (qualities of the subject, object, rules, etc.), with the aim of generating the teacher's *own account* of the system in which she works and makes sense of her site of practice. The activity system provides a slice of practice and an instantiation that we have deliberately selected to investigate the practice of the teacher. This system was then further analysed against references to care as understood from an ethics of care perspective. The findings of this analysis in relation to one teacher are presented thematically below together with an overview of the case study site and the teacher participant.

The Case

Sutton Community School

Sutton Community School is located in an outer suburb of Melbourne, Australia, with 110 students and around 55 staff; around half of these are teachers, while the rest have leadership, administrative and auxiliary roles. All of its students fall in the lowest quartile of social disadvantage in the country and the school is not required to report against standardised assessment benchmarking because it consistently falls below the minimum grade average threshold (Australian Curriculum, Assessment and Reporting Authority 2013). The school subscribes to a particular 'passion-based' curriculum which proports to meet all the students learning objectives by teaching them through subjects, ideas, topics and possible futures that the student is 'passionate' about. The teacher is expected to help the students link this learning to experiences within the community, which include mentor relationships and accessing other organisations and resources. The students write letters and apply for funding for special projects to develop their learning within the school.

The particular properties of Sutton Community School create a population of students who have previously found themselves marginalised in one way or another in mainstream schooling. The school population is defined by its 'otherness' and being an 'alternative' within the broader school system. As the school principal, Annette, explains:

> There's as many reasons [that the students are at this school] as there are kids in the school. The work was going too fast and they couldn't keep up. It's better to be a clown so I can get thrown out. Kids were mean to me. Nobody understood me. I thought everyone was out to get me. So you've got kids on the autism spectrum here, kids with severe language disorders, severe behaviour disorders, ADHD, ODD, conduct disorder. Cutters, suicidal ideation, borderline personality disorder, intellectual disability, justice issues.
>
> (Annette, Principal Interview)

Mary and an instance of teacher practice

In her late twenties and a teacher for almost three years, Mary worked at Sutton in the year before this study as substitute for regular teachers on leave. Her role now (at Sutton) is her first full-time contract teaching position. She completed part of her secondary school education in an Australian International school in a large Asian city and has an undergraduate degree in arts and a master's degree in teaching. She describes herself as having been a 'goody-two shoes' student and rarely referred to her family or friends throughout her interviews. She did, however, make frequent references to other staff at Sutton who she described as 'incredibly supportive'. She job-shares the teaching of the class we observed two days a week while alternating with another teacher in the study, Lucy. Her other three days of teaching are on another campus of the school which is part of a residential program for young people living in out-of-home care facilities.

The classroom is a large room with large windows on either side. The students filter in slowly, often later than expected. The students are in this classroom for the whole year and do not shift classrooms for different subjects and specialists. They sit at small tables, in pairs or separately, and move the tables around the room regularly. Students regularly move out of their seats, sometimes sitting on the floor in small groups, and there are regularly empty chairs because attendance is irregular. Students will often move from seat to seat and conduct conversations amongst themselves during each class. They also regularly check their phones and sometimes take calls in class, stepping outside to the front steps by the classroom door once they have answered to continue the call, which is often still audible to the rest of the class. Many of the students are dressed in jeans or sweatpants, t-shirts and 'hoodies' and use their hoods to hide their faces, sometimes with their heads on their desks.

The vignette that follows provides a brief example of interaction between the teacher and students in this class, representative of the 'activity' we typically see unfolding within this classroom space. It serves as an example of the interactions, tensions and struggles we see exemplified throughout our observational data of Mary's teaching practice. The lesson involves the students having to provide outlines for three possible stories, and answering the questions: Who? What? Where? When? and How?

Mary moves to Stu, who has his hoodie up and head on the desk. He does not acknowledge her as she sits next to him in the empty student's desk to his left. She attempts to engage him with his work but he refuses to look up at her.

MARY: Hi Stu, how you doing? Have you got your book because I saw that you had your book open? [2-second pause] Stu, can I have a look at your book? Would you mind? [1-second pause] Shake your head if you wouldn't mind. [4-second pause] Or is it easier to nod if it's ok that I look at your book? [2-second pause] Ok, I'm going to have a peak.

Picks up the pencil that is resting on the top of the container and puts it away. [2-second pause]

An altercation happens between two other students on the other side of the room. Mary stays seated next to Stu but banter ensues for another four minutes and meanwhile Stu has started writing in his book. Mary does not convince the other students to settle; she sighs and turns her attention back to Stu. Stu rips the page from his book and slowly methodically starts to fold it. He does not look at Mary, but stares ahead smirking. He crumples the paper into a ball. Another student turns and passes his book to Mary. She reads it

MARY: [To other students] Cool! Love it!

Stu throws his paper across the room at Grant.

MARY: Stu, Don't do that, mate. *[To Grant, who is staring angrily at Stu.]* Turn around, face the front. Do your story.

She continues to comment on the other student's work. He has written about knights and Stu speaks for the first time.

STU: If it's historical, he eats his blood.

MARY: That's very graphic.

OTHER STUDENT: Naw, he destroys his kingdom.

MARY: Okay *[writing in the student's book]*, we might add that in.

They continue to talk and meanwhile, Stu rips another paper from his book and crumples it. Mary ignores this and continues to talk to the other student. He throws it at Grant again, but misses.

MARY: Can you please stop throwing things, Stu? You were getting on to a good start. Keep going.

STU: Okay, I'll work . . .

MARY: Yeah . . .

STU: If you go away.

MARY: Ok, I'll just do this [motioning to the other student's book] and then I'm gone.

STU: Nah, go away or I'm not . . . working . . . ever.

Mary continues to work with the other student and give him feedback on the work. She stands to unlock the safe with the laptops in it so that the other student can use one to work on his individual learning plan [ILP] now that he has completed the writing exercise. After five minutes and working with one other student and passing out computers, she relocks the safe, explaining that she doesn't want the boys who are being disruptive to get their computer til they finish their writing task. She returns to Stu, standing over him.

MARY: Stu, can I please have a look at what you've done, even if you just flash it open to me?

STU: No.

MARY: Yeah?

STU: No.

MARY: Please?

STU: Nooooo.

MARY: 'Cause I'd love for you to get started on your ILP.

STU: No.

MARY: Please, 'cause I need to see your work first. Even if you've got one.

STU: No.

MARY: Because I know you don't enjoy writing.

STU: No.

MARY: *[Looking at her watch, and then at the wall clock.]* Ok, I'm going to come back in . . . two minutes . . . . I'm going to ask to see it again.

STU: *[Takes his book out and slaps it down on the desk.]* How about you just look at it?

MARY: That would make me so happy.

STU: That way you can just leave me alone.

MARY: Great, then you can get out your laptop and start working on your ILP.

STU: Will you just shut the fuck up and stop bugging me?

MARY: I will, because you will be working on your ILP.

STU: I'm going to hurt you in a minute.

MARY: *[in a low voice]* We don't want threats here mate. *[Changing tone, and after glancing at his book]* Cool, awesome, all right, do you want your laptop?

Without waiting for a reply, she moves to collect the laptop from the safe. She does not speak with Stu for the remainder of the lesson, which lasts for an hour and twelve minutes longer.

Analysis: The student object in Mary's practice

The difficulty Mary is having in working with Stu in this vignette was typical of her interactions with the students in this classroom. She speaks her understanding of Stu in saying that she 'knows' he does not like writing, but she treats the task as non-negotiable and takes a series of cajoling steps which result in a verbally abusive response from him. In reflecting on this incident later, Mary explains that when Stu is feeling overwhelmed it is better for him to work on work that he has 'contributed to', but she does not pursue this observation further. In Mary's second interview, she contextualises her beliefs as to why her students are resistant to the work she is asking them to do, saying:

> A lot of these kids struggle with their self-confidence because they haven't fitted into a mainstream school. They see a failure, or they lack the self-confidence and they don't – because of that lack of confidence – they don't feel as motivated to participate.

She recognises the priority that must be placed on 'positive relationships' for the students. She describes one student who had been refusing to go to school for two years, but has been pretty regular with attendance at Sutton. When asked why she thought this might be, Mary explains:

> He's said that this is the first time I've had friends, that I've had close friends, this is the first time that he's ever had friends and he wants to keep them and wants to keep building those relationships and that's what's kept him coming and staying when he's hating everything else apparently.

It is understood that the students have had past negative experiences in mainstream schooling and Mary explains it as the students not 'fitting in', often also using phrases such as 'X's lack of confidence in his/her ability' to describe why students react negatively to learning tasks she sets:

> The type of students we're working with and what they're capable of. If they don't feel supported then they shut down. If they don't feel capable of it then they shut down so we need to really make it tiny steps I think.

As seen here, Mary sees her students as experiencing barriers to learning due to difficult past schooling experiences and sees their difficult behaviour as a manifestation of this. She also acknowledges that this is not like her own experience of being a student. Mary describes her past self as a school student who was known for 'always doing the right thing', drawing on her own experiences of schooling to help make sense of their current circumstances which she describes in contrasting terms to this. This is perhaps not surprising, as Lortie (1975) has long recognised the impact of teachers' own schooling experience in their development into the teachers they become.

With respect to caring, then, Mary feels she needs to work to help her students through the anxiety that manifests itself in their opposition to doing work, to help them feel better connected with the school and achieve doing the material she presents them. As evident in the example of practice presented, though, this is not being realised, and we instead see frustration on both sides.

The first tension – *rules* and *artefacts*: Finding students' 'passions'

During the structured recall interviews, Mary frequently refers to the students and their passions, expressing difficulty and frustration with students who cannot identify their passion. As noted above, the school relies on a 'passion-based curriculum' approach which aims to engage students in the classroom and beyond by having them identify passions which then act as the vehicle through which their learning occurs. For example, the principal describes an example of a student who loves skateboards and has done several terms of work on skateboard ramps and skateboard designs, etc. When discussing curriculum, Mary refers to the national curriculum only once, whereas she makes frequent reference to passion-based learning as 'the curriculum' that she, as a teacher, is expected to deliver. In activity theory, 'rules' refer to the expectations and conventions – both formal and informal, explicit and implicit – that regulate certain types of practices that can unfold within the system (Engeström 1987). Here a significant rule becomes evident – an expectation that Mary adopt a personalised teaching approach, driven by students' 'passions' – which has its origins in the principal's view of good teaching being 'student driven and centred' (Annete in Phase One interview) – perhaps best summed up in the maxim she herself offered: 'I don't care how much you know until I know how much you care'. However, this rule also becomes the source of a key systemic tension.

In the sequence of three classes observed across a two-week period mid-semester, students spent most of the class time finding YouTube videos or chatting to each other – ostensibly about 'their passions' – such as finding pictures from the Internet and sending them to print so they can paste them in their learning portfolios. While this is happening, Mary and her classroom assistant, Judy, roam the classroom talking to students independently about what they are doing and encouraging the students to 'document' their passions in their portfolios. Mary identifies herself as being literacy-focussed and she expresses a desire to work more on the students' research skills; however, her literacy-focussed lesson does not draw on their passions because she feels many of the students need to review some fundamental writing skills.

During the class from which the vignette is drawn – one that she refers to as being her 'worst ever' – she attempts to get the students to do a literacy task where they complete story outlines that do not incorporate their identified passions at all. She explains that while *she* thought it would be fun, it ended up being 'stressful, frustrating, and tedious'. Throughout the class there was much resistance to the task, indicating it to be a poor pedagogical choice, with one student exclaiming, 'I did this in primary school' and two students having a physical altercation for which they were suspended the next day. Reflecting on the lesson, Mary reasons:

> Perhaps if I'd had a more engaging . . . or an activity that they felt was more relevant to them, then perhaps they would have been able to engage

more and then there would have been more cooperation and general better behaviour in the classroom.

When asked, 'How do you know that it wasn't engaging for them? What makes you make that decision?', Mary laughs while simultaneously shedding tears and replies:

> The battles I had to fight to persuade some of them to do their work. The . . . just outright refusal. A lot of them don't enjoy writing and I knew this idea of creative writing would be difficult for them and would already have a bit of resentment, but I thought the shorter condensing it down would simplify it a bit and make it a bit quicker and therefore less painful for them.

A tension between the rule of 'passion-based learning' and the actual identification and use of these passions to develop appropriate artefacts to mediate a more successful teaching/learning relationship with their students becomes evident here. This is represented in the figure below as the dotted tension line between the rule and the artefact.

Helping the students to identify these passions involves a deep knowledge of the students and their interests, which itself develops through the personal connectedness expected between the teachers and their students. To help understand the situated nature and root of this tension within Mary's practice, a second source of tension becomes apparent between the rule of passions-based learning and the division of labour.

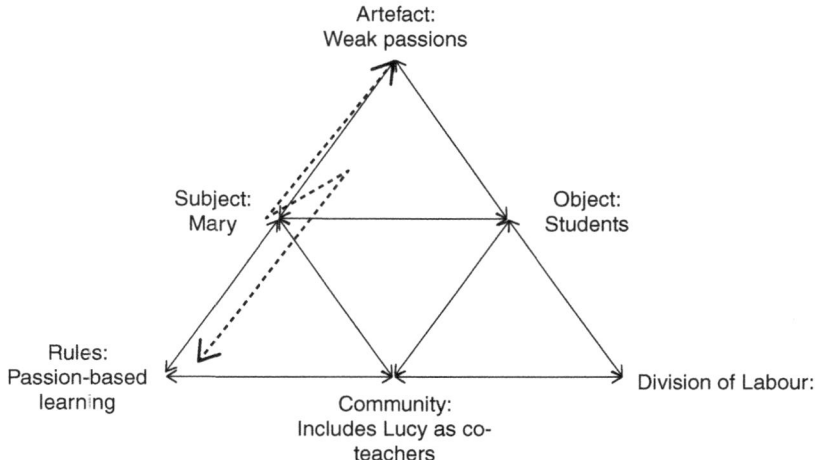

Figure 13.2 Finding Student Passions

The second tension – *division of labour* and *rules*: Weakening the subject/object relationship

Referring to the organisation of the school's approach to passion-based learning, Lucy (the class's other teacher) explains: 'If you actually read the book [i.e., the official curriculum materials], it says the advisor must stay with the class and move up with them every year so they never change advisor'. Yet as indicated earlier, Mary and Lucy have a job-sharing arrangement. Each teacher spends two days a week in the classroom being examined in this study as the 'sole' teacher on whichever day they are there, while each of their other three teaching days are spent at an off-campus residential program for students in the care of the state where students are described as being often violent and unpredictable. When asked how this routine came about, Lucy explains that this was the principal's decision because 'they just needed to break it up, because it's a really intense project down there [at the residential unit] as well'. Mary also points to problems in the way their time is divided and expectations of the curriculum: 'we've got three different [teachers] in that room, that's too distracting, too disruptive for the students and for me, being in there'. In her account of the system that she occupies, this contradiction between expectations of how staff time should be allocated to each individual class group, and the complex job-sharing arrangement in place between herself, Lucy and a third teacher who covers the remaining day of each week, impacts on Mary's ability to connect with the students in the way she would like:

> It took a long time to build up connections with them and even still, I'm only seeing them for two days a week so it's not a great deal of time. If there was the consistency of staying in there, I feel I'd be able to do a whole lot more.

This becomes the root of the problem evident in the first systemic tension highlighted earlier; that is, insufficient time with her students (Tension 2) means Mary's understanding of her students is insufficient to make pedagogical decisions about what 'passions' will be most effective to fulfil the curriculum design and goals (Tension 1). Ultimately, the end result is a breakdown in the fundamental relationship between *subject* and *object* (the solid grey line in Figure 13.3, below). From an ethic of care perspective, this breakdown is of critical significance. In the absence of a positive, strong relationship Mary is not able to know her students. In missing the opportunity to engage with the passions and passion-based learning due to the systemic tensions evident in this setting, Mary also misses the opportunity in caring for them, to hear their voices, as those receiving that care.

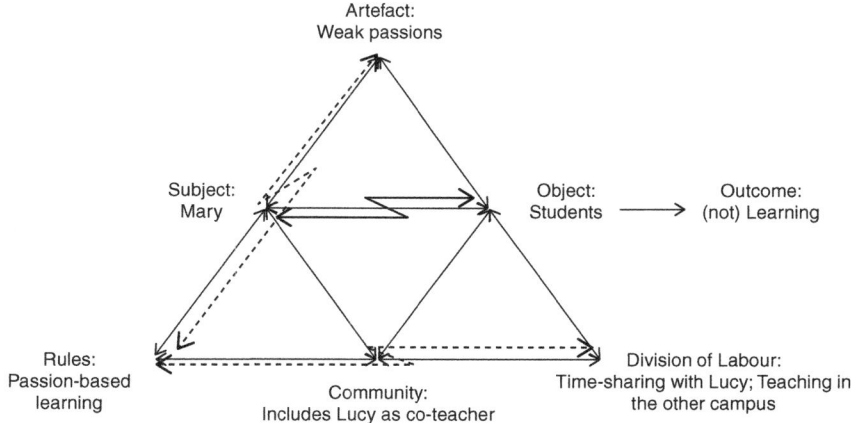

Figure 13.3 Weakening the Subject/Object Relationship

Conclusion

This chapter has focused on the tensions that arise within the practices of care within teaching, analysed through the lens of activity theory from an ethics of care perspective. A theoretical analysis of the activity system permits a deeper understanding of practice in relation to its context and, in this case, how it has led Mary to be positioned in relation to her students in a way that is disconnected. This disconnection, in turn, makes the development of a care relationship difficult. Through the analysis it becomes clear that Mary's difficulties in relating to her students manifest – not only in the poor pedagogical choices she makes in teaching in misidentifying which passions might provide a better basis to facilitate more successful engagement and outcomes from learning – but also the organisation of time and job-sharing that facilitates opportunities to develop that knowledge in the first instance. Activity theory provided us with analytical framings to 'make sense of the materiality of human practice' (Miettinen et al. 2012, p. 350) within which Mary was situated as a novice teacher attempting to understand and know her students.

In doing so, it also made visible and concrete where new possibilities for change might lie in terms of interrupting what has otherwise become accepted as the invisible (and inevitable) habituality of practice, and the 'primacy of routinized, pre-reflective and/or unconscious, embodied actions and dispositions to actions' (Miettinen et al. 2012, p. 348). Through the analysis, it becomes possible to reveal where tensions lie between the material and ideal – how things are, and how Mary wants things to be. As Hatch (1997) puts it: 'contradictions do not speak for themselves, they become recognized when practitioners articulate and construct them in words and actions' (in Engeström & Sannino 2011, p. 373). In this example of Mary's practice, the analysis allowed us to expose how *rules* and the *division of labour*, in particular, work in connection with (or against) the realisation of caring practices (Zemblylas et al. 2014): Mary is trying to care for her students but lacks opportunities to develop stable long-term regular relationships with them because the labour is organised in a way that fractures her capacity to identify the types of pedagogical decisions needed to fulfil the aims of the curriculum.

Affirmed through this analysis is the need for strong relationships with the students and rigorous planning and teaching as the basis for care within teaching. When Mary explains that giving 'student voice' a stronger place in her practice brings a better dynamic, she echoes the assertions of Tronto (2013): that successful caregiving requires as much voice as possible to be provided to the care-receiver – in this case, her students. By identifying the tensions in the dialectic between the teacher-subject and student-objects in this system, the contradictions in the system develop a strong argument for importance of students' voice in pedagogical and care practices. Significantly, in our return to the school for the final-stage interview at the end of the year, Mary explains that the students are currently working together to plan a end-of-year formal and she observes: 'So it has changed and I think giving more power to the student voice has led to a better dynamic in this classroom'.

Notes

1 Pseudonyms have been used throughout for all participants and any personal or institutional identifiers.
2 See, for example, Groenhout (2004), Held (2005) and Zemblylas.

References

Anderson, L., Stillman, J., Beltramo, J., Struthers, K., & Gomez-Najarro, J. (2015, April). From stimulated recall to scaffolded reflection: Using video-mediated interviewing to learn about teachers' sense-making and navigation of education policy. Paper presented at the annual meeting of the American Educational Research Association, Chicago, IL.

Ashwin, P 2012, *Analysing teaching-learning interactions in higher education: Accounting for structure and agency*, Continuum, London.

Australian Curriculum, Assessment and Reporting Authority 2013, *My school*, retrieved 13 May 2016, <http://www.myschool.edu.au/>.

Blunden, A 2009, *Vygotsky and activity theory: The object in Leontyev, Engeström and Vygotsky*, retrieved 13 May 2016, <https://http://www.academia.edu/5262910/Vygotsky_and_Activity_Theory>.

Bozalek, V 2014, *Activity theory, Authentic learning and emerging technologies: Towards a transformative higher education pedagogy*, Routledge, London.

Bozalek, V & Lambert, W 2008, 'Interpreting users' experiences of service delivery in the Western Cape using a normative framework', *Social Work*, vol. 44, no. 2, pp. 107–120.

Centre for Activity Theory and Developmental Work Research 2005, *Cultural-historical activity theory*, retrieved 13 May 2016, <http://www.edu.helsinki.fi/activity/pages/chatanddwr/>.

Cross, R 2010, 'Language teaching as sociocultural activity: Rethinking language teacher practice', *Modern Language Journal*, vol. 94, no. 3, pp. 434–452.

Daniels, H & Edwards, A 2013, 'School leaders and learning cultures in school: The case for intelligent leadership' in D Hung, KYT Lim & S Lee (eds) *Adaptivity as a transformative disposition for learning in the 21st century*, Springer, Singapore, 109–119.

Engeström, Y 1987, *Learning by expanding: An activity-theoretical approach to developmental research*, Orienta-Konsultit, Helsinki.

Engeström, Y 1999, 'Activity theory and individual and social transformation', in Y Engeström, R Miettinen & RL Punamäki (eds), *Perspectives on activity theory*, Cambridge University Press, Cambridge, pp. 19–38.

Engeström, Y 2001, 'Expansive learning at work: Toward an activity theoretical reconceptualization', *Journal of Education & Work*, vol. 14, pp. 133–156.

Engeström, Y 2008, *From teams to knots: Activity-theoretical studies of collaboration and learning at work*, Cambridge University Press, Cambridge & New York.

Engestrom, Y & Sannino, A 2011, 'Discursive manifestations of contradictions in organizational change efforts: A methodological framework', *Journal of Organisational Change Management*, vol. 24, no. 3, pp. 368–387.

Fisher, B & Tronto, J 1990, 'Toward a feminist theory of caring', in EK Abel & MK Nelson (eds), *Circles of care: Work and identity in women's lives*, State University of New York Press, Albany, NY, pp. 35–62.

Folbre, N 2008, *Valuing children: Rethinking the economics of the family*, Harvard University Press, Cambridge.

Gass, SM & Mackey, A 2000, *Stimulated recall methodology in second language research*, L. Erlbaum Associates, Mahwah, NJ.

Gilligan, C, Gardiner, J, Germain, CB, Reardon, B, Tronto, JC, Stack, CB, Lips, H, Ruddick, SM, Black, KN, Brown, BB, Benjamin, J & Bate, B 1982a, *In a different voice: Psychological theory and women's development*, Harvard University Press, Cambridge.

Gilligan, C, Langdale, S & Lyons, N 1982b, *The contribution of women's thought to developmental theory: The elimination of sex bias in moral development research and education (Final report)*, Harvard University, National Institute of Education, Cambridge.

Gilligan, C, Lyons, N & Hanmer, TJ (eds) 1989, *Making connections: The relational worlds of adolescent girls at Emma Willard School*, Harvard University Center for the Study of Gender, Education and Human Development, Emma Willard School, New York.

Gilligan, C & Richards, DAJ 2008, *The deepening darkness*, Cambridge University Press, New York.

Gilligan, C & Wiggins, G 1987, 'The origins of morality in early childhood relationships', in J Kagan & S Lamb (eds), *The emergence of morality in early childhood*, University of Chicago Press. Chicago, IL, pp. 227–305.

Groenhout, R 2004, *Connected lives: Human nature and an ethics of care*, Rowman & Littlefield, Langham, NY.

Hasan, H & Kazlauskas, A 2014, 'Activity theory: Who is doing what, why and how' in H Hasan (ed.), *Being practical with theory: A window into business research*, THEORI, Wollongong, AUS, pp. 9–14.

Hatch, MJ 1997 'Irony and the social construction of contradiction in the humor of a management team', *Organization Science*, vol. 8 no. 3, pp. 275–288.

Held, V 2005, *The ethics of care: Personal, political, and global*, Palgrave Macmillan, Oxford.

Hennick, MM, Hutter, I & Bailey, A 2011, *Qualitative research methods*, SAGE, Los Angeles, CA.

Lortie, DC 1975, *Schoolteacher: A sociological study*, University of Chicago Press, Chicago, IL.

Miettinen, R, Paavola, S & Pohjola, P 2012, 'From habituality to change: Contribution of activity theory and pragmatism to practice theories', *Journal for the Theory of Social Behaviour*, vol. 42, no. 3, pp. 345–360.

Nicolini, D 2012, *Practice theory, work, and organization: An introduction*, Oxford University Press, Oxford.

Noddings, N 2002, *Starting at home: Caring and social policy*, University of California Press, Berkeley, CA.

Noddings, N 2013, *Caring: A relational approach to ethics & moral education* (2nd ed.), University of California Press, Berkeley, CA.

Rowe, V 2009, 'Using video-stimulated recall as a basis for interviews: Some experiences from the field', *Music Education Research*, vol. 11, no. 4, pp. 425–437.

Stetsenko, A & Arievitch, I 2004, 'The self in cultural-historical activity theory: Reclaiming the unity of social and individual dimensions of human development', *Theory & Psychology*, vol. 14, no. 4, pp. 475–503.

Tronto, JC 1993, *Moral boundaries: A political argument for an ethic of care*, Routledge, New York.

Tronto, JC 2013, *Caring democracy: Markets, equality, and justice*, New York University Press, New York.

Vygotsky, LS, Luriia, AR & Rossiter, E 1992, *Ape, primitive man, and child: Essays in the history of behavior*, Harvester Wheatsheaf, New York.

Walker, M & Unterhalter, E 2007, *The capability approach: Its potential for work in education*, Palgrave Macmillan, New York.

Zemblylas M, Bozalek, V & Shefer, T 2014, 'Tronto's notion of privileged irresponsibility and the reconceptualisation of care: Implications for critical pedagogies of emotion in higher education', *Gender & Education*, vol. 26, no. 3, pp. 200–214.

Section 4

Professional practice, public policy and education

Chapter 14

Bad research, bad education

The contested evidence for evidence-based research, policy and practice in education

Michael A. Peters and Marek Tesar

Introduction

The birth of educational research is both strongly related to the systematic collection of data by the state (something that could be referred as *state-istics*), as well as to the early experimental psychological laboratories, which were established by Wilhelm Wundt in Leipzig, William James at Harvard and G. Stanley Hall at Johns Hopkins University in the nineteenth century. These psychological laboratories paved the way for the grounding principles of experimental psychology, and of experimental psychology as applied to education. At the beginning of the twentieth century John Dewey and Edward Thorndike formulated two radically different and enduring conceptions of educational science that shaped our contemporary education. While Thorndike wedded his behavioural psychology to the newly emerging techniques of statistical analysis to produce a technocratic theory of schooling and to inform industrial management, Dewey, by contrast, focused on constructing a form of science that modelled learning processes on the practice of a democratic community of students and teachers as problem-solvers. Thorndike's and Dewey's two competing visions, or 'paradigms', are still pervasive today. Thorndike's vision remained dominant in educational research until the turn to practice, which followed the work of Wittgenstein, Bourdieu and others, and infused particular approaches into the social and cultural sciences in the 1970s and beyond. In teacher education, this turn also coincided with the early stages of the process of the merger, incorporation and integration of teachers colleges, and therefore of teacher training and education, with universities. This chapter thus focuses on the turn to practice in educational research, theories of pedagogy, and the recent move toward the state mandating of evidence-based policy and practice. Furthermore, it contextualises this turn to practice in educational research, theories and policy by examining the 'birth' of educational research in the English-speaking world, the historicity of the discipline of education, and the influences and legacies of the scholarship of Dewey and Thorndike.

An historical understanding provides an important background for the educational research landscape. The historical context of the United States is linked with President Woodrow Wilson, when, in 1916, he established the National Research Council to encourage and support organised research; however, there was rarely support for educational research and development until the 1950s (Leedy 1973). Historical milestones such as World War II, the Cold War, Russia's satellite Sputnik, desegregation, the Vietnam War and other national and international concerns all contributed to the low level of funding and focus of educational research and development (R&D). The *Brown vs. Board of Education* 1954 decision, *Civil Rights Act* of 1964, *Elementary and Secondary Education Act* of 1965 (ESEA), *Equal Opportunity Act* of 1965 (EOP), National Science Foundation (NSF), Educational Research and Development Centers (R&D), Regional Educational Laboratories (RELs), Desegregation Assistance Centers and Title I and Head Start Programs were all created as a response to a crisis or event impacting American and world society (Simon-McWilliams 2007).

The birth of educational research

The 'birth' of educational research does not lie in a history of ideas but the history of form and the epistemological rupture that establishes a new 'paradigm' or 'episteme' by legitimizing a related repertoire of practices. Nietzsche (1872/1994) – in his *The Birth of Tragedy: Out of the Spirit of Music* – discusses the history of the tragic form in Greek theatre, an art form that transcended the pessimism and nihilism of a fundamentally meaningless existence, and introduces the philosophical concept from Greek mythology of the 'Apollonian' and 'Dionysian' as a dialectic historical framing of whether reality is governed and ordered by forms or not. Nietzsche's contribution here is focused on an historical form. In the twentieth century, Foucault presented what could be called an epistemological rupture, in his works such as *The Birth of the Clinic* and *The Birth of Biopolitics*. *The Birth of the Clinic* traces the development of the medical profession, and specifically the institution of the hospital. Foucault coined the term *medical gaze* to denote the dehumanizing medical separation of the patient's body from the patient's person (identity). The birth of modern medicine was not simply the dawning of a new empirical system but a decisive shift in the structure of knowledge:

> The clinic – constantly praised for its empiricism, the modesty of its attention, and the care with which it silently lets things surface to the observing gaze without disturbing them with discourse – owes its real importance to the fact that it is a reorganization in depth, not only of medical discourse, but of the very possibility of a discourse about disease.
>
> (Foucault 1963/1973, p. xix)

The birth of the clinical science of medicine is part of a deep structural shift – an episteme – where one epistemological era gives way to another and where the observations and analysis depended on accepted practices of the episteme. The taxonomic era gave way to the organic historical era, hence the use of 'birth' in the title; the clinic had no origins, but simply and suddenly arrived. Through the birth of the medical gaze, Foucault chronicled how the 'medical gaze was organized in a new way. . . . [I]t was no longer the gaze of any observer, but that of a doctor supported and justified by an institution, that of a doctor endowed with the power of decision and intervention' (Foucault 1963/1973, p. 109). Thus, the concept of 'birth' as part of an archeology of knowledge, where Foucault argues that medicine, or the modern concept of medicine, established its 'birth' into the late eighteenth century:

> In order to determine the moment at which the mutation in discourse took place, we must look beyond its thematic content or its logical modalities to the region where 'things' and 'words' have not yet been separated, and where – at the most fundamental level of language – seeing and saying are still one. We must reexamine the original distribution of the visible and invisible insofar as it is linked with the division between what is stated and what remains unsaid: thus the articulation of medical language and its object will appear as a single figure.
>
> (Foucault 1963/1973, p. xii)

The birth of educational research is a history of the educational profession, public education and pedagogy, educational psychology and the science of measurement and testing, first at the national level and more recently at the global level, involving international scale comparisons and rankings of 'achievement' across the disciplines. But it is also a history of human experience, of human subjectivity, of the reconstitution of 'students' and 'teachers' and the experience of politics, bodies and systems. By locating the birth of educational research within all these frameworks, it also becomes a critical history of public education in the world, the emergence of governmentality, regulated social spaces and eventually self-regulated bodies.

As argued above, the birth of modern educational research is associated with psychology, and with Wilhelm Wundt who opened the Institute for Experimental Psychology at the University of Leipzig in Germany in 1879. This was the first laboratory dedicated to psychology, and its opening is usually thought of as the beginning of modern psychology, with Wundt regarded as the father of psychology (McLeod 2008). Wundt's experimental method of the psychology lab established psychology as a separate field of study with its own methods and questions. Wilhelm Wundt's support of experimental psychology also set the stage for behaviouristic and cognitive paradigms, and many of his experimental methods are still used today. Wundt's students later became prominent psychologists, including Edward Titchener, James McKeen Cattell, Charles Spearman,

Granville Stanley Hall, Charles Judd and Hugo Munsterberg. One of them, Granville Stanley Hall (1844–1924), earned the first doctorate in psychology in the United States, with William James serving as his supervisor. In 1883 he established the first experimental psychology laboratory at Princeton and became the President of Clark University and Professor of Psychology and Pedagogy. In 1887 he also founded the *American Journal of Psychology*, and in 1892 became the first president of the American Psychological Association. In the paper *The contents of children's minds on entering school* (1893), he discusses reasons behind, and the methods used in, tests given to school children on admission to school to measure general knowledge. He argues, for instance, that

> it seems not too much to infer [t]hat there is next to nothing of pedagogic value the knowledge of which it is safe to assume at the outset of school-life. Hence the need of objects and the danger of books and word-cram.
>
> (Hall 1893, p. 27)

The first American psychologist to directly address educational issues was William James (1842–1910). Marchetti (2011, p. 134) in his review work, *James, Nietzsche and Foucault on Ethics and the Self*, asks what James, Nietzsche and Foucault have in common; he concludes that it is the question of 'what does it take to have a moral experience?', and the 'answer' to this concern is the *form* of the answer 'to take care of one's own self.' As he argues, what James, Nietzsche and Foucault share is

> a conception of ethics as an activity of self-care. According to these authors, individuals constitute themselves as ethical subjects by being attentive to the experiences and thoughts that are transformative of the way in which they conduct themselves.
>
> (Marchetti 2011, p. 134)

While Nietzsche and Foucault can be considered to trace the problem back to the history of Western culture, James addresses the problem of modern ethical thought through empiricism and rationalism. James perceives a focus on the moral psychology and epistemology on which moral experiencing is grounded, while Foucault considers the historicity of its understanding by the subjects involved. The varieties of ethical experience are what Rorty argues,

> ties Dewey and Foucault, James and Nietzsche together . . . the sense that there is nothing deep down inside us except what we have put there ourselves, no criterion that we have not created in the course of creating a practice, no standard or rationality that is not an appeal to such a criterion, no rigorous argumentation that is not obedience to our own conventions.
>
> (Rorty 1982, p. xlii)

A brief history of research on education

James begins his talks to Cambridge teachers in July 1892 by declaring to the teachers in his audience that they hold the future of the country in their hands, and cautioning them that knowledge of psychology does not ensure effective teaching (James 1916). He warned them of a great error in thinking that scientific psychology could offer them teaching strategies or instructional methods they could readily incorporate into their teaching. After all, 'psychology is a science, and teaching is an art; and sciences never generate arts directly out of themselves' (James 1916, pp. 7–8). Further, he argued that what psychology can do is to

> save us from mistakes. It makes us, moreover, clearer as to what we are about. We gain confidence in respect to any method which we are using as soon as we believe that it has theory as well as practice.
>
> (James 1916, p. 11)

Christoph Wulf (2003) argues that educational research and science in Europe, in the 1970s and 1980s, was one of the most developed areas of disciplines, both in the humanities and social sciences. He claims that

> no doubt . . . it is in Germany that educational science developed as a scientific discipline in its own right, when humanist pedagogics, empirical educational science and the Critical Theory of the Frankfurt School merged. Indeed, these three different paradigms have played such an important part in shaping educational science that it is essential that their convergence be reconstructed and critically reflected.
>
> (Wulf 2003, p. 9)

The historicity of the discipline of education (and its relevance for an understanding of educational practice) was originally charted within the framework of humanist pedagogics. Education was first conceived following a model of the pedagogical relationship as a process of interaction between an adult and a youth. Thus, humanist pedagogy defined itself as a theory of education. Later on, however, the empirical form of educational science tried to differentiate itself from humanist pedagogics by developing its views on the significance of educational practice. Dilthey (as cited in Wulf 2003, p. 57) argues that 'Education can only be deduced from the aims of "life"; and morality has not been able to define these aims in a manner universally recognized'. From this demonstration of the primacy of 'life' over ethics, Dilthey deduced the primacy of educational practice over moral discourses. While it is clearly about the relationship between theory and practice, it supports the primacy of practice over theory, which led to the premise that the idea and grounding of any theoretical or scientific educational knowledge is deduced from educational practices and realities. Hence, educational science became first and foremost not a theoretical discipline, but a practical one. As Wulf (2003, p. 16) argues, 'by casting itself as a historico-social theory of practice at the service of this practice, this new educational science wants to contribute to the improvement of practice. This self-affirmation has taken the shape of a critique'.

The institutionalisation of research on education

The founding of Johns Hopkins University as the first research university in 1876 set the stage and range of the new elite research universities, such as the University of Chicago, Stanford University and others. As Lagemann (1989) points out, these institutions suddenly became the frontrunners in conducting research and disseminating new knowledges that led to major changes in understanding of the professions, and became identified as places where educational research thrived at the end of the nineteenth century. During this time period, there was a belief that the social world could be 'acted on and changed through scientific principles' (Popkewitz 1998, p. 4), and where teaching professions became closely embodied in various forms of scientific analysis and planning. This way of re-imagining and re-structuring higher education in the United States, from a sole focus on the practitioner's teaching to the new focus on something that included both teaching and research, led to new understandings and the birth of new schools of thought, and different approaches to science, including education.

The inter-war years in the twentieth century were times of transformation for educational research. By the year 1915, the field of education had been established at universities with more than half of the 600 institutions of higher education in the United States offering courses on education. The growth of doctoral-level research and studies had increasing enrolments only comparable at that time to the field of chemistry. While faculty at institutions such as Harvard, Teachers College and the University of Chicago, which had dominated the educational research landscape decades earlier, continued to make significant contributions to the study of education, there were scholars at many other institutions that were generating additional valuable contributions to educational research scholarship. The rise of university-based educational research formed educational research capabilities as a very rich and diverse interdisciplinary field, with boundaries that were being pushed and shifted over time. These were the foundations of a system that was producing educational knowledge, and they were organised and traditionally managed through universities' faculties of education, which were established from the early twentieth century to concentrate and deepen educational knowledge. This coincided with the professional field of education that has transitioned from an apprenticeship model to specialist teachers colleges, which were run by state departments of education. However, in the 1960s, stand-alone teachers colleges were reformed as colleges of advanced education. In the 1990s these colleges were amalgamated with existing faculties and schools of education or configured into new universities.

The 1990s was the decade of mergers and amalgamations of tertiary education institutions in the English-speaking world. The United Kingdom, for instance, undertook some twenty-five mergers since 1994, including three teachers colleges merging with universities: Moray House Institute of Education merged with The University of Edinburgh in 1998; St Andrew's College of Education merged with The University of Glasgow in 1999; and Northern College of Education merged with Aberdeen and Dundee Universities in 2001. During the period from 1987–2004 in Australia there were over eighty institutions that through merger or amalgamation became integrated with some thirty-two state universities. Teacher education in New Zealand was 'for more than a century the preserve of independent stand alone Teachers' Colleges', as Alcorn (2008, p. 1) argues, and is now, 'following recent mergers, largely university based'. The overall push to perform in a new research culture is a new concept because in the country prior to the 1990s there was a clear split between practitioner-teacher training colleges linked with practice in schools, and the universities that fostered a research culture. There remains a tension between these groups, and arguments refer to being theoretically blind, on one side, or irrelevant for a real classroom or policy on the other. As Alcorn argues, practitioners are

> often disappointed that research studies do not provide a firm basis for policy intervention or for classroom practice . . . because all learning is contextually based, it is impossible for educational research to come up with firm answers to troubling questions that will work in any situation.
> (Alcorn 2008, pp. 3–4)

The period from 1991 to 2007, a mere sixteen years, was the era of mergers between universities and colleges of education in New Zealand. Hamilton Teachers College was the first, amalgamating with the University of Waikato in 1991 to be followed by the Palmerston North College of Education (formerly known as Palmerston North Teachers College), which merged with Massey University in 1996. By the mid-2000s, Auckland and Wellington Colleges of Education became amalgamated with the Universities of Auckland and Victoria (Wellington), respectively. The remaining stand-alone Colleges of Education at Christchurch and Dunedin, formally known as the Christchurch and Dunedin Colleges of Education, respectively, were merged with the Universities of Canterbury and Otago in 2007. It is interesting to note that the Dunedin College of Education was the first college to be founded in New Zealand in 1876 and in 2007 the last to be amalgamated, thus ending a tradition of specialist stand-alone teachers colleges of over 130 years (Alcorn 2008). In 2004 there were reportedly '31 providers and 156 different programmes of initial teacher education in New Zealand' (Cameron & Baker 2004, p. 17) offering

75 programmes for primary school teaching and 32 programmes for secondary teaching. 'Prior to 1989', observe Cameron and Baker (2004, p. 16), 'initial teacher education was almost entirely restricted to six colleges of education, offering a three-year primary Diploma of Teaching, a shortened two-year primary Diploma of Teaching for those with degrees, and a one-year post-degree secondary Diploma of Teaching'.

Two paradigms of educational research

The beginning of the twentieth century was dominated by paradigms from two thinkers: John Dewey from philosophy and E. L. Thorndike from psychology, who shaped the landscape of research scholarship, educational thought and educational practice. Dewey developed his progressive notions of education, which influenced practitioners to alter traditional educational practices (Lagemann, 1989). His legacy is influential even in contemporary times, when a lot of debates in education are focused on, and framed around, the traditional and progressive philosophies and concepts. On the other hand, Thorndike was influential in pursuing and acknowledging the 'laws of learning', published studies and texts around the psychology of arithmetics, and developed what became known as a count of common words. This resulted in the idea of practices to enhance the development of basal readers, and assessment of the difficulty of reading materials. His impact is also visible in contemporary scholarship. These diverse visions were well explored by Soltis (1988), and in Tomlinson's (1997) work, where he analyses the art of teaching and its transformation into a science.

While Dewey promoted a commitment to democracy and community that was made manifest through cooperation, holistic curriculum and instruction, and minimal individual assessment, Thorndike believed in individualizing education, breaking curriculum down to its lowest skills or conceptual elements, and then, through behavioral objectives, putting it back together. Such an approach was facilitated by the mass use of individual tests of various sorts, as Theobald and Mills (1995) argue. Thorndike's views seemed to reflect the lived experiences of education and schooling of adults, and from these paradigmatic struggles he emerged as an influential player who was able to speak to and capture the perception of what was public education. Dewey's ideas were also influential and he was able to influence a number of scholars who followed him, kept his ideas alive and carved out a foothold at the margins of educational thought. In the midst of the twentieth century, this movement came closer to a position that would enable and be suitable for direct engagement.

Lagemann (1989, p. 185) argues that 'one cannot understand the history of education in the United States during the twentieth century unless one realizes that Edward L. Thorndike won and John Dewey lost'. In the juxtaposition of these two thinkers, the primary reasons that 80% of education reforms proposed and implemented over the past half-century have yielded such insufficient, and often even poor results become visible. The mechanistic view of learning espoused by Thorndike dominated the last half of the twentieth century in so-called school reforms. With the signing of the *No Child Left Behind Act* (NCLB) in 2002, it was as if Thorndike's ghost marched at the head of the reform parade. To emphasize their distinction from each other further, Thorndike saw human subjects in the image of the machine, while Dewey perceived human subjects as the image of life. In this sense, both Dewey's and James' scholarship and thinking reflect the foundation and the core of the modern scientific method, while Thorndike's lens can be viewed directly as 'scientistic', in the sense that it is strongly attached to, and places too much value on, what could be easily counted. This is a built-in conflict in policies such as the NCLB, between purportedly Deweyan ends and Thorndikean means. And this tension is fundamental even in the contemporary educational landscape, as Thorndike's legacy overpowered Dewey's philosophy.

Popkewitz (2011), in what nowadays might be seen to be the construction of the subject that made possible the welfare state by producing more precise and accurate knowledge of individual behaviours, was to improve the nation's human resources by enabling the fittest to profit the most from schooling. Thorndike's references to the range of abilities among children and to equal practice opportunities gave scientific sanction to liberal theories regarding individual freedom and self-actualisation. However for Dewey, the learning of science as 'habits of the mind' was to create conditions for the mode of life considered necessary for the democratic process. That mode of life simultaneously constituted the inscription of the American enlightenment hopes that connected with the technological sublime, placing science and technology as the apotheosis of reason.

The turn to practice

Theories of practice do not only shape what we accept as 'true' and 'normal', but also implicitly constitute a set of politico-ethical choices. The use of the notion of 'practice' in education often figures as an unanalysable 'given' in educational research, and it is perceived as the bedrock of educational activities which are generally regarded as self-evident. *Practice* is part of a new orthodoxy in education prioritising the practical over the theoretical, which informs programmes of teacher education and associated research. This notion of educational practices includes an emphasis on cultural construction and post-empiricist theory that describes the new constellation of studies in educational research as they have developed over the postwar period and especially since the 1970s.

The intellectual forbears of these practices can be considered to be Aristotle and Marx. The origins of the turn to practice are an account of practical reason beginning, perhaps, with Aristotle (2000), who in the *Nicomachean Ethics* (Book VI) talks of *phronesis* as the ability to use the intellect practically, as a form of practical reason. It is also important when arguing for the turn to practice to mention

Marx for his materialist social ontology that has influenced thinkers like Heidegger, as well as contemporary practice theorists like Bourdieu (1977, 1990, 1998) and Freire (1972). His texts are strewn with references to the priority of the practical, as the second thesis on Feuerbach reads: 'The question whether objective truth can be attributed to human thinking is not a question of theory, but a *practical* question' (Marx 1959b, p. 283). He also argues elsewhere that 'life is not determined by consciousness, but consciousness by life' (Marx & Engels 2001, p. 47), or 'it is not the consciousness of men [sic] that determines their being, but on the contrary, their social being that determines their consciousness' (Marx 1959a, p. 182).

Some of the elements of practice theory are embedded in the notion that practice reflects the 'cultural turn' in philosophy and theory and therefore emphasizes the focus on cultural (and linguistic) practices. This implies a central focus on 'the practitioner' and practitioner knowledge, especially within the idea of reflective practice, the use of which is carried over to so-called 'communities of practice' and theories of 'situated learning'. The term has been used to signal the priority of the practical over the theoretical in educational research, theory and activities. Thus, educational activities are primarily practical engagements-with-others-in-the-world; it implies that learning and teaching are fundamentally social activities, and thus 'doings' or performances without 'inner' processes. This notion of practice draws attention to context, forms of contextualism and 'contexts of use'. The use of 'practices' also highlights *pragmatics* in general, both in linguistic and cognitive theory, such as the view of practices as pragmatically grounded. These theoretical tendencies derive from a largely unexamined shift in philosophy and social theory to focus on *practices* as the underlying concept of cultures and communities, which coordinates sociopolitical order and structures social reality.

There are a number of theories of educational practice: Aristotle's notion of practice as *phronesis* or practical judgement; Marx's, and later Freire's, practice as *praxis*; Dewey's practice as *problem-solving*; Heidegger's practice as *lived experience* (life-world phenomenology); Bourdieu's practice as *habitus*, and Schön and Argyris' practice as *reflection in action*. In Wittgenstein and Heidegger it is an attempt to overcome the object/subject dualism and to 'highlight non-propositional knowledge and illuminate the conditions of intelligibility' (Schatzki et al. 2001, p. 1). This is a way of avoiding the dualism of action and structure as well as the determinism of the objectified social structures and systems of Bourdieu and Giddens. *Practices* provide a means for theorizing language as a discursive activity against structuralist and semiotic notions of language as a structure or system, as reflected in the work of Derrida and Foucault. Social studies of science use the notion of practices to counter representational accounts of science, such as in the work of Rouse and Pickering, and to challenge 'humanist dichotomies between human and nonhuman entities' (Schatzki et al. 2001, p. 1). The posthumanist trend, especially in science and technology studies, wants to construe practices as involving an interface with machines and scientific instruments, and to de-centre the human subject. While there is, as Schatzki claims, 'no unified practice approach' (Schatzki et al. 2001, p. 2), most theorists identify practices as fields of human activity defined as the skills, or 'tacit knowledges' or presuppositions that underlie activities. Schatzki further argues:

> most practice theorists would agree that activity is embodied and that nexuses of practices are mediated by artefacts, hybrids and natural objects, disagreements reign about the nature of embodiment, the pertinence of thematizing it when analyzing practices, the sorts of entities that mediate activity, and whether these entities are relevant to practices as more than mere intermediaries among Humans.
>
> (Schatzki et al. 2001, p. 2)

Forms of human activity are anchored in accounts of the body and typically theorists will maintain 'bodies and activities are "constituted" within practices' (Schatzki et al. 2001, p. 2). In so doing, practice theorists tend to adopt a materialist social ontology emphasising the way human activity depends on shared skills or understandings, typically viewed as embodied. The priority of practical engagement is grounded in the fundamental philosophical claim that involves the assertion of the priority of practical engagement and understanding of the world over any form of theoretical contemplation, understanding or speculation. The priority of practical engagement and understanding follows from an emphasis on the body and on embodied knowledge, rationality and understanding, which takes place through the skilled body, through the acquisition of shared embodied know-how (Peters & Besley 2006).

Wittgenstein came to accept in his later work that philosophy, like language, was 'just a set of indefinitely expansible social practices' (Rorty 1993, p. 344). Rule-following might seem to be a paradigm case of rationalism, yet for Wittgenstein rule-following is a practice and its normative aspect derives from the consensus between different rule-followers, which can be understood only in naturalistic terms as facts about our 'natural history'. The concept of *practice* is one of the key concepts in Wittgenstein's later philosophy. It partly replaces his earlier talk about the inexpressible, and his argument was that the practice must speak for itself. To follow a rule is what Wittgenstein calls a *practice*, and the sketched analysis of this concept makes us understand better how it is possible to apply a rule without the support of another rule. It also makes us realize in what sense one is justified in talking about *tacit* knowledge in connection with the application of concepts and rule-following in general. Rorty further argues:

> Early Heidegger and late Wittgenstein set aside the assumption (common to their respective predecessors, Husserl and Frege) that social practice – and in particular the use of language – can receive a noncausal, specifically philosophical explanation in terms of conditions of possibility. More generally, both set aside the assumption that philosophy might explain the unhidden

on the basis of the hidden, and might explain availability and relationality on the basis of something intrinsically unavailable and unrelational.

(Rorty 1993, pp. 347–348)

Despite their differences in style and outlook it is no longer surprising or unusual to classify Wittgenstein, and particularly his later work, and Dewey, as both belonging to the same family of pragmatism, understood in a broad sense. They both express a common position, which can be roughly defined as claiming 'the primacy of practice' even though, in the end, they have a different view of what this appeal to practice means, a question that concerns the very nature of philosophy itself. Heidegger was to emphasise the practical over the theoretical and also claimed to find his source for firsthand practical understanding in Aristotle (Sheenan 1993). As Hall (1993, p. 128) notes, 'the practical world is the one that we inhabit first, before philosophizing or engaging in scientific investigation' and further 'the world in the traditional sense can be understood as derivative from the practical world'. Heidegger's emphasis on the priority of the relational context of practical activity is also mounted as a critique of traditional Cartesian ontology which pictures the world as comprising subjects as minds whose mental representations, or ideas, attempt to capture an independent, material, reality. Philosophy and science, in this view, is concerned with ways of guaranteeing the accuracy of our representations. Furthermore, Heidegger questions both the possibility and the desirability of making our everyday understanding absolutely explicit. In his work he introduces the notion that the shared everyday skills, concerns and practices into which subjects are socialized provide the conditions necessary to make sense of the world and of everyday lives. All intelligibility presupposes something that cannot be fully articulated, and, in this sense, deals with the knowing-how rather than a knowing-that. At the deepest level such knowing is embodied in subjects' social skills rather than concepts, beliefs and values. Heidegger argues that our cultural practices can direct our activities and make our lives meaningful only insofar as they are and stay unarticulated background practices. As Heidegger puts it in a later work, *The Origin of the Work of Art*, 'Every decision . . . bases itself on something not mastered, something concealed, confusing; else it would never be a decision' (cited in Dreyfus 1993, pp. 293–294).

Competing views of the turn to practice

Following Dreyfus (1993), and our above analysis, it is possible to identify five competing views of practice and the extent to which they are unified or dispersed, and integrated or disseminatory. These five approaches form a rich set of connections between theories of practice and the ethico-political commitments they embody. The first one is *stability*, and it emerges from the work of Wittgenstein and Bourdieu. The practices are relatively stable and resist change. Change may be initiated by innovators, or be the result of 'drift', but there is no inherent tendency in the practices for this to happen. The consequence is either a conservative acceptance of the status quo or revolutionary prescription of change. These notions are particularly visible in Bourdieu's works *Outline of a Theory of Practice* (1977) and *The Logic of Practice* (1990). The second approach is *articulation*, represented by Hegel and Merleau-Ponty. The practices have a telos of clarity and coherence, and become increasingly more refined as our skills develop. This leads to political progressivism, albeit with the recognition that the path to progress will not always lead in that direction.

The third one is Appropriative Gathering, *Ereignis*, based on Dreyfus' reading of the later Heidegger. When practices run into anomalies, we make an originating leap, drawing on marginal or neighbouring practices and so revising our cultural style. This supports those who can best bring about such change within a liberal democratic society, such as entrepreneurs, political associations, charismatic leaders and culture figures. The fourth one is *dissemination and difference* based on Derrida's work. While there are many equally appropriate ways of acting, and each new situation calls for a leap in the dark, the consequence is then a sensitivity to difference, to loosen the hold of past norms on present and future action, and to become aware of the leaps we make rather than covering them up with whiggish history. The fifth one is Foucault's *problematization*, where practices develop in such a way that contradictory actions are felt to be appropriate. Attempts to fix these problems lead to further resistance. This leads to a hyperactive pessimism: showing the contingency of what appears to be necessary and engaging in resistance to the established order.

These five approaches to educational practices are thus phenomenological (Wittgenstein, Heidegger, Dreyfus) in that they call for practices to be non-cognitive, nonconceptual and prelinguistic; Marxist (Bourdieu and Passeron), where they are seen as telic or praxical; positivist, where practice is 'practical' or 'applied theory'; cognitive, where practice is perceived as 'reflection in action' (Schön); ethical (Aristotle, Kant), where practice is seen as practical judgment or engagement; classical pragmatism (James, Dewey, Peirce), where practice is considered to be a problem-solving or a 'community of inquiry'; and poststructuralist, where practice is perceived as problematization (Foucault) or difference (Derrida). Turner's (1994) *The Social Theory of Practices* was a broad-ranging attack on the very idea of a 'social practice', a widely deployed concept in the philosophy of social science, social theory and the social sciences themselves. He claims that practices 'are the vanishing point of twentieth-century philosophy' (Turner 1994, p. 1) and further argues that:

> In postfoundationalist writings in the humanities, the diversity of human practices has become a place-holder or filler in the slot formerly occupied by the traditional 'foundationalist' notions of truth, validity and interpretive correctness. Truth, validity, and correctness are held to be a practice-relative rather than practice-justifying notion.
>
> (Turner 1994, p. 9)

Concluding comments

Critiques of evidence-based research, policy and practice in education are emphasised by Shahjahan (2011), who offers an anti-colonial perspective. This position argues that proponents of evidence-based education unknowingly promote a colonial discourse and material relations of power that continue from the American-European colonial era. This colonial discourse is evident in at least three ways: (1) the discourse of civilizing the profession of education, (2) the promotion of colonial hierarchies of knowledge and monocultures of the mind, and (3) the interconnection between neoliberal educational policies and global exploitation of colonised labour. Therefore, the call for the decolonising implications of revealing some of the colonial vestiges in educational policy, research and neoliberal reform are very important in contemporary times. A sense of practice has always been central to critical and interpretive policy studies, both as a theoretical construct and as an object of inquiry. Much work has been put into conceptual and methodological issues and the field has developed quickly as a result. But what makes for an effective descriptive account of 'practice'? How should we develop case studies in order to make practice available for interrogation, discussion and reflection, both by researchers and by practitioners themselves? The elusive concept of practice is increasingly establishing itself as a vital perspective in policy analysis. Practice-based accounts conceptualise policy as more or less typified patterns of day-to-day activity and stress the negotiated and performative character of public policy, the situatedness of knowledge and the role of materiality (bodies and artefacts) in policy making. In recent years the number of such accounts has grown to an extent that we can veritably speak of a 'practice turn' in policy analysis.

Collecting better evidence about what works best and establishing a culture where this evidence is used as a matter of routine can improve outcomes for children and increase professional independence. A knowledge of educational research enhances opportunities for teachers to become part of an evidence based profession, by embedding research into everyday practice; making informed decisions independently; and fighting off the odd spectacle of governments telling teachers how to teach, because teachers can use the 'good quality' evidence that they have helped to create to make their own informed judgments. Understanding the history of educational research, its birth and paradigm wars, and the ways in which teachers and education still work with their fall-outs can really help us to achieve this.

References

Alcorn, N 2008, 'Evidence and education: The braided roles of research, policy and practice in New Zealand', *NZ Annual Review of Education*, vol. 17, pp. 5–23.

Aristotle 2000, *Nicomachean Ethics* R Crisp (ed. & trans), Cambridge University Press, Cambridge, UK.

Bourdieu, P 1977, *Outline of a theory of practice* R Nice (trans), Cambridge University Press, Cambridge, UK.

Bourdieu, P 1990, *The logic of practice* R Nice (trans), Polity, Cambridge, UK.

Bourdieu, P 1998, *Practical reason: On the theory of action*, Stanford University Press, Stanford, CA.

Cameron, M & Baker, R 2004, *Initial teacher education: Research on initial teacher education in New Zealand 1993–2004 literature review and annotated bibliography*, New Zealand Council for Educational Research, Wellington, NZ.

Dreyfus, H 1993, 'Heidegger on the connection between nihilism, art, technology, and politics', in C Guignon (ed.), *The Cambridge companion to Heidegger*, Cambridge University Press, Cambridge, UK, pp. 289–316.

Foucault, M 1963/1973, *The birth of the clinic: An archaeology of medical perception* AM Sheridan-Smith (trans), Pantheon, New York, NY.

Freire, P 1972, *Pedagogy of the oppressed* MB Ramos (trans), Penguin, Harmondsworth, UK.

Hall, GS 1893, *The contents of children's' minds on entering school*, E. L. Kellogg & co, New York & Chicago, IL.

Hall, H 1993, 'Intentionality and world: Division I of *Being and Time*', in C Guignon (ed.), *The Cambridge companion to Heidegger*, Cambridge University Press, Cambridge, UK, pp. 122–140.

James, W 1916, *Talks to teachers on psychology, and to students on some of life's ideals*, Holt, New York, NY.

Lageman, E 1989, 'The plural worlds of educational research', *History of Education Quaterly*, vol 29, no. 2, pp. 184–214.

Leedy, HA 1973, 'Research', *The world book encyclopedia Vol. 16*, Field Enterprises Educational Corporation, Chicago, IL, pp. 238–239.

Marchetti, S 2011, 'James, Nietzsche and Foucault on ethics and the self', *Foucault Studies*, no. 11, February, pp. 126–155.

Marx, K 1959a, 'The eighteenth Brumaire of Louis Bonaparte', in LS Feuer (ed.), *Marx and Engels: Basic writings on politics and philosophy*, Doubleday, Garden City, NY.

Marx, K 1959b, 'Theses on Feuerbach', in LS Feuer (ed.), *Marx and Engels: Basic writings on politics and philosophy*, Doubleday, Garden City, NY.

Marx, K & Engels, F 2001, *The German ideology part one, with selections from parts two and three, together with Marx's "Introduction to a Critique of Political Economy"*, International Publishers, New York, NY.

McLeod, SA 2008, *Wilhelm Wundt*, Psychology Articles for Students, retrieved 22 April 2016, <www.simplypsychology.org/wundt.html>.

Nietzsche, F 1872/2004, *The birth of tragedy: Out of the spirit of music*, Penguin Classics, London, UK.

Peters, MA & Besley, T 2006, *Building knowledge cultures: Education and development in the age of knowledge capitalism*, Rowman & Littlefield, Lanham, MD.

Popkewitz, T 1998, 'The culture of redemption and the administration of freedom as research', *Review of Educational Research*, vol. 68, no. 1, pp. 1–34.

Popkewitz, T 2011, 'Curriculum history, schooling and the history of the present', *History of Education: Journal of the History of Education Society*, vol. 40, no. 1, pp. 1–19.

Rorty, R 1982, *Consequences of pragmatism*, University of Minnesota Press, Minneapolis, MN.

Rorty, R 1993, 'Wittgenstein, Heidegger, and the reification of language', in C Guignon (ed.), *The Cambridge companion to Heidegger*, Cambridge University Press, Cambridge, UK, pp. 337–357.

Schatzki, TR, Cetina, KK & Savigny, E 2001, *The practice turn in contemporary theory*, Routledge, London, UK.

Shahjahan, RA 2011, 'Decolonizing the evidence-based education and policy movement: Revealing the colonial vestiges in educational policy, research, and neoliberal reform', *Journal of Education Policy*, vol. 26, no. 2, pp. 181–206.

Sheenan, T 1993, 'Reading a life: Heidegger and hard times', in C Guignon (ed.), *The Cambridge companion to Heidegger*, Cambridge University Press, Cambridge, UK, pp. 70–96.

Simon-McWilliams, E 2007, 'Federal support for educational research and development: The history of research and development centers and regional educational laboratories', *The Journal of Negro Education*, vol. 76, no. 3, pp. 391–401.

Soltis, JF 1988, 'Dewey and Thorndike: The persistence of paradigms in educational scholarship', *Canadian Journal of Education (Revue canadienne de l'éducation)*, vol. 13, no. 1, pp. 39–51.

Theobald, P & Mills, E 1995, 'Accountability and the struggle over what counts', *The Phi Delta Kappan*, vol. 76, no. 6, pp. 462–466.

Tomlinson, S 1997, 'Edward Lee Thorndike and John Dewey on the science of education', *Oxford Review of Education*, vol. 23, no. 3, pp. 365–383.

Turner, S 1994, *The social theory of practices: Tradition, tacit knowledge, and presuppositions*, University of Chicago Press, Chicago, IL.

Wulf, C 2003, *Educational science: Hermeneutics, empirical science and critical theory (European studies in education 18)*, Waxmann, Münster; New York; München & Berlin.

Cases

Brown vs. Board of Education 1954, US Supreme Court

Legislation

Civil Rights Act 1964, US Congress
Elementary and Secondary Education Act of 1965 (ESEA), US Congress
Equal Opportunity Act of 1965 (EOP), US Congress
No Child Left Behind Act of 2002 (NCLB), US Congress

Chapter 15

Deliberations on the deliberative professional

Thought-action provocations

Trevor Gale and Tebeje Molla

Introduction

Our intentions in this chapter are deliberative, perhaps even repetitive. We purposefully canvas the literature on professionalism for its account on what it means to be a deliberative professional. Our ambition in revisiting these claims is to encourage the reader, and ourselves, to slow down – to create space for contemplating claims of deliberativeness and to subject these claims to scrutiny. After all, that is the deliberative thing to do. We particularly want to consider what the literature has to say about how the deliberative professional comes into being. In Amartya Sen's (2009) terms, we are interested in the functionings – the beings and doings – of the deliberative professional as well as in *deliberation* as a capability to be developed, which is sorely needed by professionals working in the 'liquid' times of late capitalism (Bauman 2005).

Throughout, we maintain a distinction between 'deliberate' and 'deliberative', 'deliberateness' and 'deliberativeness'. We think the first of each couplet draws attention to intentionality of thinking and action, whereas we take 'deliberative' and 'deliberativeness' to *also* mean thoughtfulness. As we discuss, we see this thoughtfulness as retaining an important aspect of deliberation in thought and action. Similarly, we use 'deliberation' as a capability that is intentional and thoughtful, not just the intentionality implied in the capability of 'deliberateness'. While we acknowledge that some in the literature (e.g., Trede & McEwen 2012) would also claim thoughtfulness in the meaning they ascribe to deliberate, we see our use of *deliberative* and *deliberativeness* as a correction of this work.

The chapter is organised into two main parts. We begin by addressing three questions: what is deliberation; what is professionalism; and, by extension, what is the deliberative professional? We add our own answers to those provided in the literature and offer our own reading and organisation of their responses. Our deliberations are thus summative, evaluative and manipulative. We build on this account in the second part of the chapter to consider ways in which universities and other sites of higher education might advance the development of the deliberative professional. In brief, we argue that this necessarily requires a 'pedagogy of discomfort' (Boler 1999; Boler & Zembylas 2003; Zembylas 2008). We see discomfort as a pedagogical approach aimed at disruption, which can cause (would-be) professionals to re/consider their position. We also understand this pedagogy as intentional (i.e., deliberate) and potentially positive.

As a way of illustrating the efficacy of a pedagogy of discomfort for developing the deliberative professional, we draw briefly on a three-year research project funded by the Australian Research Council (ARC). The project focused on discerning the social justice dispositions of Australian secondary school teachers (n=16) and head teachers/principals (n=10) working in advantaged and disadvantaged schools in Brisbane and Melbourne. Dispositions – the constitutive elements of the habitus – were theorised as 'structured structures predisposed to function as structuring structures' (Bourdieu 1977, p. 72). In other words, dispositions are both the product of practices of the field in which agents are located, and generative structures through which agents produce practices in accordance with the field. Thus, drawing on Bourdieu, the project understood social justice dispositions as being able to be read from and read into practice and, drawing on Cultural Historical Activity Theory (CHAT), we sought to develop a systematic account of teacher and head teacher/principal practice to better inform that reading. In this chapter, we particularly draw from the deliberately provocative techniques of stimulated 'consciousness awakening' (Bourdieu 1990), 'stimulated recall' (Calderhead 1981) and stimulated critique, which we used as tactics to provoke these professionals to name their previously unconscious social justice dispositions. Relevant to the discussion in this chapter, we see these techniques as not only productive of useful data, but also as having pedagogical effect: specifically, generating a deliberativeness in our research participants' that is characteristic of a pedagogy of discomfort.

These matters of how to develop the professional *capability* of deliberation are taken up in the second part of the chapter, following our recount of the functionings of the deliberative professional (cf. Sen 2009). In this respect, we take our lead from Walker and McLean (2013) who similarly worked backwards from functionings, although in our case our intention is to identify the aspects of being deliberative and professional that might inform a pedagogy aimed at developing deliberativeness in professionals.

The deliberative professional

The literature on the deliberative professional is steeped in notions of deliberative democracy (Bohman & Rehg 1997; Elster 1998), particularly in the dialectic relation between 'thinking' and 'action'. Each informs the other; both are functions of being capable (Sen 2009) of deliberation: that is, to deliberate and to be deliberative.

Deliberative thinking

For the deliberative professional, *to deliberate* involves thoughtfulness and purposefulness: the careful consideration of circumstances or issues and a weighing up of the relative merits of all available or known options and possible responses before making a judgment or decision. But it is not enough simply to know. To know only one thing or one way is a limited knowing and may simply lead to one-dimensional action (Marcuse 1991). To truly be considered, the social world needs to be understood as diverse. Its complexity requires professionals to be conscious of explanations derived from sometimes-conflicting social constructs such as class, race and gender. In attending to these diverse ways of knowing, deliberative thinkers also require epistemic resources to help them sort through the complexities of their worlds and an appreciation of power relations that inform 'how knowledge is produced, circulated and approached in distinct ways in different knowledge communities' (Nerland & Jensen 2012, p. 104). To deliberate also requires an investment of time (Sobrekke & Englund 2011): a slow approach to deliberative pursuits (Hartman & Darab 2012). Time features in what it means to deliberate and also in what it means to develop the deliberative professional – matters to which we return below.

On this point, many of the accounts in the literature on the deliberative professional resonate with Daniel Kahneman's (2011, p. 38) conception of 'deliberate thought' (outlined in his now seminal text, *Thinking, Fast and Slow*). In his book, Kahneman defines deliberate thought as necessarily 'slow' if it is to be truly 'deliberate, effortful, and orderly' (p. 48). That is, slow thinkers do not do what fast thinkers do, just more slowly (Hartman & Darab 2012). Instead, they take time to 'compare objects on several attributes, and make deliberate choices between options' (Kahneman 2011, p. 90). In fact, Kahneman's monograph is written primarily as a warning against fast thinking, which he describes as intuitive and impressionistic and leading to 'the unfortunate tendency to treat problems in isolation, and . . . [to be] shaped by inconsequential features of choice problems' (p. 41). Fast thinkers jump to conclusions that are ill informed. They do not do the mental work required to identify all the available information and consider its relative merits before taking a position. They are the antithesis of the deliberativeness that characterises the deliberative professional.

Deliberative action

However, it is not enough just to be deliberative in one's thinking. Deliberation is also about translating thinking into action. For the deliberative professional, *to be deliberative* is to act on one's convictions, with conviction. Just as deliberations are not meant to remain just an idea, action is not simply activity but is intentional and purposeful, similar to how Bourdieu defines practice (Bourdieu 1977, 1984; Warde 2004). Still, deliberative professionals cannot do whatever they have a mind to. Socio-cultural, historical, political, economic and material contexts set boundaries on what can be thought and done. In Sen's (2009) terms, the 'agency freedoms' of the deliberative professional are always curtailed, albeit differently in different contexts.

In a study that investigated the work-based learning of computer engineering professionals and the knowledge domains of the profession, Nerland (2008) showed that professional communities have distinctive knowledge cultures, highlighting differences in professional learning. Every 'professional knowledge culture' is distinctive in its 'knowledge objects' and ways of knowing. Thus, when students embark on becoming a professional, they enter into 'professional communities' that 'differ in the extent to which their collective ways of knowing rest upon scientific achievements, upon personal experiences and reflexivity, or upon processes of codification' (Nerland 2008, p. 52). The epistemic resources informing the deliberations of professionals can be quite different depending on the knowledge cultures of the profession. In turn, their different 'epistementality' (Knorr Cetina 2006) frames their practices. In other words, all professionals are engaged in practice, but their deliberative action can look different across, if not within, professional boundaries.

We think that this line of reasoning raises three interrelated issues in conceiving of the thinking and action required of the deliberative professional. First, and to reiterate what has already been noted, deliberative action is derived from deliberative thought. The fact that actions can vary from profession to profession or from professional to professional is not at issue. In fact, the deliberative nature of action is called into question when professional actions are always the same. There are implications here for the development of deliberation-capable professionals: i.e., it is unlikely to be achieved simply by teaching the functions associated with deliberation, as a way of generating uniform actions consistent with professional communities. Instead, it requires the creation of *opportunities* (Walker & McLean 2013) to deliberate and to be deliberate. Second, deliberative thought is derived from deliberative action. Schön (1983, p. 280) argues that 'doing extends thinking in the tests, moves, and probes of experimental action, and reflection feeds on doing and its results'. It is an argument for 'reflection-in-action' as much as for 'reflection-on-action' (Schön 1983). Burgh et al. (2006) also make this point when deliberating over the ethics of research. They contend that in moments of ethical dilemma in research, pre-deliberated thoughts (i.e., ethical standards or norms) do not always provide adequate direction for deliberative action. Instead, 'the *direction* of the inquiry . . . will be revealed by the *progress* of the inquiry' (2006, p. 28, emphasis added). It is in the doing that thinking emerges. In their extended comments, Burgh et al. (2006, p. 28; emphasis in original):

> disagree that justification for ethical decision-making requires any overarching normative position. Our contention is that ethical decision and action requires *deliberative justification*. That is, faced with an ethical problem that is of genuine concern the direction of the inquiry, and the ways in

which normative theories might enter into the inquiry, will be revealed by the progress of the inquiry rather than being preordained.

Third, and building on this argument, the dialectic relation between deliberative thinking and action suggests a logic with elements akin to Bourdieu's logic of practice. For Bourdieu, practice has a logic distinct from the logic of science. As Burgh et al. (2006) observe, scholastic knowledge comes 'preordained': it is 'a mode of thought that works by making explicit the work of thought' (Bourdieu 1990, p. 91) and thus privileges thinking over action. In contrast, the logic of practice 'can only be grasped in action, in the temporal movement that distinguishes it' (Bourdieu 1990, p. 92). Similarly, deliberations cannot be predetermined. They must be thought in relation to specific moments of action, in 'reflective conversation with the situation' (Schön 1983).

Deliberative professionalism

This logic of deliberation – the dialectic interplay between thought and action, in situ – is at the heart of what it means to be a professional. Professionals are engaged in fields of practice, but they do not simply act in these fields on the instruction of others. Professional work involves a degree of 'artistry' (Schön 1983): in bringing knowledge and skills from a particular epistemic culture together with insight into the particularities of a given situation, to inform practice. Such work is not technical-instrumental but 'inherently discretionary' (Flynn 1999, p. 23). Yet while being *capable* of deliberation, some professionals are 'restricted', others 'extended' (Hoyle 1974) in their *capacities* to deliberate and to be deliberative.

Drawing on and extending Hoyle (1974), Menter et al. (2010) suggest that this restricted-extended continuum (of professional capacity for deliberation) produces four models of professionalism, although these overlap or are somewhat cumulative particularly towards one end:

1   The *effective* professional is characterised by technical accomplishment and measurement.[1] It is the preferred model of current accountability and performativity regimes (Mahony & Hextall 2000) and corresponds with government standardisation of professional practice aimed at achieving national priorities. There is little to no recognition of contextual differences or choice in what practices to employ, while the expertise of knowledge domains and professional communities is overlaid, even usurped, by an explicitly political dimension.

2   The *reflective* professional has more capacity for deliberation, with an emphasis on carefully considering the particulars of a context in order to discern what techniques should be applied. The approach has most recently been taken up in teacher education as a clinical model of teaching, with teaching understood as 'a clinical-practice profession such as is found in

many allied health professions' (McLean Davies et al. 2013, p. 93). In this clinical form, the model is reflective but also interventionist in orientation, sharing some aspects of the effective professional, and is derived from a medical conception of triage: an initial assessment and prioritisation of 'problems' that are then addressed by following standard procedures. There is capacity for deliberation but this is confined to determining what the problems are (based on pre-existing research), which are the most pressing and which pre-learned interventions match the problems at hand.

3   The *enquiring* professional is – unlike the clinician – not just a user of expert knowledge and skills but also a producer of them. Such professionals are engaged in systematic enquiry (research), which serves as a vehicle for coming to know the epistemological bases of their practice and for improving that practice. Enquiring professionals are also part of an enquiring professional community with which they share the results of their research deliberations.

4   The *transformative* professional exhibits characteristics from both the reflective and enquiry models, although transformative professionals are more *reflexive* (i.e., critical reflection of self and of the social) than *reflective*, and are committed to enquiry that contributes to change, not just new understanding. There is thus a moral and 'activist' (Sachs 2003) dimension to the transformative professional.

It is this fourth model of professionalism that grants the most capacity for deliberation. Deliberative professionals are primarily agents for 'transformation' of the social (Sachs 2003); they are 'public-good professionals' (Walker & McLean 2013). Judith Sachs (2003, p. 146) describes activist professionalism similarly as 'not self-interested; its concern is with wider issues of equity and social justice . . . [it] challenges not only dominant interests but also the beliefs and practices that sustain power in everyday life'. Thinking and acting in ways that transform social and economic inequities goes beyond simply adjusting (for) inequitable outcomes. As Nancy Fraser (1997, p. 23; emphasis added) explains:

> By affirmative remedies for injustice I mean remedies aimed at correcting inequitable outcomes of social arrangements *without disturbing the underlying framework that generates them*. By transformative remedies, in contrast, I mean remedies aimed at correcting inequitable outcomes precisely by *restructuring the underlying generative framework*. The crux of the contrast is end-state outcomes versus the processes that produce them.

This distinction between correcting inequitable outcomes and restructuring frameworks that generate them, draws attention to the kind of deliberations – the thinking and action – required of the deliberative professional and names the strategy behind what it means to be an transformative professional (Sachs 2003).

Developing deliberation as a professional capability

There are at least three elements in this description of the deliberative professional that hint at what it takes to develop deliberation as a capability. First, developing deliberative professionals takes an *investment of time*; time to do as well as time to think, given that thinking is provoked by action. Second, deliberative professionals also need to be *exposed to opportunities* in which to deliberate and to be deliberative; opportunities that are varied, by context and epistemology (cf. 'epistemological equity' Dei 2010). And third, deliberative professionals need to be *challenged to critically reflect* on the inequities of social, political and economic arrangements, how they are implicated in these arrangements and how they might act to transform them. We think that the first of these elements is required for the second and the second is required for the third. While we focus in this section on the third, the first and second are also implicated. Our interest is specifically in the design of pedagogy for would-be deliberative professionals to engage in critical reflection. According to Taylor (2009, p. 7), this entails:

> questioning the integrity of deeply held assumptions and beliefs based on prior experience. It is often prompted in response to an awareness of conflicting thoughts, feelings, and actions and at times can lead to a perspective transformation.

Critical reflection makes it possible for professionals to identify, examine and transform 'theories-in-use' (Schön 1983). Without conscious inquiry and reflection, much of the tacit knowledge and assumptions underpinning what practitioners do remains unknown. For instance, in order for professionals to be transformative, they need to assume a critical position to scrutinise the complexities of identity formation as well as its manifestations and consequences in everyday life (Roberge 2011).

From our perspective, a 'pedagogy of discomfort' (Boler 1999; Boler & Zembylas 2003; Zembylas 2008) is most suited to provoking this critical reflection within professionals. Discomforting pedagogies are both social and critical. They engage learners in 'collective witnessing', 'mutual exploration' and 'deliberate listening' (Boler 1999), informed by the wider collective interests of an activist professionalism, and they embrace the seemingly contradictory aims of: (1) *discomfort* – invoking pedagogic actions directed at disorientating learners in order to unsettle 'cherished beliefs and assumptions' (Zembylas & McGlynn 2012, p. 56); and (2) *comfort*–invoking pedagogic actions directed at creating an environment for learners to share cherished beliefs and assumptions without fear of ridicule or condemnation. Both discomfort *and* comfort – or what Zembylas and McGlynn (2012, p. 45) refer to collectively as 'controlled discomfort' – are needed in order to provoke the reflexivity required of deliberative professionals.

Drawing on research outlined above, we propose three pedagogical 'tactics' for provoking deliberativeness: stimulated 'consciousness awakening' (Bourdieu 1990), 'stimulated recall' (Calderhead 1981; Stough 2001) and stimulated critique. As noted, these are derived from data generation techniques utilised in our research on teachers' social justice dispositions and match the three stages of our research, which included purposeful conversations (pertaining to social justice) with: (1) head teachers/principals, aimed at uncovering the authority for teachers' practice; (2) teachers, aimed at uncovering teachers' reasons for their own classroom practices (captured on video); and (3) teachers, aimed at eliciting teachers' assessment of the classroom practices of other teachers (captured on video). As well as producing data for the research, the conversations also proved to be pedagogical encounters for both researchers and research participants. Conversation extracts illustrative of these three stages are utilised below. All three participants (Glenn, Brett and Angela)[2] are sourced from one elite private school – here referred to as Heyington College – a K-12 school with well above average student academic achievement.[3] While being an elite school with outstanding student results, Heyington also took pride in its social justice programs and in the commitments by its teachers and students to social justice endeavours.

Stimulated 'consciousness awakening'

In the first stage of the project, we were interested in identifying the authority of/for school teachers' practices, particularly those described as socially just. This was researched at two interrelated levels: the *deferral* of authority (i.e., what sources of authority informed the school's commitments to social justice) and the *conferral* of authority (i.e., how the school's commitments to social justice were conveyed to and instilled in teachers). While we sought official accounts of these from head teachers/principals, we were also interested to unmask contradictions and inconsistencies in these accounts in order to discern how the deferral and conferral of authority for social justice worked in practice. Thus, in our conversations with the 10 head teachers/principals in our study, we employed a tactic of reflecting back what head teachers/principals said to us in conversation, in ways that juxtaposed what appeared to us as potentially contradictory or inconsistent aspects of their dialogue. In particular, we were concerned to juxtapose stated beliefs and actions, offering as little assessment as possible beyond our juxtaposition as a way of encouraging head teachers/principals to reflect and comment. Our aim was to stimulate what Bourdieu (1990) describes as a 'consciousness awakening' – given that dispositions (the habitus) sit at the level of unconsciousness and between belief and action.

For instance, in the course of our conversation with Glenn (the head teacher/principal of Heyington College), we discussed his background as a young adult and early teacher, how his philosophies of society and education differed now from then, and how they differed from some of the teachers he employs at his school. Later in the conversation we juxtaposed this discussion with the school's practice of offering selective scholarships to students from ostensibly poor backgrounds, as illustrative of the school's social justice practice:

INTERVIEWER: You spoke earlier about some of the leftist humanist backgrounds of some of the teachers in the school as being a good thing.

GLENN: Yeah, absolutely.

INTERVIEWER: How does that fit with you now being more to the right? I'm particularly thinking about the way in which you describe social justice as being about making sure that opportunity is created for people from poorer parts of society, through scholarships and so on. But in practice aren't you just choosing people for scholarships who are going to fit your school?

GLENN: Yes, that's true, yeah. I feel uncomfortable using the word fit, but in fact it's true. No, I can't argue with it. We do tend to award scholarships to students of a very similar background to our student population, which doesn't quite match our social justice intentions. That's why I feel uncomfortable about it.

In this brief encounter, the pedagogical effect of the stimulated consciousness awakening is evident in Glenn's recognition of contradiction and inconsistency between beliefs and actions. While Glenn acknowledged the contradiction here, later in our conversation he indicated a willingness to 'live with it' – neither attempting to ignore or resolve the 'problem', demonstrating a pragmatism in being able to see past the 'allure of certainty' (Schulz 2010) as necessary for justifying (social justice) practices. This too seemed to be a consciousness awakening for Glenn.

We think that there are insights here for being a deliberative professional. In practice, differences in thinking and action are not always easily resolved. Sometimes no resolution appears possible, at least not thought possible, and yet this should not render the deliberative professional immobile, unable to act. As noted above, thinking feeds on action (Burgh et al. 2006; Freire 1998; Schön 1983). It is through doing that Glenn seeks to prompt his thinking. There are lessons too for pedagogy aimed at critical reflection. Deliberative professionals need *opportunities* that elicit contradiction and inconsistency, and *time* to deliberate over them, if not to resolve them.

As experiential learning theorists such as John Dewey (1938) argue, uncertainty creates opportunity for professional practitioners to critically examine their lived experiences: 'prompted by a sense of uncertainty or unease, the reflective practitioner steps back to examine this experience: What was the nature of the problem? What were my intentions? What did I do? What happened?' (Osterman & Kottkamp 1993, p. 3). Pedagogies of discomfort, then, embrace contradiction and tension as valuable learning experiences, and are instrumental in promoting uncertainty though questioning the status quo and problematising what is taken for granted. They feed on what Nicholls describes as the postmodern condition of 'creative uncertainty' and 'openness to the possibility of thinking otherwise' (Nicholls 2012, pp. 361–362).

Stimulated recall

In the second stage of our research we video-recorded the lessons of 16 teachers (three lessons each, over three days usually within the same week) and at the end of each lesson[4] entered into conversation with the teachers, using excerpts or clips from the video as stimulus for the conversation (approximately three clips per conversation). The clips – between 1 and 3 minutes each in length – were selected by the researchers on the basis that they represented practices that were either informed by or antithetical to social justice. At the end of each clip, we invited the teachers to comment on what they saw and to talk about what they were thinking at the time. We did not offer the teachers our own assessment of their practices and often found that their comments changed our own views. Instead, we used the video clips as a device to stimulate post-active (i.e., evaluative) thinking – as a way of jolting memories and initiating 'reflection-on-action' (Schön 1983).

Our intention in using 'stimulated recall' as a device for generating research data was to elicit 'the logic of practical knowledge' (Bourdieu 1990) rather than normative accounts of the issue in question. The video clips provided participants with a way to revisit the thinking behind what they were doing at a particular time and place, rather than to fall into rehearsed accounts of practice. This enabled us to 'summon up' unspoken or unconscious rationales for action so that these could be examined. At the same time, our conversations became authentic pedagogical encounters for our participants. Often these encounters also provoked wider-ranging discussion about social justice ideals, goals and needs.

In a conversation with Brett (a teacher at Heyington College), we replayed a video clip of him organising students into small groups to undertake a learning activity. In the process, he also selected two students to work with him on activities in isolation from other students and from each other. In conversation about this later, his decision to do this did not appear to be informed by a learning or behavioural issue. Indeed, Brett was not overly forthcoming with an explanation apart from the activities suiting the interests of the students concerned. The next day, our conversation with Brett began as follows:

INTERVIEWER: Has anything stuck in your mind since we spoke last time?
BRETT: A little bit. I haven't thought too much about you guys . . . [but] it's probably stuck in my mind how I treated Ruth and Mark and just having them outside of it [the class]. That was probably one thing that stayed with me a little bit.
INTERVIEWER: What did you think about that?
BRETT: Probably from you guys bringing it up, whether I did the right thing or whether I had excluded them.

Brett acknowledges here that our interactions with him created opportunity for him to reflect on his practice. But it is also important to note the role of the passage of time in this pedagogical encounter. We began with a question often asked of participants at the start of our second and third conversations: whether the participant had had cause to reflect on anything raised in earlier conversations. Our expectation was that the passage of time between the two might give rise to further deliberation, including deliberations on practice and on our discussions about that practice. As can be seen in the conversation extract above, the stimulated recall enabled Brett to be self-reflective about the 'excluded' students and to deliberate on whether this was a practice he should continue. Zembylas and McGlynn (2012) similarly note that discomfort and unsettling of taken-for-granted views and assumptions is a necessary condition for social change.

Stimulated critique

In the third stage of our project, we held a second round of conversations with our 16 teachers, on this occasion stimulated by video clips of the practices of other teachers in our research. Each teacher viewed between four and 12 second-stage clips,[5] depending on the time available for the conversation and the length of their response to each clip. The first four clips were illustrative of four different social justice principles; the second group of four clips repeated these principles, as did the third group. While we invited the teachers to comment on what they saw as 'interesting' in the clips and to explain what they would do if they were in the place of the teacher in the video, most also offered an assessment of the practical and ethical merits of the practices they witnessed. We were less interested in the substance of these assessments and more interested in what they revealed about the disposition of the teacher with whom we were conversing. Our intention was to stimulate critique, that is, 'both criticism and reasoned reflection' (Dant 2003, p. 7), but with the purpose of revealing what informed this critique so that this could become part of the dialogue. We deliberately selected video clips of practices that we thought might provoke a response, juxtaposed with what we knew of the teacher's own context and practice.

In one of these conversations, we showed Angela (another teacher at Heyington College) a video clip of a teacher employed at a similar school teaching students of a similar upper-secondary year level, but utilising a classroom practice more common among younger age groups. The following exchange arose as a result of us drawing this practice to Angela's attention:

INTERVIEWER: She's got the students on the floor and they're not very young children.

ANGELA: Yeah, no that wouldn't work for me.

INTERVIEWER: You wouldn't do that?

ANGELA: Occasionally . . . but generally I just wouldn't do that. It depends if it's just a one-off thing.

INTERVIEWER: What is it about sitting on the floor?

ANGELA: Obviously for her – well, I'm assuming that she's thinking it's a way of connecting or relaxing or having a bit of fun, or injecting some interest in the class. I'm also very practical though. I'd be like 'that's really uncomfortable and they can't write properly, and if they're on carpet the highlighter [pen] is not going to work', and 'do you want them to annotate the sheet because, try writing on carpet on top of the paper' . . . it would depend on the students as to how well they respond to that, so they might be like 'we're on the ground, we're relaxing, therefore I don't have to engage in a more serious way. I can relax and be passive and hear only what she's saying rather than doing things' . . . if she does that all the time that might be normal. If you're doing it infrequently it just gives a sense, if you're on the floor, that it's something that's a bit fun and that you can relax. It's setting a different tone, and it's just not my style.

Here Angela is making a judgment about the impracticality of the students' seating arrangements, particularly given the age and size of the students involved, that it is not conducive to the students doing their work. In Angela's view, the arrangements inhibit active participation in learning experiences. But she is also making a moral judgment, that some seating arrangements send signals to students about the importance of the work to be done. In this case, Angela ponders whether sitting on the floor, particularly if it is irregular, suggests that the work is less important: it sets the wrong 'tone'; it undermines the business of the classroom.

Such conversations provoke professional deliberations that otherwise would remain hidden or unconsidered. A pedagogy of discomfort makes it possible for these to be revealed (to professionals themselves and to those involved in their development) and then once revealed, to be subjected to a critique of critique or what Gardiner (2000) refers to as 'reflexive critique'.

Conclusion

As we have indicated in this chapter, before we can educate the deliberative professional, we need to be clear on what the deliberative professional is. Throughout we have reasoned that the core feature of deliberation is the dialectic relationship between thought and action, and that this itself is synergistic with the work of the professional. Thus defined, deliberation is the hallmark of professionalism. Although, we acknowledge that some forms of professionalism allow for deliberation more than others and, thus, the less deliberative professions are subject to claims of de-professionalisation (e.g., the restriction on professionals to be simply 'effective'). It is the transformative professional that resonates most strongly with our conception of deliberativeness. The deliberative professional is informed and thoughtful, but also an activist, particularly with respect to leading the charge against structures that generate social inequalities and injustices.

We have also noted that development of the deliberative professional requires greater emphasis on the capability of deliberation than on its functionings. The pedagogical focus needs to be on 'opportunity freedom' not just on 'agency freedom' (Sen 2009). This requires an investment of time and the creation of opportunities, if critical reflection and deliberativeness are to become the norms for deliberative professionals. Indeed, we have suggested that pedagogies directed first at the development of critical reflection necessarily imply the other two. Critical consciousness is uppermost in the deliberative mind. One question that we have sought to address in this chapter is how such critical reflection or critical consciousness can be achieved. In our view, these need to be provoked into development through a pedagogy of discomfort. Drawing on what originally were data generation techniques in our research on school head teachers/principals and teachers, we posed three pedagogical tactics directed at discomforting would-be professionals, which we referred to as stimulated consciousness awakening, stimulated recall and stimulated critique. Common to all is a strategy to create opportunities that stimulate professionals-in-the-making to: (1) recognise and name their beliefs and actions; (2) juxtapose the contradictions in these; and then to (3) allow them time to sort through the inconsistencies. We understand this 'sorting through' as not just an intellectual exercise but also a matter for action. Thinking about the injustices of the world can be provoked through and informed by experiences of these injustices, and pedagogies aimed at developing deliberative professionals need to include the creation of opportunities for these to be experienced. That said, 'reflection-in-action' (Schön 1983) is the aim, not just action.

However, beyond a relatively technical argument about the *what* and the *how*, we have said little about *why* the deliberative professional and their development is something towards which we should aspire. It is in fact hard to imagine a moment in recent times when deliberative professionals of the kind described herein have been more needed. Social inequality is growing everywhere. Recently, Oxfam (2014a, 2014b) reported that the bottom half of the world's population owns the same as the richest 85 people in the world and that in the UK, the five richest families are worth more than the country's poorest 20% combined (about 12.6 million people). According to the European Central Bank (Vermeulen 2014), the richest 1% own up to 37% and 33% of the national wealth in the US and Germany, respectively. Similarly in Australia, in 2011/12, the top 20% of households owned 61% of the national wealth, and while the share of other net worth quintile groups decreased, the share of the net worth held by the highest net worth quintile increased from 59% in 2003–04 to 61% in 2011–12 (ABS 2013, p. 6).

This is not just food for thought. Professionals of all kinds are implicated in this widening gap between rich and poor, as instruments 'affirming' this oppression and also subjected to it. However, with commitments to social transformation for the betterment of all, their interests are not just personal. The deliberative professional also has a responsibility to act on behalf of others to restructure the underlying framework generating these inequitable outcomes (Fraser 1997). This would normally require considerable deliberation, including an investment of time to contemplate what is happening and how it could be redressed. Yet in the context of rapid change in the workplace and accelerated technological progress in general, 'reflection-on-action' (after-the-event thinking) has increasingly become a challenge. Professionals are now required to think while doing. The norm must now be 'reflection-in-action'. The challenge has become how to think slow, in fast times. In the face of 'postmodern anxieties,' the deliberative professional needs to capitalise on uncertainties, tensions and contradictions rather than rush to certainty.

At one and the same moment, these challenges are the very reason we need deliberative professionals and are also the greatest challenge to their development. This is the emergent future that beckons them at the same time as it heralds their demise. This chapter is one response to these challenges, one deliberative act performed amidst the hurry of contemporary life. Many more responses will be needed if we are to truly educate the deliberative professional.

Acknowledgements

We acknowledge the Australian Research Council for its financial support of the project (DP130101297 *Social Justice Dispositions Informing Teachers' Pedagogy*) from which data in this chapter is drawn, and the generous participation of teachers and head teachers/principals. The research team included Trevor Gale (Chief Investigator), Russell Cross (Chief Investigator), Carmen Mills (Chief Investigator), Stephen Parker (Research Fellow), Tebeje Molla (Research Fellow) and Catherine Smith (PhD candidate).

Notes

1 See Skourdoumbis and Gale (2013) for a critique of research advocating the effective classroom teacher model.
2 Pseudonyms are used in this chapter for the head teacher/principal, the two teachers and the school.
3 As measured by Australia's National Assessment Program – Literacy and Numeracy (NAPLAN) test, administered annually across the nation to students in Years 3, 5, 7 and 9.
4 Throughout the project the videoed lessons ranged across several subject areas: mathematics, health and physical education, English, religious education, sociology, history and so on. However, our interest was in identifying social justice dispositions, which we did not consider were overly influenced by particular subject areas.
5 To preserve the anonymity of the teachers involved, two sets of twelve clips were used: the Brisbane set was shown in Melbourne and vice versa. In addition, all teachers signed agreements to reveal to the research team if they recognised any teacher, student or school and to agree to keep these particulars confidential. No such recognition was declared.

References

ABS [Australian Bureau of Statistics] 2013, *Household wealth and wealth distribution, Australia, 2011–12*, retrieved 28 April 2016, <http://www.ausstats.abs.gov.au>.
Bauman, Z 2005, 'Education in liquid modernity', *Review of Education, Pedagogy & Cultural Studies*, vol. 27, no. 4, pp. 303–317.

Bohman, J & Rehg, W (eds) 1997, *Deliberative democracy: Essays on reason and politics*, The MIT Press, Cambridge, MA.

Boler, M 1999, *Feeling power: Emotions and education*, Routledge, New York.

Boler, M & Zembylas, M 2003, 'Discomforting truths: The emotional terrain of understanding difference', in P Trifonas (ed.), *Pedagogies of difference. Rethinking education for social change*, Routledge Falmer, London, pp. 107–130.

Bourdieu, P 1977, *Outline of a theory of practice*, Cambridge University Press, New York.

Bourdieu, P 1984, *Distinction: a social critique of the judgement of taste*, R Nice (trans), Routledge & Kegan Paul, London.

Bourdieu, P 1990, *The logic of practice*, R Nice (trans), Polity Press, Cambridge.

Burgh, B, Field, T & Freakley, M 2006, *Ethics and the community of inquiry: Education for deliberative democracy*, Thomson Social Science Press, Melbourne, AUS.

Calderhead, J 1981, 'Stimulated recall: A method for research on teaching', *British Journal of Educational Psychology*, vol. 51, no. 2, pp. 211–217.

Dant, T 2003, *Critical social theory: Culture, society and critique*, Sage Publications, London.

Dei, GJS 2010, *Teaching Africa: Towards a transgressive pedagogy*, Springer, New York.

Dewey, J 1938, *Experience and education*, Macmillan, New York.

Elster, J (ed.) 1998, *Deliberative democracy*, Cambridge University Press, Cambridge.

Flynn, R 1999, 'Managerialism, professionalism and quasi-markets', in M Exworthy & S Halford (eds), *Professionals and the new managerialism in the public sector*, Open University Press, Buckingham, pp. 18–36.

Fraser, N 1997, *Justice interruptus: Critical reflections on the 'postsocialist' condition*, Routledge, New York.

Freire, P 1998, *Pedagogy of hope*, Continuum, New York.

Gardiner, ME 2000, *Critiques of everyday life*, Routledge, London.

Hartman, Y & Darab, S 2012, 'A call for slow scholarship: A case study on the intensification of academic life and its implications for pedagogy', *The Review of Education, Pedagogy and Cultural Studies*, vol. 34, no.1–2, pp. 49–60.

Hoyle, E 1974, 'Professionality, professionalism and control in teaching', *London Educational Review*, vol. 3, no. 2, pp. 13–19.

Kahneman, D 2011, *Thinking, fast and slow*, Farrar, Straus and Giroux, New York.

Knorr Cetina, K 2006, 'Knowledge in a knowledge society: Five transitions', *Knowledge, Work and Society*, vol. 4, no. 3, pp. 23–41.

Mahony, P & Hextall, I 2000, *Reconstructing teaching: Standards, performance and accountability*, Routledge Falmer, London.

Marcuse, H 1991, *One-dimensional man: Studies in the ideology of advanced industrial society* (2nd ed.), Beacon Press, Boston, (Original work published 1964).

McLean Davies, L, Anderson, M, Deans, J, Dinham, S, Griffin, P, Kameniar, B, Page, J, Reid, C, Rickards, F, Tayler, C & Tyler, D 2013, 'Masterly preparation: Embedding clinical practice in a graduate pre-service teacher education programme', *Journal of Education for Teaching: International Research and Pedagogy*, vol. 39, no. 1, pp. 93–106.

Menter, I, Hulme, M, Elliot, D, Lewin, J, with Baumfield, V, et al. 2010, *Literature review on teacher education in the 21st Century*, Scottish Government, Edinburgh.

Nerland, M 2008, 'Knowledge cultures and the shaping of work-based learning: The case of computer engineering', *Vocations and Learning*, vol. 1, no. 1, pp. 49–69.

Nerland, M & Jensen, K 2012, 'Epistemic practices and object relations in professional work', *Journal of Education and Work*, vol. 25, no. 1, pp. 101–120.

Nicholls, DA 2012, 'Postmodernism and physiotherapy research', *Physical Therapy Reviews*, vol. 17, no. 6, pp. 360–368.

Osterman, KF & Kottkamp, RB 1993, *Reflective practice for educators: Improving schooling through professional development*, Corwin Press, Inc., Newbury Park.

Oxfam 2014a, *A tale of two Britains* [Press Release], retrieved 27 April 2016, <http://policy-prac tice.oxfam.org.uk/publications/a-tale-of-two-britains-inequality-in-the-uk-314152>.

Oxfam 2014b, *Working for the few: Political capture and economic inequality*, retrieved 27 April 2016, <http://policy-practice.oxfam.org.uk/publications/working-for-the-few-political-capture-and-economic-inequality-311312>.

Roberge, J 2011, 'The aesthetic public sphere and the transformation of criticism', *Social Semiotics*, vol. 21, no. 3, pp. 435–453.

Sachs, J 2003, *The activist teaching profession*, Open University Press, Buckingham.

Schön, D 1983, *The reflective practitioner*, Basic Books, New York.

Schulz, K 2010, *Being wrong: Adventures in the margin of error*, Ecco – HarperCollins, New York.

Sen, A 2009, *The idea of justice*, Belknap Press of Harvard University Press, Cambridge, MA.

Skourdoumbis, A & Gale, T 2013, 'Classroom teacher effectiveness research: A conceptual critique', *British Educational Research Journal*, vol. 39, no. 5, pp. 892–906.

Sobrekke, TD & Englund, T 2011, 'Bringing professional responsibility back in', *Studies in Higher Education*, vol. 36, no. 7, pp. 847–861.

Stough, LM 2001, 'Using stimulated recall in classroom observation and professional development', paper presented to the Annual Meeting of the American Educational Research Association, Seattle, WA, 10–14 April 2001.

Taylor, EW 2009, 'Fostering transformative learning', in J Mezirow & EW Taylor (eds), *Transformative learning in practice: Insights from community, workplace and higher education*, Jossey-Bass, San Francisco, pp. 3–17.

Trede, F & McEwen, C 2012, 'Developing a critical professional identity: Engaging self in practice', in J Higgs, R Barnett, S Billett, M Hutchings & F Trede (eds), *Practice-based education: Perspectives and strategies*, Sense Publishers, Rotterdam, pp. 27–40.

Vermeulen, P 2014, *How fat is the top tail of the wealth distribution?*, Working Paper Series No. 1692, European Central Bank, Frankfurt.

Walker, M & McLean, M 2013, *Professional education, capabilities and the public good: The role of universities in promoting human development*, Routledge, Hoboken, NJ.

Warde, A 2004, *Practice and field: Revising Bourdieusian concepts*, CRIC Discussion Paper No. 65, University of Manchester, Manchester.

Zembylas, M 2008, 'Engaging with issues of cultural diversity and discrimination through critical emotional reflexivity in online learning', *Adult Education Quarterly*, vol. 59, no. 1, pp. 61–82.

Zembylas, M & McGlynn, C 2012, 'Discomforting pedagogies: Emotional tensions, ethical dilemmas and transformative possibilities', *British Educational Research Journal*, vol. 38, no. 1, pp. 41–59.

Chapter 16

The temptations and failings of teacher effectiveness research

Provocations of a 'practice perspective'

Andrew Skourdoumbis and Julianne Lynch

Introduction

In this chapter we engage critically with teacher effectiveness research (TER). Like others before us, we argue that TER employs a reductive view of teaching and that the uptake of its tools and products can potentially have negative impacts on teachers and teaching. Like others, we argue that TER overly emphasises teachers' classroom-based pedagogic behaviours as predictors of student achievement, but we also problematise the assumptions underpinning the processes and products of TER: that classroom-based pedagogic behaviours can be documented, assessed and indeed manipulated in meaningful and straightforward ways. TER has been critiqued from many angles[1]. By engaging with the tenets of practice theory, we provide a critique from an onto-epistemological basis; that is, the philosophical sensibilities of a 'practice perspective' are used as a basis to critique the assumptions TER makes about what teaching is, and how it might be known and shaped. We suggest that the theoretical sensibilities of practice theory call for alternative approaches that would support more productive engagements with the complexities of teaching: engagements that would potentially be more supportive of transformational agendas in school education than those offered by current manifestations of TER. We do not do this by adopting a particular practice theory. Instead, we draw on the practice writings of Reckwitz (2002), Thrift (1996, 2007) and Schatzki (2012) – all of whom provide analyses of commonalities to be found amongst diverse practice theories – to articulate our 'practice perspective'.

The argument unfolds in three parts. First, we describe TER and discuss why TER has appeal to education policy makers and administrators in current times. Second, we draw on understandings common to practice theories to argue that more nuanced conceptualisations of teaching practice are needed rather than those TER currently offers. The concluding section discusses the distinctive contribution that practice theory can bring to critiques of TER and speculates about ways forward. In our view, TER needs to move beyond its scientistic approach to determinations of cause-effect relations between individual teacher behaviours and student achievement, and instead to engage in truly experimental enterprises (after Thrift et al. 2010). Such enterprises would engage teachers themselves in explorations of TER's aims, tools and methods, and outputs, not as *objects of* inquiry or as *subject to* change agendas, but as agents within the complexity of professional practice.

TER – Background, key features and appeal

Our aim in this section is to provide an overview of the key features of TER, identifying the significant characteristics of TER as an approach to knowledge production and discussing why these characteristics support the influence that TER currently enjoys. This provides the basis from which to bring a practice perspective to bear on TER.

TER is a research field that aims to identify the behaviours of classroom teachers that positively influence student learning. The teaching performance of individual classroom teachers is the proxy measure of influence in TER, the aim being to 'establish empirically the relationship between teacher behaviour and student achievement' (Grant & Drafall 1991, p. 31). Gage's 1972 study *Teacher Effectiveness and Teacher Education* contributed significantly to a scientific approach to understanding teaching and provided the foundation for numerous well-known studies in the area (e.g., Berliner 1979; Evertson 1982; Good & Brophy 1986; Stallings 1985). Gage's work established an experimental model of 'research on teaching', focusing on the 'study of relationships between variables, at least one of which refers to a characteristic or behaviour of a teacher' (Gage 1972, p. 16). Classroom observations of what 'good teachers did in their classrooms' (Imig & Imig 2006, p. 171), particularly regarding the types of teaching strategies used with students to enhance learning, are characteristic of much of the early work in TER. This work was behaviourist in its orientation, hence the focus on observable aspects of practice (Muijs et al. 2014). Later studies continued this focus on observable behaviours, but took advantage of large-scale data sets of student standardised test scores[2], where researchers correlated gains made in learning against particular instructional or curricular initiatives (see Ballou & Podgursky 2000; Goldhaber & Brewer 2000; Hanushek 1997).

While some TER studies focus on the influence of teacher characteristics on student learning, most focus on teacher practices or 'what goes on in the classroom' (Konstantopoulos & Sun 2014, p. 314). The overwhelming majority of these studies employ a process-product model of teaching and learning, aiming to identify associations between the processes of teaching practice and the product of student achievement (see Anderson et al. 1979; Konstantopoulos & Sun 2014; Muijs et al. 2014). The body of work in this area is now vast (see Seidel & Shavelson 2007, for a comprehensive list; also Muijs et al. 2014). Quantitative research designs tend to predominate, incorporating systematic classroom observations and student testing. Random and non-random data sets (teachers, students and schools) are often used. Variables or parameters measured (usually individual student learning) are thought to vary across more than one level (e.g., at the individual student level and/or classroom group level). Linear and non-linear regression analyses are used on data sets depending on the context of the study, with the latter gaining in favour with advances in computer software. Typical findings centre on correlating student learning (test score achieved) against teaching strategies used. Teaching practice is usually disaggregated and characterised according to type (e.g., direct, interactive, small group and so on) (see Muijs et al. 2014; Seidel & Shavelson 2007). The findings of TER studies generally indicate that particular teaching strategies, styles or behaviours have greater effects on student learning than others (see Good & Brophy 1986).

While the process-product approach has typified TER (Muijs et al. 2014), studies are diverse in how they characterise teaching (see Seidel & Shavelson 2007). That said, most studies tend to report overall estimates of teaching effectiveness giving an impression of homogeneity across studies, something that Seidel and Shavelson (2007, p. 485) argue is misleading. Commenting on recent trends of meta-analyses across TER studies and the combination of results from different meta-analyses, Muijs et al. (2014) note that common criticisms include TER's underestimation of the extent to which different classroom factors might interact and also the extent to which factors external to the classroom (e.g., at the school organisational level) might interact with aspects of classroom practice. Although this latter criticism is partially mitigated by current developments in multi-level studies that seek to model student, classroom, school and system effects, the teacher – particularly observable teacher instructional behaviour – remains a central focus (Muijs et al. 2014).

Seidel and Shavelson suggest that developments in TER have enabled more refined analyses of teaching effects on student achievement, particularly through the use of large-scale surveys and sophisticated statistical algorithms and models to analyse 'teaching patterns or regimes instead of single teaching acts' (2007, p. 458). Statistical approaches allow researchers to control for 'extraneous variables' so that teacher effects on student achievement can be isolated (Seidel & Shavelson 2007, p. 458). A second trajectory noted by Seidel and Shavelson adopts a discipline specific slant in that researchers focus on the teaching practices employed in 'specific knowledge domains' (2007, p. 458). In other words, a key consideration for teacher effectiveness researchers using this approach resides in identifying the particular teaching strategies germane to individual disciplines – for example, mathematics, science, geography and so on. Other recent developments in TER include value-added modelling (see Imig & Imig 2006; McCaffrey et al. 2004) that compares student growth over time, and contextual value-added models that account for context (e.g., gender and family circumstances) (UK Department for Education 2012). These developments represent a growing sophistication in TER methods and how the object of inquiry is specified in ways that continue a focus on the disaggregation of teaching and a removal of teacher behaviours from contexts that are 'accounted for'. In many ways, TER is a compelling and attractive approach to researching teaching with a view to developing implications and products that support educational improvement. Three features that contribute to its attractiveness to policy makers in current times are its scientism, its appeal to common sense, and its 'fit' with the logics of audit that predominate in current managerial practices. Each of these features is discussed below, providing a partial explanation for why a very particular way of understanding teaching and very particular approaches to researching teaching have been so influential on education reform policies and associated strategies for shaping the teaching profession.

Allure of scientism

There is an appearance of a straightforward scientific logic in how TER reports its findings on the teaching practices that enhance student achievement. TER has a distinctive methodological core, favouring quantification and numerical data and findings, and employing study designs and analysis methods that derive from the conventions of scientific knowledge production, particularly models developed within medical science[3]. The trappings of scientific method are evident – large-scale randomised designs, quantification and statistical testing, and the removal of the intricacies of the practice of research methods from accounts of research outcomes and products – and provide authority to accounts (e.g., Ballou et al. 2004; Muijs & Reynolds 2005). These characteristics of TER are consistent with the hegemonic knowledge production practices of the current times, where large-scale randomised control studies are lauded as the 'gold standard' in education research, and indeed legislated within some jurisdictions as a defining characteristic of rigorous scientific methods in education research[4].

Through the adoption of scientific method, TER therefore presents itself as a neutral umpire, one that seeks to uncover the facts about teaching and learning (Goldhaber & Anthony 2007; Rivkin et al. 2005), an approach consistent with what Hammersley (1992) described as a *naïve realist* ontology. The absolutist descriptions that are characteristic of TER research outputs offer a sense of predictability about teaching and learning, consistent with populist understandings of scientific research as developing absolute truths through objective replicable research processes (see Davies 2000). Through processes of objectification and quantification[5], the approaches taken up by TER recalibrate the world such that practices – that might be otherwise unassailable – become easily comparable with each other and against standards. Within TER, the scientific paradigm is rarely presented as problematic because engagements with methodological assumptions are substituted with method considerations, such as the conditions and relative power of particular sampling processes and statistical tests. This is despite the proliferation of criticisms along paradigmatic lines since the inception of TER (Doyle 1977). TER presents its methods as holding great promise for developing objective accounts of 'what works' in classroom teaching and learning, and there is an unquestioned assumption from within TER scholarship that its outputs translate into applicable solutions (see, for example, Hattie 2012). If the practices of classroom teaching and learning are seen as fixable (like a specimen on a microscope slide), as independent of our research apparatus, and therefore as objectively knowable, then we can assay them in the service of shaping them and their effects. Such assumptions have long been criticised within educational research (e.g., Fenstermacher 1978), yet the allure of the promise of TER to deliver a clear reading of the effects of teaching 'variables' and to lead to answers about how things ought be done in classrooms, persists.

Teachers as easy targets

Inequities in educational achievement are a perennial problem that has received longstanding attention from educational researchers from diverse research traditions. In current times, this problem is married with economic concerns, with policy agendas focusing both on the resourcing of education systems – that value is being derived from resources that are invested – and on the resourcing of national economies through the production of workforces (see Henry et al. 2012; Office for Official Publications of the European Communities 2004). Within Australia – and fuelled by readings of national and international standardised testing in reading, science and mathematics (e.g., the National Assessment Programme in Numeracy and Literacy; the Programme for International Student Assessment; Trends in Mathematics and Science Study and Progress in International Reading Literacy Study) – there is also a perceived problem of underperformance in average student achievement. While some have argued that this problem of underperformance is a constructed crisis that serves political ends (Grek 2013; Lingard 2011) and others have problematised the popular and sometimes misleading *readings* of the results of these testing regimes (e.g., Gorur & Wu 2015), they serve as compelling evidence for arguing that educational reform is needed. As a perennial and 'wicked' (Rittel & Webber 1973) educational problem, there are no quick fixes – either to inequity in educational achievement or to underperformance across schools, systems or countries – and many of the factors known to correlate with low test scores (e.g., socio-economic conditions, access, rurality, curriculum alienation, parental connections to school, student language skills[6]) are recognised as recalcitrant in the face of policy-led reforms. Amongst the obvious suspects in a narrative of crises and underperformance, teachers – their preparation and the work they do – appear more amenable to policy intervention than, say, the socio-economic circumstances of individual students, the cultural attitudes of students to school or the broader economic and social conditions prevalent in societies.

A focus on the practices of teachers as the source of problems and of possible solutions shifts responsibility of student achievement away from the policy and funding arrangements of governments, making it the private concern of individual schools and teachers. Teachers represent easy targets whose work can be scrutinised within episodes and timeframes that make sense within educational systems (lessons, school terms, school years) and can be measured indirectly via student test scores. The assumption that only teachers and their teaching practices are open to policy influence, and that the socio-economic background of students is not open to influence, for example, has been strongly critiqued by scholars who recognise the focus on teaching as at best a 'quick fix' and at worst scapegoating (e.g., Connell 2009).

A focus on the influence of individual teachers is also consistent with common sense popular understandings of the role of teachers in students' learning and lives. In his 2012 State of the Union address, US President Barack Obama stated, 'Every person in this chamber can point to a teacher who changed the trajectory of their lives' (Obama 2012). The assumptions underpinning this comment are clear: teachers can effect significant change in the lives of their students, and we are all able to recognise and name this influence and to observe the effect it has. Thus the underlying assumptions and the aims of TER are both convenient in terms of short-term policy responses and consistent with popular imaginings and common sense understandings of teaching as both an important determinant of outcomes for students and as knowable in everyday ways. However, the practices of TER are not *everyday* in this sense, and while TER analytical methods often comprise a series of complicated mathematical algorithms, the messages delivered in its conclusions are uncomplicated: the classroom teaching behaviours of individual teachers contribute to student achievement, and researchers can determine which pedagogic actions will produce desirable effects and what types of teacher attributes support such actions.

Making teaching auditable

A core consideration of TER is precise determinations of 'what works' to improve student achievement. Within TER, classroom teaching practices and the teacher qualities that support them (teacher skills, understandings and attributes) stand out as the school-based input of maximum impact on student achievement. Measuring instructional performance against standardised achievement levels can be used to distinguish effective from ineffective practices and so TER itemises what it deems are the most important variables of interest in enhancing learning[7]. This type of research and knowledge base has strong appeal to policy makers and managers in that, if teaching is knowable, it is also auditable and can be standardised.

The outcomes of TER and the potential uses of TER products fit well with the logics and processes of accountability and control found in contemporary approaches to governance and management[8]. The effects of such logics and associated management practices have arguably been felt most in government-funded social services – such as education – where regimes of measurement, codification, testing and reporting have increasingly featured as tools for initiating top-down change and ensuring compliance, while also butting up against traditions of independence and self-regulation (Mockler & Groundwater-Smith 2009). Amenable to such agendas is the assumption within TER that teaching practice is observable and quantifiable in straightforward ways, that it varies independently of other influences, that there are direct cause-effect relationships (inferred from statistical correlations) between teaching and learning (vis-a-vis, student achievement), and that the products that emerge from TER can be applied to the attributes and actions of individual classroom teachers. Many TER studies systematise teaching practice by charting what are considered productive practices to enhance student learning[9]. For example, Robinson (2004) moves from outcomes of TER research to propose a list of skills, understandings and traits associated with effective teachers. The purpose of this charting of teacher attributes is to support abstract descriptions of effective teachers and effective teaching, where effectiveness is understood to reside in behaviours positively related to student achievement. Similarly, other researchers like Muijs et al. (2014) suggest that effective teachers engage in particular types of behaviours that maximise opportunities to learn and time spent on tasks. These behaviours include adhering to a particular lesson sequence that is understood as characteristic of effective teaching. Many frameworks that are produced from TER imply a staged enactment of teaching, where particular types of classroom actions are best undertaken in particular sequences, thus supporting evaluations of practice that seek to determine how well teachers adhere to specified instructional sequences (see Scheerens & Bosker 1997). Thus the tools and processes of TER allow for particular manifestations of teaching practice to be checked and measured against codifications of actions deemed effective.

Within such approaches, the classroom is constructed as isolated and complete[10]. The focus is on individual teachers in their classrooms – other possible variables are accounted for and erased. This exerts pressures on teachers to make themselves auditable against TER tools and processes. Emerging within broader contexts of evaluative systems of performance and appraisal (Lingard et al. 2013), such inquiries into teaching practice and its effects on student achievement have a quality assurance feel. A primary consideration is one of verification, where it is possible to monitor teachers' behaviours to determine whether obligations to students are being met. Holding sway is the ingrained absolutism of quantitative single measures given authority by external agencies and investigators. While mathematical certainties potentially lend a firm logic to the student achievement problem, research representations of what passes for effective teaching practice can easily translate into an exercise of rules that will express and govern teachers. Such effects have been long recognised in relation to audit processes and cultures[11].

Reclamations of teaching practice: A 'practice perspective'

Having outlined the key features of TER and gestured towards its limitations, we now outline how a 'practice perspective' offers avenues for more generative engagements with teaching practice, engagements that are more likely to embolden new interpretations of what teaching is and can be. To do this, we do not adopt a particular theoretical framework. Nor do we rework a particular TER approach. Instead, following Reckwitz (2002, p. 257), we use the key tenets of practice theory as a 'sensitizing "framework"' to discuss critically how TER frames and produces teaching practice and what the alternatives might be.

With the rise of interest in practice theory, numerous scholars have provided accounts of what constitutes a practice theory or a practice perspective. In this chapter we draw predominantly on Reckwitz (2002), Thrift (1996, 2007) and Schatzki (2012) to describe a 'practice perspective'. Among these accounts, characteristics seen as part of the common ground of practice theory include: (1) the location of practice in an inter-individual domain instead of as something that belongs to individual human subjects; (2) an understanding of agency as emerging through ongoing relations between entities, where these relations are also constitutive of the entities themselves, including human subjects; (3) an embrace of the non-cognitive, including the corporeal and affective; and, (4) a recognition of the material force of discourse, where representations are understood to act in relation with other entities in co-constitutive ways. Each of these characteristics is discussed below as a basis for critiquing TER.

Reckwitz (2002, p. 246) explains that practice theory 'situates the social in a different realm from those of other cultural theories' because, instead of understanding practices to belong to individuals, individuals are understood to participate *in* and effectively 'carry' practices. He explains that practices involve a complex interconnection between and coordination of bodily activities, mental activities, things, knowledge, emotions and know-how, and he emphasises that, within a practice perspective, practices 'cannot be reduced to any one of these single elements' (p. 250). Schatzki makes a similar point when he argues that practices are an important aspect of human life and 'must be understood as forms of, or as rooted in, human activity – not the activity of individuals, but in practices, that is, in the organised activities of multiple people' (Schatzki 2012, p. 13). Within a practice approach, the purposeful actions of an individual cannot be separated from what Schatzki (2012, p. 16) describes as 'a bundle of practices and arrangements'. Schatzki argues that these 'bundles' exceed the individual, encompassing complex arrays of people, objects and discourses that interrelate in ways that are often difficult to account for. Thrift, in his discussion of non-representational theory, provides a useful definition of practices that both notes their extra-individual character and points to an underlying ontology of dissipation, striated by world-making movements:

> . . . if we are looking for something that approximates to a stable feature of a world that is continually in meltdown, that is continually bringing forth new hybrids, then I take practice to be it. Practices are productive concatenations that have been constructed out of all manner of resources and which provide the basic intelligibility of the world: they are not therefore the properties of actors but of the practices themselves.
>
> (Thrift 2007, p. 8, citing Schatzki)

This location of practices outside of individual actors has been highly influential in contemporary understandings of professional practice,[12] and in ways that contrast dramatically with the assumptions and approaches of TER. From a practice perspective, practices are comprised of more than actions performed by a human body – 'actions presuppose practices' (Thrift 2007, p. 8). And changing practices involves more than an instrumental decision by a human agent to do things differently. Participation in a practice brings teachers into relation with complexes of meanings, materials and bodies that extend beyond the teachers' bodily actions, beyond the walls of their individual classrooms and indeed beyond the walls of their particular schools. When teachers act, they do so in relation to the manifold logics, movements and ambitions of a complex, expansive, interconnected and mutually constituted array of entities, including:

- The other human bodies present in classrooms (students, support staff, classroom helpers);
- The mental and emotional activities of these other human bodies, and still more human bodies located outside of the classroom (principals, parents, government ministers, education researchers);
- The tangible non-human objects present in the classroom (desks, books, technology, walls); and
- Tangible non-human objects found outside of the classroom (other rooms and resources, other sites, students' homes and belongings, the material arrangements found in other agencies).

This relational understanding of practice heads off presumptions of self-contained, instrumental human subjects who can unproblematically change their practices, what Wilkinson and Kemmis (2015, p. 343) refer to as a 'rationalistic, means-end paradigm' in relation to educational leadership. Instead, the human subject is constituted through practices, including the discursive practices of researchers and policy makers.

Thrift also emphasises movement as an important theme in contemporary understandings of human life: the relational co-constitution of entities is ongoing. This is a significant shift away from modernist conceptualisations and approaches to inquiry that emphasise states of being. Within practice theory, both activity and subjectivity are conceptualised as 'in motion' – as an ongoing forming of actors, relations, assemblages[13] – through which practices can be reproduced and transformed. By focusing on states of effectiveness, TER enacts teaching as an accomplishment, eliding its emergent character and the ongoing work (of which TER is now a part) involved in producing teaching and teachers. TER effectively takes teaching practices out of time, translating them into abstract discursive representations, denuded of temporality.

TER also neglects non-cognitive aspects of teaching – focusing on observable enactments of discrete practices, understood as governed by a rational subject. This is a naïve empiricism, without scope or the tools to engage with other types of material – for example, the non-cognitive, corporeal or affective aspects of teaching practice. Although recent developments in TER have seen the inclusion of broader conceptions of student learning outcomes in TER studies – for example, the inclusion of student self-concept and metacognitive behaviours (Muijs et al. 2014) – the framing of teaching remains closely focused on observable behaviours. With its behaviourist beginnings and tools, TER fails to engage with the less easily observed and measured aspects of teacher practice (such as emotion and intuition), or aspects of teaching and learning events that do not fit with an individualised notion of these practices (such as how affects might circulate around classrooms or in and out of classrooms). These are integral aspects of classroom life that remain outside of the TER apparatus and therefore do not feature in TER accounts of effective teaching practice.

Practice theories usually elaborate an explicit critique of Cartesian realist onto-epistemologies where a singular, objective reality is assumed to both exist independently of our knowledge-making practices and to be knowable and representable in straightforward ways. That practices escape our attempts to represent them is echoed by numerous practice scholars. In his discussion of commonalities among diverse practice theories, Schatzki notes that a common tenet is an understanding of human activity that 'rests on something that cannot be put into words' (Schatzki 2012, p. 14). Thrift also notes that 'there is always something that lies outside knowledge. There is always something that cannot be described' (Thrift 1996, p. 34). Such comments derive from a fundamental questioning of the whole enterprise of modernistic knowledge production as based on a separation of a knowing subject from the object that is known. Practice theories characterise practices as exceeding the research apparatus that we use to objectify them. And more than this, they point to the world-making contribution of our knowledge-making practices and products. Thrift explains that 'representational *effort* is always firmly embedded in a contextually specific process of social negotiation' (Thrift 1996, p. 8, citing Curt). Similarly, Barad, elaborating on the onto-epistemological implications of quantum physics, explains that,

> ... there is something fundamental about the nature of measurement interactions such that, given a particular measuring apparatus, certain properties *become determinate*, while others are specifically excluded. Which properties become determinate is not governed by the desires of will of the experimenter but rather by the specificity of the experimental apparatus.
>
> (Barad 2007, p. 19)

These views of knowledge and of knowledge-making practices challenge scientised constructions of teaching and teachers within TER by recognising the indeterminate aspects of teaching practice(s) and also the force that representations of teaching/teachers – and the processes and apparatuses involved in researching, assessing and reporting upon teachers' classroom work – can exert. The implications of the reductions and elisions enacted by TER go further than failing to incorporate important aspects of teaching practice. They manifest in discursive representations of teaching and related intellectual tools that become part of the teaching assemblage, acting back on the objects of TER inquiry. The representations of effective teaching produced by TER interact with other representations, and other entities and processes, to affect what teaching is known to be and potentially what teaching might be in the future. TER tells a quantitative story about the efficacy of teaching practices and their inferred connections to student achievement. Although this framing of teaching practice might be presented as a useful 'snapshot' of 'what works', the influence of this story has serious ramifications for our conceptualisation of teaching and learning and how we engage and speak about these practices. The representations deployed in the processes and products of TER can potentially contribute to a re-shaping of the profession when these representations become part of the complex of meanings, materials and bodies that comprise teaching. The imbrication of these representations within the practices of teaching can be seen in current times as teachers' work is increasingly entangled with logics, artefacts and indeed practices that seek to define teaching through, for example, curriculum and assessment policy, teacher education and accreditation policy, school-level audit, and teacher performance and review.

Conclusion: Where to from here?

In this chapter we have provided a description and critique of teacher effectiveness research, its assumptions and presumptions. We have identified its defining characteristics and discussed how these might explain, at least in part, the influence that TER currently has in educational policy and administration. Importantly, the uptake and influence of TER positions teachers as a matter for concern, and does so in what we argue are reductive ways, where observable classroom-based pedagogic actions of individual teachers are taken as constitutive of teaching – what they are, should and can be. A practice perspective challenges the underlying assumptions of TER, particularly in relation to:

- Its focus on the impact of individual teachers and their classroom behaviours;
- Its positioning of teachers as sovereign change-agents in charge of their own teaching behaviours – and through those the learning behaviours and outcomes of students;
- Its presumption to represent teaching practices as codified matrices of actions; and
- Its failure to engage critically with its own contributions to limiting what teaching is seen to be and how the futures of teaching are envisaged.

We argue that a 'practice perspective' — where practices are conceived as extra-individual, relational, emergent and subject to ongoing formation and reformation — offers a more affirmative and more generative platform from which to engage teachers as professionals.

This critique of TER is easily made from a practice perspective platform, but how do we move forward if the purposes and processes of TER and the understandings and questions supported by practice theory are incommensurable? What does a practice perspective offer that other critiques of TER do not? The subjectivising tendencies of TER are well argued by researchers and commentators who see TER processes, products and uptake into management tools as an erosion of teachers' professional freedoms and responsibilities. But practice theory does not reinstate the sovereign professional. Instead, a more expansive understanding of subjectivity and agency is supported. How might these more expansive understandings dialogue with TER in productive ways? These are difficult questions. While it is easy to critique TER from a practice perspective, the tenets of a practice perspective do not translate easily into approaches to inquiry into teaching[14], or into empirical research approaches that might appeal to policy makers or indeed produce products that do. While we don't offer answers to these difficult questions, we conclude by noting two initial moves through which the tenets of a practice perspective might inform alternative ways of narrating teaching and new ways that teachers might engage (always partially) with their own practices and TER.

The first of these moves (and possibly also the second) concerns the material-discursive politics of TER, which currently position teachers as *subject to* TER. Through its processes and products and the uptake of these in policy and management practices, TER enters the teaching assemblage, and does so in ways that risk particular effects. A practice perspective suggests that the representations of TER should be seen as material-discursive actors — they are *both* feeble representational attempts *and also* powerful mediators. In accounts of TER, these two faces of representation are rarely promoted as a matter for attention. Instead, any feebleness of TER representations is dealt with at the superficial level of limitations of method, but without explicit epistemological framing. Additionally, the power of TER is dealt with, again superficially, as a matter of statistical power of processes and also practical usability of products, but without engagement with the part that TER might play in non-instrumental world-making. We believe that the value of TER accounts might be enhanced — and potentially damaging *effects* ameliorated — if these problematics were an explicit feature of accounts of TER 'findings'. Engaging with onto-epistemology has emerged as a key concern of practice theory and a characteristic element of accounts of phenomena that draw upon practice theory, and TER could well benefit from this and the generative questioning and experimentation that follows.

The second move — related to how we might work with TER accounts — concerns the relationship of TER to teacher professional learning. Muijs et al.

(2014) point out how teacher professional development is oddly missing from much TER – this is 'odd' because the warrant for the research is more often than not centred on how teaching practice might be improved. They also note that traditional approaches to teacher professional learning can fail to engage teachers in effective ways because the goals and content of the learning are identified by someone external to teaching and the teacher or group of teachers being taught, such as a policy official or researcher. Contemporary understandings of effective teacher professional learning incorporate principles of professionalism, where learning is seen as an integral part of the lives of teachers, which is grounded in local school communities and founded on teacher-led inquiry (Doecke et al. 2008). This is not simple work where established scripts and strategies ('what works') can be injected into teacher practice. It is complex work that involves professional investment and risk taking, where teachers engage in and with their own practices in new ways, understanding that many actors are involved in 'teaching' and that representations of 'teaching' are always partial, situated and perspectival, but powerful nonetheless. Within such an approach (i.e., teachers embracing a practice perspective), TER could potentially feature as providing generative material and intellectual tools and processes for teachers, supporting home-grown teacher inquiry, professional learning, and the development of school and classroom solutions (recognised as contingent and partial). However, such a move can only happen if the first move supports a problematisation and expansion of the object of TER (the individual rational teacher in his or her own classroom). More expansive understandings of teaching would not only engage teachers in productive ways, but would be more consistent than narrower conceptions with the ways that contemporary schools operate, and with the ways that classroom teaching and learning articulate beyond the walls of the classroom and beyond the school gate.

Following this view and the moves noted, a reclamation of teaching practice involves teachers, school education administrators, policy makers and other stakeholders in school education recognising that research accounts are material-discursive entities that are situated, political, partial and necessarily (openly) reductive – that they are both feeble *and* powerful; and, that they can and do play roles in change, but that these roles materialise in local events and situations in emergent and unpredictable ways. This requires a new experimentalism that puts the well-tried tools of TER to work in brave new ways. Thrift, when writing about non-representational theory, promotes a move away from established methods towards experimental work, talking of developing what he calls new 'emancipatory spaces' that 'can act both as interventions and as cultural probes' (Thrift et al. 2010, p. 197) and suggesting that when we inhabit such spaces, we can think in different ways by 'simultaneously measuring them out differently and by producing new and unexpected alliances out of that work of measurement' (p. 198). Might teachers reinvent TER?

Notes

1 For example, Imig and Imig (2006) discuss the historic divide between 'essentialists' and 'progressivists'.
2 Despite the widely recognised narrowness of such measures – for more on this, see Wu (2016).
3 See Peters and Tesar (2017) for an historical account of the influence of evidence-based medicine on educational research.
4 We refer to the much-criticised *US Education Sciences Reforms Act of 2002* (USA) (National Research Council 2002).
5 See Pianta et al. (2007) for details about various observation models used in teacher effectiveness research.
6 See for example Jorgensen (2012) and Teese and Polesel (2003).
7 For a comprehensive list of some of these variables, see Seidel and Shavelon (2007).
8 See Power (1999) for an influential account of these logics and processes.
9 For example, Cheng and Tsui (1999), Evertson (1982), Good and Brophy (1986), Mortimore et al. (1988), Muijs (2006), Muijs and Reynolds (2005) and Robinson (2004).
10 While some studies also incorporate student (e.g., Kane & Staiger 2012) and parent evaluations (e.g., Master 2013), these components are more often than not treated as add-ons to observations of teachers.
11 For example, Power (1999, p. 8) argues that audit is not a passive undertaking, but instead 'actively shapes the context in which it operates'.
12 See for example Kemmis (2009), who also cites Schatzki.
13 This focus on imminence is particularly evident in inquiries informed by the theoretical work of actor-network theory and also the philosophies of Deleuze and Guatarri.
14 See Trowler (2014) for discussions of this challenge and associated methodologies.

References

Anderson, C, Evertson, C & Brophy, J 1979, 'An experimental study of effective teaching in first-grade reading groups', *Elementary School Journal*, vol. 79, no. 4, pp. 193–223.

Ballou, D & Podgursky, BM 2000, 'Reforming teacher preparation and licensing: Continuing the debate', *Teachers College Record*, vol. 102, no. 1, pp. 5–27.

Ballou, D, Sanders, W & Wright, P 2004, 'Controlling for student background in value-added assessment of teachers', *Journal of Educational and Behavioural Statistics*, vol. 29, no. 1, pp. 37–65.

Barad, K 2007, *Meeting the universe halfway: Quantum physics and the entanglement of matter and meaning*, Duke University Press, Durham.

Berliner, DC 1979, 'Tempus educare', in P Peterson & H Walberg (eds), *Research in teaching*, McCutchan, Berkeley, CA, pp. 120–135.

Cheng, YC & Tsui, KT 1999, 'Multimodels of teacher effectiveness: Implications for research', *The Journal of Educational Research*, vol. 92, no. 3, pp. 141–150.

Connell, R 2009, 'Good teachers on dangerous ground: Towards a new view of teacher quality and professionalism', *Critical Studies in Education*, vol. 50, no. 3, pp. 213–229.

Davies, P 2000, 'The relevance of systematic reviews to educational policy and practice', *Oxford Review of Education*, vol. 26, no. 3–4, pp. 365–378.

Doecke, B, Parr, G, North, S, Gale, T, Long, M, Mitchell, J, Rennie, J & Williams, J 2008, *National mapping of teacher professional learning project* (final report), Department of Education, Employment and Workplace Relations, Canberra, ACT.

Doyle, W 1977, 'Paradigms for research on teacher effectiveness', *Review of Research in Education*, vol. 5, pp. 163–198.

Evertson, CM 1982, 'Differences in instructional activities in higher and lower achieving junior high English and math classes', *Elementary School Journal*, vol. 82, no. 4, pp. 329–351.

Fenstermacher, GD 1978, 'A philosophical consideration of recent research on teacher effectiveness', *Review of Research in Education*, vol. 6, pp. 157–185.

Gage, NL 1972, *Teacher effectiveness and teacher education. The search for a scientific basis*, Pacific Book Publishers, Palo Alto, CA.

Goldhaber, D & Anthony, E 2007, 'Can teacher quality be effectively assessed? National board certification as a signal of effective teaching', *Review of Economics and Statistics*, vol. 89, no. 1, pp. 134–150.

Goldhaber, D & Brewer, DJ 2000, 'Does teacher certification matter? High school teacher certification status and student achievement', *Educational Evaluation and Policy Analysis*, vol. 22, no. 2, pp. 129–146.

Good, TL & Brophy, JE 1986, 'School effects', in MC Wittrock (ed.), *Handbook of research on teaching*, Macmillan, New York, pp. 570–620.

Gorur, R & Wu, M 2015, 'Leaning too far? PISA, policy and Australia's "top five" ambitions', *Discourse: Studies in the Cultural Politics of Education*, vol. 36, no. 5, pp. 647–664.

Grant, JW & Drafall, LE 1991, 'Teacher effectiveness research: A review and comparison', *Bulletin of the Council for Research in Music Education*, no. 108 (Spring, 1991), pp. 31–48.

Grek, S 2013, 'Expert moves: International comparative testing and the rise of expertocracy', *Journal of Education Policy*, vol. 28, no. 5, pp. 695–709.

Hammersely, M 1992, *What's wrong with ethnography: Methodological explorations*, Routledge, London.

Hanushek, EA 1997, 'Assessing the effects of school resources on student performance: An update', *Education Evaluation and Policy Analysis*, vol. 19, no. 2, pp. 141–164.

Hattie, J 2012, *Visible learning for teachers: maximizing impact on learning*, Routledge, London.

Henry, D, Drysdale, P, Livingstone, C, Denton, John WH, de Brouwer, G, Gruen, D & Smith, H 2012, *Australia in the Asian century white paper*, Commonwealth of Australia Canberra, retrieved 11 May 2016, <www.defence.gov.au/whitepaper/2013/docs/australia_in_the_asian_century_white_paper.pdf>.

Imig, DG & Imig, SR 2006, 'The teacher effectiveness movement: How 80 years of essentialist control have shaped the teacher education profession', *Journal of Teacher Education*, vol. 57, no. 2, pp. 167–180.

Jorgensen, R 2012, 'Exploring scholastic mortality among working class and indigenous students: A perspective from Australia', in B Herzelman, J Choppin, D Wagner & D Pimm (eds), *Equity in discourse for mathematics education: Theories, practices and policies*, Springer, Dordrecht, pp. 35–49.

Kane, TJ & Staiger, DO 2012, *Gathering feedback for teaching. Combining high-quality observations with student surveys and achievement gains*, Bill and Melinda Gates Foundation, Seattle, WA.

Kemmis, S 2009, 'Understanding professional practice: A synoptic framework', In B Green (ed.) *Understanding and Researching Professional Practice*, Sense Publishers, Rotterdam, pp. 19–38.

Konstantopoulos, S & Sun, M 2014, 'Are teacher effects larger in small classes?', *School Effectiveness and School Improvement*, vol. 25, no. 3, pp. 312–328.

Lingard, B 2011, 'Policy as numbers: Ac/counting for educational research', *Australian Educational Researcher*, vol. 38, no. 4, pp. 355–382.

Lingard, B, Martino, W & Rezai-Rashti, G 2013, 'Testing regimes, accountabilities and education policy: commensurate global and national developments', *Journal of Education Policy*, vol. 28, no. 5, pp. 539–556.

Master, B 2013, 'What can parents tell us about teacher quality? Examining the contributions of parent perspectives in comparison to a portfolio of alternative teacher evaluation measures', PhD Thesis, Stanford University Center for Education Policy Analysis, retrieved 11 May 2016, <https://cepa.stanford.edu>.

McCaffrey, D, Lockwood, JR, Koretz, DM & Hamilton, LS 2004, *Evaluating value-added models for teacher accountability*, RAND, Santa Monica, CA.

Mockler, N & Groundwater-Smith, S 2009, *Teacher professional learning in an age of compliance: Mind the gap*, Springer, retrieved 11 May 2016, <http://link.springer.com/book/10.1007/978–1–4020–9417–0>.

Mortimore, P, Sammons, P, Stoll, L, Lewis, D & Ecob, R 1988, *School Matters*, Open Books, Somerset Wells.

Muijs, D, Kyriakides, L, van der Werf, G, Creemers, B, Timperley H & Earl, L 2014, 'State of the art – Teacher effectiveness and professional learning', *School Effectiveness and School Improvement: An International Journal of Research, Policy and Practice*, vol. 25, no. 2, pp. 231–256.

Muijs, D 2006, 'Measuring Teacher Effectiveness: Some methodological reflections', *Educational Research and Evaluation*, vol. 12, no. 1, pp. 53–74.

Muijs, D & Reynolds, D 2005, *Effective teaching: Evidence and practice*, Sage Publications, London.

National Research Council 2002, 'Scientific research in education', RJ Shavelson & L Towne (eds), *Committee on Scientific Principles for Educational Research*, National Academy Press, Washington DC.

Obama, B 2012, *State of the union address*, The Whitehouse, USA, retrieved 11 May 2016, <https://www.whitehouse.gov/the-press-office/2012/01/24/remarks-president-state-union-address>. Office for Official Publications of the European Communities 2004, *Facing the challenge: The Lisbon strategy for growth and employment (Kok Report)*, Luxembourg, retrieved 19 February 2016, <http://ec.europa.eu/research/evaluations/pdf/archive/>.

Peters, M & Tesar, M 2017, 'Bad research, Bad education: The contested evidence for evidence-based research, policy and practice in education', in J Lynch, J Rowlands, T Gale, and A Skourdoumbis (eds), *Practice theory and education: Diffractive readings of professional practice*, Routledge, UK, pp. 231–246.

Pianta, RC, Hamre, BK, Haynes, NJ, Mintz, SL & La Paro, KM 2007, *Classroom assessment scoring system manual, middle/secondary version*, University of Virginia, Charlottesville, VA.

Power, M., 1999. *The audit society: Rituals of verification*, Oxford University Press, New York, NY.

Reckwitz, A 2002, 'Toward a theory of social practices: A development in cultural theorizing', *European Journal of Social Theory*, vol. 5, no. 2, pp. 243–263.

Rittel, HWJ & Webber, MM 1973, 'Dilemmas in a general theory of planning', *Policy Sciences*, vol. 4, no. 2, pp. 155–169.

Rivkin, SG, Hanushek, EA & Kain, JF 2005, 'Teachers, schools and academic achievement', *Econometrica*, vol. 73, no. 2, pp. 417–458.

Robinson, W 2004, *Power to teach*, Woburn Press, London.

Schatzki, TR 2012, 'A Primer on Practices. Theory and Research', in J Higgs, R Barnett, S Billett, M Hutchings & F Trede (eds), *Practice, education, work and society*, Sense Publishers, Rotterdam, pp. 13–22.

Scheerens, J & Bosker, R 1997, *The foundations of educational effectiveness*, Oxford University Press, London.

Seidel, T & Shavelson, R 2007, 'Teaching effectiveness research in the past decade: The role of theory and research design in disentangling meta-analysis results', *Review of Educational Research*, vol. 77, no. 4, pp. 454–499.

Stallings, J 1985, 'Effective elementary classroom practices', in MJ Kyle (ed.), *Reaching for excellence: An effective schools sourcebook*, National Institute of Education, Washington, DC.

Teese, R & Polesel, J 2003, *Undemocratic schooling. Equity and quality in mass secondary education in Australia*, Melbourne University Press, Melbourne, AUS.

Thrift, N 1996, '"Strange country": Meaning, use and style in non-representational theories', in *Theory, Culture & Society: Spatial formations*, Sage Publications Ltd, London pp. 1–51.

Thrift, N 2007, *Non-representational theory: Space, politics, affect*, Routledge, London.

Thrift, N, Harrison, P & Anderson, B 2010, '"The 27th letter": An interview with Nigel Thrift', in B Anderson & P Harrison (eds), *Taking-place: Non-representational theories and geography*, Ashgate, London, pp. 183–197.

Trowler, PR 2014, 'Practice-focused ethnographies of higher education: Method/ological corollaries of a social practice perspective', *European Journal of Higher Education*, vol. 4, no. 1, pp. 18–29.

UK Department for Education 2012, *A technical guide to contextual value added 2007 and 2008 model*, retrieved 11 May 2016, <http://www.education.gov.uk/performancetables/schools_08/s3.shtml>.

Wilkinson, J & Kemmis, S 2015, 'Practice theory: Viewing leadership as leading', *Educational Philosophy and Theory: Incorporating ACCESS*, vol. 47, no. 4, pp. 342–358.

Wu, M 2016, 'What national testing data can tell us', in B Lingard, G Thompson & S Sellar (eds), *National Testing in Schools*, Routledge, UK, pp. 18–30.

Index